Maintaining
The New Audience
For Theatre

The History of ASSITEJ
The International Association of Theatres for Children and Youth
Volume III
(1991–2005)

MAINTAINING THE NEW AUDIENCE FOR THEATRE

The History of ASSITEJ
The International Association of Theatres for Children and Youth
ASSITEJ/l'Association Internationale du Théâtres pour l'Enfance et la Jeunesse
Volume III
(1991–2005)

NAT EEK, PhD
College of Fine Arts
University of Oklahoma
Honorary President of ASSITEJ
President of ASSITEJ, 1972–1975
Santa Fe, New Mexico, USA

with
KIM PETER KOVAC, MFA
Producing Director
Theatre for Young Audiences
John F. Kennedy Center
Vice-President of ASSITEJ, 2008 to present (2014)
Washington, DC. USA

and
KATHERINE KRZYS, MFA
Curator – Child Drama Collection
Arizona State University
Curator, ASSITEJ/USA & ASSITEJ/Int'l, 1985 to present (2014)
Tempe, Arizona, USA

SANTA FE

On the Cover: *The Tale of Haruk*, Performance Group Tuida (Hwacheun, Korea), Directed by Bae Yosup, performed by Kim Suah, Hwang Hyeran, Choi Jaeyoung, Jung Hyunsuk, photo by Lee Seunghee, 2009, courtesy of Kim Woo Ok. Photograph preparation by Konrad Eek.

© 2014 by Nat Eek, PhD.
All Rights Reserved.

No part of this book may be reproduced in any form or by any electronic or mechanical means including information storage and retrieval systems without permission in writing from the publisher, except by a reviewer who may quote brief passages in a review.

Sunstone books may be purchased for educational, business, or sales promotional use. For information please write: Special Markets Department, Sunstone Press, P.O. Box 2321, Santa Fe, New Mexico 87504-2321.

Book and Cover design › Vicki Ahl
Body typeface › WTC Our Bodoni
Printed on acid-free paper
∞

Library of Congress Cataloging-in-Publication Data

Eek, 1927-
Discovering a new audience for theatre : the history of ASSITEJ, the International Association of Theatre for Children and Youth / by Nat Eek, with Ann M. Shaw, and Katherine Krzys.
   v. cm
Includes bibliographical references.
Contents: v. I. 1964-1975
ISBN 978-0-86534-660-4 (v. 1 : pbk.: alk. paper)
   1. International Association of Theatre for Children and Young People–History.
I. Shaw, Ann M. (Ann Marie), 1930- II. Krzys, Katherine. III. Title
PN2015E45 2008
792.02'2609-dc22
                                2008010550

Contents: v. III. 1991–2005
ISBN: 978-0-86534-987-2 (v. III : pbk. : alk. paper)

WWW.SUNSTONEPRESS.COM
SUNSTONE PRESS / POST OFFICE BOX 2321 / SANTA FE, NM 87504-2321 /USA
(505) 988-4418 / ORDERS ONLY (800) 243-5644 / FAX (505) 988-1025

This History is dedicated to ASSITEJ, to its leaders, and its National Centers and their members who gave of their time, their money, and their devotion to a firm belief in the art of the theatre for young people, making it an artistic equal to adult theatre.

With this concluding Volume of *The History of ASSITEJ* the authors feel it appropriate to offer an additional dedication to all those who made its completion possible. Their loyalty, their incisiveness, their promptness in reply, all made this the easiest but largest of Volumes to write. We four, Kim Peter Kovac, Ann M. Shaw, Katherine Krzys, and Nat Eek, thank you from the bottom of our archives.

CONTENTS

Volume III
(1991–2005)

FOREWORD / 9
INTRODUCTION / 31

PART VI / 35
THE CHANGING OF THE GUARD/CUBA 1993

The World at the Time / 38
The Status of ASSITEJ in 1990 / 39
Executive Committee Meeting of ASSITEJ/Budapest, Hungary/23-27 January 1991 / 42
Executive Committee Meeting of ASSITEJ/Lyon, France/5-8 December 1991 / 53
Executive Committee Meeting of ASSITEJ/Nairobi, Kenya/8-11 November 1992 / 57
XIth World Congress of ASSITEJ/Havana, Cuba/22-27 February 1993 / 66
Executive Committee Meeting of ASSITEJ/Frankfurt, Germany/1-5 December 1993 / 77
Executive Committee Meeting of ASSITEJ/Caracas, Venezuela/19-24 September 1994 / 84
Executive Committee Meeting of ASSITEJ/Seattle, Washington, USA/7-14 May 1995 / 91
Executive Committee Meeting of ASSITEJ/Brisbane, Australia/9-16 June 1996 / 100
Interim 1995–1996 / 106
XIIth World Congress of ASSITEJ/Rostov-on-Don, Russia/1-8 October 1996 / 107
A Summary of 1991–1996 / 121

PART VII / 135
RETRENCHMENT AND NEW GROWTH BEYOND

The World of 1996–1997 / 136
Executive Committee Meeting of ASSITEJ/Lima, Peru/13-17 August 1997 / 137
Executive Committee Meeting of ASSITEJ/Biel, Switzerland/26-31 October 1997 / 142
Interim/October 1997–April 1998 / 148
Executive Committee Meeting of ASSITEJ/Haifa, Israel/ 11-15 April 1998 / 151
Executive Committee Meeting of ASSITEJ/London, England/27 February-3 March 1999 / 156
XIIIth World Congress of ASSITEJ/Tromsø, Norway/11-18 June 1999 / 164
The World of 2000 (The Millennium) / 179
Executive Committee Meeting of ASSITEJ/Dallas, Texas, USA/11-13 February 2000 / 180
Executive Committee Meeting of ASSITEJ/Harare, Zimbabwe/8-11 December 2000 / 186
A Historic Perspective / 193
Executive Committee Meeting of ASSITEJ/Tokyo, Japan/19-24 July 2001 / 194
Executive Committee Meeting of ASSITEJ/Rio de Janeiro, Brazil/1-7 March 2002 / 204

XIVth World Congress of ASSITEJ/Seoul, Korea/23-26 July, 2002 / 212
A Summary of 1997–2002 / 227

PART VIII / 235
BUILDING THE FUTURE

Executive Committee Meeting of ASSITEJ/Zagreb, Croatia/22-27 October 2002 / 236
Interim Fallout/2002 / 242
Executive Committee Meeting of ASSITEJ/Aberystwyth, Wales, UK/25-30 March 2003 / 244
Executive Committee Meeting of ASSITEJ/Vienna, Austria/23-28 September 2003 / 255
Executive Committee Meeting of ASSITEJ/Amman, Jordan/13-17 April 2004 / 262
Executive Committee Meeting of ASSITEJ/Cape Town, South Africa/2-8 September 2004 / 272
Executive Committee Meeting of ASSITEJ/Adelaide, Australia/7-12 April 2005 / 281
XVth World Congress of ASSITEJ/Montreal, Canada/21-30 September 2005 / 289
Executive Committee Meeting of ASSITEJ/Frankfurt, Germany/2-6 December 2005 / 308
A Summary of 2003–2005 / 312
The World of 2005 / 322
A Leadership Evaluation / 324
The World of ASSITEJ in 2013 / 328

CONCLUSION / 329
THE AUTHORS / 330

APPENDICES

APPENDIX A – List of Officers and Honorary Members (1965– 2005) / 331
APPENDIX B – Biographies of Principal Officers, Leaders, and Members (1991–2005) / 334
APPENDIX C – List of International/World Congresses of ASSITEJ (1965–2011) / 366
APPENDIX D – List of Executive Committee Meetings of ASSITEJ (1965–2005) / 367
APPENDIX E – List of Members of the Executive Committee of ASSITEJ by Terms (1965–2014) / 369
APPENDIX F – The Constitutions of ASSITEJ / 372
    The 1965 Constitution / 372
    The 2005 Constitution, as amended / 382
    The 2011 Constitution, as amended / 389
APPENDIX G – History of the Formation & Suspension of National Centers (1991–2005) / 399
APPENDIX H – The Current Election Process of ASSITEJ (2005 & 2011) / 401
APPENDIX I – The ASSITEJ/International Award for Artistic Excellence / 404
    (The Former Honorary Presidents Award) – 1993–2011
APPENDIX J – The 30th Anniversary of ASSITEJ (1995) / 408
    (Speeches by Former Secretary General Rose-Marie Moudoués and Former President Dr. Ilse Rodenberg)

APPENDIX K – "Welcoming Speech" by President Michael FitzGerald (1996) / 417
APPENDIX L – "The Tromsø Declaration" / 420
APPENDIX M – "A Presentation" by Marián Lucky / 421
APPENDIX N – Letter of Jan Skotnicki / 422

NOTES / 426
BIBLIOGRAPHY / 434

FOREWORD TO VOLUME III
by
Niclas Malmcrona
Vice-President, ASSITEJ/Sweden
Secretary General of ASSITEJ (1999-2008)
Honorary Member of ASSITEJ/Int'l

Openness, including communication, professionalism, effectiveness, networking.

Those were the key words of the work and life of ASSITEJ when I became involved in the work of ASSITEJ—a new ASSITEJ. My involvement coincides to a large extent with the period that this Volume III of *The History of ASSITEJ* covers.

ASSITEJ as an organization had moved from "an originally progressive organization to one which gradually stagnated and refused to keep up with the development of the times", not moving forward to meet the new times of the 1990's and later into the new century. Fortunately this journey towards modern times was started during the Xth World Congress in Stockholm in 1990, and gradually moved forward from there.

From 1990 to 1996 the Constitution was modernized, the issue of languages was resolved, and ASSITEJ turned from being a Western/Euro-centered organization to a truly international network.

When I was elected Secretary General in 1999, I wanted to continue the work that was started by Michael Ramløse, Secretary General (1990-1996), and Michael FitzGerald, President (1993-1999). ASSITEJ needed and deserved to have an effective professional leadership, and an Executive Committee that responded and listened to its members.

In 1990 forty-one (41) countries were members of ASSITEJ. In 2008 ASSITEJ had seventy-five (75) member countries on all six continents. In 1999 I felt it was extremely important to turn ASSITEJ into a truly international organization. Truly international to me means to have a membership in all parts of the world-on all continents. It means also that all countries-all members-have the possibility to make their voices heard.

Together with Harold Oaks, President (1999-2002), I travelled to Hwange in Zimbabwe in 2000. African countries were increasingly part of the international stage, both regionally and globally. It is universally accepted that development must pay attention to culture and its various manifestations in the arts, or become one-dimensional and limited by definition.

Against this background, the African Network Project of ASSITEJ/Int'l took place. In Africa altogether 16 regional meetings and regional workshops (including three ASSITEJ/Int'l EC Meetings) were held in 14 countries from 2000-2007. The focus of the network was not necessarily to advance individuals specifically, but to improve strategies concerning children's and young people's theatre, so that successful platforms for education, debate, and social development were established.

This work took place in Africa, but the experiences gave important knowledge for working in other parts of the world. Wolfgang Schneider, President (2002-2012) contributed to this work with his extensive travelling, and since the beginning of the new century, ASSITEJ/Int'l has met on all six continents.

In 1999 in Tromsø, Norway three or four ASSITEJ centers had e-mail addresses. No center had a web-page. The main tool for communication, if you wanted to be quick, was FAX. Sometimes it was sufficient with a letter—with a stamp and an envelope—it took a couple of days to get to another country in Europe—a little bit longer if it was going to another continent. From 1990 ASSITEJ has steadily improved its communication through Newsletters, distribution of Minutes of Meetings, the ASSITEJ Annual and magazine, the web-site, Facebook, and more.

In 2013 we are all connected day and night, but still the personal encounters are the most important. Being part of a network means not only to *get*—more importantly it also means to *give*. You'll never get more back than you give away. We all understand the problems we face with organizing, funding, networking, and limited resources—but that is why we have ASSITEJ—to share experiences.

This is also the place to give credits to and to thank Nat Eek (Honorary President of ASSITEJ), Ann Shaw (Honorary Member of ASSITEJ), Katherine Krzys (Curator of the ASSITEJ/USA Archives at Arizona State University), and Kim Peter Kovac (Vice President of ASSITEJ/USA and Producing Director at the Kennedy Center in Washington DC). Your work and dedication to record the history of ASSITEJ from 1965 to 2005 is outstanding! The history is part of the future, and with the common knowledge of our past, we will build a sustainable network. To share experiences!

ASSITEJ is an organization and network for professional performing arts practitioners from all parts of the world. We work under different conditions, we work in different traditions, we work in different styles. We have different tastes, different opinions, different understandings of good quality.

In addition, we all share the love of the performing arts, the belief in good theatrical art for children and youth, the right for the younger generation to aesthetic and cultural experiences. To me—and, as I believe to ASSITEJ—one of the important things is to be open and inclusive. Only if we are open to each other, to each other's art, can we develop and grow—and that way we can make ASSITEJ stronger.

Be open and inclusive with each other as colleagues and working partners. Be open and truthful to our children, our audiences, and recipients of our work. These are the reasons we are working with the performing arts for children and youth.

This is how we will celebrate the 50th year Anniversary of ASSITEJ in 2015!

—/s/ Niclas Malmcrona

Förord till Volym III
av Niclas Malmcrona
Vice ordförande, Svenska ASSITEJ
Generalsekreterare i Internationella ASSITEJ 1999–2008
Hedersmedlem i Internationella ASSITEJ

Öppenhet, inkluderande kommunikation, professionalism, effektivitet, nätverk. De här orden var nyckelord i ASSITEJs verksamhet när jag började arbeta med ASSITEJ – ett nytt ASSITEJ. Mitt arbete med ASSITEJ sammanfaller till stor del med den period som denna volym III av *The History of ASSITEJ* täcker.

Som organisation hade ASSITEJ ändrats, från att vara en "ursprungligen progressiv organisation till en som gradvis stagnerade och vägrade att följa med i tidens gång", och som inte kunde möta 1990-talets nya tider och senare det nya seklet. Förändringen mot nyare tider började på den 10:e Världskongressen i Stockholm 1990 och fortsatte sedan gradvis därifrån.

Under tiden från 1990 till 1996 förändrades stadgarna, språkfrågan löstes och ASSITEJ förändrades från en västerländsk/europeisk organisation till ett reellt internationellt nätverk.

När jag 1999 valdes till generalsekreterare ville jag fortsätta det förändringsarbete som startades av Michael Ramløse, generalsekreterare (1990–1996) och Michael FitzGerald, president (1993–1999). ASSITEJ behövde och förtjänade ett effektivt, professionellt ledarskap och en exekutivkommitté som svarade och lyssnade på sina medlemmar.

1990 hade ASSITEJ 41 medlemmar och 2008 hade ASSITEJ 75 medlemmar på alla kontinenter. Jag kände 1999 att det var extremt viktigt att förändra ASSITEJ till en sant internationell organisation. För mig betyder sant internationell att det finns medlemmar i alla delar av världen – på alla kontineneter. Det betyder också att alla länder – alla medlemmar – ska ha möjlighet att göra sin röst hörd.

Tillsammans med Harold Oaks, president (1999–2002) reste jag 2000 till Hwange i Zimbabwe. Afrikanska länder var i allt högre utsträckning en del av den internationella scenen, både regionalt och globalt. Det är allmänt accepterat att utvecklingen måste ta hänsyn till kultur och dess olika uttryck för att inte bli endimensionell och per definition begränsad.

Mot den här bakgrunden skapades Internationella ASSITEJs afrikanska nätverk. Mellan 2000 och 2007 arrangerads 16 regionala möten och workshops i 14 olika länder. Syftet med nätverket var inte i första hand att utveckla den individuella kapaciteten, utan att förbättra strategier inom scenkonst för barn och unga så att framgångsrika plattformar för utbildning, debatt och social utveckling skapades.

Detta arbete skedde i Afrika, men erfarenheten gav viktig kunskap för arbete i andra delar av världen. Wolfgang Schneider, president (2002–2012) bidrog till detta arbete med ett vidsträckt resande och sedan början av 2000-talet har ASSITEJ förlagt sina möten till alla kontinenter.

I Tromsø 1999, hade tre eller fyra ASSITEJ-center en e-postadress. Inget center hade en hemsida. Det viktigaste redskapet för kommunikation, om man ville vara snabb, var faxen. Ofta fick ett brev—med kuvert och frimärke – duga. Det tog några dagar att nå ett annat land inom Europa och lite längre om det skulle skickas till en annan kontinent. Sedan 1990 har ASSITEJ stadigt förbättrat kommunikationen genom nyhetsbrev, distribution av protokoll, ASSITEJs årsbok, hemsidan, Facebook och mycket annat....

Idag 2013 är vi alla uppkopplade dag och natt, men fortfarande är det personliga mötet det allra viktigaste. Att vara del av ett nätverk betyder inte bara att man *får* – mer viktigt är att *ge*. Man får aldrig tillbaka mer än man ger. Vi har alla problem med bidrag, nätverkande och begränsade resurser – men det är för det vi har ASSITEJ – till att dela erfarenheter.

Här är också platsen att ge ett erkännade till och tacka Nat Eek (Hederspresident i ASSITEJ), Ann Shaw (Hedersmedlem i ASSITEJ), Katherine Krzys (Kurator vid ASSITEJ/USAs arkiv vid Arizona State University och Kim Peter Kovac (Vicepresident i ASSITEJ USA och Producing Director vid Kennedy Centre i Washington DC). Ert arbete och er hängivenhet i att dokumentera ASSITEJs historia från 1965 till 2005 är enastående! Historien är en del av framtiden och med en gemensam kunskap om vår dåtid kan vi bygga ett hållbart nätverk—för att dela erfarenheter.

ASSITEJ är en organisation och ett nätverk för yrkesverksamma scenkonstnärer i alla delar av världen. Vi arbetar under olika förhållanden, vi arbetar inom olika traditioner och vi arbetar inom olika stilarter. Vi har olika smak, olika åsikter och olika förståelse av god kvalitet.

I tillägg delar vi kärleken för scenkonst, tron på god scenkonst för barn och unga, rätten för en ung generation till estetiska och kulturella erfarenheter. För mig – och, tror jag – för ASSITEJ är en av de viktigaste sakerna att vara öppen och inkluderande. Bara om vi är öppna mot varandra och mot varandras konst kan vi utvecklas och växa – och på så sätt göra ASSITEJ starkare.

Var öppna och inkluderande mot varandra som kollegor och arbetspartners. Var öppna och ärliga mot barnen, vår publik och mottagare av vårt arbete. Detta är anledningen att vi arbetar med scenkonst för barn och unga.

Så ska vi fira ASSITEJs 50-årsjubileum år 2015!

In Swedish by Niclas Malmcrona

Préface au volume 3
par Niclas Malmcrona,
vice-président de l'ASSITEJ Suède,
secrétaire générale de l'ASSITEJ (1999-2008)
Membre Honoraire de l'ASSITEJ Internationale

Franchise, inclusion dans la communication, professionnalisme, effectivité, travail en réseau.
Voici les mots-clé dans le travail et l'existence de l'ASSITEJ, de la nouvelle ASSITEJ, quand j'ai adhéré à l'association. Mon engament dans l'association se situe largement dans la période que couvre ce volume 3 de l'histoire d'ASSITEJ.

Assitej comme organisation avait évolué « d'une organisation au départ progressive à une qui s'était graduellement engourdie et qui refusait de suivre le développement des temps. » Elle avait cessé d'aller en avant à la rencontre des années 1990 et du nouveau siècle. Heureusement ce mouvement vers les temps modernes a commencé dans le X ème Congrès Mondiale à Stockholm en 1990, et petit à petit a continué de se développer.

Entre les années 1990 - 1996 la Constitution a été modernisé, la question des langues a été réglée et l'ASSITEJ occidentale-européenne est devenue un réseau vraiment international.

Quand j'ai été élu secrétaire général en 1999, je voulais continuer le travail commencé par Michael Ramlose, secrétaire général (1990-1996) et de Michael FitzGerald, président de l'association (1993-1999). L'ASSITEJ méritait et avait besoin d'une direction effective et professionnelle et un Comité exécutif qui écoute et répond aux membres de l'association.

En 1990 il y avait 41 pays membres dans l'ASSITEJ. En 2008 l'ASSITEJ rassemblait 75 pays membres sur tous les six continents. En 1991 j'ai pensé qu'il était absolument nécessaire de faire de l'ASSITEJ une organisation réellement internationale. Pour moi réellement internationale, c'est d'avoir des adhérents dans tous les coins du monde, dans tous les continents. Cela voulait dire aussi que tous les pays, tous les membres aient la possibilité d'être entendus.

En 2000 j'ai fait un voyage à Hwange à Zimbabwe avec le président Harold Oakes (1999-2002). Les pays africains montaient de plus en plus sur scène aussi bien dans le réseau régional que globale. Partout dans le monde on soutient l'idée que le développement doit prendre en compte la culture et ses différents manifestations dans l'art, autrement il devient limité et simpliste.

Voir ces circonstances le projet du réseau africain de l'ASSITEJ International a eu lieu. Entre les années 2000-2007 on a organisé 16 rencontres et ateliers dans 14 pays différents, avec 3 réunions du comité exécutif de l'ASSITEJ incluses. Le focus du réseau n'était pas d'avancer les artistes individuels sinon d'améliorer les stratégies du théâtre pour enfants et jeunes gens. Ainsi a-t-on établi des scènes de rencontre pour l'éducation, la discussion, le débat et le développement social.

Ce travail a eu lieu en Afrique, mais cette expérience nous a aidé à travailler dans d'autres parts du monde. Le président Wolfgang Schneider (2002-2012) a contribué à ce travail lors de ces innombrables voyages et au début du nouveau siècle ASSITEJ International a enfin couvert les six continents.

En 1999, quand on a organisé le Congrès International à Tromssö, Norvège, seulement trois ou quatre centres nationaux avaient une adresse « e-mail ». Aucun centre n'avait de page web. La façon la plus rapide pour envoyer des messages était un FAX. Parfois il suffisait d'envoyer une lettre avec enveloppe et timbre, cela prenait 2-3 jours en Europe, un peu plus longtemps pour les autres continents. Depuis 1990 ASSITEJ n'a cessé de développer sa communication à travers les lettres d'info, la publication des procès-verbaux, le livre annuel et les magazines, la page web, le facebook, et autre. En 2013 nous sommes en contact jour et nuit, mais, il faut l'admettre, le contact personnel est le plus important. Etre membre d'un réseau ne signifie pas seulement de recevoir mais aussi de donner. Tu ne recevras pas plus que tu auras donné. Nous connaissons tous des problèmes d'organisation, de financement, de travail de réseau et des ressources limités, mais c'est pourquoi nous avons l'ASSITEJ pour partager nos expériences.

C'est ici que je veux donner crédit et remerciements à Nat EEK (président honoraire de l' ASSITEJ), à Ann Shaw (membre honoraire de l' ASSITEJ), à Katherine Krzys (déléguée de l'ASSITEJ Etats Unis et archiviste) et Kim Peter Kovac (vice- président de l 'ASSITEJ Etats Unis.

Votre travail et zèle à rédiger l'histoire de L'ASSITEJ de 1965 à 2005 est incomparable!
L'histoire fait partie du futur et avec la connaissance commune de notre passé nous pouvons construire un réseau tenace.

L'ASSITEJ est une organisation et un réseau pour les professionnels des arts de scène de tous les coins du monde. Nous travaillons dans des circonstances différents, nous avons des traditions différentes, nous travaillons de manières différentes. Nous avons des goûts différents, des opinions différentes, de différentes conceptions de bonne qualité.

Mais, nous aimons tous les arts de scène, nous croyons dans le bon théâtre pour les enfants et la jeunesse, et nous déclarons le droit de la jeune génération aux expériences culturelles et esthétiques.

Pour moi, comme je crois qu'à l'ASSITEJ aussi, une des choses les plus importantes est d'être ouvert et inclusif. Seulement si nous sommes ouverts envers l'un et l'autre, généreux envers l'art de l'autre, nous pourrons développer et grandir et de cette manière rendre l'ASSITEJ plus forte.

Etre ouverts et inclusifs avec nous autres comme collègues et partenaires de travail. Etre ouverts et honnêtes envers nos enfants et nos jeunes, nos publics et le cible de notre travail. C'est pourquoi nous travaillons dans les arts de scène pour les enfants et la jeunesse. De cette manière nous allons célébrer les 50 ans de l'ASSITEJ en 2015!

/s/ Niclas Malmcrona
Translated by Katariina Metsälampi (Finland)

Никлас Мальмкрона
Вице-президент Шведского центра АССИТЕЖ
Генеральный секретарь АССИТЕЖ (1999-2008)
Почетный член АССИТЕЖ

ПРЕДИСЛОВИЕ

Открытость, взаимодействие, профессионализм, эффективность, нетворкинг

Эти ключевые слова, характеризовали существование и деятельность АССИТЕЖ, когда я начал работать в этой организации – в новой АССИТЕЖ. Период моей работы в основном совпадает с тем периодом, который охватывает настоящий, третий том Истории АССИТЕЖ. Изначально прогрессивная, АССИТЕЖ постепенно превратилась в организацию, которая отличалась застоем и нежеланием быть современной и идти навстречу новым временам в 90-е годы и, позже, в новый век. К счастью, это путешествие навстречу современности началось на X Конгрессе АССИТЕЖ в Стокгольме, в 1990 году, и с тех пор, постепенно, это движение вперед нарастало.

За период с 1990 по 1996 годы стал более современным Устав АССИТЕЖ, была решена проблема перевода на другие языки, из организации, ориентированной на Западную Европу, АССИТЕЖ превратилась в по-настоящему полноценное международную сеть.

Когда в 1999 году меня избрали Генеральным Секретарем, я хотел продолжить работу, начатую Генеральным секретарем Микаэлем Рамлезе (1990-1996) и президентом Майклом Фицжеральдом (1993-1999). АССИТЕЖ нуждалась в эффективном и профессиональном руководстве, а также ейбыл нужен Исполнительный Комитет, который бы слышал своих членов и откликался на это.

В 1990 году АССИТЕЖ входила 41 страна. В 2008 году их стало 75, представлявших все 6 континентов мира. В 1999 году я считал чрезвычайно важным, чтобы АССИТЖ стала действительно настоящей международной организацией. По моему мнению, настоящая международная организация должна иметь членов во всех частях света, на всех континентах. Это означает, что все страны-члены организации имеют возможность быть услышанными.

Вместе с президентом Харольдом Оаксом (1999-2002) я посетил Хараре в Зимбабве в 2000 году. Африканские страны все больше становились частью международной жизни, как на региональном, так и на мировом уровне. Общеизвестно, что для полноценного развития общества требуется внимание к проблемам культуры и ее различным проявлениям в искусстве, иначе общество становится однолинейным и ограниченным по определению.

На таком фоне стартовал проект АССИТЕЖ «Нетворкинг в Африке». С 2000 по 2007 годы в 14 странах Африки было проведено 16 региональных встреч и лабораторий (в том числе 3 заседания Исполкома АСИТЕЖ). Целью этой сетевой работы было не обязательное специфическое продвижение отдельных участников, а улучшение стратегий в области театра для детей и молодежи. Были успешно заложены основы для развития образования, дискуссий и общественного развития.

Эта работа была проведена в Африке, но полученный там опыт дал важные знания для последующей работы в других частях мира. Президент Вольфганг Шнайдер (2002 – 2012) внес большой вклад в эту работу благодаря многочисленным посещениям разных стран – с начала текущего века встречи АССИТЕЖ состоялись на всех шести континентах.

В 1999 году, к Конгрессу в Тромсе в Норвегии, только 3 или 4 центра имели свой электронный адрес. Ни у одного центра не было своего веб-сайта. Основным способом быстрого обмена информацией был факс. Иногда достаточно было написать письмо, положить его в конверт и приклеить марку. Проходило два дня, и оно уже было в любой стране Европы, если же оно было послано на другой континент, требовалось немного больше времени. С 1990 года АССИТЕЖ постоянно улучшала связи со своими центрами с помощью распространения новостных бюллетеней, протоколов заседаний и встреч, Ежегодника АССИТЕЖ, журнала АССИТЕЖ, веб-сайта, сети Фейсбук и др.

Теперь, в 2013 году, мы находимся на связи и днем и ночью, однако самое важное - это личные встречи. Быть частью сети означает не только «получать», более важно, что это также означает «давать». Никогда нельзя получить назад больше, чем даешь. Нам всем понятны проблемы, с которыми мы сталкиваемся, занимаясь организационной деятельностью, финансированием, нетворкингом, имея ограниченные средства. Но именно для этого и существует АССИТЕЖ, она предоставляет возможность делиться опытом.

На этом месте мне хотелось бы воздать должное и поблагодарить Ната Ика (Почетный президент АССИТЕЖ), Энн Шоу (Почетный член АССИТЕЖ), Катарину Кшиз (Куратор архивов АССИТЕЖ/США в Университете штата Аризона) и Кима Питера Ковача (Вице-президент АССИТЕЖ/США, худрук Кеннеди центра в Вашингтоне, штат Колумбия). И отметить их невероятную преданность делу, выразившуюся в желании написать историю АССИТЕЖ с 1965 до 2005 года. История – это часть будущего и, основываясь а наших общих знаниях о нашем прошлом, мы построим серьезную сеть. для обмена опытом!

ASSITEJ - это организация и сеть для профессионалов - действующих практиков исполнительского искусства, работающих в разных частях света. Мы работаем в разных условиях, в разных стилях и на основе разных традиций. У нас разные вкусы, разные мнения, разное понимание хорошего качества.

Плюс к этому, нас всех объединяет любовь к исполнительскому искусству и вера в качественное театральное искусство для детей и молодежи, а также вера в то, что молодое поколение имеет право на эстетический и культурный опыт. Для меня, а также, думаю, и для АССИТЕЖ, самое главное - быть открытым и восприимчивым. Только, если мы будем открыты друг к другу, к искусству друг друга, мы сможем развиваться, расти и сделать нашу организацию сильнее.

Быть открытыми и прислушиваться к коллегам и партнерам по работе. Быть открытыми и честными по отношению к нашим детям, нашим зрителям, к тем, кому предназначена наша работа. Все это лежит в основе нашего желания работать в области исполнительского искусства для детей и молодежи

Никлас Мальмкрона
Translated by Galina Kolosova (Russia)

PRÓLOGO PARA EL VOLUMEN III
POR
Niclas Malmcrona
Vice Presidente de ASSITEJ /Suecia
Secretario General de ASSITEJ (1999-2008)
Miembro Honorario de ASSITEJ/ Int'l

Apertura, incluyendo comunicación, profesionalismo, eficacia, interconexión
Esas eran palabras claves del trabajo y la vida de ASSITEJ cuando recién comenzaba con el trabajo de ASSITEJ-un nuevo ASSITEJ. Mi conexión con ellos coincide en gran parte con el período de este Volumen III que cubre *La Historia de ASSITEJ*.

ASSITEJ como organización ha crecido de una organización originalmente progresiva a una que gradualmente se ha estancado y ha rehusado a mantenerse con el desarrollo de los tiempos actuales", al no moverse hacia adelante para acercarse a los nuevos tiempos de los años noventas y más tarde con la llegada del nuevo siglo. Afortunadamente su viaje hacia los tiempos modernos comenzó durante el Décimo Congreso del Mundo en Estocolmo en 1990 y graduablemente se ha movido hacia adelante desde allí.

Desde 1990 a 1996 se modernizó la Constitución, el problema sobre el idioma se resolvió y ASSITEJ se transformó de una organización centrada en Europa Occidental a una red verdaderamente internacional.

Cuando fui elegido Secretario General en 1999, yo quise continuar el trabajo que había comenzado Michael Ramløse, Secretario General (1990-1996) y Michael FitzGerald, Presidente (1993-1999). ASSITEJ necesitaba y merecía tener un liderazgo más efectivo y profesional, y un Comité Ejecutivo que respondiera y escuchara a sus miembros.

En 1990, cuarenta y un (41) países eran miembros de ASSITEJ. En 2008 tenía setenta y cinco (75) países miembros en todos los seis continentes. En 1999 sentía que era extremadamente importante transformar ASSITEJ en una organización verdaderamente internacional. Para mí verdaderamente internacional significaba tener miembros en todas partes del mundo – en todos los continentes. Esto, al mismo tiempo quería decir que todos los países
– todos sus miembros – tuvieran la posibilidad de ser escuchados.

Conjuntamente con Harold Oaks, Presidente, (1999-2002) viajé a Hwange en Zimbabue en el año 2000. Los países africanos se hacían más visibles en el escenario internacional, tanto regionalmente como en forma global. Es universalmente aceptado que el desarrollo ponga atención en la cultura y en sus variadas manifestaciones de arte, o de lo contrario, pasa a ser, por definición, unidimensional y limitado.

Ante estos antecedentes, nació el proyecto de las Redes Africanas de ASSITEJ/Int'l.

El total de 16 reuniones africanas y talleres regionales (incluyendo 3 de ASSITEJ/Int'l EC Meeting) se llevaron a cabo en 14 países entre el año 2000 a 2007. El enfoque de la red no era necesariamente capacitar a individuos específicos, sino a mejorar las estrategias relacionadas con los niños y jóvenes del teatro, de modo que se establecieron exitosas plataformas para educación, debate y desarrollo social.

Este trabajo se realizó en África, pero las experiencias arrojaron importantes conocimientos para trabajar en otras partes del mundo. Wolfgang Schneider, Presidente (2002-2012) contribuyó a su trabajo con extensos viajes y a principios del nuevo siglo ASSITEJ/Int'l había conocido los seis continentes.

En 1999 en Tromsø, Noruega, tres de los cuatro centros de ASSITEJ tenían direcciones de correos electrónicos. Ninguno de los centros tenía una página en la Internet. La principal herramienta de comunicación, si Ud. la necesitaba rápido era el FAX. A veces era suficiente con una carta-con un sobre y un sello postal-pero tomaba algunos días en llegar de un país a otro en Europa-un poquito más de tiempo si quería alcanzar a otro continente. Desde 1990 ASSITEJ ha mejorado su comunicación a través de boletines, distribución de minutas de reuniones, la revista anual de ASSITEJ, su sitio en la Internet, Facebook y mucho más....

En 2013 estamos todos en contacto día y noche, pero todavía los encuentros en persona son los más importantes. Ser parte de la red, no solamente significa recibir – pero lo más importante es dar. Nunca se recibe tanto como cuando se da. Todos comprendemos los problemas que tenemos con la organización, reunión de fondos, interconexión y recursos limitados – pero por eso tenemos ASSITEJ-y compartimos las experiencias.

Este es también el lugar para agradecer y reconocer a Nat Eek (Presidente Honorario de ASSITEJ) Ann Shaw (Miembro Honorario de ASSITEJ), Katherine Krzys (Conservadora de los Archivos de ASSITEJ/USA en la Universidad del Estado de Arizona) y Kim Peter Novak (Vicepresidente de ASSITEJ/USA y Director Productivo en el Kennedy Center de Washington D.C.) Su dedicación al trabajo para conservar la historia de ASSITEJ desde 1965 hasta 2005. ¡Ha sido sobresaliente! La historia es parte del futuro, con un conocimiento común de nuestro pasado, construiremos una red sostenible compartiendo las experiencias.

ASSITEJ es una organización y red para profesionales de las artes de la representación de todas partes del mundo. Trabajamos bajo diferentes condiciones, distintas tradiciones y diferentes estilos. Tenemos gustos diferentes, opiniones diferentes y entendemos la buena calidad de diferentes maneras.

Además, todos compartimos la devoción por el arte de la representación, la creencia de un buen arte para los niños y jóvenes, el derecho que tienen las generaciones más jóvenes a experiencias estéticas y culturales. Para mí-y creo que para ASSITEJ-una de las cosas más importantes es ser abierto y global. Solamente si estamos abiertos entre nosotros, hacia el arte de todos nosotros, podemos desarrollarnos y crecer – y así hacer de ASSITEJ una organización fuerte.

Ser abierto y ser global entre nosotros mismos como colegas y compañeros de trabajo. Ser abiertos y agradecidos hacia nuestros niños, nuestras audiencias y receptores de nuestros trabajos. Estas son las razones por qué trabajamos con las artes de la representación para los niños y la juventud.

¡Así es como celebraremos el aniversario número 50 de ASSITEJ en 2015!

Translated by Isabelle C. Jennings (USA)

VORWORT ZU BAND III

von

Niclas Malmcrona

Vizepräsident, ASSITEJ Schweden
Generalsekretär ASSITEJ (1999–2008)
Ehrenmitglied ASSITEJ International

Offenheit in Verbindung mit Kommunikation, Professionalität, Effizienz und vernetztem Arbeiten

Das waren die Prinzipien der ASSITEJ, als ich anfing, für die Vereinigung zu arbeiten – eine neue ASSITEJ. Meine Tätigkeit fällt größtenteils in den Zeitraum, der in diesem dritten Band der Reihe *The History of ASSITEJ* (Die Geschichte der ASSITEJ) beschrieben wird.

Die ASSITEJ entwickelte sich von „einer ursprünglich fortschrittlichen Vereinigung zu einer Organisation, die immer mehr stagnierte, nicht mit der Zeit ging" und auch nicht in den 90er Jahren oder später im neuen Jahrhundert ankam. Glücklicherweise begann die Reise in die Neuzeit während des 10. Weltkongresses in Stockholm und setzte sich danach Schritt für Schritt weiter fort.

In den Jahren von 1990 bis 1996 wurde die Satzung modernisiert, das Sprachproblem gelöst und die ASSITEJ von einer westlich/europäisch ausgerichteten Vereinigung in ein wirklich internationales Netzwerk umgewandelt.

Als ich 1999 zum Generalsekretär gewählt wurde, wollte ich das Werk von Michael Ramløse, Generalsekretär (1990–1996), und Michael FitzGerald, Präsident (1993–1999), fortführen. Die ASSITEJ benötigte und verdiente eine effiziente, professionelle Leitung sowie einen Vorstand, der die Mitglieder der Vereinigung anhörte und auf sie einging.

Im Jahr 1990 hatte die ASSITEJ 41 Mitgliedsländer, 2008 waren es 75 auf allen sechs Kontinenten. Ich spürte 1999, dass es enorm wichtig war, die ASSITEJ in eine wirklich internationale Organisation zu verwandeln. Wirklich international heißt für mich, dass es Mitglieder auf allen Kontinenten in allen Teilen der Welt gibt. Es bedeutet auch, dass alle Länder – alle Mitglieder – die Möglichkeit haben, angehört zu werden.

Im Jahr 2000 reiste ich mit Harold Oaks, Präsident von 1999 bis 2002, nach Hwange in Simbabwe. Die afrikanischen Länder betraten zunehmend die internationale Bühne, sowohl im regionalen als auch im globalen Kontext. Es ist allgemein anerkannt, dass Entwicklung immer im Einklang mit Kultur und deren verschiedenen Erscheinungsformen in der Kunst einhergehen muss, ansonsten wird sie definitionsgemäß eindimensional und beschränkt.

Vor diesem Hintergrund wurde das African Network Project der ASSITEJ International initiiert. Zwischen den Jahren 2000 und 2007 fanden in Afrika 16 regionale Treffen und Workshops (einschließlich drei Treffen des Exekutivausschuss der ASSITEJ International) in 14 Ländern statt. Im Netzwerk ging es nicht vordergründig um die besondere Förderung des Einzelnen, sondern vielmehr darum, die Strategien im Bereich des Kinder- und Jugendtheaters so zu verbessern, dass erfolgreiche Plattformen für Bildung, Diskussionen und soziale Entwicklung geschaffen werden konnten.

All dies geschah zwar in Afrika, brachte aber auch wertvolle Erkenntnisse für die Arbeit in anderen Teilen der Welt. Wolfgang Schneider, Präsident von 2002 bis 2012, leistete hierzu mit seinen zahlreichen Reisen einen großen Beitrag. Seit Beginn des neuen Jahrhunderts gab es auf allen sechs Kontinenten Treffen der ASSITEJ International.

Im Jahr 1999 hatten in Tromsø, Norwegen, nur drei oder vier ASSITEJ/Zentren eine E-Mail-Adresse. Keines hatte eine Internet-Seite. Der Hauptweg für schnelle Kommunikation war das Fax. Manchmal genügte auch ein Brief – mit Stempel und Umschlag – der in innerhalb Europas mehrere Tage und in Länder auf anderen Kontinenten noch etwas länger benötigte. Seit 1990 hat die ASSITEJ ihre Kommunikation durch die Veröffentlichung von Newslettern, Protokollen der Sitzungen, Jahrbüchern, Magazinen, die Website, Facebook und anderes mehr immer weiter verbessert.

Im Jahr 2013 sind wir nun Tag und Nacht miteinander verbunden, aber die persönlichen Begegnungen sind noch immer am wichtigsten. Als Teil eines Netzwerkes bekommt man nicht nur mehr, man gibt auch mehr. Man bekommt nie mehr, als man selber gibt. Wir alle verstehen die Probleme, denen wir in der Organisation, der Finanzierung, im Netzwerk und mit begrenzten Mitteln gegenüberstehen, aber genau dafür haben wir die ASSITEJ – um Erfahrungen auszutauschen.

An dieser Stelle möchte ich die Arbeit von Nat Eek (Ehrenpräsident der ASSITEJ), Ann Shaw (Ehrenmitglied der ASSITEJ), Katherine Krzys (Kuratorin der Archive der ASSITEJ USA an der Arizona State University) und Kim Peter Kovac (Vizepräsident der ASSITEJ USA sowie Produzent und Regisseur am Kennedy Center in Washington, DC) würdigen und ihnen herzlich danken. Ihr Einsatz für die Aufzeichnung der Geschichte der ASSITEJ von 1965 bis 2005 ist einfach herausragend! Die Geschichte ist Teil unserer Zukunft und mit dem Wissen über unsere Vergangenheit können wir ein nachhaltiges Netzwerk aufbauen. Um Erfahrungen auszutauschen!

Die ASSITEJ ist eine Vereinigung und ein Netzwerk für professionelle darstellende Künstler aus der ganzen Welt. Wir arbeiten unter verschiedenen Ausgangsbedingungen, mit verschiedenen Traditionen, auf verschiedene Art und Weise. Wir haben verschiedene Geschmäcker, verschiedene Meinungen, verschiedene Ansichten bezüglich guter Qualität.

Zudem teilen wir jedoch alle die Liebe zu darstellender Kunst, den Glauben an gutes Theater für Kinder und Jugendliche sowie das Recht der Jugend auf ästhetische und kulturelle Erfahrungen. Für mich – und ich glaube, auch für die ASSITEJ – ist einer der wichtigsten Aspekte, dass die Vereinigung offen und integrativ arbeitet. Nur wenn wir einander offen begegnen und offen sind für die Kunst des Anderen, können wir uns weiterentwickeln und wachsen – und so die ASSITEJ stärken.

Seid als Kollegen und Partner offen im Umgang miteinander. Seid offen und ehrlich zu unseren Kindern, unserem Publikum, den Empfängern unserer Arbeit. Das sind die Gründe, warum wir im Bereich der darstellenden Kunst für Kinder und Jugendliche arbeiten.

In diesem Sinne werden wir auch den 50. Jahrestag der ASSITEJ im Jahr 2015 begehen.

Übersetzung: Gisa Schönfeld (Germany)

第Ⅲ巻発刊によせて

ニクラス・マルムクローナ

　公開性、　情報交流、　専門性、　実効力、　ネットワーク：
　これらの語は私がアシテジ活動に参加するようになった時、いわば新しいアシテジのキーワードでした。その時期こそ、まさに本書「アシテジの歴史；第Ⅲ巻」の時代です。
　アシテジは、組織としては、当初の進歩的団体から次第に行き詰まって時勢の進展に追いつけなくなり、1990年代から次の新世紀に向けての時代の要望に応えられない状態でした。幸運にも、1990年に第10回アシテジ世界大会がストックホルムで開催されて新しい動きが芽生え、そこから次第に前進が始まります。
　1990年から1996年にかけて規約が時代に合わせて改正され、言語問題も解決し、アシテジは西欧中心の組織から真に国際的なネットワークへと転換しました。

　私は1999年にアシテジ事務局長に選任された時、前事務局長ミケル・ラムローズ(1990-1996)、前会長マイケル・フィッジェラルド(1993-1999)の路線を受け継いで行こうと思いました。アシテジは有能な専門的指導力と、会員の声に耳を傾ける理事会を必要としていました。
　1990年のアシテジ会員数は41ヵ国、そして2008年には会員数75ヵ国となり、世界の六大陸全てに広がりました。1999年の時点で私はアシテジが真の国際組織になることが極めて重要であると考えました。真に国際的とは、私の考えでは全世界の六大陸すべてに会員がいることであり、その全会員の意見が反映されるということです。

　当時会長であったハロルド・オークス(1999-2002)と共に、私は2000年にジンバブエのフワンゲに行きました。その頃、アフリカ諸国はアフリカ地域内でも世界的にも次第に頭角を現しつつありました。発展するときに重要なことは、文化とその多様な芸術表現を大切にすることであり、そうしなければ一方的で偏向してしまうことは周知の事実です。
　その認識にもとづいて、世界アシテジのアフリカ・ネットワーク計画が発足しました。2000年から2007年の間に、アフリカの14の国において、16の地域で集会やワークショップ、さらにアシテジ理事会も3回開催されました。この計画の意図は、個々の進展というよりも、児童青少年演劇への理解を深めることにあり、その結果として教育や討議、社会発展のための有意義な土台が築かれました。

　これはアフリカでの実例ですが、その体験は世界の他の地域における活動にも貴重な貢献をもたらしました。アシテジ会長のオルフガン・シュナイダー(2000-2012)はこの体験をもとに広く各地を訪れ、現在アシテジは21世紀初頭以来、六大陸全てに会員が存在します。
　1999年ノルウェーのトロムソでの第13回世界大会の時点で、Eメール・アドレスを持っていた会員センターはわずか3、4ヵ国だけで、ウエブページは皆無でした。緊急の場合の情報連絡手段は主にFAXでした。通常は封筒や切手による郵便が主流でしたが、ヨーロッパ地域内でも2、3日かかり、他の大陸との間ではもっと長くかかりました。

1990年以降、アシテジは情報交流の改善をはかり、会報アシテジ・ニュース、各会議の議事録配布、年報、ウエブサイト、フェイスブックなどの手段を活用しています。

　2013年の今、私たちは皆、昼も夜もつながっていますが、それでもやはり個人的な出会いは最も大切です。ネットワークの一員になるということは、そこから何かを得るというだけでなく、さらにより重要なことは、そこに何かを与えるということなのです。あなたは自分が与えるもの以上に多くのものを得ることはないでしょう。私たちの前には、組織や資金、ネットワークなど種々の多くの問題がありますが、それだからこそ、経験や知識を分かち合うアシテジという場が存在するのです。

　そこはまた信頼と敬意を共有する場でもあり、ここで次の方々に感謝を捧げます：
ナット・イーク（Nat Eek；アシテジ名誉会長）
アン・ショウ（Ann Shaw；アシテジ名誉会員）
キャサリン・クリス（Katherine Krrys；アリゾナ州立大内アメリカ・アシテジ文書館館長）
キム・ピーター・コバック（Kim Peter Kovac；アメリカ・アシテジ副会長、ケネディ・センター制作部長）
これらの方々は1965年から2005年までの世界アシテジの歴史において実に献身的な活動をされました。歴史とは未来の一部をなすものであり、そして私たちは共通の過去認識の土台の上にこそ堅固なネットワークを築くことができます。経験を共有するために！

　アシテジは全世界の舞台芸術専門家たちの組織、ネットワークです。私たちは皆それぞれ異なる状況、異なる伝統の下で、異なるスタイルで働いています。皆それぞれ趣向も、意見も、特質判断の見解も異なります。
　それでも私たちは皆、舞台芸術への愛と、優れた児童青少年演劇への熱意、そして若い世代が美的・文化的経験を享受する権利への活動を共有しようとしています。
私は、アシテジにとって最も重要なことの一つは、開放的であり包容力を持つことだと思います。私たち自身相互に、そして相互の芸術に心を開き合うことこそが、今後の成長発展を可能にし、またアシテジをより強固にしていくのです。

　同労の仲間としてお互いを受け入れましょう。また子どもたち、観客、仕事の関係者たちにも誠実、率直に対応しましょう。それは私たち児童青少年演劇の世界で働く者の叡知です。

　このようにして私たちは2015年のアシテジ設立50周年祝賀の時を迎えましょう！

ニクラス・マルムクローナ（Niclas Malmcrona）：
　スエーデン・アシテジ副会長、アシテジ前事務局長（1999-2008）、世界アシテジ名誉会員

Translated by Fusako Kurihara (Japan)

Mau okhuza pa bukku lacitatu
Wolemba ndi
Niclas Malcrona
Othandizira akumpando wa ASSITEJ Sweden
Ndiponso a Kalembera a ASSITEJ (1999-2008)
Ndiponso a Membala a ASSITEJ

Kugwira ncito poonekera, kulankhulizana, kugwira ncito munjira yo lungama, ndiponso kusewenzera pamodzi

Awo ndiwo anali mawu akuru a ncito la kabungwe ka ASSITEJ pamene ine ndinakhala ogwapo pa ncito imeneyi ya ASSITEJ watsopano. Kugwapo kwanga kunabwera panthawi imene buku imeneli ili kuyanganapo. Iyi buku ndi lacitatu la mabuku oyangana pa ncito la ASSITEJ kucokera ku ciyambi.

Bungwe la ASSITEJI linasinthadi kucokera kukhala bungwe lopita patsogolo ndikukhala bungwe imene inali kulephera kugwira ncito ndi kusintha. Bungweli lina lephera kupita patsogolo ndi ncito la tsopano mu caka ca 1990. Komadi co khoma ndi cakuti ulendo olowa mu nthawi ya tsopano unayamba mu caka cimeneci ca 1990 ku Msonkhano wa Khumi wa maiko amene ali ma membala a ASSITEJ. Msonkhanowu unacitika mu mzinda wa Stockholm ku dziko la Sweden.

Kucokera mu caka ca 1990 kufikira mu 1996 buku la malamulo la ASSITEJ lina sinthidwa kuti likhale logwilizana ndi zocitika zatsopano. Bvuto la malilime ogwiritsidwa ncito ndi ASSITEJ linatha. Ndiponso bungweli linakula ndi kukhala lopezeka padziko lonse la pansi. Pamene ndinasankhidwa kukhala Kalembera mu 1999, ndinapitiriza ndi ncito imene anacita a Michael Ramlose, amene anali Kalembera kucokera mu caka ca1990 kufikira mu 1996. Ramlose anakhala ali kugwira ncito imeneyi ndi a Michael Fitzgerald, amene anali a kumpando a ASSITEJ kucokera mu caka ca 1993 ndikufikira mu 1999. ASSITEJ linali lofunitsitsa kukhala ndi atsogoleri okhwima, ogwira ncito mwaubwino ndiponso omvera maganizo a ma membala a bungwe la ASSITEJ.

Mu caka ca 1990 bungwe la ASSITEJ linali ndi ma membala mu maiko makhumi anai ndi limodzi (41). Mu caka ca 2008 bungweli linali ndi ma membala mu maiko ofika pa 75. Mu caka ca 1999 ndinakhala ndi ganizo lakuti cinali cofunikira ndithu kuti ASSITEJ likhale bungwe la anthu onse pa dziko la pansi, kuthanthauza kuti likhale ndi ma membala kucokera ku mizinda losiyana siyana la padziko la pansi. Ganizo langa linali lakuti ma membala onse kucokera ku maiko amitundu yosiyana siyana akhale olankhulapo pa ncito la bungwe lathu.

Conde mu caka ca 2000 ndinakhala ndi ulendo opita ku mzinda wa Harare ku Zimbabwe ndi wankumpando wa ASSITEJ bambo Harold Oaks. Bamboyu anali vamumpando wa bungweli kucokera mu caka ca1999 ndikufikira mu caka ca 2002. Tinaona kuti maiko a mu Afrika anakhala ogwapo pazocitika padziko la pansi. Anthu onse a padziko ali obvomekezana kuti mkhalidwe ndi mwambo wa anthu zili zofunikira kuti za masewera zipite patsogolo.

Kucokera mu caka ca 2000 ndi kufikira mu caka ca 2007 ndinakhala ogwirizana ndi maiko a mu Afrika pa ncito la ASSITEJ. Conde misonkhano yosiyana siyana inakhala yocitika mu maiko khumi ndi anai a mu Afrika. Tinakhala ndi cigwirizano mu Afrika ndiponso ncito la ASSITEJ linapita patsogolo. Ngakhale ncitoli linacitikira mu Afrika, zimene zinacitika zinatipatsa nzeru zocita zimenezi mu mizinda ina ya padziko lapansi. Wakumpando wa bungwe la ASSITEJ, bambo Wolfgang Schneider, anakhala ogwapo pa ncito limeneli pakutenga maulendo ambiri ku mizinda yosiyana siyana.

Mu caka ca 1999 mu mzinda wa Tromso ku dziko la Norway ma membala ambiri anali kugwirisa ncito ma lamya ndiponso tinali ndibvuto lo patsana mauthenga. Tinalinso kugwiritsa ncito ma kalata amene anali kutenga masiku ambiri kuti afike. Komabe lero zinthu zakhala zosintha cifukwa ca internet. Lero ndi capafupi ku patsana mauthenga ndiponso tilikudziwa zimene zili kucitika mu maiko a ma membala athu.

Tsopano ndifuna kuyamikira ndi kuonga anthu awa pancito labwino limene anacita lolemba zimene zinacitika mu bungwe la ASSITEJ kucokera mu caka ca 1965 kufikira mu caka ca 2005: Nat Eek, Ann Shaw, Katherine Krzys, ndi Kim Peter Kovac. Titaziwa zimene zinacitika kale tizakhala oziwa zocita kutsogolo.

ASSITEJ ndi bungwe limene libweretsa anthu pamodzi ocekera ku maiko osiyana siyana, ndiponso ali ndi maganiso ndi makhalidwe osiyana siyana. Ndiponso tonse tili okonda ncito ya masewera a ana ndi anyamata. Cikhulupiriro canga ndiponso ca ASSITEJ ndicakuti bungwe lathu lizakula ndi kulimba ngati ma membala onse akhala ogwapo ndiponso ocita ncito zao poyera osati munjira yobisala.

Khalani omasuka ndiponso ogwirizana pa ncito lanu. Tikhale omasuka ndiponso okamba coonadi ku ana athu, ku anthu oyangana masewera athu, ndiponso awo olandira zincito zathu. Ndiye cifukwa cace tiri ogwapo pa ncito yocita masewera okwendeletsa ana ndiponso acinyamata ndi asikana.

Iyi ndiyo njira imene tizakondwereramo cikumbuso ca Makhumi Asanu cakuyamba kwa ncito la ASSITEJ ca caka ca 2015!

Translated in Chinyanja (Zambia) by Cheela Chilala, PhD

INTRODUCTION
by Nat Eek

Sources

Since we have now arrived at the final volume of this three-part *History of ASSITEJ*, our sources have expanded considerably. First of all, records of the various meetings are not only accessible, but can be easily duplicated and forwarded. Photographs of the various meetings and their participants can easily be sent via e-mail in a *pdf* file. Most of the participants are alive and leading active theatrical lives. All of this made compiling this history much easier than the first two volumes. It also made for more communication and more writing!

Eek began his association with ASSITEJ in 1965 at its Founding Conference in Paris, continued it through his Presidency to 1975, and has attended all but one of the World Congresses up to and including that in Montreal, Canada in 2005. Only the Moscow Congress of 1984 was missed. Since then he has attended the World Congress in Copenhagen/Malmö in 2011.

Shaw first attended ASSITEJ in 1972 at the Canada/USA joint Congress in Montreal, Canada and Albany, New York, USA. As a member of the US Center she attended the Spanish Congress in 1978. Then as President of ASSITEJ/USA, she began attending all ASSITEJ meetings in 1978 as an elected Member of the EC and one of its Vice-Presidents. She went off the EC in 1988, but continued attending all the Congresses up to and including Montreal, Canada in 2005. Altogether Eek and Shaw have attended every one of the Congresses from the beginning of ASSITEJ in 1965 up through 2005.

For the writing of Volume III, we have asked Kim Peter Kovac to join our team. Kovac became acquainted with ASSITEJ by first attending the German Director's Seminar in the GDR in 1986. He joined the Board of ASSITEJ/USA (now TYA/USA) in 1998, and was appointed their International Representative in 2001. He attended his first ASSITEJ World Congress in Seoul, Korea in 2002. He was elected Vice-President of TYA/USA in 2002, and then served as their President from 2004–2008. From 2005–2008 he served on the ASSITEJ/Int'l Executive Committee, first as a Counselor, and then as a Member, and was elected as a Vice-President of ASSITEJ/Int'l from 2008–2014. He has been an invaluable source of first hand information, as well as contributing to the writing, editing, and proofing of this manuscript. His contributions have helped us conclude Volume III on a high note.

The attendances of Eek, Kovac, Shaw, and Krzys at these final Congresses in 1991–2005 provide a compendium of personally witnessed activities and events of ASSITEJ/Int'l, although Eek and Shaw attended few if any of the EC and Bureau Meetings in 1991–2005, but Kovac started attendance in 1986,and was on the EC as of 2005.

Also, we have relied extensively on younger eyes and fresher insights in detailing these meetings. In addition, the following people who were involved significantly in ASSITEJ have both contributed to and helped edit the manuscript: Michael Ramløse, Niclas Malmcrona, Michael FitzGerald, Harold Oaks, Wolfgang Schneider, Meiki Fechner, Galya Kolosova, Ivica Šimič, Vicky Ireland, Kim Woo Ok, Fusako Kurihara, and Cheeli Chilala.

Organizational Pattern of the History: This History has been completed in three volumes. Volume I covered the first ten (10) years of the existence of ASSITEJ, the time when Eek was an officer and most active in the organization, and was published in 2008. Volume II covered the next fifteen (15) years of the existence of ASSITEJ, the time when Shaw was an officer and most active in the organization, and was published in 2011. Volume III covers the final fifteen (15) years of this History, ending with the Canadian Congress in Montreal in 2005, and is being published in 2014. All three volumes have been written in chronological order starting with the early informal meetings of 1957. They now conclude in 2005, and it will up to other scholars to continue the History of ASSITEJ/Int'l.

As in the past two volumes, there is a narrative of all the Executive Committee and Bureau meetings over the years, as well as the results of those meetings. Anything significant that occurred between meetings is also listed, usually under the title of "Interim", which includes major world events that affected the tenor of the meetings and the activities of ASSITEJ. There are also Interim sections between major meetings that describe some of the activities of the Association and the world.

At the end of every few years there is a Summary listing the salient points, achievements, failures, disappointments of that time in the progressive history of the Association. Comments on historical events, personal experience, and observations are added to the Summaries whenever appropriate.

If the reader wishes to get a complete but simplified overview of the History of ASSITEJ, it is recommended that he or she go from Summary to Summary, thus avoiding many of the finer details. Hopefully the reader will then want to go back and read this History in greater detail.

The History concludes with a summing up of the past and future of ASSITEJ as of 2005, then its current status in 2013, and its possible future direction. Some comment has been added on the World Congress in Adelaide, Australia in

2008 and that of 2011 held in Copenhagen, Denmark and Malmö, Sweden.

Appendices: Separate Appendices follow the same pattern as the two previous Volumes: the dates of meetings, locations, major individual participants, and countries participating. Also in the Appendices are copies of the original (1965), and the current Constitution of ASSITEJ (2005). Because of the major changes made to the Constitution at the Copenhagen/Malmö World Congress, the current Constitution (2011) has been included. Other items too lengthy to include in the body of the History are also added.

Conference Titling: Consistency in terminology has been difficult in that many different terms were used interchangeably and in some cases indiscriminately. Many times this was a result of improper translation. In terms of titling, the archives show a mixture of terms—conference, general assembly, congress, world congress. The initial meetings to form ASSITEJ were called conferences. Since the organizational structure of ASSITEJ was patterned after the United Nations, the word General Assembly began being used for the proposed future gatherings. That in turn was abandoned for the term International Congress by the Prague meeting in 1966. For clarity in this History, the Paris meeting is called the Constitutional Conference. Meetings after Paris are designated as International Congresses, and then World Congresses after 1990. The term World Congress emerged after the Stockholm meeting in 1990, undoubtedly prompted by the incredible increase of national centers around the world promoted by the Nordic Centers. The governing rules of the Association are called both the Statutes and the Constitution.

The meetings within a Congress have been called Plenary Sessions, General Assemblies, Discussion Sessions, etc. For the sake of clarity the term General Assembly has been used whenever all the delegates at the Congress met together.

Abbreviations: To avoid writing out the term Executive Committee each time, the abbreviation EXCOM was used in Volumes I and II. The official minutes of the organization after 1990 uses the abbreviation EC, and for consistency EC has been used throughout Volume III. Since the creation of Commissions which evolved into Working Groups, and have proved to be very active, the abbreviations of C+number andWG+number are used many times to avoid writing out the name.

The abbreviations FGR for the Federal Republic of Germany, GDR for the German Democratic Republic, USSR for the Union of Soviet Socialist Republics, and USA for the United States of America have been used. As countries were consolidated, separated, and/or changed in name, the new name has always been used with a single identification of the old name at the time of the change. Then the new name is used consistently. For example: USSR became Russia, Georgia,

Ukraine, etc.; Czechoslovakia became the Czech Republic and Slovakia; FGR and GDR became Germany; and Yugoslavia became Croatia, Serbia, etc. In Vol. III UK has been used consistently for Great Britain.

Participants are first mentioned by their full name, and after that the narrative uses their last name. Usually no formal titles are used, only the titles of the elected officers of the ASSITEJ Association.

Spellings of words throughout are American rather than British, since the authors are American and wanted to avoid a mixture of styles.

Meeting Narrative: Each meeting's narration begins with a listing in bold type of dates, locations, officers, participants, countries represented, members absent, and special items of information. The notes on the meeting itself usually follow this order: agenda, discussion, motions or decisions, special presentations, special events or performances seen, and finally a brief evaluation.

Summaries: Personal brief biographies, anecdotes, historic notes, comments and evaluations on the meetings and performances presented are all given in the Summaries to put the actions taken in proper perspective. More complete Biographies of the current ASSITEJ World Leaders (1991–2005) are in Appendix B, which also indicates where earlier Biographies can be found in Volumes I and II.

Notes: Notes are placed at the end of the Volume after the Appendices to avoid interrupting the narrative. The font used throughout the manuscript is Times New Roman in a variety of fonts.

Authors' Caveat: This History is written from the perspective of a citizen of the United States of America, and should be judged accordingly. However, the authors have tried to be as objective as possible in their observations and judgments, while keeping an international perspective. Also, we have tried to keep the narrative human and personal, and any errors of fact are certainly not deliberate but those of the authors.

The authors hope that this document will prove to become a rich and accurate resource of the history of an important international theatre organization, and we are grateful for the privilege of attending the actual events and recording this history in writing.

PART VI

THE CHANGING OF THE GUARD/CUBA 1993

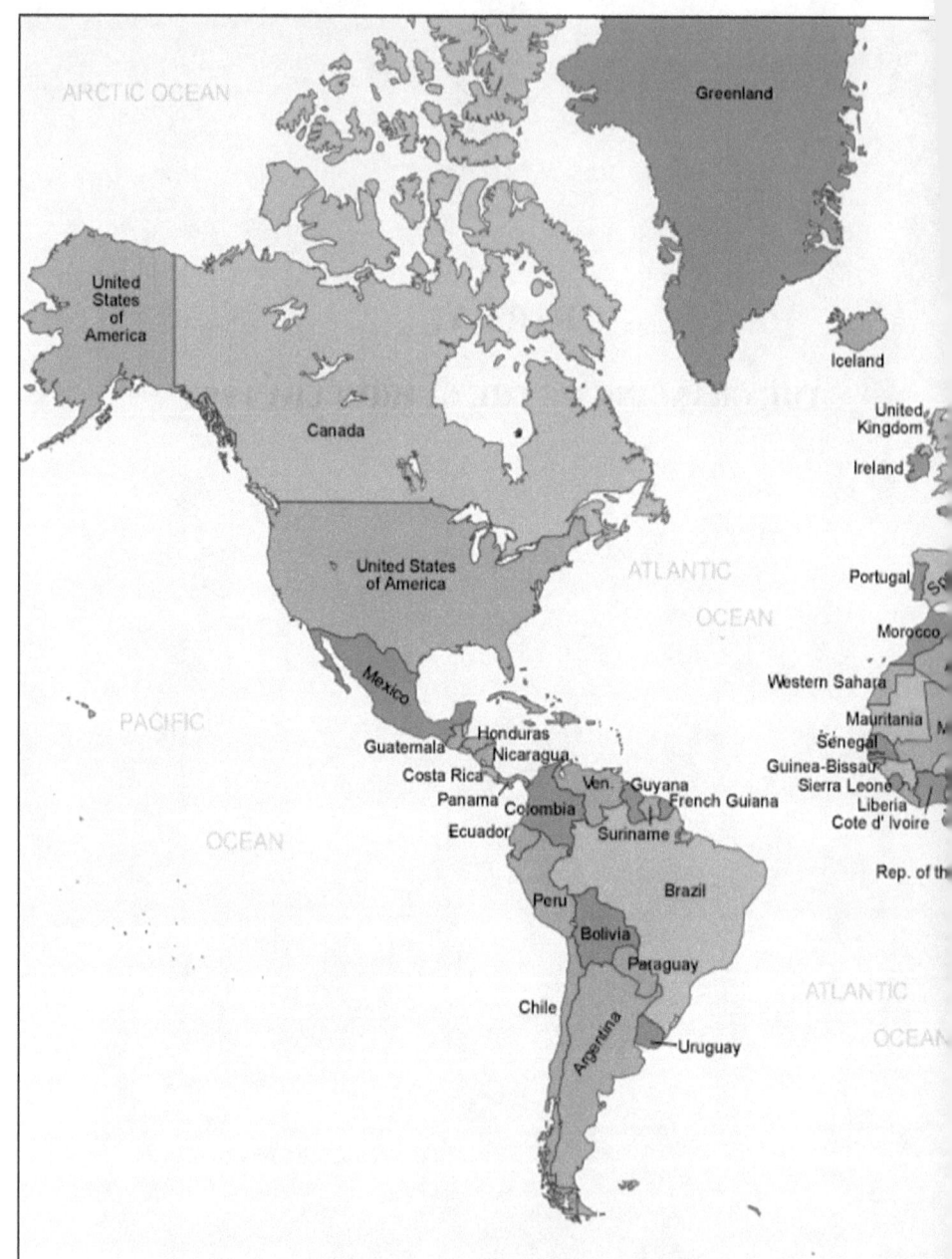

The world of 1991.

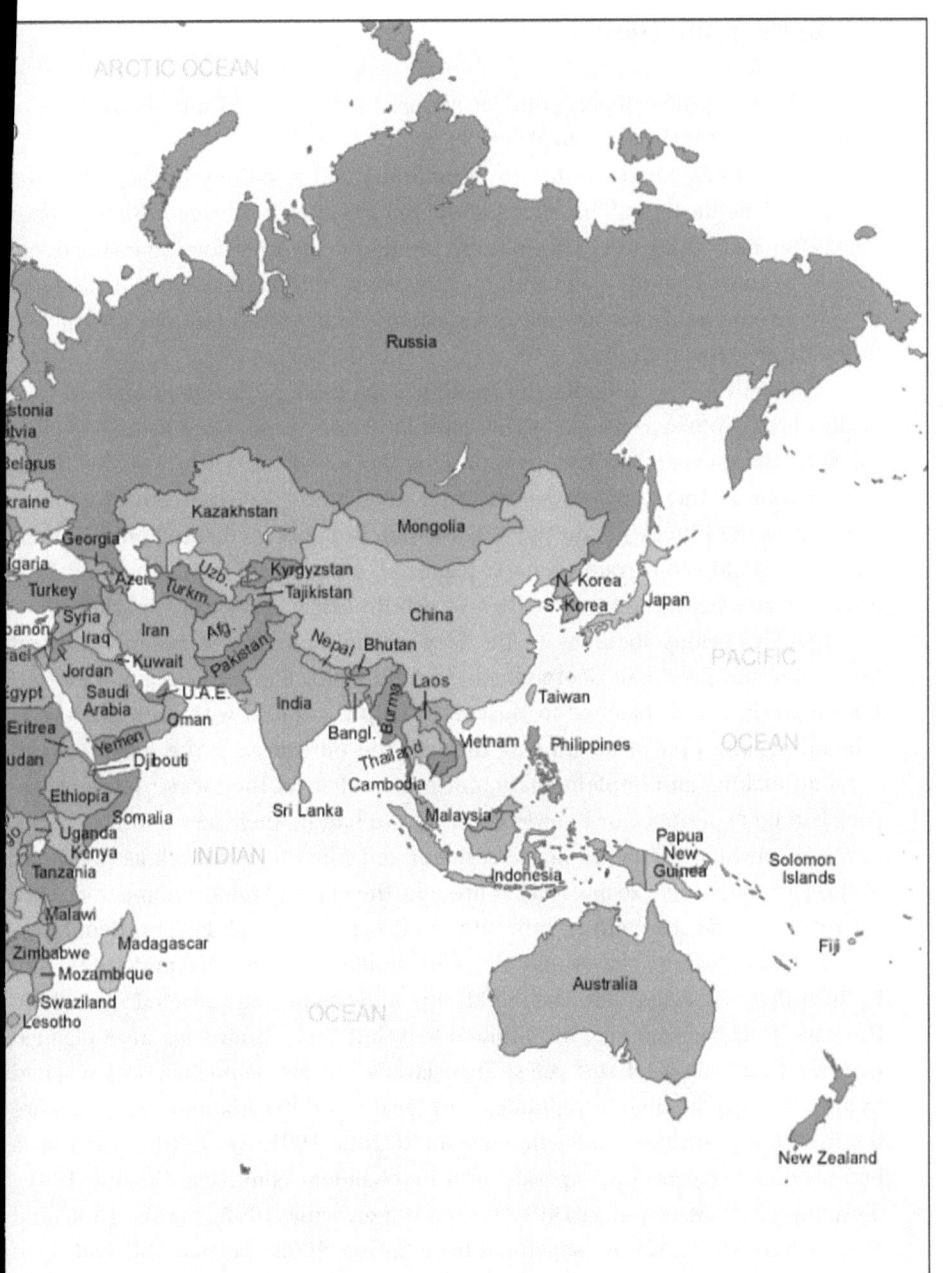

The world of 1991.

The World at the Time[2]

The most electrifying political element of the 1990s was the decline of communism from Germany to Mongolia.

After a 45-year division into Communist and non-Communist states, the collapse of the Berlin wall in 1989 and the reunification of Germany on 3 October 1990 after forty-five years of separation, brought currency reform and support to the newly unified country, and with it came a new solidity in Europe. At the same time in a remarkable gesture the new Germany sent $10 billion in economic aid to the former Soviet Union.

The Soviet Union under the tenuous leadership of President Mikhail Gorbachev broke into separate countries, with Lithuania, Latvia, and Estonia leading the way. Russia had become a republic with Georgia, the Ukraine, Moldavia, Armenia, and others separating into individual units, defying central control. Under President Boris Yeltsin the New Russian Republic embarked on a 500-day plan that would see private property legalized, government subsidies abolished, price controls lifted, and the creation of private banks and a stock market.

On a curious footnote to the May summit meeting between President Gorbachev and President George Bush (USA) in 1990, White House Chief of Staff John Sununu was dispatched to Moscow to help them deal with such matters as scheduling, the flow of documents through the bureaucracy, the techniques of decision-making and implementation of policy. Many of the former leftist countries had no experience or knowledge of how to handle their new political world.

Meanwhile, Vaclav Havel as President and Alexander Dubcek as Chairman of the Parliament of Czechoslovakia brought the country toward democracy with relative ease, and the country split into the Czech and Slovak Federal Republics.

Poland had a non-communist government in place by mid-1989, and Lech Walesa, the hero of the Solidarity movement, was elected President. Hungary, Bulgaria, Albania, all followed suit, but their economies were plagued with food and materiel shortages. Yugoslavia's bid for democracy was plagued by the diversity in their 6 republics and local wars. Croatia and Slovenia were the first to declare their independence on 25 June 1991. As of 2012, Yugoslavia had become six peaceful, separate, and independent countries: Croatia (1991), Slovenia (1991), Macedonia ((1991), Bosnia-Herzegovina (1992), Serbia (1906),and Montenegro (1906). Kosovo separated from Serbia (2008), but was still waiting to be recognized by the UN.

During these upheavals China was relatively quiet, lifting martial law in January 1990 after the Beijing student riots of June 1989. Mongolia embarked upon political reform. However, Cuba was not swept up in the winds of change, but its $5 billion subsidy from the Soviets was at risk.

In the Mideast Saddam Hussein's forces moved into Kuwait, which brought on UN sanctions against him, and forced the U. S. Military intervention plus forty-three other nations to protect Saudi Arabia and especially American interests in the Persian Gulf.

In South Africa Nelson Mandela, the Black Nationalist leader, was freed from prison after 27 years, and he began an international tour to raise money for the African National Congress, and to encourage Western governments to maintain sanctions against the South African government. In 1991 the South African Parliament voted to repeal the legal framework for apartheid. Three years later Mandela was elected its President.

Nobel Prizes went to Pres. Mikhail Gorbachev of the Soviet Union for his initiatives in promoting international peace, championing political change in Eastern Europe, and helping end the Cold War; and to Octavio Paz as the first Mexican to win the Prize for Literature for his poetry and essays, "...impassioned writing with wide horizons, characterized by sensuous intelligence and humanistic integrity."

On the visual art front the Robert Mapplethorpe exhibit of photography, which had been cancelled at the Corcoran Gallery of Art in Washington, DC, USA, which was now being shown in Cincinnati, Ohio, was indicted by a grand jury on obscenity charges. However, a U.S. Judge forbade law enforcement officials from closing the exhibit, which then broke records for attendance at the museum.

Pierre Renoir's painting "Au Moulin de la Galette" was sold to Japanese business man Ryoei Saito for 78.1 million US$, the second highest price paid for any painting.

On 22 April 1990 over 200 million people in Europe, Asia, Africa, and the Western Hemisphere participated in Earth Day, founded in 1970, in what was believed to be the biggest grass-roots celebration ever.

"Batman" was the top grosser movie, and notable works of fiction included *Cat's Eye* by Margaret Atwood and *The Remains of the Day* by Ishiguro Kazuo, which won the Booker Prize. The top TV series in the USA was *60 Minutes* with Mike Wallace.

The Status of ASSITEJ/Int'l in 1990

At the Stockholm, Sweden World Congress in 1990 there was a complete changing of the guard. At this Congress Rose-Marie Moudoués (France) after 25 years of devoted volunteer service was replaced by Michael Ramløse (Denmark) as Secretary General. Helpfully funded by the Nordic Council of Ministers of Culture, he brought with him an excellent staff, modern equipment, and electronic communication, so the Minutes from each Congress have proved to be quite accurate.

One of Ramløse's first duties as the new Secretary General was to get complete communication going between the Secretariat and the National Centers. No records yet had been transferred from the Paris Office, so in a sense he had to start from scratch with the ASSITEJ records based on those in the Danish Center. Else-Marie Mandøe, on his staff, did an excellent job over the years, with the promptness and accuracy of the Minutes of each meeting.[3]

Immediately, Ramløse sent a questionnaire to all the member centers requesting the Name of the Center, Address, Telephone Number, FAX Number, Name of Contact Person, Office Hours, and Bank. He also asked for their contact's Private Address and Phone. This information was then immediately sent to all the other Centers.

Later, at the request of the Danish Secretariat, a few of the Paris records were transferred to Denmark and to the official Archives in Frankfurt, Germany. (See Summary of 1991 for the complete history of the Archives.)

At the very beginning of the change in leadership under Ramløse, each center was paying its dues, had an address for correspondence, and was in conformity with the Constitution, or received a notice to pay up, or they were no longer a Center of ASSITEJ/Int'l.

Accepting the fact that some centers which were reorganizing were still active national centers, there were 41 active National Centers and 5 Corresponding Centers making a total of 46 National Centers in 1990.[4] These were:

National Centers – 41
    Algeria
    Argentina
    Australia
    Austria
    Belgium
    Brazil
    Bulgaria
    Canada
    Cuba
    Czechoslovakia
    Denmark
    Ecuador
    Federal German Republic (FGR)

Finland
France
German Democratic Republic (GDR)
UK
Greece
Hungary
Ireland
Iran
Israel
Italy
Japan
Mexico
Netherlands
Norway
Paraguay
Peru
Poland
Portugal
Romania
Spain
South Korea
witzerland
Taiwan
Turkey
USA
USSR
Venezuela
Yugoslavia

<u>Corresponding Centers – 5</u>
India
Kenya
Madagascar
Mongolia
Sri Lanka

1991
EXECUTIVE COMMITTEE MEETING OF ASSITEJ
Budapest, Hungary/23-27 January 1991[5]

Present:
President Adolf Shapiro (USSR), VP Michael FitzGerald (Australia), VP Jürgen Flügge (Germany), VP Eddy Socorro (Cuba), Secy-Genl Michael Ramløse (Denmark), Treasurer Paul Harman (UK).

Members: Marián Lucky (Czechoslovakia), Rose-Marie Moudoués (France), Benvenuto Cuminetti (Italy) Deputy for Franco Passatore, Yohei Hijikata (Japan), João Luiz Sousa (Portugal), Mårten Harrie (Sweden), Harold Oaks (USA).

Executive Assistant: Else Marie Mandøe (Denmark).

Budapest, Hungary. All Budapest EC photos courtesy of Harold Oaks, ASU Archives, Tempe, AZ, USA.

The bridge between Buda and Pest, Hungary

Mme. Rose-Marie Moudoués (France) at the EC Meeting,
Budapest, Hungary, 23 January 1991.

(left to right) Mrs. Galina Kolosova and President Adolf Shapiro (Russia) at the EC Meeting, Budapest, Hungary, 23 January 1991.

President Shapiro opened the meeting and welcomed everyone, expressing his concern that in view of the present war in the Persian Gulf [1990–1991—the invasion of Kuwait by Iraq and the USA's involvement] as well as the troubles in the USSR, everyone should be aware of the importance of work with children and of bringing different cultures together. Art is common to everyone.

Adoption of the Minutes from the EC Meeting during the Congress in Stockholm, Sweden in 1990: Luiz (Portugal) protested that the Minutes did not mention the suggestions of counselors which had been brought up at the meeting. Ramløse stated that these corrections had been sent out, so with this correction, the Minutes were adopted.

Information on the Hungarian Center: This item was temporarily postponed until later.

Report of the Secretary General: For clarification it was stated that the Secretary General has the right to vote in the EC even though it is a paid office. However, he is being paid by the Nordic Ministries of Culture, not by ASSITEJ/Int'l.

All members of the EC were asked to name their deputy in the event they could not attend a meeting. If the President is absent, the Statutes state that a Vice-President will preside.

The EC decided to send an official letter to Ilse Rodenberg confirming her appointment as Honorary President. Luiz suggested she could join any EC meeting, but that decision was postponed.

The Bureau: FitzGerald presented his opinion that the duties of the Bureau were as follows:

- It should be efficient and act in accordance with Art. 11 of the Statutes.
- It should meet only in connection with EC meetings to prepare those meetings.
- The Chairs of the Commissions should meet with the Bureau for the sake of efficiency.

He indicated the Bureau looked forward to being a well-functioning instrument for the Association.

The ASSITEJ Archives: The Paris Archives were to be transferred by the Danish Secretariat as follows: in October the current records would go by truck to Copenhagen, and the remaining archives to Frankfurt. Dr. Wolfgang Schneider would be in charge of the Archives in Frankfurt where all technical facilities were available, and all members may use them accordingly. After all material had been transferred from Paris, hopefully all centers would send their information to the Archives in Germany.

New Centers:

- A center in **Iceland** was established in 1990, with 4 professional theatre companies, 3 theatre institutions, and 3 non-professional companies. They have applied for membership, and the Secretary General was present at their first meeting. Luiz criticized the fact that their application papers were not sent in advance to the EC members. The President has been informed according, and he recommends that all application papers will be sent to the EC members.

However, FitzGerald stated that it is merely important that the Secretary General is assured that everything in a new application is in order, and that he informs the EC of that assurance. Papers do not have to be sent to all the EC.

Iceland was admitted as a new Full Member unanimously.

- **Kenya:** This corresponding center had now applied for full membership. There was considerable discussion about the problems of the documentation needed and its translation, which can be difficult for the Secretariat. Some felt the applicant should pay for a translation before the application is sent in. Harrie felt that the nations that had been encouraged to join put an obligation on ASSITEJ to admit them. The EC accepted FitzGerald's statement that the assurance of the Secretary General was sufficient, and Kenya was admitted as a Full Member.
- **Venezuela:** A new theatre school had recently been started as well as a theatre for young people. Those involved had formed a center with Carlos Jimenez as President, and now wished to become a member of ASSITEJ. They were informed there was already a center, which was unknown to them, but it had not paid its dues for four years. The EC decided that a letter from the Secretariat must be sent to the old center requesting a response within 3 months, or that center would be dissolved. If there was no response, then the new center could be admitted as a member.
- **Peru:** The Peruvian Center is active, with Myriam Reàtegui/President who attended the Stockholm Congress. Supported by the government, it organizes festivals, etc. but has no contact with the children's theatres in the country, except for Nosotros, Reàtegui's own theatre. The Secretary General has urged them to find an internal solution. The major problem is that Peru has not paid dues over the years, and is now asked to fund the debt before admittance. The Secretary General recommended that the debt to ASSITEJ/Int'l be released. According to Sousa new members have been admitted to the Peruvian Center, and hopefully an election in November 1991 will solve their problems.

President Shapiro concluded the discussion that the EC and ASSITEJ/Int'l cannot interfere with internal problems in the Centers according to the Statutes. The Centers must be reminded that all theatres can join a Center if they so wished.

"**Ghost Centers**": The following Centers had not paid their dues in four years: Algeria, Argentina, Brazil, Ecuador, Iran, Iraq, Paraguay, Sri Lanka, Turkey, and Venezuela, even though Iran, Iraq, Sri Lanka, Turkey, and Venezuela have been in contact with the Secretariat.

In the discussion which followed the EC decided that the Secretary General should write each one asking for a reply within 3 months. If no answer was received, that Center would be considered dissolved, and other people in that country could form a new Center and apply for membership to ASSITEJ/Int'l. Hijikata asked for the letter's tone to be gentle, and was assured by the Secretary General that it would be diplomatic.

The Working Program 1990–1993: The EC confirmed the Working Program as that which was adopted at the Stockholm Congress. The main items were:

- Improvement of information
- Improvement of artistic exchange
- A new system of subscription
- Review the Constitution so that all countries of the world could belong

Co-options and Appointments of Counselors: In accordance with the wishes expressed at the General Assembly at the Stockholm Congress to open up the world to ASSITEJ/Int'l, the Bureau recommended the co-option of Kim Woo Ok (Korea) and the appointment of Penina M'Lama (Tanzania) as a Counselor.

Hijikata recommended Kim Woo Ok as a very competent person, and the Korean Center as very active. Also, he felt that Japan alone is not sufficient representation for Asia.

Penina M'Lama was highly recommended by the Union of African Performing Artists. She was well known for her liaison work and as an ASSITEJ representative to African countries. Her appointment would mean that all continents would be represented in ASSITEJ.

After the discussions Kim Woo Ok was co-opted unanimously, and M'Lama was appointed as a Counselor without vote to the EC.

Counselors for the Commissions: They were selected as follows:

Commission on Artistic Problems: Jürgen Flügge (Germany) as Chair; Marián Lucky (Czechoslovakia), João Luiz Sousa (Portugal), Franco Passatore (Italy), Kim Woo Ok (Korea), Angela Chaplin (Australia), Mary Hall Surface (USA), and Maurice Yendt (France) as members. The new Commission requested then that all Centers send annual reports to the EC about their artistic work, and then stressed the importance of the ASSITEJ themes:

- Each theme should be distinct at ASSITEJ Festivals and "Theatres of the World" Festivals
- All Centers should attempt to have seminars for directors, actors, etc. based on the chosen theme

- A pamphlet should be published every three years about how the activities carried through on the theme
- Regional festivals should utilize the theme in their work
- Establish regional international work to examine the themes
- Discover what the artistic theme can mean to the developing countries in their specific situations

Finally the Commission expressed their desire to have a number of meetings in common with the Liaison Commission.

Commission on Liaisons: The EC confirmed Michael FitzGerald (Australia) as Chair, Mårten Harrie (Sweden), Yohei Hijikata (Japan), Adolf Shapiro (Russia), Eddy Socorro (Cuba), Arun Agnihotri (India) as members, and Carlos Jimenez (Venezuela) and Penina M'Lama (Tanzania) as counselors.

Cuba had suggested Maria Navarro as a counselor, but she had been rejected for the EC by a majority in the General Assembly at Stockholm, and Harrie commented that her work in the Commission previously had not been satisfactory. FitzGerald felt that a Latin American member would be preferable as well as being close as possible to the problems. Carlos Jimenez was mentioned, and he could be moved from the Artistic Commission to the Liaison Commission. Navarro was defeated by a vote of: For – 4; Against – 7; and Abstentions – 2. Jimenez was appointed.

FitzGerald was accepted unanimously as the Chair, and he specified that the Commission would work for regionalization and ASSITEJ projects common to all commissions.

In its meeting the Commission had also discussed:

- The need of constant contact to organizations in those regions independent of personal contacts
- The importance of sending representatives to seminars, festivals, and congresses in these regions, or finding people to represent the EC and to report back
- The possibility of having the EC meet in Africa, Asia, or Latin America, and Africa was a possibility in 1992, which the EC approved
- Reaffirmed the practice of inviting observers to attend EC meetings

Shapiro also suggested that the Commission try to re-establish relations with China, even though money for dues was difficult for them, and the Commission agreed to try. Also, the Commission recommended Arun Agnihotri (India) as a new member, which was approved.

Commission on Statutes: The Bureau had recommended that the Secretary General present to the EC at the next meeting suggested revisions to the current Statutes, which needed to be modernized and revised. The EC appointed Michael Ramløse and Rose-Marie Moudoués to do this.

Commission on Finances: The Secretariat: Its costs were entirely covered by the Nordic countries. The accounts showed a deficit of 3,000 British£ because of the costs of establishing the Secretariat. This cost was covered by TEATERCENTRUM I DENMARK.

- **ASSITEJ:** The account had been transferred from France to a new account in UK, and the balance on 1 January 1991 was 18,700 British£. Ramløse commented that subscriptions were high since many Centers had paid up to 2-3 years of unpaid dues ahead of time in order to have the right to vote at the Stockholm Congress.[6] Also, some had already paid for 1991. These accounts were approved by the EC.
- A preliminary draft of the 1991–1992 Budget was presented, and the Financial Commission requested that 10,000 British£ be kept in the bank as a reserve. The Commission was to present a new budget taking the needs of the EC and the Commissions into account.
- **Fund Raising:** The Commission suggested that each center add 10 US$ for each member in their centers so that ASSITEJ could approach UNESCO and business firms to seek matching funds. The Commission then suggested approaching UNESCO for funds to assist emerging countries with their dues. They also asked that the other Commissions come up with fund-raising ideas. Oaks and Ramløse were instructed to work out such a letter for UNESCO.
- The Treasurer informed the EC that next year each Center would receive a form that would allow them to transfer their dues automatically in the amount of 250 US$ (50 British£) into the ASSITEJ/Int'l bank account.
- Lastly, it was proposed to consider a reduction of dues to 200 US$, with the addition of 10 US$ for each member of the center. This would not penalize smaller centers. It was left to the financial Commission to explore this possibility, since it would have to be adopted by the next General Assembly.

Regionalization: One of the functions of ASSITEJ was to help regional centers to get together to encourage international exchange, but this required a change in the Statutes. It was decided that this would be one of the functions of the Liaison Commission; Sousa asked that a paper be presented to the EC outlining the plan before their next meeting.

Nordic Center Proposal: Presented by Harrie, the Nordic Centers (Norway, Sweden, Iceland, Finland, and Denmark) proposed to have 3 seminars in Africa, Asia, and Latin America in order to develop relationships among these continents. Those organizations involved would be asked to fund the project. The EC accepted the proposal, and gave them the mandate to proceed with the project.

ASSITEJ/Int'l Newsletter: After considerable discussion the Secretary General accepted the responsibility for the edition of a Newsletter, but Ramløse pointed out that the suggested 1,000 British£ may not cover the costs.

Flügge requested that *all* member theatres of a Center should get the Newsletter, and this was the responsibility of each Center.

The EC decided that the Secretariat would edit and distribute an ASSITEJ Newsletter, preferably 4 times a year, with full responsibility with a budget of 1,000 British£.

Theatres of the World: 3-14 June 1991 had been designated as a "Theatre of the World" Festival (RITEJ) in Lyon, France. There were no candidates yet for 1992 and beyond. Kenya had made inquiries, but the title required that the producer had had at least one successful world festival prior to such designation. The Secretary General recommended that the Kenya Festival be designated as an "ASSITEJ Project". The Secretary General was instructed to look for future candidates.

ASSITEJ/Int'l Projects: In the discussion on the term "ASSITEJ Project", the EC determined to have the Commission on Artistic Problems come up with a proper definition.

The Cuban Congress in 1993: Socorro reassured the EC that the Congress would take place in Havana, Cuba in February 1993, and preparations were progressing. It would be a small festival, with 4–5 Latin American companies performing. The raising of money was difficult so they decided on a selective festival, rather than a world one. They were also planning workshops, readings, and seminars to show off different sides of Cuban theatre work.

Socorro has been assured that all countries can participate, and it will be easy for everyone to get a Visa. However, communication might be a problem as mail and telephone connections are bad. The EC decided that the Congress should run 10 days, and the Cuban Center could fix the dates.

Future Meetings of the EC: Since there were no invitations, Maurice Yendt was asked if Lyon would extend an invitation, despite the short notice. Even though Yendt was interested, Moudoués suggested that a meeting in France would be possible in November. The EC decided to wait until they heard from France.

There was discussion of a meeting in Africa, and to lessen the financial burden the EC members could pay their own expenses. Sousa mentioned that there were 5 Portuguese-speaking countries in Africa who work together to organize festivals, seminars, and congresses. He would be happy to help with the necessary contacts.

No decision was made.

Miscellaneous:

- **Children's Theatre in Portugal:** Children's theatre has been without subsidy for 2 years, but recently 3-4 companies had received money from the Ministry of Culture. Sousa asked that ASSITEJ write the Ministry to thank them for this support.
- **German Report:** As a result of the fall of the wall, ASSITEJ/Germany plans to unite the East and West Centers. They plan to write new statutes by taking the best of each country. Theatres can then join, and there will be an election for the EC representative in early June. There is considerable risk that the 5 theatres in the GDR will have to close, but the theatres must restructure to become more efficient. The "Theater der Freundschaft" is seriously threatened by this situation. The EC will try to put international pressure on the German Government.
- **Honorary President's Award:** Nat Eek (USA), Honorary President of ASSITEJ, had presented the concept of the Award to the General Assembly in Stockholm in 1990. Oaks informed the EC that the Award will be made in 1993, and the amount set aside was 1,000 US$. A draft of the rules and regulations would be presented to the EC at a later date.
- **Theatre School in Cuba:** Socorro gave a description of the International Theatre Training School of Latin America, which was supported by Cuba and other Latin American countries. Now 2 ½ years old, it has a good reputation but they do not offer any education on children's theatre. Socorro asked that ASSITEJ/Int'l write a letter which would acknowledge their good work, but which would encourage an awareness of children's theatre in their country.
- **The Hungarian Center:** Janos Meszner, President of the Center, had distributed a paper listing their activities at the first meeting of the EC. He now expressed his wish to the EC that the new Arany Janos Theatre, which had just reopened during the EC meeting, could be a stimulant to

ASSITEJ. Hoping for many international activities, it planned to invite the best plays for young people to many of their international activities. He also expressed his gratitude to the EC for allowing them to host the meeting, and welcomed everyone to return at another time.

President Shapiro thanked Meszner and everyone who had helped to make the meeting possible in Hungary, and especially for their hospitality. In closing Shapiro reminded the EC of the projects which had been approved at this meeting, and expressed the hope that their next meeting would be even more efficient.

1991
EXECUTIVE COMMITTEE MEETING OF ASSITEJ[7]
Lyon, France/5-8 December 1991

Present:
President Adolf Shapiro (USSR/Latvia), VP Michael FitzGerald (Australia), VP Jürgen Flügge (Germany), VP Eddy Socorro (Cuba), Sec. Gen. Michael Ramløse (Denmark), Treasurer Paul Harman (UK).

Members: Marián Lucky (Czechoslovakia), Rose-Marie Moudoués (France), Benvenuto Cuminetti (Italy) for Franco Passatore, Yohei Hijikata (Japan), João Luiz Sousa (Portugal), Kim Woo Ok (Korea), Mårten Harrie (Sweden), and Harold Oaks (USA).

Counselors: Angela Chaplin (Australia), Mary Hall Surface (USA), and Maurice Yendt (France).

Observers: Wasonga Eliud (Kenya); América Alonso, Jacqueline Russo, and Roberto Stopello (Venezuela); and Nguyen Van Phuc (Vietnam).

Executive Assistant: Else Marie Mandøe (Denmark).

Lyons, France. Courtesy of Harold Oaks. Archives, ASU, Tempe, AZ, USA.

The meetings were held at the Théâtre des Jeunes Années, hosted by Maurice Yendt.

President Shapiro welcomed the members of the EC. He expressed optimism about the condition of the Association, and that there was a widening of its activities around the world. In his Report he mentioned visiting festivals and talking with theatre personnel in Vietnam, the Netherlands, Portugal, Belgium, Turkey, France (Lyon), Japan, and Russia, as well as attending a seminar of directors of Eastern European companies this past fall.

Secretary General's Report: Ramløse reported as follows:

- Franco Passatore (Italy) has had to resign due to his health, and Claudio Massari would take his place.
- The Newsletter costs were being covered by the Secretary General's Budget. Information is needed from all centers.

News of the Centers:

- **Venezuela** has an international festival and was very active. They were accepted as a member by the EC.
- Ramløse had met with the **Philippines'** Educational Theatre representatives, and they would be sending in full application materials.
- **Uruguay** was approved for acceptance, provided they met the requirements.
- **Chile** was accepted as a full member.
- The status of **Cyprus** in the UN was being questioned. Was it one or two nations? This was being investigated.
- The **USSR** is a complicated situation. It will remain as the USSR Center for the time being. However, Lithuania wants its own national center. Estonia and Latvia will remain with the Soviet Union. Shapiro was currently attending the meeting on a USSR Passport, but at the next meeting he would report what passport he would be using!
- The **Peru** situation was unclear. The Cuban theatre troupe was not allowed to play at their Festival. Contacts are trying to clear up the situation.
- **Brazil** has been inactive for a long time. Two groups left Stockholm to reactivate the Center, but they are not cooperating with each other. It's a power struggle.
- **"Ghost Centers"** – those which appear inactive and have not paid their dues for several years. The Secretary General will send letters to Algeria Argentina, Bulgaria, Ecuador, Greece, Iran, Iraq, and Paraguay.

Ramløse closed his report saying there had been a proposal to add Spanish as an official language of ASSITEJ, but such an addition would be an economic problem, and there was no budget available to cover the cost.

The World Congress in Cuba: Socorro reported that the dates had been set for 22-27 February 1993 at the Conference Hall in Havana. The Festival in conjunction with the Congress would be held in three cities—Havana, Santa Cruz, and Montezuma, so that visitors could see provinces as well as Havana. Costa Rica, Puerto Rico, Columbia, and Venezuela had all accepted invitations to present productions. They will focus on Latin American Theatre.

There will be Workshops for actors, theatre teachers, and on contemporary theatre. There would be discussion groups and play readings at midnight. Travel arrangements must be made early, and Shapiro and Ramløse were scheduled to visit Cuba in February 1992, and report back to the EC.

Vietnam Center: They would be hosting a seminar in Hanoi 8-14 September 1992, and were expecting 100 delegates, including three from the USA. Focus would be on theatre for young audiences in developing countries. While they requested support money from ASSITEJ/Int'l, they were now asking delegates to pay for their own travel, lodging, and food. Vietnam would pay for travel within the country.

Kenya Center: The Kenya Center has offered to host the EC in Nairobi 8-15 November 1992. There will be 10 performing companies from Kenya and 10 from other African nations. They are inviting representatives from several other centers, for a total of 400 delegates. Funding is not yet in place, and the EC expressed concern that the plans were too large. However, the EC accepted the invitation from Kenya for their next meeting.

Reports on Regional Activity:

- **Japan** reported on festivals in Sado Island, and their 23-26 July 1992 All-Japan Association Festival in Kobe. In January 1994 there will be an International Festival in Okinawa.
- **Cuba** will have a regional meeting in connection with the 1993 Congress.
- **Sweden** will host regional meetings prior to the Cuban Congress for under-developed countries.
- **Australia** will be holding a festival in November 1993.
- The **USA Center** will have an International Festival in May 1994 in Seattle, Washington.
- **Venezuela** had a major festival in April 1992, and will have another one in 1993.

- **Korea** reported that it is now the only divided country, and there is no contact between North and South Korea. They requested that a representative from North Korea be invited to Cuba, so that the two representatives could meet and discuss ways to cooperate.

President Shapiro closed the meetings with the comment, "We must find ways to unite the children of the world!"

1992
EXECUTIVE COMMITTEE MEETING OF ASSITEJ[8]
Nairobi, Kenya/8-11 November 1992

Present:
President Adolf Shapiro (Latvia/Russia), VP Michael FitzGerald (Australia), VP Jürgen Flügge (Germany), VP Eddy Socorro (Cuba), Sec. Gen. Michael Ramløse (Denmark), and Treasurer Paul Harman (UK).
Members: Yohei Hijikata (Japan), Kim Woo Ok (Korea), Mårten Harrie (Sweden), and Harold Oaks (USA).
Counselors: Penina M'Lama (Tanzania), Arun Agnihotri (India).
Observers: Marjorie MacLean (Canada) and Wolfgang Schneider (Germany).
Members absent: Marián Lucky (Czechoslovakia), Rose-Marie Moudoués (France), Benvenuto Cuminetti (Italy), João Luiz Sousa (Portugal).
Counselors absent: Angela Chaplin (Australia), Mary Hall Surface (USA), Carlos Jimenez (Venezuela), and Maurice Yendt (France).

Executive Assistant: Else Marie Mandøe (Denmark).

Nairobi, Kenya, Africa.
All Nairobi, Kenya. photos Harold Oaks, ASU Archives, Tempe, AZ, USA.

EC Meeting Building, Nairobi, Kenya, Africa, 8 November 1992.

A performance at the EC Meeting in Nairobi, Kenya, November 1992.

(left to right) Members of the EC at the Nairobi Meeting: Kenya driver, Eddy Socorro (Cuba), Adolph Shapiro (Russia), Michael Ramløse (Denmark), Michael FitzGerald (Australia), Else Marie Mandøe (Denmark), Marjorie MacLean (Canada).

EC Treasurer Paul Harman (UK) at the Nairobi Meeting.

Agenda: The following Agenda was approved by the EC:

- Approval of the Minutes from the EC Meeting in Lyon, December 1991
- Report on activities since the Lyon Meeting
- Report on Kenya Center
- Secretary General's Report
- Report on the Havana Congress in 1993
- Invitations to host the 1996 Congress
- Modernization of the Statutes
- Finances
- Dues – 1993–1996
- Working Program – 1993–1996
- Artistic theme – 1993–1996
- New Member Centers
- ASSITEJ/Peru for Festival '93 in Lima, Peru
- "ASSITEJ World Project" – Application from ASSITEJ/Germany
- Miscellaneous

Along with the distribution of the Agenda, the Members received in English and French a carefully worded Voting Procedure for approval prior to the Congress. It was the first time that the procedure had been written down instead of being given verbally by the Secretary General at the time of the election.

Sunday, 8 November 1992

Report of the President: President Shapiro thanked the Nordic Centers for their support of the Seminar in Hanoi, Vietnam and for their support of the EC Meeting in Kenya. He also commented on the Artistic Commission's Meeting in Venezuela as a key to ASSITEJ/Int'l's future in Latin America, building relationships and assisting festivals.

He once and the Secretary General twice had been to Cuba to check on arrangements for the 1993 Congress. Lastly he expressed pride in their creation of a Working Program for this term, and its being successfully carried out.

The Hanoi Seminar: It was an intensive and tight program—a total of 40 speeches in 4 days, 20–25 papers per day, with no time for discussion of the papers, sharing of situations between centers, or interaction of the guests. Kim Woo Ok (Korea) commented it was very frustrating, too tight a schedule, and no chance to meet and talk with the local people.

ASSITEJ/Kenya:[9] James M. Mudavadi (Kenya) was the Artistic Director of their Center, and gave a report on their theatre activities. Their Center was three years old, and this was the first time that the ASSITEJ EC had had a meeting in Africa. The Nairobi Players was their main support group. About 20 groups belong to their Center, but they are not permanent.

They mostly produced plays based on books assigned to young people to read. They come to see the plays rather than read the books. "Aids Education" is one of their current projects. "Things You Don't Talk About" is about sex education, but they are forbidden to go to the schools. There is a TV tape which is played in community centers. Other play concerns are about Drug Problems Among the Youth, Conservation, and Environment, and are for children ages 4–12 years old.

They have an International Festival planned for September 1993, which is supported by their Ministry of Culture. Unfortunately the Ministry is more interested in supporting sports events.

They hope their center can become an African Center that reaches out to the rest of Africa.

Membership:

- **Cyprus** had applied, had four professional companies, and was accepted as a Member.
- **The Philippines** had applied for Full Membership, had three professional companies, and was accepted as a Member.
- **The Ukraine** had 38 companies—professional, amateur, and independent. There were 8 in Kiev alone. They were accepted as a Member.
- **Kyrgyzstan** had 2 professional companies, and was accepted pending submission of a complete application. They did not qualify at the moment.
- **Georgia**'s application was incomplete, but they were accepted pending completion of the application forms.
- **Croatia** was requesting membership, and the name Yugoslavia must be cancelled from all memberships. They were accepted pending completion of the new application.
- **Lithuania** was seeking application, since they were already accepted by the ITI.
- Mrs. Zvjezdana Ladika (formerly of **Yugoslavia**) had written to delete that country's name from all correspondence and the directory. They would have to wait until the UN makes a decision re: country names.
- **ITI/Brazil** had last corresponded in February 1992, and São Paulo was at their September Meeting. They have not been heard from since.
- **Greece** was fully paid up, but the center was reorganizing.

- **Iran** had sent a brief letter as of 10 June.
- **Iraq** had sent a letter in April, but no word since.
- **Peru** had 33 theatre groups, was to sponsor a 1993 Festival, and was the bank for all their companies. It was a good response.
- **Portugal** has many problems.
- **Ireland** has only 3 companies, limited work, and tight finances.

An Invitation: Rostov-on-Don, Russia has written the Secretariat that they would like to host the 1996 ASSITEJ World Congress as part of their Festival.

Report on Activities: (See Summary 1991–1996).

Modernization of Statutes: The following Amendments to the Constitution were approved by the EC for presentation to the General Assembly at the Cuban Congress. These were added onto the changes approved at the 1990 Stockholm Congress. Most of them were cosmetic and for clarification, with some amendments proposed by the USA Center. The most important were:

- Art. 9. 3 – Add ...*and must be given in writing*
- Art. 9. 9 – Add ...*selected by vote of the Executive Committee.*
- Art. 9. 13 Par. 1 – ...*in this order: The Secretary General is elected first and presides over the election of the Treasurer, representatives of additional countries to the Executive Committee and of the President.*
- Par 3 – ...*A country may have only one representative on the Executive Committee.*
- Par 5 – ...*who shall be nominated in a meeting of the new Executive Committee.*
- Art. 10. 9 – ...*selected by vote of the Executive Committee*
- Art. 10. 10 – ...*All motions are carried*

Dues: The EC approved an increase of Dues to $300 for Regular Membership and $100 for Hardship/Beginning Membership (up to 5 years). They then recommended two levels: $500 and $100, and a center could choose its level. A request for an exception could be made to the EC.

Monday, 9 November 1992

The Secretary General reported on the Finances.

- Requested that the Financial Report be issued with the announcement of the EC Meeting, so members had time to analyze it.
- There should be a 3-year Report and a 1-year budget projection.

- Projected income: Dues—a total of 50 national centers: 25 @ $100, 10 @ $500, 15 @ $250 for a total of $10,750.
- Centers more than 6 months in arrears lose the right to vote in the General Assembly.
- Dues will be $100 for the term of 1994–1996. Members who can are encouraged to pay up to $500 per year. Members in financial difficulty may apply to the EC for an exception.

Report of the Liaison Commission:

- Recommended Regional Co-operation rather than "regionalization"
- More exchanges with other countries
- Obsolete equipment should be sent to under-developed countries for further use
- The two languages used should be English and French
- *The French Review* support should be discontinued. Use the money for short term grants or for projects
- Germany has published a reference book of 100 contemporary plays. The German ASSITEJ Archives are available for the use of all
- Suggested Theme: Theatre for Cultural Survival, with Theatre for the Disabled as a sub-theme

Report of the Promotion & Publication Commission:

- A new promotional pamphlet has been printed
- Need to look for more creative ways in the use of finances
- Announced the Okinawa International Festival for Young Audiences 6-13 February 1994, expecting 50,000 spectators with 20–30 national productions and 20–30 international productions

RITEJ Festival: Suggested that the Artistic Commission review ways to use this event more fully.
Peru Festival '93: Requested $31,000 from ASSITEJ/Int'l to support the Festival, which would be 50% of the cost. The EC denied their request for lack of money but encouraged the Festival.
Miscellaneous:

- **German Application for "World Project" Designation:** The German

Center requested this designation for two conferences: 1) 3-5 December 1993 in Frankfurt for a Playwriting Conference with 5 playwrights from 5 continents; and 2) 26-28 March 1993 in Esslingen, Germany for a Directors Seminar (previously held in Berlin, GDR) with 5 playwrights (from Belgium, Netherlands, Portugal, Italy, and Germany) to meet with 10 directors on "How to develop a play—a work in progress".
- **Next EC Meeting:** Proposed to meet with the Playwright's Conference in Frankfurt in December 1993. Also in Kenya in August 1993 and in Australia in August 1994.

Tuesday, 10 November 1992

The Review: The EC decided to end their support of the French magazine, and seek an annual publication of a bibliography of books in this area. It will be done by the German Center.

EC Meeting in Cuba: The date was set at 21-22 February 1993 as part of the Cuban Congress. Future EC Meetings were suggested in Perth, Australia and Frankfurt, Germany.

Wednesday, 11 November 1992

Cuban Congress in 1993: Socorro presented an update. Special invitations will come from the Minister of Culture. Korea and the USA had a problem with diplomatic relationships. Could be resolved by receiving a special invitational letter from the ASSITEJ Secretary General. They would need to send the Secretariat a name and address list, and indicate who the official three delegates were. Socorro would need immediately from each attendee: name, address, profession, Passport Number and date of issue, plus a photo-copy of each front page. The costs of the 3 official delegates would be covered by the Cuban Center. The Congress is only in Havana with other city tours after.

There will be 25 performances, 15 of which will come from Cuba, and others from Finland, Angola, Argentina, Mexico, Peru, and Denmark. There is also a possibility of productions from Spain, Venezuela, Puerto Rico, and Chile. The Latin American companies will be paid so they have money for travel to the Congress, but they would stay in private homes.

Candidates for the EC: The following Centers and individuals had been nominated for election to the EC:

Australia – Michael FitzGerald
Cuba – Eddy Socorro
Denmark – Michael Ramløse and as Secretary General
France – Maurice Yendt

Germany – Jürgen Flügge
Italy – Graziano Melano
Japan – Yohei Hijikata
Korea – Kim Woo Ok
USA – Harold Oaks and as Treasurer
Vietnam – Pham Thi Thanh

Future Congress in 1996: They had received an invitation from Rostov-On-Don which would be confirmed in 14 days, and a potential one from Latvia. A possible one from India, but without a Festival. Japan perhaps in 1999.

This concluded the deliberations of the EC, and President Shapiro thanked all the members for their diligence as well as their presence so far from home. He also thanked Kenya for their excellent hospitality.

1993
XIth WORLD CONGRESS OF ASSITEJ[10]
Havana, Cuba/22–27 February 1993

The EC Meeting in Havana, Cuba prior to the first meeting of the General Assembly:

Present:
President Adolf Shapiro (Russia), VP Michael FitzGerald (Australia), VP Jürgen Flügge (Germany), VP Eddy Socorro (Cuba), Sec. Gen. Michael Ramløse (Denmark), Treasurer Paul Harman (UK).
Members: Rose-Marie Moudoués (France), Yohei Hijikata (Japan), Kim Woo Ok (Korea), Marián Lucky (Slovakia), Mårten Harrie (Sweden), Harold Oaks (USA).[11]

Counselors: Penina M'Lama (Tanzania) and Maurice Yendt (France).
Members absent: Arun Agnihotri (India), João Luiz Sousa (Portugal), Angela Chaplin (Australia), Carlos Jimenez (Venezuela), and Mary-Hall Surface (USA).

Executive Assistant: Else Marie Mandøe (Denmark).

Havana, Cuba – 1993,
all photos courtesy of Harold Oaks, ASU Archives, Tempe, AZ, USA.

EC Member and host Eddy Socorro and his son, Havana, Cuba, 1993.

A performance at the ASSITEJ World Congress in Havana, Cuba in 22-27 February 1993.

In the EC Meeting prior to the first meeting of the General Assembly, the following Centers were approved and accepted as members, making them eligible to vote: Russia, Estonia, Czech Republic, Slovak Republic, and Zimbabwe. There was considerable discussion about the legitimacy of the Kenya Center.

The General Assembly
Presiding:
President Adolf Shapiro (Russia), VP Michael FitzGerald (Australia), VP Jürgen Flügge (Germany), VP Eddy Socorro (Cuba), Sec. Gen. Michael Ramløse (Denmark), Treasurer Paul Harman (UK).
National Centers present: Australia, Austria, Belgium (by proxy to the Netherlands), Canada, Croatia (by proxy to Germany), Cuba, Czech Republic (by proxy to Slovakia), Denmark, Estonia, Finland, France, Germany, Greece (by proxy to Denmark), Hungary, Iceland, Israel (by proxy to UK), Italy, Japan, Kenya (by proxy to Japan), Korea, Netherlands, Norway, Peru, Poland, Portugal (by proxy to France), Russia, Slovakia, Spain, Sweden, Switzerland, Turkey, UK, USA, Venezuela, Vietnam.
Corresponding Center: Tanzania.
Executive Assistant: Else Marie Mandøe (Denmark).

Eddy Socorro, President of ASSITEJ/Cuba and Vice-President of ASSITEJ/Int'l, welcomed the delegates and expressed the hope that the Congress would be both productive and successful. President Adolf Shapiro expressed his gratitude to the Cuban Center for organizing the Congress, reminding all the delegates of their united faith in theatre for young audiences, whose aim was to improve life on our planet and make it more beautiful.

Honorary President Ilse Rodenberg greeted the delegates and wished them success in their endeavors. Honorary President Nat Eek stated that continuity and tradition should go hand in hand, and presented a special box with a gavel for the President to use to preside over the Congress. The box was engraved with the names of all the Past Presidents with space for the names of those to come.

Secretary General Michael Ramløse then took the stand and presented the outgoing EC and the Commissions to the Assembly. The EC had recommended the following three persons to serve on the Voting Commission: Rose-Marie Moudoués (France), Jacqueline Russo (Venezuela), and Maggi Miles (Australia), and they were approved accordingly.

Thirty-four Centers were certified to vote, making a total of 104[12] possible votes. This made 52 votes the simple majority. For constitutional changes a majority of 68 (or 2/3rds) was required. Proxies as declared were accepted.

Minutes of the 1990 Congress in Stockholm: These Minutes were adopted unanimously.

Report of the EC for 1990–1993: The Report had been distributed to the Membership prior to the Congress. In his remarks Shapiro emphasized the importance of theatrical art in the world of youth who today were witnessing a world of cruelty, death, and famine. Theatre is an art *for* humanity!

Ramløse added that just prior to the Congress the EC had added the following centers as full members of ASSITEJ/Int'l: Czech Republic, Estonia, Russia, Slovak Republic, and Zimbabwe.

The Report was adopted unanimously.

Treasurer's Report: Harman's Report had been distributed ahead of time, and his Report for 1990–1992 was passed unanimously.

Amendments to the Statutes: Copies of the recommended changes had been distributed by the required three months ahead of time to the members. Little debate was expected. The Secretary General recommended voting on the changes as a whole, which would require a 2/3rds vote for adoption. The result of the vote was: Yes – 93; No – 4. All the amendments were passed, and would take effect following the close of the Congress.

Amendment Proposed by ASSITEJ/Kenya: Ramløse presented the Kenya proposal since they were not able to attend the Cuban Congress. Essentially it asked for ASSITEJ/Int'l to broaden the requirements for membership in order to include indigenous theatre in its membership.

The ensuing discussion was long and thorough. On the recommendation of Oaks, Ramløse concluded that "...the new EC must work very carefully and thoroughly on this issue in order to present to the General Assembly in 3 years a balanced and well prepared proposal for the accommodation of African theatrical tradition within the framework of ASSITEJ/Int'l without demolishing the fundamental principles of the Association."

Items for Discussion from the Centers:

- **Regional Co-operation:** Anne van Otterloo (Netherlands) presented the example of a practical cooperation in a Manager's Seminar between the Netherlands and Russia. She urged all centers to think of practical, not theoretical, ways to cooperate in the artistic field. Flügge recommended cooperative projects related to the "theme" of the next Congress, a sort of network within ASSITEJ/Int'l. Harman commented that many networks remain exclusive, rather than open to all which was always the

aim of ASSITEJ. Yendt suggested examining all ASSITEJ networks to see if they are meeting the needs of the members.
- **Spanish as an Official Language: Fernando Rojas** (Spain) introduced the concept by saying that 22 countries and about 350 million persons speak Spanish as their official language. The Secretary General concluded that languages can only be considered in the context of the needs of ASSITEJ in connection with its work.
- **Commission on Artistic Activities:** Yendt felt that most of the Commission's work has been theoretical, and now the EC should look into the possibility of a periodical dealing with artistic problems on a practical basis.

Working Program 1993–1996: The General Assembly had approved an ad hoc commission to work on the Working Program based on the proposal which the EC had sent out in advance. The Members of the Commission were: Michael FitzGerald (Australia/Chair), Anne van Otterloo (Netherlands), Maurice Yendt (France), Fernando Rojas (Spain), Jeremy Turner (UK), and Jacqueline Russo (Venezuela). Sundry comments included wanting relations with UNESCO stated in the program. FitzGerald informed them that all comments would be included, and the Commission would find practical ways of accomplishing the tasks.

Dues 1994–1995–1996: Oaks of the Financial Commission presented the Report. Dues for 1993 would remain at 250 US$ for Full Membership and 50 US$ for Corresponding Membership. The new rates would be in effect as of 1994. Essentially Dues would be 100 US$, but encouraged those centers that could would pay up to 500 US$. Centers in financial difficulty could apply to the EC for exceptions. The proposal was adopted unanimously.

Budget 1994–1996: As Treasurer Harman had distributed the Budget ahead of time. Oaks commented that the need for the Reserve was to provide financial support when the Nordic subsidy expired after 1996. The Budget was adopted unanimously.

Artistic Theme 1993–1996: Flügge of the Artistic Commission presented their recommendation that "Theatre for Survival" be adopted as the "artistic theme" for the next three-year term. All centers should cooperate in its usage, but there was no "official" interpretation. The Assembly adopted the Theme.

Site of 1996 Congress: There were three invitations for hosting the 1996 Congress: Rostov-on-Don, Russia; Kinshasa, Kenya; and Harare, Zimbabwe. Shapiro stated that the city Rostov-on-Don and the Russian Center would be able to meet all the requirements of the Congress. They had conducted international festivals in 1989 and 1991. There were several world class hotels. They would be able to meet all the financial obligations, and would be able to help delegates with financial difficulties. There were no presenters from Kenya or Zimbabwe.

In the discussion which followed Harman urged that every delegate should bring something of theirs to the Congress to share, and they must respond to the diversity of the membership. Van Otterloo asked that the EC work out a list of criteria for hosting a Congress. The Assembly expressed their desire to hold a Congress in Africa, and hoped they would offer an invitation for 1999.

The General Assembly accepted the invitation from Rostov-on-Don to host the 1996 World Congress of ASSITEJ.

The Elections/27 February 1993

On 25 February two days prior to the elections, the Candidates for the Secretary General, the Treasurer, and all the EC Members-elect were presented to the General Assembly. That same day there were artistic discussions on the theme of the Congress.

Candidates for Election:
Secretary General – Michael Ramløse (Denmark).
Treasurer – Harold Oaks (USA).
Executive Committee – Australia (Michael FitzGerald); Canada (Marjorie MacLean); Cuba (Eddy Socorro); France (Maurice Yendt); Germany (Jürgen Flügge); Italy (Graziano Melano); Japan (Yohei Hijikata); Korea (Kim Woo Ok); Norway (Helge Andersen); Peru (Myriam Reàtegui); Poland (Maciej Wojtyszko); Russia (Adolf Shapiro); Slovakia (Marián Lucky); Spain (Maria Navarro Blanco); Turkey (Tamer Levent); Vietnam (Pham Thi Thanh).

The Elections: The Secretary General reminded the delegates that a total of 104 votes could be cast, with 53 votes constituting a majority for election. The votes were as follows:

Secretary General: Michael Ramløse for re-election: Yes – 96; No – 6.
Treasurer: Harold Oaks: Yes – 98; No – 3; Invalid – 1.
Executive Committee: There was a total of 16 nominees for the EC. Those elected were:

		Rank Order
Australia (Michael FitzGerald)	70 votes	7
Canada (Marjorie MacLean)	84 votes	3
Cuba (Eddy Socorro)	84 votes	4
France (Maurice Yendt)	70 votes	8
Germany (Jürgen Flügge)	52 votes	12

Italy (Graziano Melano)	59 votes	10
Japan (Yohei Hijikata)	99 votes	1
Korea (Kim Woo Ok)	81 votes	5
Norway (Helge Andersen)	72 votes	6
Russia (Adolf Shapiro)	90 votes	2
Slovakia (Marián Lucky)	53 votes	11
Vietnam (Pham Thi Thanh)	68 votes	9

Those not elected were:
UK (Tony Goveia)	47 votes
Poland (Maciej Wojtyszko)	35 votes
Spain (Maria Navarro Blanco)	18 votes
Turkey (Tamer Levent)	47 votes

The President: There were three (3) candidates for President. The vote was:
Michael FitzGerald	52 votes, Elected
Adolf Shapiro	40 votes, Not elected
Eddy Socorro	10 votes, Not elected

The Vice-Presidents: There were four (4) candidates for the three Vice-Presidents. The vote was:
Marjorie MacLean	73 votes, Elected
Jürgen Flügge	42 votes, Not elected
Eddy Socorro	60 votes, Elected
Maurice Yendt	55 votes, Elected

This concluded the elections.

The General Assembly

While the ballots were being tabulated, President Shapiro recognized the important work that former Secretary General Rose-Marie Moudoués had done over 25 years of her volunteer service. She was now stepping down as a Member from the EC, having been a member since the start of ASSITEJ/Int'l in Paris in 1965. The General Assembly applauded her warmly.

Miscellaneous:

- Michael FitzGerald (Australia) announced that <u>LOWDOWN</u>, the Australian magazine, was being sent to all Centers, and please notify him if they did not get one.
- Nat Eek (USA), as promised at the Stockholm Congress, presented the statutes governing the Honorary President's Award to the General Assembly. The Award will be given to an individual theatre group or theatre artist for artistic excellence in theatre for children and youth.

- The Award consisted of 1,000 US$, an engraved silver goblet, and a bottle of champagne. Nominations were to be sent to the USA Center when requested. Eek's initiative was highly appreciated by the General Assembly, and warmly applauded.[13]
- Judit Benedek (Sweden) read the draft on a resolution on child abuse, which expressed the deep concern of all its members at the growing incidence of the many forms of child abuse, and urged governments to redress the situation in order to guarantee children of the world their basic rights to food, shelter, security, education, and cultural and artistic activities. The General Assembly adopted it, and instructed the Secretary General to send it to all the governments in the ASSITEJ countries.

Closing Session:

In the final session President FitzGerald expressed his thanks to the Voting Commission for their excellent work. He gave great thanks to the Cuban Center and the organizers of the Congress for doing an excellent job, in spite of the difficulties encountered in Cuba at the present time. He hoped it would not be too long before ASSITEJ returned to this part of the world, and gave especial thanks to Eddy Socorro.

He closed saying that he hoped he would see everyone again at Rostov-on-Don in Russia in 1996.

The New Executive Committee Meeting/27-28 February 1993[14]

Present:

President Michael FitzGerald (Australia), VP Marjorie MacLean (Canada), VP Eddy Socorro (Cuba), VP Maurice Yendt (France), Sec. Gen. Michael Ramløse (Denmark), Treasurer Harold Oaks (USA).

Members: Helge Andersen (Norway), Jürgen Flügge (Germany), Graziano Melano (Italy), Yohei Hijikata (Japan), Kim Woo Ok (Korea), Adolph Shapiro (Russia), Marián Lucky (Slovakia), and Pham Thi Thanh (Vietnam).

Executive Assistant: Else Marie Mandøe (Denmark).

President FitzGerald welcomed the members of the new EC to the meeting.

He opened the discussion by asking for recommendations regarding the co-option of candidates. The EC decided to co-opt Jacqueline Russo (Venezuela) and Penina M'Lama (Tanzania) with vote. They also recommended Wolfgang Schneider (Germany) and Anne van Otterloo (Netherlands) as Counselors.

At this same meeting President Michael FitzGerald with the blessing of the General Assembly re-created the Commissions as a means to get individual projects of concern handled in an efficient and on-going manner. Later the Commissions' names were changed to Working Groups (WG), and have continued to be so designated to this date.

President Vladimir Adamek (1975–1978) was the first to use the concept of Commissions to involve the entire EC in the handling of the business of ASSITEJ. However, President Ilse Rodenberg (1978–1987) did not continue this practice. It was up to FitzGerald and Ramløse to revive the Commissions, and put them to very active use.

From the beginning of their creation a Chair was appointed and members of the EC, plus other Members if desired, were added to the Commissions (WG), and continued so for the 3-year term between Congresses. Occasionally another Working Group with a specific task was appointed, and then dismissed when its project was completed or superseded.

* * *

For clarity in Volume 3, the authors have codified the numbers and names of the Commissions/Working Groups throughout the rest of the text to avoid confusion, since their identification by title in the Minutes is not always the same.

Accordingly, the names, numbers, and content titles of the following entities are used in Volume 3 as follows:

Commissions:
C1 – Policy & Public Relations Commission
C2 – Communication Commission
C3 – Artistic Commission
C4 – Publications & Information Commission
C5 – Congress Commission
C6 – Language Commission & Catalog of Scripts
C7 – Finance & Statutes Commission

Working Groups:
WG1 – Policy
WG2 – Communication & Networking
WG3 – Artistic
WG4 – Publications & Information
WG5 – Congress & Archives
WG6 – Language & Catalog of Scripts
WG7 – Finance, Dues, Fund-Raising, & Statutes
WG8 – Iraq War

Over the years some areas were moved or added to another Commission or Working Group, such as Archives and Networking.

***

FitzGerald then asked for the members of the new EC to volunteer to sit on the various Commissions. He appointed Members of the EC to the newly established Commissions as follows:

- **C1 – Public Relations Commission:** Marjorie MacLean (Chair), Graziano Melano, Anne van Otterloo
- **C2 – Communication Commission:** Was [apparently] not appointed, or perhaps combined under Publications
- **C3 – Artistic Commission:** Eddy Socorro (Chair), Jürgen Flügge, Pham Thi Thanh, Kim Woo Ok
- **C4 – Publications Commission:** Maurice Yendt (Chair), Yohei Hijikata, Marián Lucky, Wolfgang Schneider
- **C5 – Congress Commission:** Not [apparently] appointed, since the Congress was discussed as a separate item with the current Chair being the person in charge of the Congress
- **C6 – Language Commission:** Michael FitzGerald (Chair), Adolph Shapiro, Jacqueline Russo
- **C7 – Finance Commission:** Harold Oaks (Chair) and Michael Ramløse
- **C7 – Statutes Commission:** Michael Ramløse (Chair), Helge Andersen, Penina M'Lama

For practical reasons the Commissions on Finance and Statutes should work together.

Meeting the next day and including both co-opted members and counselors, the EC had three items on their Agenda: 1) Report from the preceding EC; 2) Future Meetings; and 3) Work of the Commissions.

The EC approved the Bureau's decision to release Peru from their 1991–1992 dues, but requested that they pay their 1993 dues. They also accepted Angola as a potential member.

Under future meetings, they accepted the Frankfurt invitation to meet there in conjunction with their Playwrights Forum from 1-5 December 1993. There were three additional invitations: Matanzas, Cuba in 1994; Seattle, Washington, USA in May 1995; and possibly Venezuela in September/October 1995. They agreed that priority should always be given to a country not visited before, and that any Center may offer to host the EC, the only condition being that they would provide accommodations and meals.

The President then asked for reports from the Commissions, and they were as follows:

- **C1 – Public Relations:** Information about ASSITEJ will be sent to large cultural and political organizations in the world, ensuring a point of reference in each of the 6 continents. Also they would make a list of invitees for the next Congress. They would also inform governments of the importance of theatre for young people. They would work closely with Vladimir Chigishev, the Artistic Director of the Festival in Rostov. They would look for a new Logo to express their new spirit, and would seek money to fund these plans.
- **C3 – Artistic Commission** would meet in Lyon in June, and make Theme proposals before 1 November. They will try to involve Chigishev in their Commission as he plans the next Congress.
- **C4 – Publications** would seek advice from the centers on what kind of magazine ASSITEJ needed. They would concentrate on only one project – a newsletter, a yearbook, or a periodical.
- **C6 – Language Commission** would consider other models for the use of languages, e. g. the concept of "working languages". They would investigate how other world organizations have solved the language problem.
- **C7 – Finance** would contact UNESCO and UNICEF to seek funding. Their primary goal would be to seek funding for the Secretariat in 1996. Oaks was to prepare a paper on funding possibilities.
- **C7 – Statutes** would ask all centers to make suggestions re: changes in the Statutes to solve the African dilemma of different cultural traditions in theatre. They would also look at election procedures.

FitzGerald closed the meeting with the statement that he hoped their endeavors would give rise to a wider involvement from all centers, so that the 1996 Congress would demonstrate artist-driven work to the world. He wished for all to enjoy a fruitful cooperation during the next three years.

1993
EXECUTIVE COMMITTEE MEETING OF ASSITEJ[15]
Frankfurt, Germany/1-5 December 1993

Present:
President Michael FitzGerald (Australia), VP Marjorie MacLean (Canada), VP Eddy Socorro (Cuba), VP Maurice Yendt (France), Sec. Gen. Michael Ramløse (Denmark), Treasurer Harold Oaks (USA).

Members: Jürgen Flügge (Germany), Graziano Melano (Italy), Yohei Hijikata (Japan), Kim Woo Ok (Korea), Helge Andersen (Norway)), Adolph Shapiro (Russia), Marián Lucky (Slovakia), Penina M'Lama (Tanzania), Jacqueline Russo (Venezuela), Pham Thi Thanh (Vietnam).

Counselors: Wolfgang Schneider (Germany), Anne van Otterloo (Netherlands), Vladimir Chigishev (Russia).

Executive Assistant: Else Marie Mandøe (Denmark).

Christmas Fair at Frankfurt, Germany in December 1993. All Frankfurt photos courtesy of Harold Oaks, ASU Archives, Tempe, AZ, USA.

(left to right) Ilse Rodenberg (Germany), Cristel Hoffman (Germany), Kim Woo Ok (Korea) at the Reception for the EC, Frankfurt, Germany, 5 December 1993.

Suzanne Osten (Sweden) and Michael FitzGerald (Australia).

President FitzGerald welcomed the members of the EC, the Counselors, and the invited guests: Razi Amitai (Israel) and Xenia Kalogeropoulou (Greece). The revised Agenda was accepted.

The Minutes of the Meetings in Cuba in February 1993 were approved as distributed. **Report of the Secretary General:** Upon investigation Ramløse found that ASSITEJ/Int'l had neither a C-status nor B-status with UNESCO, despite all its various applications over some 28 years. He met with Torben Krogh, a member of the NGO-Commission (Non-Government Organizations) in UNESCO, and he was told that ASSITEJ could apply for B-status, although an already existing C-status is usually required. Ramløse will pursue this.

During the various sessions at the Congress, the EC attended and took part in the "Playwrights' Forum" which focused on international playwrights. There was a presentation of and reading of texts by playwrights from Australia, Cuba, USA, Russia, and Japan.

News from the Centers:
- **Kenya** had withdrawn its World Project application.
- **Zimbabwe** had promised a report on their recent Festival.
- **Mexico** announced that their center had been reorganized and re-energized, and a new head had been appointed. Russo will contact them.
- **Bulgaria** had not responded for two years. ASSITEJ/Int'l had dissolved their Center. Then ASSITEJ/Int'l will try to contact Bulgaria through ITI.
- **Brazil:** José Caldas had made attempts to form a center, but it was difficult with no permanent theatre groups. Russo would keep contact.
- **France:** Rose-Marie Moudoués has been replaced by Maurice Yendt as President of ASSITEJ/France. She has been named Honorary President of ASSITEJ/France, and Ramløse will write her a letter of congratulations.
- **Spain:** Maria Navarro has resigned as President of ASSITEJ/Spain, and the new President is Eduardo Galán. He has requested that a member from Spain be appointed to the Commission on Languages, and Socorro has reminded the EC that there had been a proposal from Spain at the General Assembly on languages.
- **Angola:** While an ASSITEJ Center has been established, no application has yet been received. The Secretariat had decided to list them as a Corresponding Member.
- **India:** They are moving toward Full Membership.
- **Tanzania:** Their Center is very active. Their recent Festival hosted a child audience of 3–4,000.

- **Ghana:** MacLean has been in correspondence with them, and has encouraged them to form a center.

Partner Centers: There were three (3) cooperative centers of ASSITEJ working very productively at the current time: Finland/Estonia; Australia/The Philippines; and Denmark/Ukraine.

Russian Center: Adolph Shapiro had recently been elected as President of ASSITEJ/Russia, and the theatres in Russia were working despite the difficult situation. FitzGerald asked them to be very open about any problems they were encountering, so other centers could help them.

Shapiro outlined the situation. The economic situation is difficult but theaters are working well, and are receiving help from the state. President Yeltsin has exempted artistic organizations from tax payments. A decentralization in theatre life has taken place, and theatres in small towns get more support now. Re: the Congress – there are good hotels in Rostov; there will be no Visa problems; and the event will receive support from the Ministry of Culture.

ITI World Congress: Flügge had handed out a Report urging ASSITEJ/Int'l toward a closer cooperation with ITI. He recommended that ASSITEJ/Int'l make a presentation at their next ITI World Conference.

Latin American: Russo gave a report indicating that networking was happening but extremely slowly. Socorro urged the EC to meet in Venezuela in order to cement Latin American contacts. He also commented that the situation for children in Cuba continued to be difficult. Hijikata recommended that ASSITEJ/Int'l bring this to the attention of the UN.

Taiwan: Ramløse brought the attention of the EC to the fact that Taiwan had been granted a center in ASSITEJ wrongfully, since it was not a separate country from China. Its Center would be dissolved, and they would be informed accordingly.

China: Over the years strenuous efforts had been made to have China join ASSITEJ/Int'l. Originally they balked at the size of the Membership Fee. Now it appeared that they were no longer interested in participation. Pham Thi Thanh would contact them for discussion.

Reports from the Commissions:
- **C1 – Commission on Public Relations:** The Commission had devised a plan of promotion starting immediately and continuing up to the beginning of the Rostov Congress: 1) a Logo for ASSITEJ; 2) a large mailing list drawn from all the centers; and 3) a new informational brochure. The cost estimate was 10,100 US$. The EC approved the project, its cost,

requested the Commission to submit a written Project Description to the EC. MacLean explained that an artist in Vancouver, B.C. in Canada was designing the Logo on a *pro bono* basis.

- **C3 – Commission on Artistic Activities:** Only 6 questionnaires re: the Congress had been returned.
- **C4 – Commission on Publications:** The Commission recommended endorsement of *The ASSITEJ Yearbook* concept starting in 1995, which they did. A proposal for a Video Library would be presented at the next EC Meeting.
- **C6 – Commission on Language:** The EC had invited Benvenuto Lumber (the Philippines), a learned linguist to participate in the discussions of the Language Commission. This was possible since the EC had decided at a earlier meeting that they could call in special counselors for just the meeting on a subject on which they needed expert advice.[16] Paul Harman (UK) had recommended in a report that ASSITEJ adopt the concept of English as its "Working Language", since it was the most universally used and accepted language globally. This would avoid the term "official language". Then the host country could add its language as the "host language". This became the 1+1 principle of language selection. The EC was to comment on this recommendation.
- **C7 – Commission on Finance:** In 1993 the Bureau had authorized the expenditure of 2,500 US$ for the publication of TABLAS to be made available at the Cuban Congress. An additional 900 US$ had been requested and granted. Invoices for Dues had been sent to all the Centers. The Commission estimated the 1994 income at 11,400 US$. The EC accepted the request from Georgia to exempt them from payment. Finally the Commission was concerned about Secretariat expenses as of 1997, and this was put on the Agenda for the next meeting.
- **C7 – Commission on Statutes:** The EC endorsed the Commission's proposal on the requirements for hosting an EC Meeting. They would prepare one on hosting a Congress for the next EC Meeting. The Commission was still to discuss the African concern on the definition of "professionalism" which denied many countries admission to membership. Ramløse and Andersen from the Commission would meet and attempt to draft a definition that would solve the dilemma.

ASSITEJ World Projects 1994: The EC approved that this designation be given to both the "3rd International Women Playwrights Conference" in Adelaide, Australia, and to "Interplay '94" in Townsville, Australia.

ASSITEJ World Congress 1996 Update: Ramløse reminded the EC of their obligation to help the Congress organizers with projects, plans, and assistance. A joint proposal suggested a presentation of work from each of the 6 continents. Representatives were selected as follows: Australia – Michael FitzGerald; Latin America – Jacqueline Russo and Eddy Socorro; North America – Harold Oaks; and Marjorie MacLean; Africa – Penina M'Lama, Marjorie MacLean, and Maurice Yendt; Europe – Graziano Melano; Asia – to be chosen from recommended names.

M'Lama reminded them of the right of the Russian Center to accept or reject a proposal. Melano stressed the need for change where needed. People must be motivated to come.

A special Congress Commission was set up: Ramløse as Chair, Kim, Melano, Chigishev, with the Russian Center to appoint someone.

They also decided to ask ASSITEJ/Russia to set the dates in October 1996.

Future EC Meetings: FitzGerald reminded the EC of their decision in Cuba to always favor holding meetings around the world. Invitations had been received from Switzerland and Venezuela. Because of the opportunity to meet with Latin American countries, the Venezuelan invitation was accepted, and they were to communicate the date as soon as possible.

ASSITEJ/USA offered to host the EC Meeting 7-14 May 1995 in Seattle, Washington, USA. A Festival was also being planned. This invitation was accepted.

Invitations for 1996 had come from both UK and Australia. The UK invitation proposed a Meeting in the South West region of England in order to promote and develop theater for young people in England, as well as hosting a Festival. The Australian invitation proposed meeting in Melbourne in May 1996, as part of their New Wave Festival, giving delegates a chance to see productions from Australia and Asia. The EC accepted the Australian invitation.

Miscellaneous:

- ASSITEJ/Peru had requested a financial grant of 31,000 US$ to support their Festif-94. Ramløse had met with Myriam Reàtegui that fall to discuss their need to cut down the size of the project (a suggestion which the festival organizers did not approve), to seek other funding since ASSITEJ/Int'l did not fund local projects, and Socorro had suggested seeking support from the theater school in Peru.
- President FitzGerald thanked the EC for their presence and hard work. In the future he suggested for the sake of efficiency that they all bring their comments and ideas regarding any items on the Agenda, consider them

carefully, and prepare what they had to say. All reports should be given to the Secretariat ahead of time for duplication and distribution.

During the Meetings the members of the EC were able to visit the celebrated "Wineachtsmarkt" (Christmas Market) in Frankfurt, which is a tradition in all German towns and cities.

At their final meeting President FitzGerald thanked the German Center and their staff warmly, who had been admirably efficient and had provided such a good working environment. Schneider thanked them all for coming to Germany. The meeting was adjourned.

1994
EXECUTIVE COMMITTEE MEETING OF ASSITEJ[17]
Caracas, Venezuela/19-24 September 1994

Present:
President Michael FitzGerald (Australia), VP Marjorie MacLean (Canada), VP Eddy Socorro (Cuba), VP Maurice Yendt (France), Sec. Gen. Michael Ramløse (Denmark), Treasurer Harold Oaks (USA).

Members: Yohei Hijikata (Japan), Kim Woo Ok (Korea), Helge Andersen (Norway), Adolph Shapiro (Russia), Penina M'Lama (Tanzania), Jacqueline Russo (Venezuela).

Counselors: Wolfgang Schneider (Germany), Benvenuto Lumber (the Philippines).

Members absent: Jürgen Flügge (Germany), Graziano Melano (Italy), Marián Lucky (Slovakia), Pham Thi Thanh (Vietnam).

Counselors absent: Anne van Otterloo (Netherlands), Vladimir Chigishev (Russia).

Executive Assistant: Else Marie Mandøe (Denmark).

Penina M'Lama (Tanzania) at the EC Meeting in Caracas, Venezuela, September 1994. All photos courtesy of Harold Oaks, ASU Archives, Tempe, AZ, USA.

Wolfgang Schneider (Germany)

Yohei Hijikata (Japan)

The Bureau met for one hour on Sunday, 18 September 1994 to set the agenda.

Monday, 19 September 1994, 9 am to 1 pm

The Secretary General had sent out the following Agenda:

- Adoption of the Minutes from the EC Meeting in Frankfurt, Germany, December 1993
- Secretary General's Report
- ASSITEJ/UNESCO relationship
- TABLAS – Havana Congress Report
- Reports from the Commissions
- World Congress 1996
- Secretariat after 1996
- Reports from the Commissions – 2 decisions
- Miscellaneous

President FitzGerald welcomed the members of the EC and the Counselors, and gave a special welcome to the invited guests from Latin America: Argentina, Mexico, Nicaragua, Peru, and Uruguay. He addressed special thanks to the Nordic Agencies—SIDA and DANIDA—for enabling their presence with their financial support.

FitzGerald noted the death of Natalia Sats, distinguished Member of Russian children's theatre as well as ASSITEJ, at the age of 90 in Moscow. He also announced with regret the untimely death of Wasonga Eliud, one of the anchors of ASSITEJ/Kenya. He had sent letters of condolences to both.

The Minutes of the EC Meeting in Frankfurt in December 1993 were accepted as amended. However Ramløse reminded the EC of the new rule for expediency that Minutes were adopted as delivered if no corrections had been received within three months, and then would be distributed to the centers.

The President's Report: FitzGerald expressed concern at the lack of response from the EC to the questions posed by the President's Report on its distribution. If they did not respond, their ideas could not be included in the final report!

The Secretary General's Report: News from the Centers:
- **The Icelandic Center** is in the process of reorganization, a new Board had been elected, and contact should soon be restored.
- **Zimbabwe** plans to set up a center with a professional staff, and has asked Andersen and Ramløse for assistance, and were advised to set up offices with IATA and IDEA. They will meet with Titus Moetsabi, President of ASSITEJ/Zimbabwe, in Norway in October for discussions.
- **Turkey** has good contacts with the Secretariat, but too much is centralized around Tamer Levent, head of ASSITEJ/Turkey. They have been advised to decentralize.

- In **Brazil** there is good theatre for young people, and contacts have been established. However, there are severe rivalries between São Paulo and Rio de Janeiro. Maurice Yendt will go to Rio, and hopes to clear up some of the confusions. FitzGerald has asked him for a report on his visit.
- **The Netherlands** has financial problems, and van Otterloo is no longer associated with ASSITEJ/Netherlands, but can continue as a Counselor to ASSITEJ/Int'l if she will represent Dutch interests and ASSITEJ/Netherlands agrees to her appointment.
- **Cuba** just celebrated its 20th Anniversary, and Sara Miyares Ramos is its new President. Eddy Socorro will continue as its representative until 1996. ASSITEJ/Cuba has been given the Cuban Xavier Oliviera Medal for its work for children and young people.
- **Hungary** has notified the Secretariat that the Arany Janos Theatre has been closed, and Janos Meszner, President of ASSITEJ/Hungary, is now director of one of the puppet theatres in Budapest.
- **New Centers: China** was accepted as a new Full Member of ASSITEJ, and notice was given that new centers will be set up in Argentina and Nicaragua.
- Letters have been sent to **Indonesia, Malaysia, New Zealand, Singapore,** and **Thailand** with information about ASSITEJ encouraging them to become members.
- The **Caracas** Meeting has allowed the EC to have closer contact with the Latin American Centers, and the presence of representatives from Argentina, Cuba, Mexico, Nicaragua, Peru, Uruguay, and Venezuela was extremely helpful.
- Maurice Yendt has made contact with the following French-speaking countries: **Algeria, Burkina Faso, Cameroon, Central Africa, Ethiopia, Ghana, Mali, Morocco, Senegal, Tunis, Uganda,** and **Zaïre.** Theatre for children is not formalized in these countries, and there are usually financial problems. The French Center will continue to work these contacts.
- **ASSITEJ/Belgium** urged the EC to consider accepting a center in Bosnia, but the EC decided to hand over action and the initiative to the Belgian Center.

Under the Publications Commission the Secretariat has published the ASSITEJ Festival Guide. While there are flaws, it is extremely useful. An updated edition for 1995 will be distributed in December 1994.

Once more the EC has applied for a status Class B Membership in UNESCO. This application has been well strategized and planned. It will probably be considered in the spring of 1995.

1996 World Congress: In planning their 1996 Congress at Rostov-on-Don the Russian Center agreed to the following:

- The dates had been set at 1-8 October 1996, with the General Assembly on 4-8 October.
- Adolf Shapiro was President of the Organizing Committee, with Galina Kolosova as Secretary. 1995 was set as the year to raise funding.
- There would be a variety of theatre activity for children and young people.
- The artistic program would be representative of all parts of the world.
- At their own expense centers were asked to contribute performances, workshops, exhibitions, receptions—anything that would be of interest to the delegates.
- There would be 8–10 Russian performances, and hopefully 6 international performances representing all 6 continents, selected by the Artistic Commission. The selection would be coordinated with the Theme: "Theatre for Survival".
- They hoped to have the structure in place by the EC Meeting in Seattle in May 1995.
- The Russian Center guaranteed that all participants would get the necessary documents to be able to enter the country.

C1 – Commission on Public Relations was producing a new mailing list, and working on the design of a new logo. The Commission needed mailing lists from all the centers to add to their Master List. MacLean had worked with FitzGerald and Ramløse on the information to be included in the new brochure. It would list the Purpose of the Association, its Special Programs, the next Congress and General Assembly, the Structure of the Association, and its Future. Also, they would work out a Time Line up to the Rostov Congress.

C3 – Commission on Artistic Activities recommended that individual centers submit at their own expense a production, a project, and/or a workshop to the program of the Rostov Congress. These must be done in cooperation with the Russian Center. Deadline was 15 January 1995. The EC approved the proposal.

C4 – Commission on Publications had finalized a proposal for an ASSITEJ Yearbook, which would present the work of ASSITEJ/Int'l as well as the works of each center. It will first appear in 1996, covering the work done in 1995. The publication of TABLAS, the Special Edition on the Cuban Congress, has been subjected to cost overruns and printing delays. The Secretariat has recalled all copies to its offices, and is distributing it to the members from there.

The Commission also noted a minimal response to their questionnaire in compiling a world-wide bibliography on youth theatre. The plans for their Yearbook were proceeding. It would be produced over three years, with 1996 being the first year. It would be published in Frankfurt, 1,000 copies for 14,000 US$. The EC asked for additional recommendations re: the funding. The Commission asked the EC to consider establishing a Video Library, having centers contribute their videos. They would ask the USA Center what plans they had to tape their meeting in Seattle in 1995. The Commission would work closely with the Public Relations Commission.

C6 – Commission on Language has received replies from 17 centers, and FitzGerald will draft a response which will be brought to Seattle for discussion. The Commission will present a report and a recommendation to the EC in 1995.

C7 – Commission on Finance found centers confused by the new system, and had cut their dues accordingly. They also created a new procedure to deal with delinquent "dues payers".

The Treasurer had sent out invoices as of December 1993. Under the new rules centers were expected to pay 250 US$ per annum, but in reality were paying less. They established a new time line for payments with reminders, and if at the end of the year, there was no payment, the EC would move for expulsion. This action would occur only if there had been no response from the center. Also, only dues paying members can make nominations for the Honorary President's Award. The EC approved these decisions.

C7 – Commission on Statutes was attempting to satisfy the EC request for amendments to allow more countries to become members. The Commission stressed that the term "professional" indicates the degree of dedication to theatre work, *not* the earning of money by creating theatre.

The President asked for all the Commissions to hand in brief written reports.

The Secretariat after October 1996: FitzGerald stated that it was of prime importance to maintain the current high standard of a full-time secretariat. The EC must find ways to secure the necessary resources. He also clarified the fact that this was the responsibility of the Secretary General, and could only be approved by the General Assembly.

The EC decided to inform the members of the conditions, the costs, and the responsibilities of the Secretariat, and to encourage them to seek solutions.

The Next EC Meeting: On invitation from ASSITEJ/Australia the dates were changed to 12-18 June 1996, four months prior to the Rostov Congress. It would take place in Brisbane, Australia. The EC accepted the changes.

ASSITEJ/Germany Request: ASSITEJ/Germany requested that their International Director's Seminar that would take place 13-17 July 1995 in Freiberg be given the title *ASSITEJ WORLD PROJECT 1995*. The EC granted their request.

EC Meeting in Seattle: Oaks informed the EC that ASSITEJ/USA was preparing to host them at Seattle, Washington celebrating the 30th Anniversary of the founding of ASSITEJ. It would take place on Bainbridge Island. Ann Shaw would be responsible for the preparations of the Meeting, and Oaks was gathering material for short biographies of the current EC members.

On FitzGerald's recommendation it was decided to invite Past President Ilse Rodenberg and Past Secretary General Rose-Marie Moudoués to the Meeting. Schneider offered to help. Shaw suggested that a center take on the responsibility of creating a 10 minute visual presentation of ASSITEJ. Schneider said he would discuss the possibility with the Publications Commission.

Honorary President's Award: Nomination forms would be sent out in January 1995, with a deadline for returns by 1 November 1995. ASSITEJ/USA will receive them, select three (3) finalists, and forward their names and materials to the EC for their final choice. The Winner will be notified, and must come to the Congress at Rostov to receive the Award.

President FitzGerald closed the meeting with thanks to the Latin American guests for their attendance, warm thanks to the Venezuelan Center for their hosting the meeting and especially Jacqueline Russo, who made it possible despite many financial difficulties. He commended the EC for their hard work and dedication during the Meeting.

1995
EXECUTIVE COMMITTEE MEETING OF ASSITEJ[18]
Seattle, Washington, USA/7-14 May 1995

The EC Meeting was held in conjunction with the One Theatre World Festival sponsored by the USA Center, as well as recognizing the 30th Anniversary of the establishment of ASSITEJ in Paris, France in June 1965.

Present:
President Michael FitzGerald (Australia), VP Marjorie MacLean (Canada), VP Eddy Socorro (Cuba), VP Maurice Yendt (France), Sec. Gen. Michael Ramløse (Denmark), Treasurer Harold Oaks (USA).
Members: Jürgen Flügge (Germany), Graziano Melano (Italy), Yohei Hijikata (Japan), Kim Woo Ok (Korea), Helge Andersen (Norway), Adolph Shapiro (Russia), Marián Lucky, (Slovakia), Penina M'Lama (Tanzania), Jacqueline Russo (Venezuela), Pham Thi Thanh (Vietnam).
Counselors: Wolfgang Schneider (Germany), Vladimir Chigishev (Russia), Anne van Otterloo (The Netherlands).
Executive Assistant: Else Marie Mandøe (Denmark).

Seattle, Washington, USA, 1995.
Courtesy of Harold Oaks, ASU Archives, Tempe, AZ, USA.

Members of the EC at their Meeting in Seattle, Washington, USA on 7-14 May 1995. (Front row, left to right) Kim Woo Ok (Korea), Pham Thi Thanh (Vietnam), Michael FitzGerald (Australia); (2nd row, left to right) Wolfgang Schneider (Germany), Harold Oaks (USA), Michael Ramløse (Denmark), Anne van Otterloo (Netherlands), Helge Andersen (Norway); (3rd row, left to right) Else Marie Mandøe (Denmark), Yohei Hijikata (Japan), Penina M'Lama (Tanzania), Adolph Shapiro (Russia), Maurice Yendt (France), Vladimir Chigashev (Russia), (4th row, left to right) Marián Lucky (Slovakia), Marjorie MacLean (Canada), Graziano Melano (Italy), Jürgen Flügge (Germany), Eddy Socorro (Cuba). Courtesy of Michael FitzGerald.

Marjorie MacLean, Yohei Hijikata, Wolfgang Schneider at the EC Meeting in Seattle. Courtesy of Wolfgang Schneider.

Performance at the Seattle EC Meeting by the Seattle Children's Theatre, Linda Hartzell, Artistic Dirctor. Courtesy of Harold Oaks, ASU Archives, Tempe, AZ, USA.

The EC met on two days during the Festival: Tuesday 9 May 1995 and Wednesday 10 May 1995.

President FitzGerald welcomed the members of the EC, and thanked the US Center for the invitation to come to Seattle.

- The President noted the deaths of Hildegard Bergfeld (former President of ASSITEJ/Int'l), and Kazuto Kurihara (President of ASSITEJ/Japan) and Sozaburo Ochiai (Vice-President of ASSITEJ/Japan).
- The Minutes from the EC Meeting in Caracas in September 1994 were approved as presented, and all business arising from the Minutes was considered to be covered by the current Agenda.

New Centers:
- Argentina was accepted to Full Membership.
- Nicaragua has formed, applied for membership and was accepted.
- Singapore was accepted as a Corresponding Member.

Update on Other Centers:
- **Estonia:** A Nordic meeting of support will be held in Tallinn in the autumn of 1995. The Minister of Culture and the Mayor have been notified of the upcoming meeting.

- **Zimbabwe:** NORAD contributed money until 1999 to setup an ASSITEJ office and to organize Festivals. The Festivals are to start on the provincial level, and then move to the national level.
- **Portugal:** Yendt reported that there had been financial difficulties, but things were improving.
- **The Netherlands:** They have lost their government subsidy, and now have a new Board and have adopted a new set of Statutes. A working committee has been established with the help of Anne van Otterloo.
- **Ukraine:** Shapiro stated that heads of the centers in the former Soviet Union had been appointed from the top without informing the theatres, which might explain the lack of communication.
- **Gruzia:** Shapiro stated that their theatres there were working well, and have kept close contact with ASSITEJ/Russia.
- **Kirgizstan:** No information.
- **Austria & Switzerland:** Schneider reported that ASSITEJ/Austria had recently been reorganized, was involved in a number of projects. ASSITEJ/Switzerland was currently encouraging the writing of new plays for children.
- **Croatia:** Ramløse reported that their Center was working despite extremely difficult circumstances [the current war].
- **Tanzania:** M'Lama reported they were working on a teacher-training project through workshops, hoping to eventually write a Manual. Donations would be gratefully accepted.
- **Venezuela:** Had recently had a very successful 2nd Meeting outside of Caracas.
- **Spain:** "Market", a major Festival of theatre for young people is held annually with seminars and workshops, but has no connection with ASSITEJ. Ramløse has urged the companies to join ASSITEJ with no success so far.

Contacts with Non-Member Countries:

- **Brazil:** Yendt reported that 30–40 shows are offered each week for young people, but there is little cooperation. He stated that they are trying to form a center.
- **Asian Countries:** Malaysia and New Zealand were considering membership. Hijikata said that Japan was going to invite contributors to a Newsletter if funding can be found. Thanh (Vietnam) said they wished to establish correspondence with other Asian nations, including China.

- **African Countries:** M'Lama reported contacts with Malawi, Uganda, Cameroon, and Zambia. Apparently a Center and a Festival has been established in the Cameroon.
- **Latvia, Lithuania:** Ramløse had been in contact with them, encouraging their membership.
- **Bulgaria:** Ramløse, van Otterloo, and Lucky all had contacts there, hoping to encourage their eventual membership.
- **ASSITEJ Festival Guide 1995:** This has proved to be a useful tool for the membership. the information form was to be distributed soon.

ITI Congress in June: Russo will present a paper on ASSITEJ at the ITI World Congress in Caracas, Venezuela 24-30 June 1995.

IDEA Congress: FitzGerald will attend their Congress in Brisbane, Australia in July, and will speak about ASSITEJ, sitting on a panel dealing with international exchange.

ASSITEJ/UNESCO Relationship: Recent correspondence with them urged ASSITEJ/Int'l to make use of their affiliation with ITI. This was unacceptable. Many ITI Centers do not accept ASSITEJ. The EC decided to try to apply for UNESCO Membership once again. MacLean asked for documentation of the history of the relationship.

TABLAS: the Special Congress Edition: Socorro reported that it would be possible to obtain 600 copies through contacts in Berlin. Schneider offered to distribute the copies directly from Berlin. The German Center would send out one copy of TABLAS to each Center, and then additional copies upon request.

Naming of Deputies: Ramløse handed out forms to be filled out to the head of each center present for them to name a Deputy to replace the elected EC Member in event of him/her not being able to attend a meeting.

Job Descriptions: In preparation for his stepping down next year [1996] as Secretary General, Ramløse passed out a *job description* of the office of Secretary General. With the additions of that person being "good in communication, both orally and in writing" the EC endorsed his recommendations.

In the discussions that followed the EC dealt with the following procedures:

- A description of the task of taking on the Secretariat; Germany was willing to consider the possibility
- A job description of the Treasurer
- A job description for the EC Members
- Financial implications in relationship to obligations of all such incumbents

The EC endorsed these materials from Ramløse. FitzGerald was asked to write similar job descriptions for the Presidency and the Vice-Presidencies. Oaks was to write up the job of the Treasurer, and the Secretary General one on the Bureau.

Report on the Commissions: President FitzGerald reminded the members to bring forth their honest opinions on the work of the Commissions, so they could present "good and honest recommendations" to the General Assembly. Ramløse reminded them that nothing would change until 1996 after the General Assembly had endorsed their recommendations.

- **C1 – Commission on Public Relations:** The EC decided to use the new "Globe" logo until 1996, and then decide whether to stick with that or the alternate "spiral" design. They then decided to have the new informational brochure published in five languages: English, French, Russian, Spanish, and Japanese. This new brochure would be used up by the next Congress.
- **C3 – Commission on Artistic Activities:** For the Rostov Congress the Commission had received performance proposals from 11 countries: 22 performances covering the 5 continents, plus 6 proposals for workshops from 4 countries. They took seriously the Theme of the Congress "Theatre for Survival", and made recommendations accordingly. The Secretary General would notify the applicants of the recommendations, but all costs would have to be covered by the company or their country.
- **C4 – Commission on Publications:** The new Yearbook would be published only in English. It will contain articles on theatre for young people, information on the Centers, and general information and bibliography.
- **C6 – Commission of Language:** The ensuing discussion was lively and thorough. The decision rested on two options: Option 1: The language of the host country + English as the Working Language + any number of languages according to needs and costs; Option 2: The language of the host country + English, French, Russian, and possibly Spanish. A final draft of these proposals was to be re-written by FitzGerald for the General Assembly.
- **C7 – Commission on Statutes:** There had been an on-going and thorough discussion on the need to be a "professional" association, and to avoid using children as performers. This particularly involved the African Centers, many of which had children as performers. The Commission had returned with the following recommendation in regards to the present Statutes:

"The following categories of membership for national centers are acceptable to the International Association:
1. Professional companies of adult actors playing for children and young people, or professional theatre artists working in theatre for children and young people.
2. No changes
3. No changes
4. No changes

"In order to qualify for full membership in the Association a national center must have at least three members as defined in Category 1. Other centers with less than three members in Category 1 are Corresponding Members."

The EC endorsed this recommendation: For – 16; Abstention – 1.

- **C7 – Commission on Finance:** The Membership needed to realize that more and more financial demands were being put on the Secretariat. The new system of a basic cost of dues with Centers encouraged to send more was being abused by some centers just sending in the minimum. The question of a raising the dues higher was discussed. No action.

The President closed the discussion of the Commission Reports by asking all the Chairs to inform him of which Centers had given replies to surveys and questionnaires in their final reports. Communication between the Centers and the Secretariat is absolutely mandatory!

World Congress 1996: This report replaced that of the Congress Commission. The Russian Festival at Rostov-on-Don had been accepted as an official event, and would be given governmental support. There will be a center both in Moscow and in Rostov. The Cuban Congress had recommended limiting the number of theoretical speeches, and this was to be adhered to. The Secretary General announced the possibility of a flight from Copenhagen to Rostov Direct. A round trip ticket would cost about 650 US$, but required 200 people as a minimum. The EC approved the possibility of the flight, and the information was to be sent to all members. Flügge promised on behalf of the German Center to take care of people arriving though Frankfurt, Germany in order to catch the connection.

Shapiro noted that they were planning a "newspaper" to be published daily during the Congress. Oaks (Treasurer) advised the Russian Center to increase the Registration Fee to cover costs of booklet, newspaper, and posters.

Ramløse asked Shapiro about the rumors of all tourists submitting to an obligatory AIDS Test, but he replied that there was no indication that such a law would be passed.

Miscellaneous:

- **The Honorary President's Award:** Eek informed the EC, the Award which was announced in 1993 in Cuba, would be given to "an artist or a company who had achieved noteworthy excellence in theatre for children and young people during the previous three years." Each Center could send in one nomination from their Center by 1 December 1995. The winner would receive a check for 1,000 US$, an engraved goblet, and a bottle of champagne. Only centers whose dues are up to date are eligible to make a nomination.
- **Member of Honor:** FitzGerald proposed that Rose-Marie Moudoués be named a Member of Honor. Accepted unanimously.
- **ASSITEJ World Project:** The EC approved unanimously that the 10th Werkstatt-Tage in Halle, Germany be granted the title of "ASSITEJ World Project – 1996".
- **Future EC Meeting:** The next EC Meeting would be in Brisbane, Australia 12-18 June 1996.
- **European Network:** van Otterloo, Melano, and Schneider are the contact persons for *European Network*. They are working to combine several of the different arts. A recent project involved 5 companies entitled "The Right Shoes" and has been performed in a number of refugee camps with success.
- **Congress 1999:** Norway hopes to be able to host the next Congress in 1999 in Tromsø, Norway in May 1999.

The President thanked the EC for their efforts, and gave a special thanks to the US Center and to Harold Oaks for the preparations of the meeting and the exceptional hospitality.

The following Symposium Event, honoring the 30th Anniversary of ASSITEJ, was held along with the EC Meeting and the Festival. Invited as guests by ASSITEJ/USA for the celebration were former Secretary General Rose-Marie Moudoués (France) and former President Ilse Rodenberg (Germany/GDR). The Program indicated the following:

- Welcome by Harold Oaks to participants and guests; followed by Marilyn Raichle (Festival Director); Tom Pechar (Managing Director–Seattle Children's Theatre); Sue Donaldson (Seattle City Council Member)
- 30th Anniversary Event: Michael Ramløse (Secretary General); Ann Shaw

(ASSITEJ/USA) Stand up for ASSITEJ where people were asked to stand indicating attendance at previous Congresses
- ASSITEJ History: *The Dream of ASSITEJ* (Ilse Rodenberg); *The Birth of ASSITEJ – The Formative Years* (Rose-Marie Moudoués – read in French). (See Appendix J.)
- Video documentary – ASSITEJ/Germany Main focus on 2nd and 3rd decade
- Present Directions/New Visions (Michael FitzGerald – President)
- Roll Call & Birthday wishes
- Song – Happy Birthday (Ramløse played the piano)
- "The Ivory Circle" was presented by the Barking Gecko Theatre Company of Australia
- The Program was followed by a Birthday Celebration and dessert buffet

1996
EXECUTIVE COMMITTEE MEETING OF ASSITEJ
Brisbane, Australia/9-16 June 1996[19]

Present:
President Michael FitzGerald (Australia), VP Marjorie MacLean (Canada), VP Maurice Yendt (France), Sec. Gen. Michael Ramløse (Denmark).

Members: Jürgen Flügge (Germany), Yohei Hijikata (Japan), Kim Woo Ok (Korea), Helge Andersen (Norway), Adolph Shapiro (Russia), Penina M'Lama (Tanzania).

Counselor: Wolfgang Schneider (Germany).

Members absent: Eddy Socorro (Cuba), Marián Lucky (Slovakia), Graziano Melano (Italy), Harold Oaks (USA), Jacqueline Russo (Venezuela), Pham Thi Thanh (Vietnam).

Counselors absent: Vladimir Chigishev (Russia) and Anne van Otterloo (Netherlands).

Executive Assistant: Else Marie Mandøe (Denmark).

The bridge at Brisbane, Australia.

The EC meeting began with President FitzGerald presiding and welcoming seven delegates from China, one from India, one from Indonesia, one from Malaysia, one from New Zealand, two from Thailand, and two from the Philippines. On invitation from ASSITEJ/Australia they were there to observe the EC Meeting, attend the Out of the Box Festival, and the Asian Pacific Meeting.

Minutes from Seattle EC Meeting: The Minutes from the EC Meeting in Seattle, Washington, USA in May 1995 were approved as presented, and all business arising from the Minutes was considered to be covered by the current Agenda.

Report of the Secretary General: New Centers: Four new National Centers were accepted in membership: Brazil, Bulgaria, and New Zealand in Full Membership, with Thailand accepted as a Corresponding Member.

In an update concerning other Centers the Secretariat reported as follows:

- A meeting with a **Georgian company** needing practical and moral support in forming a Center;
- A request to contact people in **Kenya** for a Center;
- No contact with the **Madagascar** Center;
- According to Yendt **Portugal** showed no interest in joining ASSITEJ;
- The **Rumanian Center** is active with Ion Lucian as the director of a new theatre there;
- Denmark met with people from the **Ukraine** in UK and advised them to re-organize their Center;
- The Secretariat had received a subscription fee from **Zaïre** and expected more information to follow;
- The **German Center** had organized a workshop for independent companies in Germany in June, and had an international director's Seminar planned in Kiel for July 1997 with ten international directors to be invited.

There had been the following contacts with non-member countries:

- **Uganda:** They are attempting to form a Center;
- **South Africa:** There is interest in establishing a Center. Zimbabwe has a connection there, and will assist them;
- **Malaysia:** Progress is slow and the situation unstable;
- **Slovakia:** They are trying to establish outside contacts, but their situation is complicated and they may need outside support.

The Secretariat needed much more information from the Centers in order to publish the 1996 Festival Guide.

The Secretariat was still awaiting clarifications from their UNESCO relationship.

The British Center had sent out a Questionnaire on Minority Language Theatre, but is awaiting results to present a Report at the next Congress.

Job Descriptions: MacLean presented an extensive Draft of Job Descriptions of the following: The President, The Secretary General, The EC Committee Members, The Vice Presidents, The Treasurer, The Bureau, and The Commissions. There was considerable discussion, stressing the fact that the descriptions were primarily guidelines to the various jobs. There were some changes, and then the EC accepted the Paper as presented. Another example of a much-needed document well done.

Reports from the Commissions:

- **C1 – Public Relations:** 10,000 Informational Pamphlets had been printed, 8,000 of which had been distributed. The mailing list consisted of individuals and companies. The new logo has been well received, and the logo should be put on all official stationery. It was recommended to change the name of the Commission to **Communication Commission**. FitzGerald on behalf of the EC complemented the Commission on its first-class report, and stated copies of it would go forward to the General Assembly.
- **C3 – Artistic:** There was no Report, and Flügge and Schneider would contact Socorro to ask for the Report. (See Summary of 1991–1996).
- **C4 – Publications:** Schneider reported that the new Yearbook will have 125 pages and 30 photos. Cost would be 20 DEM per copy. The German Center would buy copies for all its members, and this income would help pay for the 1998 edition. The Commission recommended the continuation of: the Yearbook, the Festival guide, the ASSITEJ Quarterly Bulletin, and the setting up of an ASSITEJ video library. The EC endorsed this proposal, and FitzGerald thanked the Commission for its excellent work.
- **C6 – Language:** The EC endorsed their report to go forward to the General Assembly.
- **C7 – Finance:** The Treasurer reported more subscriptions (dues) are coming in. Yendt proposed a Dues Structure proportionate to a country's national product. This was forwarded to the New EC for consideration. Flügge recommended contacting wealthier countries to increase their subscriptions. The Treasurer was asked to locate all the ASSITEJ Funds, and seek higher rates of interest. The EC endorsed the Report.
- **C7 – Statutes:** Since their report had been distributed prior to the meeting, the EC endorsed it. Primarily it listed ways to speed up the Election process, several of which would be put to use at the Rostov Congress.

The General Assembly – Rostov 1966: The General Assembly would meet on 4, 5, and 7 of October 1996. Elections would be on 7 October. On 8 October the new EC would meet and setup the new Commissions. The President would make his oral Report from the Podium. (See Appendix K).

- **Statutes:** As a result of a vote (For – 8; Against – 1; Abstention –1) the EC decided to present only one proposed Language change: "Working languages of the World Congress and General Assembly will be the language of the host country and English and at least one other language determined by the EC according to the needs of the meeting." Also, they recommended a change in the Criteria for Membership as proposed at the Seattle Meeting to make membership easier for the African Centers, and the requirement of an annual report from each center was to be removed completely.
- The EC endorsed the **Report of the Secretary General** to be presented to the Assembly, and the President thanked Ramløse for his efficiency in all his work.
- **Working Program 1996–1999:** The EC recommended the following to be presented to the General Assembly: The Finance Commission, the Publications Commission, and the Public Relations Commission (renamed Communications Commission) should continue. The Statutes Commission should continue as required. The Language Commission had accomplished its task. The Congress Commission is very useful, and should be appointed for another 3-year term.

There was a long debate on the Artistic Commission, mostly related to the non-use of the stated Theme by the Centers. MacLean saw it as an indication of time to pause and research the membership needs. Yendt stressed the importance of maintaining an Artistic Commission, and Shapiro suggested that discussions be tied closer to specific productions, and to choose a theme of a more concrete nature.

The EC decided to continue the Artistic Commission, but to investigate membership interests, and they recommended the creation of an Administrative Commission. They also decided to recommend a survey of the membership needs and wishes by the new EC.

The Secretariat 1996–1999: Schneider reported that the German government had refused to support the Secretariat, so another solution had to be found. ASSITEJ/Germany was thanked for all their efforts on behalf of ASSITEJ.

Ramløse handed out the nomination from Austria, that of Ulli Plichta. She is currently President of ASSITEJ/Austria and a General Theater Manager, and they have applied to the government for financial support of the Secretariat. Only Austria has applied for the Secretariat. After considerable discussion, the EC decided to propose to the General Assembly that an Administrative Commission be created with responsibility for co-ordination, and the delegation duties among the Centers, the Commissions, and the EC Members.

The EC Candidates for 1996–1999: The deadline for nominations to the EC was 1 July. The EC also recommended that Harold Oaks be re-elected as Treasurer by the General Assembly, as a result of his excellent work.

Congress 1999: Proposals to host the 1999 World Congress of ASSITEJ were received from ASSITEJ/Norway to be held in Tromsø, Norway in July/August, and from ASSITEJ/Germany to be held in Berlin, Germany on 23-30 April 1999.

Both offers would be presented to the General Assembly for their vote.

Subscriptions: The EC recommended that the current Subscription rate be continued until 1999.

Rostov-on-Don Congress and Festival: Shapiro reported that the EC was to be housed at the local Intourist Hotel, opposite the "Filharmoniya" where the General Assembly would meet, along with the Workshops and Seminars. There would be two Russian keynote speakers: Theatre Critic Anatoly Smelyansky and journalist Yuri Shekochikhin. The EC recommended that Penina M'Lama be invited to be the outside Keynote Speaker, and she promised to consider it.

They also asked for other international names to be invited to come to the Congress. Ramløse announced that 2,000 US$ had been set aside for printing a daily Congress Newspaper. Shapiro announced that there would be an Opening and Closing Ceremony, the touristic offers, the "Speak Up" sessions, and the Night Club. The Honorary Presidents Award would be presented the second day of the meeting of the General Assembly (5 October).

The Secretary General announced that the Nordic Aid Agencies (DANIDA, SIDA, and NORAD) would help delegates from the following countries to attend the Congress: Chile, India, Nicaragua, Peru, Sri Lanka, Tanzania, Uganda, Uruguay, and Zimbabwe. The Agencies had decided which countries to support, and the EC could not add any other names. The President was asked to write letters of gratitude to all these agencies.

The EC endorsed the ASSITEJ/USA proposal that the Honorary President's Award be granted to Volker Ludwig from Grips Theater (Germany) and Ray Nusselein from Paraplyteatret (Denmark).

Schneider proposed to make the post Congress documentation 1996 part of the Yearbook 1998 (to be distributed in the autumn of 1997), and his generous proposal was endorsed by the EC.

Miscellaneous:

- **Future Congresses:** There was considerable discussion of the role of the EC in making decisions for the Congress planners, which sometimes involved considerable expense on the host's part. Finally it was recommended in the future it would be the Congressional Commission's responsibility to assist and make recommendations if asked by the Congress and Festival organizers.
- **Honorary Members:** Zvjezdana Ladika (Croatia) was to be recommended to the General Assembly for her to be named an Honorary Member of ASSITEJ. Also, in the future the Artistic Commission should define what "Exceptional service given to ASSITEJ" meant.
- **Future EC Meeting:** Peru offered to host the EC in Lima in connection with an International Festival of Theatre for Children and the Second Latin American and Caribbean Meeting during the first week of August 1997. The EC recommended that the invitation be passed on to the new EC.
- **Letter from Marián Lucky (Slovakia):** Lack of governmental support had forced him to close the Slovakian Center. Schneider offered to ask the ITI in Austria to make inquiries about the situation, and promised to report back to the EC.
- **Spanish Center Letter:** Spain had reacted to the announced lack of information from them at the Seattle EC Meeting, and had sent a list companies that belonged to the Spanish Center to the Secretariat.
- **Werkstatt-Tage in Halle:** The Werkstatt-Tage in Halle, Germany had been given the title "ASSITEJ World Project", and now would take place 20-29 September 1999. Flügge reported that the title had helped the organizers find sponsors.

The meeting was adjourned with President FitzGerald thanking the EC for their attendance and Ramløse for his good preparatory work. He also gave special thanks to the attendees from the Asian Pacific Meeting. Vice President Yendt expressed his gratitude on behalf of the EC to the Australian Center for organizing and hosting a very good meeting and an enjoyable stay in Australia.

INTERIM/1995-1996

In November 1995 the Secretariat issued an Information-Bulletin that gave more details about the forthcoming Congress than previous Bulletins. The "new" Russia was doing its best to provide a truly "world" Congress with the best of accommodations and appointments.

For those in the west attendance at the Rostov Congress was simplified and enhanced by the fact that the Danish Ministry of Culture forbade any of its officials to fly on Aeroflot (Russian) flights. Accordingly, the Danish Secretariat chartered a flight from Copenhagen, opening that flight to any ASSITEJ delegates. A total of 141 accepted the offer, which left on Monday 30 September and arrived in Rostov at 7 pm. It returned to Copenhagen on Wednesday 9 October. It was a Boeing 757 requiring 200 patrons. Reservations had to be made by 1 April 1996. There was also a train from Helsinki, Finland going through Moscow and on to Rostov. Visas were required. The price of the chartered flight was approximately 450 US$ per person.

The whole Congress was to be accommodated on the hotel ships on the Don River, the cabins of which could accommodate 1, 2 and 4 persons. The EC stayed at the Hotel Intourist, which was also available for tourist accommodations. The Congress offered a Package for room, breakfast, supper, and the Registration Fee. Individual package prices ran from 405–805 US$. There were extra costs for additional theatre tickets, workshops, and excursions. The Bulletin indicated that all costs were "considerably lower" than in Moscow.

The Festival as part of the Congress was to offer 6–8 Russian productions and 4–6 international ones. The only one chosen so far was a production of *Moby Dick* by the Idaho Theater for Youth (USA). Three theatre stages would be available.

The theme was stated as "ASSITEJ 1993-96: Theatre for Survival".

Russia promised an exhibition of works by Russian set designers, and there would be poster exhibits from Denmark, Finland, Iceland, Norway, and Sweden. Germany promised an exhibition which would tell the story of German Theatre for Children through posters of their productions.

There would be opening and closing Ceremonies, three informal "round-table" discussions, the first presentation of the Honorary Presidents Award, a Night Café, and a daily Newspaper highlighting the daily events, plus excursions in the Don area, and a trip to Taganrog and the Chekhov Museums, since this was his birthplace.

1996
XIIth WORLD CONGRESS OF ASSITEJ
Rostov-on-Don, Russia/1-8 October 1996[20]

The EC Meeting in Rostov-on-Don, Russia met on 2 October prior to the General Assembly Meeting:

Present:
President Michael FitzGerald (Australia), VP Marjorie MacLean (Canada), VP Maurice Yendt (France), Sec. Gen. Michael Ramløse (Denmark), Treasurer Harold Oaks (USA).
Members of the EC: Jürgen Flügge (Germany), Yohei Hijikata (Japan), Kim Woo Ok (Korea), Helge Andersen (Norway), Adolph Shapiro (Russia), Amandina Lihamba/Deputy for Penina M'Lama (Tanzania), Pham Thi Thanh (Vietnam).
Counselor: Wolfgang Schneider (Germany).
Members absent: Graziano Melano (Italy), Marián Lucky (Slovakia), Jacqueline Russo (Venezuela), Penina M'Lama (Tanzania).
Counselors absent: Anne van Otterloo (Netherlands) and Vladimir Chigishev (Russia).
Observer: Ulli Plichta (Austria).
Executive Assistant: Else Marie Mandøe (Denmark).

Rostov on Don, Russia. Photos courtesy of Harold Oaks, ASU Archives, Tempe, AZ, USA.

Delegates waiting in Copenhagen, Denmark for chartered flight to Rostov-on-Don. Courtesy of Michael Ramløse.

Outside a performance theatre, Rostov-on-Don.

Presentation of the first Honorary President's Award for Artistic Excellence: (Left to right) Nat Eek (USA – Donor & Past President), Volker Ludwig (Germany – Director), Director–Barking Gecko Theater Company (Australia), Mikhail Bartenev (Russia – Playwright), Ray Nusselein (Denmark – Theatre Artist), and Michael FitzGerald (Australia – President of ASSITEJ/Int'l) at the XIIth World Congress in Rostov-on-Don, Russia in 1-8 October 1996.

Performance of *Hamlet* (Korea).

(Left to right) Maurice Yendt (France), Myriam Reàtegui (Peru), Judit Benedek (Sweden), (peering around Vicky Ireland), Jürgen Flügge (Germany), Vicky Ireland (UK), Yoshishige Kagawa, kneeling (Japan), Helge Anderson, in back partly hidden (Norway), Tisa Chifunyise (Zimbabwe), Ullide Plichta (Austria), Michael FitzGerald (Australia), Harold Oaks (USA), Marjorie MacLean (Canada), and Kim Woo Ok (Korea). The New Executive Committee elected at the Rostov-on-Don Congress, Russia, 1996. Courtesy of Michael FitzGerald.

Accommodations for the EC were at the Hotel Intourist, and delegates were housed at Hotel Ships on the Don River.

2 October 1996

At their first meeting the EC approved the following Agenda:

- Approval of the Minutes from the Cuban Congress in 1993
- Report of the EC for 1993–1996
- Treasurer's Report
- Reports from the Commissions of the EC
- Proposals for Amendments to the Statutes (very important)
- Proposal to change the official ASSITEJ languages (very important)
- The Working Program for 1996–1999
- Elections of the EC, the Bureau, the Secretary General, and the Treasurer
- Miscellaneous requests of the National Centers

President FitzGerald welcomed the members of the current EC, which had been called to "tidy up business before the General Assembly". At this Meeting, the EC did the following:

- **Brisbane Minutes:** Approved the Minutes of the EC meeting in Brisbane, Australia 9-16 June 1996.
- **Honorary Presidents Award:** Endorsed the Bureau decision subsequent to the Brisbane meeting to accept the ASSITEJ/USA recommendations for four equal Awards of 250 US$ each. Eek had informed the EC that the Award money was to be increased to 5,000 US$ at the next Congress, that it was an ASSITEJ/Int'l Award, and he would present new recommendations at the first EC Meeting in 1997.
- **Tablas:** 600 copies of the TABLAS were now in Moscow, and would be brought to Rostov for distribution. The EC felt they could take on no more costs or take on the responsibility for bringing the copies to Rostov.
- **Verification:** Ramløse handed out a list of the delegations which specified the proxies and the number of votes for each Center.
- **Procedures:** FitzGerald and Ramløse would meet with the heads of delegations and explain the procedures. The EC will propose the following Voting Commission: Ramløse, Oaks, Andersen, and Mittelstädt. A simple majority will decide all items, except changes to the Constitution which requires a 2/3 majority. Ramløse as the retiring Secretary General will preside over the elections.
- **Election of the Secretary General:** Plichta confirmed that financial support for running the Secretariat would be coming from the Austrian government. Her name would be put forward for that office, but there can be additional nominations from the floor.
- **Honorary Members:** The EC would propose that Zvjezdana Ladika (Croatia) be made an Honorary Member of ASSITEJ. Also that Rose-Marie Moudoués (France) be named an Honorary Member. There was considerable discussion about criteria. The next EC was charged with codifying the criteria. Also they should list all those so named in the past. (See Appendix A).
- **Miscellaneous:** Flügge stated that a report from the Artistic Commission would be distributed at the meeting of the Assembly. A report of the Asian Pacific Meeting in Brisbane was handed out to the EC. Schneider asked the EC to set the price for the 1996 ASSITEJ Yearbook, and they agree upon 10 US$ per volume.

The President closed the Meeting thanking the Members for their good work. He also thanked on behalf of the entire EC the Danish Center and the Nordic Ministries for their incredible financial support during the past six years of the Secretariat. Finally, he gave particular thanks to Michael Ramløse for the extraordinary job he had done as Secretary General.

The General Assembly met intermittently from Friday 4 October to Monday 7 October.

Presiding:
President Michael FitzGerald (Australia), VP Marjorie MacLean (Canada), VP Maurice Yendt (France), Sec. Gen. Michael Ramløse (Denmark), Treasurer Harold Oaks (USA).

National Centers present: Argentina, Austria, Australia, Canada, Chile, China, Croatia, Cuba, Czech Republic, Denmark, Estonia, Finland, France, Georgia, Germany, Greece, Iceland, Iran, Italy, Italy, Japan, Korea, Mexico, Netherlands, New Zealand, Nicaragua, Norway, Peru, Poland, Russia, Sri Lanka, Sweden, Switzerland, UK, Uruguay, USA, Vietnam, and Zimbabwe.

Corresponding Centers: India, Tanzania.

Proxies: Hungary, Israel, Slovakia, Spain, Turkey, Venezuela.

Executive Assistant: Else Marie Mandøe (Denmark).

President Adolf Shapiro of ASSITEJ/Russia welcomed the delegates, and on behalf of the Russian Center thanked the delegates for allowing Russia to host the Congress. He also presented greetings on behalf of Boris Yeltsin, President of Russia, and Shapiro expressed hope for a successful meeting with many fruitful contacts. Honorary President Ilse Rodenberg sent her regrets for not attending, but gave best wishes for a successful event for all.

ASSITEJ President Michael FitzGerald welcomed the General Assembly and asked for a few moments of silence to commemorate those ASSITEJ Members who had died since the last Assembly: Hildegard Bergfeld (Germany), Christian Bleiker (Switzerland), Wasonga Eliud (Kenya), Shaun Hennessey (UK), Kazuto Kurihara and Sozaburo Ochiai (Japan), and Natalya Sats (Russia).

Voting Commission: Helge Andersen (Norway), Eckhard Mittelstädt (Germany), Harold Oaks (USA), and Michael Ramløse were appointed as the Voting Commission. Also, the Secretary General announced the total number of votes as 125, making a majority of 63 votes for election. A 2/3 majority vote or 84 votes would be required for changes in the Statutes.

Approved the Minutes of the Cuban Congress – 1993

Accepted the Report of the EC, and the Treasurer's Report

Use of Language in ASSITEJ: 1st Proposal: FitzGerald stated that the proposed change in the Statute's Language Proposal (ARTICLE 12 – Languages) could only be accepted or rejected. Essentially the Amendment stated that "Working languages at the General Assembly will be the language of the host country, English, and at least one other language as determined by the Executive Committee according to the needs of the meeting". Ramløse commented "...that the proposal offered a way to include all languages and excluding none, according to the needs of the situation." (See Appendix F – Constitution – 1996 Amended Version.)

The Assembly passed the Language Proposal, which required a 2/3's majority: Yes – 90; No – 35.

Membership Criteria: 2nd Proposal: The proposal of the EC concerning "professional" membership criteria (For example: the opening of ASSITEJ to the African practice in theatre for children and young people of using children as performers) was adopted by the Congress. The voting was: For – 122; Against – 3. (See Appendix F: the Statutes of 1965: Chapter II, Article 4.)

3rd Proposal: Required each Center to keep the Secretary General informed. The Proposal was adopted unanimously.

Working Program for 1996–1999: The Congress adopted a new working program for the coming period. The President asked that each of the delegates read the Working Program, and consider how his or her Center could contribute to the implementation of the program. Members of the Committee were FitzGerald, Flügge, MacLean, Van Otterloo, Ramløse, and Van der Boon. Their recommendations in part to the Commissions were:

- **WG2 – Communications:** Investigate a Newsletter and its costs, analyze means of communication between centers and offer solutions, make proposals on the use of technology as communication and artistic creation
- **WG3 – Artistic:** Develop a long range operating plan, examine models of successful Festivals
- **WG4 – Publications:** Update the Annual, create a dictionary of theatrical terms, collate audio/visual archival material among centers, establish a standard format
- **WG5 – Congress:** Re: the 1999 Congress, draw up a program on new processes and techniques and present the results at the Congress, discuss them through critics' forums, etc., use as a basis for workshops
- **WG7 – Finance & Statutes:** Survey the Membership–fee structure, and raise money for projects was adopted unanimously. It essentially defined the projects of the Commissions for the next three years.

Dues: The General Assembly at the Congress, on the recommendation of the EC, decided to continue the present system of subscription. This meant that the basic subscription of 1997, 1998, and 1999 would be 100 US$, and that Centers able to do so were encouraged to pay an additional membership fee up to 500 US$. The subscription rate for corresponding members was still 50 US$. The Proposed Budget was accepted unanimously.

Revised Address List: This list from the Secretariat shows an impressive 59 active National Centers with 6 Corresponding Centers.

Future Congresses: The Secretariat had received two proposals: Flügge presented a proposal for the Congress to be held in Berlin 23-30 April 1999, along with their 1999 Festival. Andersen proposed to hold the Congress in Tromsø, Norway 4-13 June 1999, along with a Nordic Festival. The result of the vote: For Tromsø – 80; For Berlin – 34; Invalid – 1. Tromsø was chosen for the 1999 Congress of ASSITEJ.

Honorary Presidents Award: Honorary President Nat Eek noted that the Award was given in memory of his wife Patricia Fulton Eek, and honored the following Honorary Presidents of ASSITEJ: Gerald Tyler (UK), Konstantin Shakh-Azizov (Russia), Nat Eek (USA), Vladimir Adamek (Czechoslovakia), and Ilse Rodenberg (Germany).

The Award was given as 4 separate prizes of 250 US$ each to Volker Ludwig (Germany), Ray Nüsselein (Denmark), *Barking Gecko* Theatre (Australia), and Mikhail Bartenev (Russia).

The Elections

At the Brisbane Meeting Secretary General Ramløse had announced that he would not run for election to that office for a third term. This meant that the considerable funding for that office supplied by the Nordic Centers would no longer be available, and that whoever took over the position would have to be well subsidized by his/her government or other sources. In the following three months there was considerable correspondence and discussion. Ulli Plichta, a young woman from Austria who managed a theatre in Vienna, emerged as a likely candidate.

Accordingly, at this Congress Ulli Plichta (Austria) was nominated to succeed Michael Ramløse as Secretary General. Her election was supported by a large, strong Austrian delegation, who said that they could afford to host the Secretariat for the next three years. There were no other nominations.[21] The outgoing Secretary General Michael Ramløse presided over the elections.

Candidates for Election:
Secretary General – Ulli Plichta (Austria).

Treasurer – Harold Oaks (USA).

Executive Committee – Australia (Michael FitzGerald); Canada (Marjorie MacLean); France (Maurice Yendt); Germany (Jürgen Flügge); Japan (Yoshishige Kagawa); Korea (Kim Woo Ok); Norway (Helge Andersen); Peru (Myriam Reàtegui); Poland (Halina Machulska); Russia (Adolph Shapiro); Sweden (Judit Benedek); Vietnam (Pham Thi Thanh); Venezuela (Jacqueline Russo); Zimbabwe (Tisa Chifunyise).

The Elections: The President reminded the delegates that a total of 125 votes could be cast with 63 votes constituting a majority for election. The votes were as follows:

Secretary General: Ulli Plichta: Yes – 96; No – 26; Abstain – 3.
Treasurer: Harold Oaks: Yes – 119; No – 6.
Executive Committee: Those elected were:

		Rank Order
Australia (Michael FitzGerald)	104 votes	4
Canada (Marjorie MacLean)	91 votes	8
France (Maurice Yendt)	77 votes	11
Germany (Jürgen Flügge)	114 votes	1
Japan (Yoshishige Kagawa)	100 votes	6
Korea (Kim Woo Ok)	80 votes	10
Norway (Helge Andersen)	104 votes	5
Peru (Myriam Reategui)	69 votes	12
Sweden (Judit Benedek)	105 votes	3
UK (Vicky Ireland)	96 votes	7
Venezuela (Jacqueline Russo)	82 votes	9
Zimbabwe (Tisa Chifunyise)	112 votes	2

Those not elected were:

Poland (Halina Machulska)	44 votes
Russia (Adolf Shapiro)	51 votes
Vietnam (Pham Thi Thanh)	27 votes

The President: Michael FitzGerald was the only candidate for the Presidency. The vote was: Yes – 106; No – 12.

The Vice Presidents: There were six (6) candidates for the three (3) Vice-Presidents, and the votes were:

| Helge Andersen (Norway) | 77 votes, Elected |
| Tisa Chifunyise (Zimbabwe) | 79 votes, Elected |

A second vote was called in order to elect the 3rd Vice President. Jürgen Flügge and Vicky Ireland withdrew their names on the grounds that the first vote had secured representation from Europe. The result of the second vote was:

Marjorie MacLean (Canada)	82 votes, Elected
Maurice Yendt (France)	41 votes, Not Elected
	2 abstentions

This concluded the elections.

Honorary Members: Both Mrs. Zvjezdana Ladika (Croatia) and Mme Rose-Marie Moudoués (France) were given the title of Honorary Member of ASSITEJ in a unanimous vote.

In closing the final session President FitzGerald thanked the Voting Commission for their good work during the elections, warmly thanked the Russian Center for their excellent work in organizing the Congress, and to the Festival organizers for a spectacular Festival. He especially mentioned Galina Kolosova for her dedication and efficiency in all the preparations.

Lastly, he gave his official thanks to Michael Ramløse for his commitment and outstanding work for ASSITEJ/Int'l during his six years as Secretary General.

New Executive Committee Meeting/7 October 1996[22]

Present:
President Michael FitzGerald (Australia), VP Helge Andersen (Norway), VP Tisa Chifunyise (Zimbabwe), VP Marjorie MacLean (Canada), Sec. Gen. Ulli Plichta (Austria), Treasurer Harold Oaks (USA).

Members: Maurice Yendt (France), Jürgen Flügge (Germany), Yoshishige Kagawa (Japan), Kim Woo Ok (Korea), Myriam Reàtegui (Peru), Judit Benedek (Sweden), Vicky Ireland (UK).

Member absent: Jacqueline Russo (Venezuela).
Executive Assistant: Sabine Prokop (Austria).

FitzGerald welcomed all the Members, and congratulated them on their election. He applauded the broad representation of countries on the new EC.

Andersen introduced Ragnhild Sørvig, Secretary of ASSITEJ/Norway, who would be the important person to contact for the next World Congress in Tromsø, Norway in 1999.

Commissions: The EC reiterated its decision to have six (6) Commissions, and appointed the following:[23]

- **C2 – Communication Commission:** FitzGerald (Chair), Plichta, Reàtegui
- **C3 – Artistic Commission :** MacLean (Chair), Benedek, Kagawa
- **C4 – Publications Commission:** Chifunyise (Chair), Flügge, Yendt
- **C5 – Congress Commission:** Andersen (Chair), Kim, V. Ireland
- **C6 – Languages:** The review of the new use of languages was assigned to the Secretary General
- **C7 – The Finance & The Statutes Commissions:** Oaks (Chair), members of the Bureau

Honorary President's Award: In light of the recent rejection and then re-acceptance of the Award, the President would present a detailed plan at the next EC Meeting. He and Eek had already conferred on the details.
Essentially the new rules and regulations stated:

1. The Award was for noteworthy excellence of an individual creative artist or company during the past three years of accomplishment
2. The Nominee must have the endorsement of his/her National Center
3. There will be a different selection committee each time
4. There can be only one winner
5. The Secretary General will notify all centers of the Award and its deadlines
6. In addition Eek had increased the Award to 5,000 US$. (See discussion of controversy in Summary: 1991-1996).

Co-option: After a lengthy discussion the EC decided to co-opt Russia as a member. Galya Kolosova was to be informed accordingly, and she was to be responsible for her own expenses. The appointment of former President Adolf Shapiro was dis-allowed as bad precedent.

Miscellaneous:

- The Membership was to be surveyed as to what their expectations of AS-SITEJ were.
- The concept of V. Ireland's proposal to create a pool of money to support other centers for translations was accepted. The requests would be run through the Secretariat. The French Center would continue to handle French translations, for which they were thanked in advance.
- The Secretary General would try to determine which centers were in financial or materiel difficulty, and bring this to the EC for possible solutions.
- The Commission on Artistic Activities would be responsible for research into contemporary trends and common threads of arts practice.
- The Newsletter Information as produced by the Danish Secretariat will be continued by the new Secretariat.
- The Netherlands Center asked for a letter from the Secretariat requesting that the Dutch Committee on Culture avoid withdrawing support money from dance theatre companies, which the EC approved.
- Uganda had applied for membership, and Chifunyise was to verify if they were eligible for full membership.

- The date of the Tromsø Congress conflicted with the Lyon RITEJ and the Vancouver, Canada Festival. The EC agreed that Norway would have to select dates most suitable to them.
- Flügge reminded the EC of the continuing need for centers to apply for ASSITEJ Festival and Project designations.
- FitzGerald reminded the EC Members that each of them had the responsibility to nominate deputies in the event that they could not attend a meeting.

The President closed the meeting by thanking all the members for their efforts which promised excellent outcomes in the future.

Following the EC Meeting, the Commissions met to define their tasks and begin their work. The Chairs were to write Reports to be included in the Agenda at the EC Meeting next in Peru.

Performances:[24] In all the productions there was great variety, a grand mixture of Russian and international companies, and plays of appeal to young children as well as teen-agers. The Russians had put together a Festival Program of tremendous appeal and high quality.

Two productions for very young children were "Washing Day" by *Theatre Pilkentafel* of Germany and "Cow, Where Are You?" produced by the *Kalmyk Youth Theatre* from Elisa, Russia. The contrast between these two productions vividly illustrated the differences in style, resources, and philosophy between "old style" Russian theatre for the young and that of western Europe.

In "Cow, Where Are You?" the young company of twelve capitalized on unique and exotic Mongol culture and traditions. In a loosely constructed 'journey' play, the young hero searches for his cow, stolen by malicious guardians. The performance was spirited and colorful but "old-fashioned".

"Washing Day" achieved its atmosphere with minimal script, cast, and scenic elements. There is really no plot. Within thirty minutes, the washing is hung up and taken down. However, the playful invention of a talented young man and woman, captures a place of wonder and delight in ordinary objects which is the dominion of happy little boys and girls everywhere.

Lars Vik, a founding member of *Grenland Friteater,* a well known actor and playwright, played "Fritjof Fomlesen", an inept jack-of-all trades whose earnest efforts not only fail, but entangle the hero in mops, pails, telephone cords, and audience members....The room rang with laughter as small boys and girls in the audience were enlisted to help Fritjof out of his predicaments.

Another highlight of the Festival was the performance of "Hamlet" by the

Street Theatre Troupe of Pusan/Seoul Korea. 17 young players, directed by Lee Youn-tak, had been working for two years on this 10th anniversary production... The director and designer combined many periods and styles in this exciting, energetic performance. The set, which was reminiscent of a European cathedral hall, was also in the shape of an ancient Korean Pyramid. The performance was riveting and very clear in plot and intent, even to an audience which did not understand Korean...The scene at Ophelia's grave was startling. Female grave diggers used skulls to present a "puppet show" with dance. Real dirt is flung upon Ophelia, who then rises up from her grave. Toward the end, the entire set, made of batik panels, collapsed.

One of the most stunning performances[25] was that of Shakespeare's "Hamlet" performed throughout their entire theatre by the Rostov-on-Don Theatre for Young Spectators, directed by Vladimir Chigishev. The audience was limited to about 20 persons, who added black gauze floor-length robes over their clothes in an anteroom before the performance began. When the play began the audience was moved through various rooms and corridors, standing or sitting where possible, viewing the various scenes as the play progressed. Particularly memorable were walking along a glass-lined corridor with Hamlet on the other side of the glass looking at you in surmise and suspicion as you walked along, the burial scene of Ophelia in the white-washed basement, the appearance of the Ghost on an outdoor balcony, passing through the narrow makeup room with the actors dressing and putting on makeup for the "play within the play", and then the audience being seated in the auditorium for the final banquet of the play's ending.

Altogether the Russians had put their best foot forward with remarkable results, some inconveniences, but supported a Congress of excellent decisions, and drew a large and delighted international audience to their "new" country.

In a letter dated 1 November 1996 retired Secretary General Michael Ramløse indicated that the General Secretariat was moving to Vienna, Austria as of that day. Ulli Plichta of the ASSITEJ/Austria Center had been elected as the new Secretary General at the Rostov-on-Don Congress, and would be starting her term of office as of the date of the letter.

Attached to this letter were:

- A résumé of the important decisions taken by the General Assembly in Rostov-on-Don
- The Statutes of ASSITEJ, updated with the amendments adopted in Rostov-on-Don

- The Working Program for 1997–99
- A revised address list
- The minutes from the EC Meeting in Brisbane, Australia in June 1996

As of 1996 the Secretariat listed the following as the National Centers of ASSITEJ:

Angola	Kyrgyzstan
Argentina	Korea
Australia	Madagascar
Austria	Mexico
Belgium	Mongolia
Brazil	Netherlands
Bulgaria	New Zealand
Canada	Nicaragua
Chile	Norway
China	Peru
Croatia	Philippines
Cuba	Poland
Cyprus	Portugal
Czech Republic	Romania
Denmark	Russia
Estonia	Singapore
Finland	Slovakia
France	Spain
Georgia	Sri Lanka
Germany	Sweden
UK	Switzerland
Greece	Tanzania
Hungary	Thailand
Iceland	Turkey
India	Uganda
Iran	Uruguay
Iraq	USA
Ireland	Venezuela
Israel	Vietnam
Italy	Zaïre
Japan	Zimbabwe
Kenya	

A total of 64 centers.

A SUMMARY OF 1991–1996

1991

The world community witnessed the extraordinary spectacle of a superpower's disintegration when the USSR under Mikhail Gorbachev broke apart into 15 independent states. In 1991 Lithuania, Latvia, and Estonia were the first to break, followed by Russia, Ukraine, and Belarus. Gorbachev was succeeded by President Boris Yeltsin in 1993, who resigned in 1999. Vladimir Putin succeeded him in his own right, and was in office until May 2008.

On 28 February 1991 the Persian Gulf War, which had been led by the USA with 34 other nations against Iraq's invasion of Kuwait, ended.

On 17 June 1991 the South African Parliament voted to repeal the legal framework for apartheid. Three years later Nelson Mandela would be elected its President.

Starting in June 1991 Yugoslavia broke up into seven independent republics which has taken over 17 years, accompanied by some savage and tragic inter-fighting in the process. Croatia and Slovenia were the first to declare their independence on 25 June 1991. Macedonia followed suit on 8 September 1991, and Bosnia and Herzegovina on 1 March 1992. On 22 May 2006 Serbia officially became independent, followed by Montenegro on 31 May of that same year. The Republic of Kosovo declared its independence on 17 February 2008, but it has yet to be officially recognized by the UN at this time of writing.[26]

With this background of unrest and change, Michael Ramløse as the newly elected Secretary General had a formidable job ahead of him in ASSITEJ.

One of the first items on the Ramløse agenda was to transfer the ASSITEJ/Int'l records.[27] Current records and financial records would go to the new Secretariat in Copenhagen, Denmark, and past records would go the ASSITEJ Archives in Frankfurt, Germany. Treasurer Paul Harman (UK) would have complete access to the financial records.

Accordingly, Ramløse and Harman visited the Secretariat in Paris. They met with Rose-Marie Moudoués for perhaps 30–40 minutes in September 1990, only to be told that there was no way that she could make the materials available on such short notice. Neither of them ever saw, had access to, or sorted the files.

In October Ramløse sent two vans with members of his staff for the transfer of "the voluminous records". There was a quick and minimal sorting of papers for Copenhagen and Frankfurt, and the two vans headed to their separate destinations, each boasting about 2 boxes of records!

To the best of our knowledge and to this day (2014), the remaining "voluminous records" of 25 years (1965–1991) of ASSITEJ history are still residing at 98 Boulevard Kellermann, Paris in the hopes of finding an archival home, either in Paris or Frankfurt or somewhere accessible to researchers and scholars.

In the meantime, Ramløse took over the office with a knowledgeable staff, modern electronic equipment, a decent budget and subsidy from the Nordic Ministries of Culture, and an all-knowing head on his shoulders. He seized the reins of government with energy and skill, dragging ASSITEJ well into the end of the century. It was time for the Association to move forward.

Ramløse was fortunate in having Adolf Shapiro as the new President. Shapiro was essentially a Russian/Latvian director of charm and skill, but most importantly he let Ramløse have his head, and did not interfere with the functioning of the Association. Essentially he was a "custodial" president for only one term. Ramløse was also fortunate in having Michael FitzGerald as 1st Vice-President, who was not afraid to articulate what needed clarity or action, yet who respected Shapiro as his President.

The first Report of the new Secretary General was important in revealing the new rules of responsibility, as well as being open and immediately responsive. The Bureau would revert to its major function of preparing the Agenda for the EC Meeting instead of making decisions for approval by the EC. Also, the Chairs of the Commissions were now to meet with the Bureau to prepare this Agenda.

In the Budapest, Hungary EC, the first since the Congress in Stockholm, Iceland was admitted as a new Center, as was Kenya, the first major African Center to join ASSITEJ. There were 10 centers that had not paid their dues for the past 4 years, and in a sense were "ghost" centers. Ramløse was instructed to write them diplomatically to get the dues paid.

After discussion Kim Woo Ok was co-opted unanimously, and M'Lama was appointed as a Counselor without vote to the EC.

Perhaps the most important approved proposal was that the Nordic Centers would jointly fund and pursue seminars in Africa, Asia, and Latin America to develop relationships among the continents.

At the EC in Lyon, France in December 1991, President Shapiro impressively listed his visits to meetings and festivals in 8 countries, two of them in Asia and six in Europe.

Venezuela, Uruguay, and Chile were accepted as member centers. The USSR was a problem since its dissolution. Lithuania wanted its own center, but Latvia and Estonia were staying with the USSR. Shapiro indicated he might be on a different passport when next they met. It was also reported that there were still eight centers who owed dues.

Cuba set the date for their hosting the next World Congress of ASSITEJ as 22-28 February 1993 in Havana, Cuba. There would be a Festival in conjunction with the Congress, and everything would focus on Latin American theater.

The Kenya Center volunteered to host the EC in Nairobi from 8-15 November 1992. There would be 10 performing companies from Kenya and 10 from other African nations. Despite their concern of the magnitude of the intended Meeting and Festival with funding not yet in place, the EC accepted their invitation.

1992

The EC meeting in Kenya was held in Nairobi as scheduled, and at the request of the new Russian Center, ASSITEJ paid the flight costs of President Shapiro. With the governmental collapses in Eastern Europe, money was very tight, and in some cases unavailable. Kolosova had written Ramløse that the Russian Center could not afford to send President Shapiro to Kenya. Ramløse asked the EC to approve travel funds for the President, which was done. João Luiz Sousa (Portugal) had also requested funding because of financial problems, but his travel was not approved since it would be a bad precedent.

The Secretariat distributed a "Voting Procedure for the Elections" for the approval of the EC, and this was the first time that the procedure had ever been written down. A major change from the verbal instructions given by the Secretary General during the elections!

Both the President and the Secretary General had been to Cuba to check on the arrangements for the Congress in 1993, and they found the Congress well planned and moving forward in its preparations. Socorro reported that there would be 25 performances, 15 from Cuba and 10 from Europe, and North and South America.

Cyprus, the Philippines, the Ukraine, Georgia, and Croatia were accepted to full membership, assuming the completion of the applications from the last two.

Rostov-on-Don, Russia had invited ASSITEJ to have their World Congress there in 1996 as part of their Festival. This invitation was to be confirmed in the next two weeks, and ultimately was accepted.

The EC voted to stop their support of *The Review* which was ASSITEJ's only official publication, coming from the French Center and of limited interest. This opened the door for the German Center to create the every two year ASSITEJ Annual.

Ten centers had nominated themselves for the election in Cuba: Australia, Cuba, Denmark, France, Germany, Italy, Japan, Korea, USA, and Vietnam.

Altogether this EC Meeting seemed to accomplish a great deal of new business, and kept pushing the Association forward. However, according to Ramløse the details of accommodation for the meetings were appalling.[28] The water supply was unreliable. The Festival was unorganized, and they saw only 3 Kenyan performances, when they were promised 10 African and 10 Kenyan ones. However, the Danish Embassy gave the EC an excellent outdoor reception.

Ramløse, FitzGerald, and MacLean had booked a safari after the meetings, and just ten minutes before they were to leave, a delegation from ASSITEJ/Kenya came forward with complaints against the Kenyan Board and wanted the three of them to meet with their Kenya Board. Although the delegation could have met with the EC anytime in the previous five days, it was now impossible on such short notice. The three of them were then accused as being "...more interested in playing tourists in Africa than in solving the problems of ASSITEJ." While many good decisions had been made by the EC, the meeting was not a pleasant one.

1993

Perhaps the most significant document of the 1990–1993 term was the Secretariat's Report of the EC Activities. That Report, which gave an overall perspective on its accomplishments, was distributed to all national centers, and became a major informational step in showing the progress of the new government of ASSITEJ through the EC.[29]

Though ASSITEJ/USA whole-heartedly supported the Cuban Congress, they soon found out that it was next to impossible to get there. Since the US paper dollar was Cuba's common informal currency, the US embargo prevented their USA delegates from taking in US dollars. Shaw corresponded with the US Treasury Department, and was told only official delegates from the USA could go provided that the Cuban government would pay all expenses within Cuba. However, they noted that the Secretariat was in Denmark, so they could send their registrations and expenditure costs in dollars to the Danish Center, who in turn could give the USA delegates that money in US dollars upon their arrival in Havana via Haitian Airlines! The first dilemma was solved!

The second dilemma occurred when the USA delegation arrived at the airport, disembarked, and then the officials would not release Treasurer Harold Oaks with the rest. In a fury Secretary General Ramløse through Socorro informed both the airport officials and other governmental officials that there would be absolutely no Cuban Congress of ASSITEJ/Int'l unless Dr. Oaks was immediately released to attend officially at the Congress. He was released about an hour later with no apology.

Much of the business in the General Assembly in Cuba had been accomplished by Reports either previously mailed or handed out at the Congress. Decisions moved forward smoothly. Of special interest were that the changes in Statutes were passed almost unanimously, but were primarily cosmetic.

As promised at the Stockholm Congress in 1990, Eek presented the new statutes governing the Honorary President's Award to the General Assembly, which had been codified at the Frankfurt EC Meeting in December 1993. The Award now was to be given to an individual theatre group or theatre artist for artistic excellence in theatre for children and youth, and the title of the Award would be the ASSITEJ Award for Artistic Excellence.

A very important and lengthy discussion occurred related to the Kenya amendment proposal that membership requirements be changed to allow the inclusion of indigenous theatre. The debate was resolved by the Secretary General stating that "...the new EC must work very carefully and thoroughly on this issue in order to present to the General Assembly in 3 years a balanced and well prepared proposal for the accommodation of African theatrical tradition within the framework of ASSITEJ without demolishing the fundamental principles of the Association." This tremendous statement would lead to the inclusion in membership of those countries with indigenous theatre, which the professional theatre members regarded as "rank amateur."

The question of Spanish as an official ASSITEJ language was raised once more with Spain stating that 22 countries and about 350 million people spoke Spanish as their official language. Ramløse resolved the dilemma by stating that languages can only be considered in the context of the needs of ASSITEJ. Later under the leadership of President Michael FitzGerald "English" was designated as the "working language" of ASSITEJ. There have been no other requests since, and at each Congress the language of the host country is always added to English as the Working Language (the 1 + 1 principle).

Judit Benedek (Sweden) presented a resolution on child abuse, which expressed the deep concern of all its members at the growing incidence of the many forms of child abuse, and urged governments to redress the situation in order to guarantee children of the world their basic rights to food, shelter, security, education, and cultural and artistic activities. The General Assembly adopted it, and instructed the Secretary General to send it to all the governments in ASSITEJ countries.

The Assembly approved holding the 1996 World Congress at Rostov-on-Don, Russia in October 1996.

In the elections of the 16 nominees the following 12 Centers were elected:

Australia, Canada, Cuba, France, Germany, Italy, Japan, Korea, Norway, Russia, Slovakia, and Vietnam. Michael FitzGerald was elected President, with Marjorie MacLean, Eddy Socorro, and Maurice Yendt as Vice-Presidents. Previously, Michael Ramløse and Harold Oaks had been elected as Secretary General and Treasurer respectively, making the EC a total of 14 members out of a possible 17.

It was clear from President FitzGerald's guidance in the first meeting of the New EC at Havana after the Congress that new leadership was in place. The Commissions were to become the guiding Working Groups of the Association, and they were expected to accomplish great and visible things.

In addition, the EC co-opted with vote both Venezuela and Tanzania. They also recommended Schneider and van Otterloo as Counselors. They also met a second time on the next day to complete all their business. In choosing meeting sites they agreed that priority must always be given to a country not visited before.

It was refreshing to see that much really "new business" was handled with dispatch.

While the Congress went on, the re-election of Fidel Castro took place. His speech as well as martial music were carried over outdoor loudspeakers, as well as room speakers and radios within the hotel. Castro was re-elected for another term by 87% of the vote. A Cuban delegate commented quietly to Eek after the results were announced that Castro had received a 93% majority vote the previous election! The delegate was pleased feeling that things were definitely changing, and there were no reprisals.

One evening the USA delegates attended a theatrical performance at the National Theater, and upon emerging from the performance on to La Plaza de la Revolución, they found no bus, no taxi, no sidewalks, only a few streetlights available, and their hotel was several miles away. The twelve of them started walking in the streets heading for the hotel when a Red Cross Ambulance drove by, and in desperation Flora Atkins signaled it to stop, and explained their plight in her minimal Spanish. While the driver was a bit reluctant, he wanted to help the visitors.

The group promised a major donation to the Cuban Red Cross. So Morris Atkins and Eek rode in front, and the rest stood among the used tires on the floor in the back of the van holding on to whatever provided a grip. The driver deposited them a few blocks from their hotel to avoid being seen transporting illegal merchandise, and Eek promptly took up a collection and gave the driver the money. Whether the Cuban Red Cross ever saw it or not is another story.

The EC meeting in Frankfurt closed the year. Once more they discovered that no progress had been made in the direction of UNESCO recognition, so the Secretary General was asked to pursue their application for status—again!

1994

Tragically ASSITEJ now had to expel the Bulgarian Center. For years Bulgaria was represented both in ASSITEJ and on the EC by Victor Georgiev, an excellent leading actor in both their childrens and adult theatre in Sophia. With the collapse of the leftist governments in the eastern countries, the destruction of the Berlin Wall, and the reformation of the USSR into separate states, many of the former Centers and their leaders disappeared along with financial subsidies which the Soviet government had provided to them. Bulgaria had no money to pay dues, and no real head of its center.

Because of the collapse of many of the eastern currencies, ASSITEJ had created partnerships, where established centers would form partnerships with those that needed assistance. Denmark and the Ukraine were such a one. This was important since the next Congress in 1996 would be in Rostov-on-Don in Russia. Shapiro presented the situation to the EC, and indicated that while there were difficulties, plans for the Congress were going forward well, and they were receiving support from the Ministry of Culture.

Ramløse brought the EC's attention to the fact that a center in Taiwan should not have been formed, since it was part of China. The EC dissolved it, and China was informed accordingly. Over the years strenuous efforts had been made to have China join ASSITEJ. Originally they balked at the size of the Membership Fee. Now it appeared that they were no longer interested in participation. Was the dissolution of the Taiwan Center to satisfy them, and once granted, China was no longer interested? We wondered!

The "official language" question was finally settled with the "1+1" principle. At all meetings English would be the Working Language plus the language of the host country. This has continued to this day.

The EC accepted the invitation of Venezuela to hold their next meeting in 1994 in conformity with their desire to always go to new countries if offered. They also accepted the USA invitation to meet in Seattle, Washington 7-14 May 1995, and the Australian invitation to meet in Melbourne in May in 1996.

As an indication of the new efficiency President FitzGerald cautioned the delegates to bring their comments and ideas related to the Agenda with them, and above all prepare what they had to say. Also, all reports were to go to the Secretariat before hand, so that they could be duplicated for distribution at the meeting.

There was considerable correspondence in 1994 between the Secretariat and Eddy Socorro (ASSITEJ/Cuba) regarding the publication of TABLAS, the official report on the Cuban Congress in 1993.[30] In the negotiations ASSITEJ/Int'l had agreed to pay 3,400 US$ for a total of 2,000 copies. 1600 were to go to ASSITEJ and 400 to the Cuban Center. Now they were informed that only 1,263 were printed. Ramløse requested that 1,000 copies be sent to ASSITEJ/Sweden, but the TABLAS people wanted to keep at least half of the copies in Cuba. Altogether it was a clear violation of all the various agreements, and a black eye for ASSITEJ/Cuba and Socorro personally. It was a mess, and never really resolved, and within two years Socorro was no longer active in ASSITEJ. To date [2014], all attempts at correspondence with him have failed.

At the Venezuela EC Meeting in September 1994 China was accepted as a Full Member of ASSITEJ. This was probably an immediate result of the dissolution of the Taiwan Center.

Chigishev presented an update on the plans for the Rostov Congress in 1996. Dates were finalized at 1-8 October 1996, with the General Assembly meeting on 4-8 October. There would be 8-10 Russian productions, and hopefully 6 international performances. The Russian Center guaranteed that all participants would get the needed documents for entry.

The Commissions all gave reports of resultant activities, which suggested they were moving forward significantly on the Working Plan.

They were reminded of the urgent need for finding a site for the next Secretariat in 1996, when Ramløse would step down as Secretary General, as well as finding the necessary financial resources. The EC approved sending these requirements to all member centers for information and possible recommendations.

They approved having their next meeting in Brisbane, Australia on 12-18 June 1996, four months prior to the Rostov Congress. Oaks reminded them that ASSITEJ/USA would be hosting the EC Meeting in Seattle, Washington, in 1995 which would celebrate the 30th Anniversary of the founding of ASSITEJ, and they were inviting Past President Dr. Ilse Rodenberg and Past Secretary General Rose-Marie Moudoués as guests for the gathering.

1995

There was only one EC meeting in 1995, and that was held in the USA in conjunction with the *One Theatre World Festival* and *The Seattle International Children's Festival* "Show Your Kids the World".

In the two meetings of the EC during the Festival and Anniversary, there were the following deliberations: At the beginning President FitzGerald noted the death of three ASSITEJ leaders – Hildegard Bergfeld (former President of ASSITEJ), Kazuto Kurihara (President of ASSITEJ/Japan), and Sozaburo Ochiai (Vice-President of ASSITEJ/Japan and Founder of their Center).

Argentina, Nicaragua, and Singapore were welcomed as new Members. The fact that there was news about 28 different old and new national centers attested to the new high level of communication.

Finally, copies of TABLAS were on their way to Berlin for distribution by the German Center. More importantly Ramløse and the EC began the process of writing job descriptions of all the elected officials in the EC.

The Commissions had been very active, and the Language Commission had brought forward the concept of 1+1, which stated that the Working languages of ASSITEJ would be the language of the host country plus English. Other languages could be added as needed. This gave excellent flexibility in languages to all the subsequent meetings.

They also began to wrestle with the problems of membership with National Centers (predominantly African) that used children and young people as performers. Ultimately the Association would accept this as a possibility which would allow membership, and ASSITEJ could become a true global international organization.

Eek announced that the Honorary Presidents Award would be given for the first time at Rostov in 1996.

Rose-Marie Moudoués was recommended to be named a Member of Honor in ASSITEJ for her long term volunteer service as Secretary General of 25 years.

This was also the occasion of ASSITEJ/Int'l's 30th Anniversary, and this was celebrated accordingly. ASSITEJ/USA had invited former Secretary General Rose-Marie Moudoués and Past President Dr. Ilse Rodenberg to attend as guests of their Center, and both had accepted. Marilyn Raichle was in charge of the Anniversary Celebration with the Seattle Children's Theatre as co-host.

The 30th Anniversary Event featured welcomes from the City of Seattle, the Seattle Children's Theatre, and Ann Shaw supervised a "Stand Up for ASSITEJ", which had participants standup for the various years of attendance at previous Congresses. Moudoués spoke (in French) on *The Birth of ASSITEJ*, and Rodenberg spoke (in English) on *The Dream of ASSITEJ*. (See Appendix J). The program closed with a dessert buffet.

Australia's Barking Gecko Theatre presented "The Ivory Circle" as part of the Festival.

1996

The EC met in Brisbane Australia in June 1996 five months before the Rostov-on-Don Congress.

At this EC Meeting on invitation from President FitzGerald, the following countries attended the EC as Observers: 7 from China, 1 from India, 1 from Indonesia, 1 from Malaysia, 1 from New Zealand, 2 from Thailand, and 2 from the Philippines.

Meanwhile Brazil, Bulgaria (new and reinstated), and New Zealand were accepted as Full Members, and Thailand as a Corresponding Member.

MacLean presented the Draft of the first ever job descriptions of the ASSITEJ Leadership, which would prove to be excellent guidelines over the years.

At this Brisbane EC Meeting C3–The Artistic Commission had no report to give, and the EC had instructed them to contact Socorro, the Chair, for a Report. Ramløse wrote much later as follows:[31]

"Michael FitzGerald, Helge Andersen, and I [Ramløse] had been to the Rostov Festival the year before (1995) where the Russians had a 'rehearsal' of the Congress program...We saw many excellent examples of what brilliant master classes the Russians would offer with top Russian artists and pedagogues, we saw some of the performances they would present, and in fact were very impressed with all the tremendous work and effort they had put into preparing the future Congress.

"Yet here at the EC Meeting the acting Chair Jürgen Flügge had said there was no report, and that the Russian Congress planners had refused to take any of the Artistic Commissions suggestions, into consideration!

"Despite the fact that Socorro, the Chair, had disappeared, the rest of the Committee had done absolutely NOTHING to do the necessary work.

"Most of the EC had no concept of the difficulties and problems that Galya Kolosova and Vladimir Chigishev were confronting to make the Rostov Congress a success... And the ASSITEJ Artistic Commission had the temerity to express their dissatisfaction IN ADVANCE – not knowing anything about the Congress, not seeking any information, not accomplishing, or even trying to accomplish anything!"

The Rostov Congress would prove to be a high-water mark of the three-year session. Delegates from 40 countries participated in the new Russia, five years after the demise of the Soviet Union. The organization had been well-thought out, and while there were more than their share of glitches, it provided great variety of excellent quality in the Festival, and the General Assembly made some excellent long range decisions.

The chartered plane from Copenhagen provided a very satisfactory trip both coming and going, although there were delays at Customs for the 141 passengers. However, it was a welcome necessity based on the fact that the Danish government forbade any of their employees to fly Aeroflot.

Unknowingly Marilyn Raichle, a delegate from the USA, gave credence to the safety concerns of the Danish government. Several months prior to the Congress in 1996, Raichle flew Aeroflot from Moscow to Rostov and back on a site visit. The trip was successful, and on her return to Moscow the plane landed safely. In her relief over her safe arrival once the plane had shut down, she failed to release her seat belt. She stood up energetically, and the seat came up with her.

The General Assembly passed major changes in the Statutes, establishing the concept of English as the Working Language plus a language of the host country, plus others as needed. Also, they changed the definitions of Membership so the African nations in particular would be able to join ASSITEJ. They were able to support the orderly transition of the Secretariat in the hands of Michael Ramløse and ASSITEJ/Denmark to those of Ulli Plichta and ASSITEJ/Austria. They selected Tromsø, Norway as the site for the 1999 Congress. The Honorary Presidents Award was presented for the first time. Zvjezdana Ladika and Rose-Marie Moudoués were each awarded the title of Member of Honor. FitzGerald closed the Assembly with acknowledging Ramløse's tremendous contribution as Secretary General, as well as the excellent financial support provided by the Nordic Ministries and Foundations.

In a letter dated 1 November 1996, one month after the Rostov Congress, retiring Secretary General Michael Ramløse indicated that the General Secretariat was moving to Vienna, Austria as of that day. Ulli Plichta of the ASSITEJ/Austria Center had been elected as the new Secretary General at the Rostov-on-Don Congress, and would be starting her term of office as of that date of the letter. This meant that the important heart and center of ASSITEJ would now be in Austria.

Ramløse had done a remarkable job of organizing, updating, and modernizing the management of ASSITEJ/Int'l. Minutes of meetings were available and distributed to all within 4–6 months after a meeting, correspondence was answered, all centers had address lists, the election system had been codified, financially the organization was solvent, although it was losing the subsidy of the Nordic Ministries, and Austria was taking on the support of the Secretariat. Success would all depend on Ms. Plichta's abilities and her country's financial support. Ramløse's act was a hard one to follow.

ADDENDUM by Nat Eek (March, 2013)

I was privileged to be sent the correspondence of Michael Ramløse's starting when he took over as Secretary General following the 1990 Congress in Stockholm, and continuing through 1996 when he stepped down as Secretary General at the 1996 Congress in Rostov-on-Don. In turn, at his request, all the materials were forwarded in March 2013 to the German Archives for permanent keeping.

Reviewing all that correspondence was daunting, but it was clear that a new era was dawning. First, Ramløse sent a questionnaire to all current National Centers for communication information, and then began an active correspondence, via FAX with everyone who wrote to the Secretariat. The bulk of the correspondence was primarily between Ramløse and President Michael FitzGerald (Australia). Ramløse was clearly on top of things, and moved decisions forward related to meetings, flight arrangements, agendas, and personal requests. The tone of the letters was always positive, but he remained open and honestly critical when appropriate.

Below are listed some of the major problems and concerns with which he dealt during his two terms as Secretary General from 1990 to 1996.

- The culpability of the Cuban Center in overcharging for the printing of TABLAS (the Report of the Cuban Congress in 1993), and then failing to provide the agreed upon number of copies. He also had to deal with the fading leadership of Eddy Socorro, an extremely likeable and hardworking head of his National Center, who could not overcome the vise of bureaucratic dishonesty and stupidity. Socorro finally just disappeared. Ultimately, in December 1995 [2 years later] they were notified that the cost of mailing the 500 available copies would be 8,000 US$! Ramløse requested that any Cubans who came to the next meetings should bring copies of TABLAS with them. The final faxed word was that the Cubans would get the copies to the Cuban Embassy in Sweden! Then "miracles of miracles" in a Fax dtd 9 June 1995, FitzGerald wrote Ramløse that he had just received a mailed copy of TABLAS in Australia from Cuba! Apparently others finally did too!
- Both Ramløse and FitzGerald were constantly on the move, attending both ASSITEJ Meetings and Festivals in many different countries, bringing the message of the re-vitalized association.
- Pursued with vigor ASSITEJ's application for Class B UNESCO Status, only once more to have it disappear into bureaucratic limbo. This status had

been pursued again and again since the founding of ASSITEJ in 1965! To date it has never been achieved.
- Worked closely with Galya Kolosova of the Russian Center to finalize the details of the Rostov Congress, despite the indifference of President Adolf Shapiro.
- Wrote to FitzGerald 13 December 1994: "There is a new year ahead – a whole new year of which nothing has been used yet. We have lots of use for it – and we will." Written and Faxed just days after his father's death from cancer!
- In a Fax dtd June 21 1995 Ramløse mailed Notice to all Centers delinquent in their dues that they "did not receive ASSITEJ/INFORMATION 14" because they were in arrears. He was obviously taking a hard-line approach to making ASSITEJ financially accountable.
- Supported a request from ASSITEJ/Germany to the German Minister for Seniors, Families, Women and Youth to support the Secretary General's position for 1997–1999.
- Provided incredible support, correspondence, advice, selection in planning and codifying the Rostov Congress in 1996.

PART VII

RETRENCHMENT AND NEW GROWTH BEYOND

The World of 1996–1997[32]

In December of 1995 UN troops were sent to Bosnia and Herzegovina to enforce the new Peace Treaty which ended that war. By spring of 1996 President Alija Izetbegovic of Bosnia, President Slobodan of Serbia, and President Franjo Tudjman of Croatia pledged to resolve any remaining difficulties over implementation of the peace treaty.

In November of 1996 Bill Clinton was elected to a second term as President of the United States, but Republicans retained control of both Houses of Congress.

South Africa adopted a permanent Constitution in May 1996 whose Bill of Right's banned discrimination on the basis or race, gender, age, marital status, pregnancy, and sexual orientation.

Boris Yeltsin of Russia despite his ill health was re-elected as President of Russia. Tony Blair (United Kingdom), the Labor Party Leader, was named Prime Minister, ending 18 years of rule by the British Conservative Party.

In Zaïre President Mobutu Sese Seko was deposed, fled into exile, and Lauent Kabila took charge.

In France the Socialist Party took over after 18 years out of power, and Lionel Jospin became Prime Minister.

After 99 years as a British Territory, Hong Kong was returned to China in July 1997. Prince Charles, Tony Blair, and Margaret Thatcher attended the handover ceremony. President Jiang Zemin of China was present.

Israel and the Palestinians continued to disagree over Israel's plan to build a settlement in Arab East Jerusalem.

The Nobel Peace Prize went to Jody Williams (USA) for her coordination of the International campaign to Ban Landmines. Russia signed the treaty, but both China and the USA were holdouts.

The Master Class by Terrence McNally won the Tony Award for Best Play, a fictional presentation of a class in voice with Diva Maria Callas. The three musicals – *Cats* (British), *Les Miserables* (French), and *Phantom of the Opera* (British) – were all successfully running on Broadway, New York City. E. R. (Emergency Room) was the top-Rated TV Show in the USA.

1997
EXECUTIVE COMMITTEE MEETING OF ASSITEJ
Lima, Peru/13-17 August 1997

Present:
President Michael FitzGerald (Australia), VP Helge Andersen (Norway), VP Marjorie MacLean (Canada), Sec. Gen. Ulli Plichta (Austria), Treasurer Harold Oaks (USA).

Members: Myriam Reàtegui (Peru), Yoshishige Kagawa (Japan), Niclas Malmcrona/Deputy of Judit Benedek (Sweden), Kim Woo Ok (Korea), Vicky Ireland (UK), Jacqueline Russo (Venezuela), Tisa Chifunyise (Zimbabwe).

Observer: Iris Pribil (Austria).

Members absent: Maurice Yendt (France), Jürgen Flügge (Germany), Bjarne Thanning (Denmark).

Counselor absent: Wolfgang Schneider (Germany).

Lima, Peru, 1997. All photos courtesy of Harold Oaks, ASU Archives, Tempe, AZ, USA.

Performance at EC meeting in Lima, Peru on 13-17 August 1997.

(left to right) Marjorie MacLean (Canada), Ulli Plichta, Secretary General (Austria), Helge Andersen (Norway.

(left to right) Kim Woo Ok (Korea), Harold Oaks (USA), Vickie Ireland (UK), Yoshishige Kagawa (Japan).

Niclas Malmcrona (Sweden).

In the Bureau Meeting of 13 August the Officers approved the Agenda as distributed, and discussed the problems of the Russian co-option, France's dissatisfaction with ASSITEJ/Int'l, and the potential breaking up of ASSITEJ/Austria, but the Bureau made no decisions for the EC.

Thursday, 14 August 1997[33]

President FitzGerald presided over the first item of business – the co-option of Adolph Shapiro (Russia). Since Shapiro had been re-elected as President of ASSITEJ/Russia, and was present at the EC Meeting, a different Russian should not be co-opted. The request was refused.

France's concerns were that the Rostov Congress Minutes were "inaccurate" in reporting Yendt's objections to the meeting and other details. The EC would ask Ramløse to redraft the Minutes to present Yendt's objections accurately, and then send them to Yendt for approval and final action at the 1999 Tromsø Congress. MacLean commented in response to these niggling concerns, "Time to grow up – accept change as part of life and process – and take joy in it!"

ASSITEJ/Austria: The Center had expressed no confidence in Ulli Plichta as Secretary General, and did not want to be represented by her, though the majority still supported their elected leaders. A German-speaking group had been formed, elected a representative who was rejected as not representing Austria. Austria was calling for a new election in October, and the dissidents had been so informed. Plichta had resigned as President of ASSITEJ/Austria, but she planned to stand for the new Board. Austria had informed Germany by letter of their displeasure over Germany's interference in their affairs.

"An informal union of German speaking countries has been formed (Germany, Switzerland, Austria) and Austrian dissidents elected a representative who was accepted by the union but was rejected by the Center as not representing Austria."[34]

In consultation with Schneider (Germany), FitzGerald was told that Germany can do what it wants, and cannot be told what to do! They were concerned about keeping contact, but did not offer support to the dissidents. He felt FitzGerald had been misinformed.

FitzGerald hoped to meet with Schneider privately before the October meeting to try to resolve the situation. If other centers have concerns, they should contact the President of ASSITEJ/Int'l.

The Rostov Minutes were adopted as distributed.

Secretary General's Report: Plichta reported that the Secretariat Office had been subleased for 3 years at 45,000 US$ per year. It was linked with the ASSITEJ/Austria office. She had facilitated the move-in to the new office. She had spent 4 days in Copenhagen familiarizing herself with the duties of the office.

News from the Centers:

- **Belgium** – Was not at Rostov. Mrs. En des Paar is the new secretary.
- **Brazil** – Alise Quaino was their new President. Would like a Mentor from ASSITEJ.
- **Croatia** – Has a new President. Festival this past spring. Plichta attended and reported it having a high level of performance.
- **Czech Republic** – Met their new President this May. Good contact.
- **Estonia** – They now have an office. Have received considerable help from Finland.
- **Hungary** – Organizing. Meeting and Festival in April. Romania, Slovakia, and Croatia attended.
- **Spain** – New response to the ASSITEJ Newsletter.
- **Angola** – Information only received through Portugal.
- **Argentina** – No response.
- **Bulgaria** – Possible "Ghost Center". Dues not paid for 7 years!
- **Cuba** – No money for dues.
- **Cyprus** – No response.
- **Ireland** – No response.

There has been no contact with the following Centers: **Kyrgyzstan, Madagascar, Mongolia, Philippines, Romania, Singapore, Thailand, Uruguay,** and **Zaïre**.

Non-center **Slovakia** had made contact, and had visited the Secretariat. **Uzbekistan** had made contact and sent in an application; they had a General Assembly in June, elected a 9-member Board; their Center is in Tashkent.

President's Report: FitzGerald acknowledged with gratitude having received airplane fare from ASSITEJ to visit Berlin in April. He reported it as a good Festival showcasing good work. He then visited the Czech Center in Prague. He met for a week in Vienna with the Arts people there. He then went to Bratislava where they were confronting problems of no production or theatre money.

On his visit to Vietnam he discovered disagreement within the center, with the "young guard" who wanted information, being told to solve their own problems. In Indonesia he met with a man who wanted to start a center, but since he had just changed jobs, the project was put on hold. In New Zealand's small center things were going well, and they were writing a Directory of their theatres that they would share with ASSITEJ. Iran was planning a tour to Russia and Zimbabwe.

Peru had severe financial problems; their groups were spread out and lacked communication. They need to seek grant support. ASSITEJ/Japan has no government support, and they finance themselves primarily by dues; it costs 20,000 yen per year ($200), and they receive $200,000 from the Yoshi Foundation.

This completed his Report.

Treasurer's Report: Oaks had handed out a complete report to all the Members of the EC. As of 10 July 1997 Total Income was 7,652.44 US$ while Total Expenditures were 13,718.13 US$. Reserves in both the British and the USA Accounts amounted to $50,441.33 US$.

Friday, 16 August 1997

The EC spent the day receiving and discussing the reports from the Commissions.

C5 – Congress Commission: Annual 1997 & Future Congress 1999: Date set at 11-19 June 1999.

C7 – Constitution/Statutes Commission: The question of term limits for the members of the EC had been raised and discussed, but the EC decided not to put the limitations in the Constitution.

New ASSITEJ Logo & Change of name: The EC accepted the new Logo and urged its use on stickers and envelopes. A name change was too costly to be considered.

UNESCO Membership: Apparently UNESCO considered ASSITEJ a Member through ITI. The EC felt they should seek an independent membership. Once more with feeling.

Honorary Membership: There were three nominations: Zvjezdana Ladika (Yugoslavia), Rose-Marie Moudoués (France), and Maria Navarro (Spain). Only Ladika was chosen.

Honorary President's Award: The President had restored the Award with the new rules and regulations recommended at the EC Meeting in Rostov in 1996 after the $1,000 Award was divided among the four Nominees.

Translations/Languages: It was recommended that an English summary be in all ASSITEJ publications.

Meetings in 1998–1999: The next EC Meeting would be in Biel, Switzerland on 26-31 October 1997. They had received an invitation to meet in Haifa, Israel in May 1998, which would celebrate their 50th Anniversary as a country. There was a possibility of a meeting in Vienna, Austria in January 1999, but it would depend on the Austrian situation at that time.

The meeting was adjourned.

1997
EXECUTIVE COMMITTEE MEETING OF ASSITEJ
Biel, Switzerland/26-31 October 1997[35]

Present:
President Michael FitzGerald (Australia), VP Helge Andersen (Norway), Tisa Chifunyise (Zimbabwe), Sec. Gen. Ulli Plichta (Austria), Treasurer Harold Oaks (USA).

Members: Jürgen Flügge (Germany), Kim Woo Ok (Korea), Niclas Malmcrona (Sweden) for Judit Benedek.

Counselors: Bjarne Thanning (Denmark), Wolfgang Schneider (Germany), Marián Lucky (Slovakia).

Members absent: Marjorie MacLean (Canada), Maurice Yendt (France), Yoshishige Kagawa (Japan), Myriam Reàtegui (Peru), Vicky Ireland (UK), and Jacqueline Russo (Venezuela).

Counselor absent: Grahame Gavin (Australia).

Biel, Switzerland EC on 26-31 October 1997. Executive Committee of ASSITEJ (left to right- front row) Ulli Plichta, Tisa Chifunyise (Zimbabwe), Mirta Lanz (Switzerland), umidentified woman in black, Niclas Malmcrona, Helge Andersen; (two in the middle) Kim Woo Ok w/ cap, Michael FitzGerald; (back row) Enrico Beeler - partially hidden (Switzerland), Jürgen Flügge, Wolfgang Schneider, Graziano Melano (Italy), Harold Oaks. Courtesy of Harold Oaks.

Ulli Plichta and her two daughters.

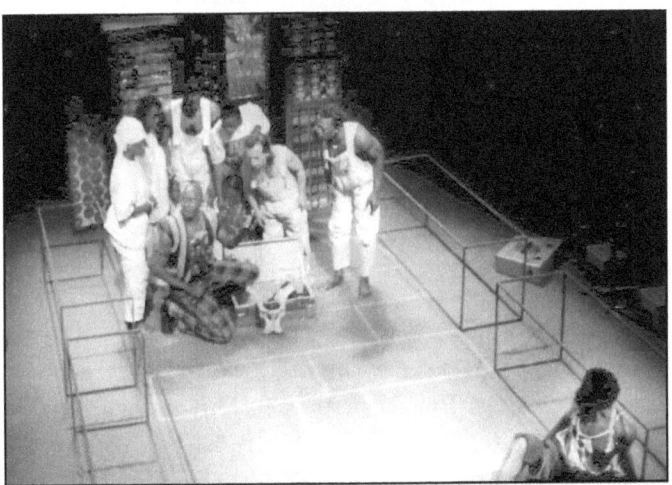
Performance at Biel EC.

The Agenda was sent from the Secretariat in Austria.
Monday, 27 October 1997
Secretary General Plichta, after one year in office, opened the meeting with informal comments about the current situation. The Austrian government had provided funds for 3 years to support the Salary for the Secretary General, travel expenses, and office expenses. She stated that the Secretary General and the Treasurer did not represent their respective countries, merely served the whole

association through their offices. [This was not true; as elected officials, they also represented their respective countries, according to the Statutes. However, this separation must have been her own interpretation.] The new Austrian Board was not working, and there were dissidents. Flügge commented that there was much less money available than the German Center had understood, and that the Austrian Center was in disarray.

There was discussion about the absent members. Zimbabwe was absent again. There had been no communication nor response from Venezuela. Peru perhaps needed a new representative.

- **Report of the Bureau Meeting**
- **Adoption of the Minutes of the EC Meeting in Lima, Peru**
  These were adopted as mailed.
- **Secretary General's Report:**
  Contact with non-member countries. Columbia had had a theatrical company member present at the Peruvian meeting.

Discussion of Centers: Gabon had requested membership. **Slovenia** had asked for more information. There had also been requests for information from **Bulgaria, Madagascar, Mongolia, Kirgizstan, Romania,** and **the Congo** (which sent in a report).

- The **Australian Center** was been cut to 1/2 time. No governmental funding. Had contacted ASSITEJ for possible support.
- The **Austrian Center** had guaranteed the following support: 200,000 (Austrian Schillings) from Dept. of Family Affairs, and 500,000 (Austrian Schillings) from Office of Cultural Affairs, all to be confirmed in writing.
- 37 Centers had sent in their annual reports of activities.[36]
- **Slovenia** had had a Festival with productions from Hungary, Czechoslovakia, Austria, and Slovenia.
- **Ghost Centers** – the EC decided that if there was no response and no contact, they would be expelled.

President's Report: He would be going to Greece, and they were interested in hosting an EC meeting in the next term (1999–2002).

Treasurer's Report: They were consolidating the fund in England with most in the USA.

Commission Reports:
- **C1: Public Relations**: On Lima and their working program
- **C2: Communications** – No report. Questionnaire will be sent out early next year
- **C3: Artistic** – No report
- **C4: Publications** – New Annual is in progress. Annual 1997–1998 and future ones

Tuesday, 28 October 1997

Honorary Members – approved the Application Form, and designated Michael Ramløse (Denmark) and Ann Shaw (USA) to be accepted as Honorary Members

Honorary President's Award: The rules and regulations had been codified in a letter from Eek which essentially placed the selection Committee and the final decision with the EC, making it definitely an ASSITEJ Award. The EC accepted the new regulations. [The name of the Award was changed to the ASSITEJ/International Award for Artistic Excellence in 2005.]

They named the judges for the Award to be given at the Tromsø Congress in 1999 as: 2 from the membership – Michael Ramløse (Denmark) and Galya Kolosova (Russia), and 2 from the EC – Vicky Ireland (UK) and Kim Woo Ok (Korea). Their report would be presented at the EC Meeting after January 1999.

They also discussed how to promote the Award.

ASSITEJ World Day: They supported the concept, but felt they should consider a different date that would fit the school year better. Perhaps March, April, May or September, October, November.

Meeting of the Commissions: Held in the afternoon.

Wednesday, 29 October 1997

Commission Reports:
- **C1 – Communications Commission:** Approved 6,490 US$ to set up an ASSITEJ Web Page, cost to be shared with the Secretariat.
- **C4 – Publications Commission:** Archives are growing. Dictionary of Children's Theatre terms is continuing. The new Annual cost 4,000 US$ from ASSITEJ, balance from the German Center, 1500 press run, 5.21 per copy US$.
- **C5 – Congress Commission (Tromsø):** Information will be sent out in spring 1998, listing alternative hotels, workshops, seminars, 2nd mailing in September to interested individuals asking for a deposit, single registration fee, dates are set as 11-19 June 1999.

- **C6 – Language Commission:** Translation: a new project for a CD, visual and sound, on the work of different theatres from around the world.

Draft of Questionnaire by Marián Lucky: Apparently Lucky had sent out a Questionnaire about theatres and funding for them. He had received information from several areas of the world: Hungary had taken over a commercial building for a theatre. Czech Republic had taken over a building for an adult theatre.

Lucky expressed concern about the funding for sports vs. the arts in countries. **Australia** reported lots of funding for sport, for the Olympics. Commented that some theatre is not relevant to the audience. **Sweden** reported they have continued good support, theatres have money, but schools do not to pay for performances. Money goes to special projects, instead of supporting the organizations. **Zimbabwe** has no government funding for theatre. Must go for private funds, and accept their agendas. Need more training in theatre. **Germany** is concerned about the audience. Relevance of "older styles" to a younger audience. Young groups producing only today's problem plays. Many new members, new playwrights, new audiences. **Korea** felt that "relevance" is their main concern. Teachers take the children to the theatre. Will they go on their own? In actor training 5 out of 15 MFA's specialize in children's theatre! They are currently working with Japan for a joint presentation at the next Asian Meeting. **Norway** brings children to the theatre, but they can choose which venue. Aging producers are a problem. Play attitudes are more for "self" rather than for others (as it was in the 1970's). Not appealing to the audience. Perhaps "everybody" shouldn't be our audience. There is no money from the government for buying shows. Groups get money for projects rather than support. Few productions for teens, many more for young children.

In the discussion that followed Schneider suggested a Magna Carta for Children – their rights for theatre. Use the nature of theatre for communication with the new child. The "new" child is a narcissistic young person – alone, little contact with others, primarily into TV and computers, while theatre encourages human contact between audience members as well as between actor and audience.

UNESCO Membership: Plichta reported membership information. An applicant is expected to have a cooperative project with UNESCO for at least 2 years. She will go ahead with an application.

Report of ITI Congress in Seoul, Korea (Kim Woo Ok): Kim reported that 173 delegates from 49 countries met for three days during 14-20 September 1997. Their subscription (dues) costs from 49,000 – 500 Fr. francs.

From USA – 12,000 US$, Germany and Japan – 10,000 US$, but most pay 500 US$. 110 countries belong with 55 qualified to vote. There are 20 in their EC, 5 in their Bureau. Currently they need to elect a President; they want to have a general election but they couldn't decide on the details, so it was postponed to the next meeting! Which will be in Strasburg; they turned down Egypt's offer.

Future ASSITEJ EC Meeting Sites:
1. Haifa, Israel – 11-19 April 1998
2. Harare, Zimbabwe – 6-9 August 1998

The EC elected to meet in Israel.

During the Meeting a total of six performances were seen.

INTERIM/October 1997–April 1998

In October 1996 at the Rostov-on-Don Congress Michael Ramløse had completed his second 3-year term as Secretary General, and chose not to run again. He had done a remarkable job of bringing ASSITEJ up to date administratively, and he would be difficult to replace.

In the discussions preparing for the next Secretary General, the members were informed that the Office would need "a full-time, professional person with enough money to pay for an office, officers, and operating costs. " It would cost between 60–80,000 US$ to run the office. Whoever would take over would undoubtedly need considerable subsidy from his/her government. While ASSITEJ/Int'l could help with dues money, it was insufficient to fund the operation. A possible solution would be to ask a national center to take on the office with whatever money ASSITEJ/Int'l could offer, and then seek additional funding from their governmental sources.[37] However, no possible candidate had emerged to date!

Ullide Plichta (Austria) was an administrator of a theatre in Vienna, and a member of the ASSITEJ/Austria Executive Committee, and appeared to have the requisite abilities. She was young, attractive, multi-lingual, an administrator, and gregarious. FitzGerald as President was assured by her that she had the full support of the Austrian Center and its delegation, as well as guaranteed financial support from the Ministry of Culture. Accordingly, she was elected to succeed Michael Ramløse as Secretary General. "The vote was unanimous since there was no other candidate!" [38]

The next EC meeting was to be held in Biel, Switzerland in October 1997, a year after the Russian Congress in Rostov. However, following Plichta's election, problems had emerged in the Austrian Center during the time between EC meetings. Oaks volunteered to go to Vienna and meet with Plichta and the ASSITEJ/Austria Board to try to resolve the difficulties. The Board had accused Plichta of making arbitrary decisions without getting clearance for them.

Oaks and his wife Ima Jean flew to Austria prior to the October 1997 EC Meeting in Switzerland. Plichta hosted the Oaks at her theatre, where her office served as the Secretariat and for ASSITEJ/Austria. Oaks also met with one or two of the Austrian Board, who were later revealed to be her supporters. Oaks was assured that everything was all right. Oaks, his wife, and Plichta took the train and later Plichta's car, stopping off to have breakfast at the home of Plichta's mother. They then proceeded to Biel, where the EC Meeting was scheduled. At this meeting Plichta assured the EC that everything was all right, but FitzGerald later wrote "... in hindsight, it was clear that Plichta made sure we met only those who supported her."[39]

Following the meeting in Biel more problems seemed to arise. A split had appeared in the Austrian Center between Community theatre and Professional theatre, and the professionals resented the fact that Plichta was granted money that they felt should have gone to companies and activities instead of the Center. In addition, she was making decisions on her own, had lost most of her supporters, there was no system of accounting in the Center, and there were debts outstanding. At the same time the ASSITEJ EC Minutes were not very detailed, Agendas arrived late and often incomplete, there was no system, and communication was sporadic.

In a phone call to Oaks on 16 December 1997 Plichta revealed to him that ASSITEJ/Austria had taken everything away, including current bills, she had been expelled from ASSITEJ/Austria, and she had resigned from their Advisory Board. She felt they "are still after her"; they had been in her computer and copied everything.[40]

Two and a half months elapsed before ASSITEJ/Austria officially notified ASSITEJ/Int'l of their actions taken on 17 November 1997, and one and a half months after Plichta's phone call to Oaks! In a letter to Oaks and ASSITEJ/Int'l dtd 9 February 1998 Ernst Reepmaker on behalf of the Executive Committee of ASSITEJ/Austria wrote as follows:[41]

"On 17 November 1997 the executive committee of ASSITEJ/Austria resolved to expulse Ulli Plichta. Present were 4 of the 5 members of the executive committee. The decision was made, by a majority, on, most seriously, the grounds of a legally and democratically highly questionable finance transaction: i.e. Ulli Plichta, at a point in time when she was neither a member of the executive committee nor in possession of signatory powers, withdrew a 6 figure (ATS [Austrian Schillings]) sum from ASSITEJ/Austria's account for which the executive committee is legally liable. There exists a receipt but no lawfully correct settlement of the accounts by Ulli Plichta for this sum...."

"The executive committee would also like to express its disappointment that no single member of the international executive committee [ASSITEJ/Int'l] seems prepared to take seriously the executive committee of ASSITEJ/Austria's view of these matters and that the above mentioned problems are viewed as arising from personal feuds...."

"Finally we feel it is important to inform you that, since November 1997, the executive committee of ASSITEJ/Austria has received *absolutely no information* relating to ASSITEJ/Int'l from the general secretariat."

In response to this and other notices of termination, President FitzGerald faxed to ASSITEJ/Austria: "...I do not know what is going on between the Stadtininitiative and Ulli which is not our business anyway...Ulli should withdraw completely from the premises so that she may continue uninterrupted her work as ASSITEJ Secretary General...I know I can count on your courtesy and professional behavior to assist this."[42]

The EC decided to have a person from Europe visit Vienna to evaluate once again the Austrian support of the Secretariat. FitzGerald on his behalf asked Vice President Helge Andersen (Norway), to go to Vienna and report on the situation. Andersen went and sent a report back to the President. On 27 March 1998 he wrote to FitzGerald: "I am sorry to say, they are not willing at all to find any solution. The only thing they want is to get rid of Ulli."[43]

Oaks wrote Eek in 2011: "The whole thing fell apart just prior to the April 1998 EC Meeting in Haifa, Israel...it was clear there was no support from Austria."[44] According to the Official Minutes of the Haifa Meeting, Plichta was present, but did not enter into the discussion, and offered her resignation at the end of the meeting.[45]

In a letter to the Membership of ASSITEJ/Int'l dated 23 June 1998 President Michael FitzGerald wrote: "I regret to inform you that Ulli Plichta has resigned as Secretary General. This is due to irreconcilable differences between her and the Austria Centre. A deteriorating situation involving a number of matters has brought the Centre to a position where it can no longer support her in the position."

He continued: "I am delighted to inform you that the Committee [the EC] has appointed Niclas Malmcrona of ASSITEJ/Sweden as Executive Officer of ASSITEJ/Int'l to manage ASSITEJ business until the Tromsø Congress." At that time a new Secretary General would be elected.

The Nordic Centers had stepped in, sent Niclas Malmcrona to the EC meeting in Biel, Switzerland, and to the EC Meeting in Haifa, Israel. He took over with greatly welcomed finances, authority, and organization. In his cover letter to his Minutes and Report of the Haifa EC Meeting[46] to the EC with copies to the Membership [undated but probably the summer of 1998], the new Executive Officer Niclas Malmcrona announced that Ulli Plichta had resigned, and he had taken over.

Following the resignation of Plichta, Stephan Rabl took over the Austrian Center and restored its credibility. Altogether Plichta had served as Secretary General for one year and five months, from her appointment in November 1996 until April 1998. (See Summary 1997–2002).

1998
EXECUTIVE COMMITTEE MEETING OF ASSITEJ
Haifa, Israel/11-15 April 1998[47]

Present:
President Michael FitzGerald (Australia), VP Helge Andersen (Norway), VP Marjorie MacLean (Canada), Sec. Gen. Ulli Plichta (Austria), Treasurer Harold Oaks (USA).

Members: Jürgen Flügge (Germany), Yoshishige Kagawa (Japan), Kim Woo Ok (Korea), Judit Benedek (Sweden), Vicky Ireland (UK).

Members absent: Maurice Yendt (France), Myriam Reàtegui (Peru), Jacqueline Russo (Venezuela), VP Tisa Chifunyise (Zimbabwe).

Counselor absent: Wolfgang Schneider (Germany).
Deputy: Niclas Malmcrona (Sweden).
Executive Assistant: Iris Pribil (Austria).
The Meeting was held at the Dan Panorama Hotel.

Bahai Temple, Haifa, Israel –1998. All photos courtesy of Michael FitzGerald.

Performance at EC meeting, April 1998.

(Left to right) Wolfgang Schneider (Germany), Orna Porat (Israel), Jürgen Flügge (Germany), and Michael FitzGerald (Australia), members of the EC at Haifa, Israel Meeting 11-25 April 1998. Courtesy of Michael FitzGerald.

Members of the EC Meeting in Haifa, Israel in 1998. (Left to right) Harold Oaks, Wolfgang Schneider, (front row) unidentified Israeli woman, Hgit Rehavi Nikolaischewski, unidentified woman, Vicky Ireland, Hideo Hijikata; (back row) Jürgen Flügge, Niclas Malmcrona, Michael FitzGerald, (behind him) Marjorie MacLean, (partially hidden) Ulli Plitchta, Kim Woo Ok, (far right) Helge Andersen. Courtesy of Wolfgang Schneider.

President FitzGerald welcomed all the Members, and thanked the Israeli Center for inviting them to have their meeting in Haifa. Neither Reàtegui nor Russo had received any governmental support for one year and were absent, and the President had sent letters supporting them to their two governments.

Also, the EC noted with concern that Yendt had been absent from all three meetings in the current term, and asked the President to write him about his intentions related to his Committee membership. Both the President and the Secretary General had sent faxes to Chifunyise and Yendt, but no replies had been received.

Report of the Meeting of the Bureau:[48]

Situation in Austria: Plichta was present during this discussion but took no part in the voting or the discussion.

President FitzGerald reported as follows: The current situation was out of hand since the election of the new Board of ASSITEJ/Austria refused to cooperate with the Secretary General any longer. They had expelled her from their Center in November 1997, and in turn she was locked out of her office. The Austrian Board justified this decision because of financial mismanagement in the accounts, as well as her personal style of management.

Since December she had worked out of her home with no financial support. This and other matters were now in the hands of a lawyer. According to the EC decision in Biel, Switzerland, Plichta was completely separated from ASSITEJ/Austria. By Austrian law the money from the Ministry was to be given to the Center and in turn given to the Secretary General for the running of the Center, and the International office. The new Austrian Board refused to do this as long as Plichta was in the position of Secretary General.

This was the situation that Andersen found on his visit in March 1998. Despite Andersen's efforts at reconciliation, the Austrian Board felt they could not justify any further financial support, and therefore were withholding payment.

The EC accepted Plichta's resignation without comment (See 1999 in the *Summary of 1997–2002*), and proposed appointing Niclas Malmcrona as the Executive Officer of ASSITEJ/Int'l from that point until the election of a new Secretary General at the 2002 Congress. His immediate duties would include: continued cooperation and support of the planning for the 1999 Congress in Tromsø, Norway and the 2002 Congress in Seoul, Korea; supervision of the Honorary President's Award; the compilation and mailing of 3 Newsletters; the completion of any current action items; and handling all the day to day duties of the office of the Secretary General. Malmcrona accepted their offer after this meeting was adjourned.

Report from the Secretariat re: the Centers:

- Nothing had been heard from Tisa Chinfunyise and **Zimbabwe**.
- **Estonia** with great support from the Nordic Centers had developed a "very active and vivid Center".
- **Germany** continues its close working relationship with **ASSITEJ/Russia**.
- **ASSITEJ/Croatia** Ivica Šimić continues doing remarkable work with his Center.
- **"Ghost Centers"** – **Congo**'s center is active and functioning; **Romania** and **Tanzania** pay their dues regularly, but provide no information; **Angola, Kirgizstan, Madagascar,** and **Mongolia** have had no contact with the Secretariat; Vicky Ireland volunteered to try to establish contact with these and other non-responding centers in Africa and Latin America.

President's Report:

- Met with members of ASSITEJ/Greece and under Xenia Papadopoulos was developing strongly and actively. They are likely to offer to host an EC Meeting in the early part of 2000.
- Oaks, V. Ireland, Schneider, and the Artistic Commission are to draft a *Magna Carta* for ASSITEJ that would detail the Association's mission in detail, for applications on grants, etc.
- Urged Centers to apply for titling under ASSITEJ "World Projects".

Questionnaire: MacLean, Kagawa, Benedek, and Malmcrona had worked out a 42 question form to be sent to all centers as of June 1998, to be returned by Sept/Oct, and results given at the next EC Meeting in 1999.

Honorary President's Award: The Secretary General was to send letters to the judges to meet the day before the next EC Meeting to select an Awardee, thus saving duplication costs of the materials and their mailing. Centers should be encouraged to send in nominations, and asked why not? if they didn't? The Treasurer was asked to get information if the award money is in a trust or other form, and if it were possible to contribute additional funds to the Award?

UNESCO Membership: The Secretary General had contacted UNESCO again to apply for membership. It was suggested to gather sponsors and supporters to push forward their request for membership.

Commission Reports:

- **C3 – Artistic:** No report
- **C4 – Publication:** Next Annual edition should come out in November 1998. A picture book was discussed but tabled.
- **C6 – Dictionary:** Not discussed. Flügge was in contact with Christel Hoffman and Wolfgang Wöhlert from ASSITEJ/Germany to collect material for publication.

Future EC Membership and Secretariat: The Centers were to be encouraged to proceed with nominations to the EC as soon as possible. Each applicant should present a written endorsement from their national center.

Future Congress: ASSITEJ/Japan announced their invitation to host the next World Congress in July/August 2002. Oaks said their invitation would be presented at the next General Assembly in Tromsø, Norway in 1999.

Future EC Meeting Sites: The EC accepted Vicky Ireland's invitation on behalf of the British Center to host the EC in London from 27 February-3 March 1999. There would be no Festival. There followed a discussion on the decline of invitations and the problem of increased costs.

Miscellaneous:

- Schneider reported on the UNESCO Meeting for cultural policy in Stockholm in March 1998
- Agreed to fix date of ASSITEJ World Theatre Day at the next Meeting
- Noted they were required to review their language requirement, which had been instituted at the 1996 Rostov Congress
- Kagawa announced the forthcoming Asian Festival from 20 July to 8 August in Tokyo and Okinawa

The meeting closed with a report from Hagit Rechavi-Nikolayevsky on the activities of ASSITEJ/Israel, a very active center with 70 active members, mostly play producers presenting a total of 300-400 performances a year!

President FitzGerald thanked Israel for hosting the meeting, which was organized in a highly professional way. They appreciated the opportunity to see a large number of plays during their festival, as well as meeting with their artists.

FitzGerald thanked Iris Pribil, Executive Assistant, for her work during her time with the EC. He also thanked Ulli Plichta for her service as Secretary General, which she had done professionally and with a fine sense of style. The EC endorsed these thanks.

1999
EXECUTIVE COMMITTEE MEETING OF ASSITEJ
London, England/27 February-3 March 1999

Present:

President Michael FitzGerald (Australia), VP Helge Andersen (Norway), VP Marjorie MacLean (Canada), Executive Officer Niclas Malmcrona (Sweden), Treasurer Harold Oaks (USA).

Members: Jürgen Flügge (Germany), Yoshishige Kagawa (Japan), Kim Woo Ok (Korea), Judit Benedek (Sweden), Vicky Ireland (UK).

Counselors: Grahame Gavin (Australia), Peter Manscher (Denmark)/Deputy for Bjarne Thanning (Denmark), Wolfgang Schneider (Germany).

Proxies: Elisabeth Kabasa (Zimbabwe) Deputy for Tisa Chifunyise (Zimbabwe).

Members absent: Maurice Yendt (France), Myriam Reàtegui (Peru), and Jacqueline Russo (Venezuela).

Observers: Guy Holland (UK) and Paul Harman (UK).

Honorary Presidents Award Jury: Michael Ramløse (Denmark), Galina Kolosova (Russia), plus V. Ireland and Kim Woo Ok.

London, England EC on 27 February-3 March 1999, Tower Bridge. Courtesy of Harold Oaks.

President Michael FitzGerald (Australia) at the London, UK Executive Committee Meeting in 1999.
Courtesy of Vicky Ireland.

ASSITEJ EC (front to back) Michael Ramløse (Denmark), Niclas Malmcrona (Sweden), Harold Oaks (USA), Vicky Ireland (UK), Kim Woo Ok (Korea), Yoshishige Kagawa (Japan), Elizabeth Kabasa (Zimbabwe), Judith Benedek (Sweden), inidentified man facing sideways behind Kabasa, Marjorie MacLean (Canada), (far right) Wolfgang Schneider (Germany), Michael FitzGerald (Australia), Jürgen Flügge (Germany), Japanese interpreter, (behind her) Peter Manscher, (Denmark), (behind him) Galya Kolosova (Russia), (behind her) Helge Andersen (Norway).
Courtesy of Vicky Ireland.

EC in session in London 1999. (Right around table)(back of head) Michael FitzGerald, (partially hidden) Helge Andersen, (standing w/camera) Harold Oaks, (seated) Kim Woo Ok, Jürgen Flügge, (hidden by Flügge) Niclas Malmcrona, Marjorie MacLean, Yoshishige Kagawa, Japanese interpreter, Wolfgang Schneider, (partially hidden) Vicky Ireland, Galya Kolosova, Judith Benedek (Sweden), Peter Manscher (Denmark). Courtesy of Vicky Ireland.

Performance at the London EC. Courtesy of Vicky Ireland.

The Agenda

The Agenda[49] covered in part the following items:
- Report of the Bureau
- Adoption of the Minutes from the Haifa Meeting
- Situation with former SG Ulli Plichta
- Report from Executive Officer Malmcrona

- President's Report
- Financial Report
- Concerns of the French Center
- Honorary Presidents Award
- Commission Reports: Artistic, Communication, Congress, Finance & Statutes, and Publication
- Report from General Assembly preparation of 2002 Congress
- Report from the Congress and Festival preparation

The Meeting

President FitzGerald welcomed the members, and thanked the British Center for their invitation. He gave a special welcome to Malmcrona as the new Executive Officer, and Kabasa, Manscher, Ramløse, and Kolosova for their special attendance.

FitzGerald reported that the Bureau had reviewed the Agenda, and added three items: the Austrian situation, and the two separate concerns of Yendt and Reàtegui. He commented that this was a complete business EC Meeting with no interruptions for a Festival.

The EC approved the Minutes of the Haifa Meeting in April 1997. MacLean pointed out that her comments in Haifa were primarily ones of extreme regret over the "loss of time and efficiency throughout the situation in Austria as well as the loss of Ulli Plichta."

Old Business: V. Ireland reported that the British Center had contacted all the "ghost centers", but had heard nothing from them yet.

- Oaks and MacLean reported that upon investigation that Malmcrona as "Executive Officer" did not have a vote, but Benedek as the Swedish Member had the vote.
- So far there were only four nominations for election to the EC: Australia, Croatia, Poland, and Switzerland. Up to 10 more nominations must be received by 10 March.
- Re: the Austrian Affair and the resignation of Plichta, FitzGerald reported that they were resolving the final payments to ASSITEJ as of the end of March 1999.

Executive Officer's Report: FitzGerald commented that once a new Secretary General was in place at Tromsø, they would concentrate on new centers.

There had been no new applications, except Nepal was interested. Malmcrona had been trying to contact South Africa. There had been only contact with Bolivia, Brazil, and Argentina. New centers are ASSITEJ's lifeline!

President's Report: All was included in the Agenda items. He had been in contact with Finland, Peru, and Japan re: singular items. He thanked Malmcrona for his excellent job as Executive Officer.

Concerns of the French Center: Yendt was Chair of the Artistic Committee and had been absent for the last four meetings "with no proxy or report." The Committee felt he had not fulfilled his obligation to ASSITEJ. Yendt felt that ASSITEJ was not dealing with ASSITEJ business properly under the statutes. The EC decided to have the Executive Officer write a letter to Yendt explaining that all had been dealt with according to the Constitution, the President had always presented the French concerns at the meetings that Yendt had not attended, the decisions had been made by the Committee, and the Committee would also like to know the names of the companies comprising the French Center with whose concerns he had had to deal. However, they decided to have these concerns available at the next Congress (Tromsø).

ASSITEJ World Day: The EC decided that their World Day should coincide with ITI's *International Children's Day*, either 18 October 1999 or 16 October 2000. This would be placed on the Agenda at the Tromsø Congress for endorsement.

ASSITEJ/Int'l Charter: The purpose of the Charter was to have a strong statement to take to potential sponsors and patrons. It should be only one page. The final draft of the Charter was to be compiled by Fitzgerald, V. Ireland, and Schneider, and would be sent to all members by the Executive Officer before 10 April. A final draft would then be presented to the General Assembly in May.

World Patrons and Sponsors: The EC agreed that as a result of the Membership Survey, the matter of patrons and sponsors should be part of the Working Program for 1999–2002.

Honorary Presidents Award: The jury members were: Kolosova, Ramløse, V. Ireland, and Kim Woo Ok. 8 Centers had made 8 nominations: Australia, Brazil, Denmark, Greece, Poland, Sweden, Switzerland, and USA. The jury met during the London EC. The jury felt that all nominees were worthy of their nomination. *The Arena Theatre Company* from Australia was chosen for the Award, and *Director Eva Bergmann* from Sweden for an Honorable Mention.

The Jury recommended in the future they would always need the following equipment: a video player (and TV which will play various formats for videos around the world), plus a CD player plus a slide projector and screen.

They had done a remarkable and fair job in their deliberations. Ramløse was to prepare a written report with recommendations as an attachment to the London Minutes.

For the future the Jury recommended: 1) Video footage of the Nominees should be provided; 2) essential written material should be in English; 3) nomination forms should be revised to give the jury all information and stress that it is given for the last three years' work; 4) the number of judges should be increased to five to ensure a majority vote; 5) there should be guidelines in event of conflict of interest of a jury member; and 6) the EC should codify the process of informing nominees of results and recognition.

UNESCO Membership: The ASSITEJ Application was in Paris and would be reviewed by UNESCO in October.

Reports of the Committees:

- **C2 – Communications Commission:** The web-site was in operation. Peter Manscher (Denmark) gave the EC a tour of <www.assitej.org>, and the EC stated that the site should be maintained and expanded. 2,500 US$ was to be set aside next year for this expansion. They also decided that a web-site presentation should be made at the Congress.
- **C3 – Artistic Commission:** MacLean distributed summary copies of the International Membership Survey. She stated that the return rate of 8% was in excess of the 3% rate considered necessary by professional survey firms to guarantee accuracy. MacLean would present a report of the survey first to members and then to the General Assembly in May. Furthermore she would mail a copy to all respondents. (See Report of the Tromsø Congress).
- The Committee felt that a Commission be set up to implement changes based on the survey's recommendations. This should be a main priority for the Working Program of 1999–2002. FitzGerald thanked the Commission and MacLean in particular on their outstanding work on the Survey.
- **C4 – Publications Commission:** Schneider handed out "hot-off-the-press" copies of the *ASSITEJ Annual 1998/99*. Centers could buy copies for sale or for their members. He said the next issue would be the 2000/2001 Annual. They were hoping to deal with the following issues: 1) the Working Program of 1999–2002: a dictionary of theatre terms; 2) a compilation of biographies of 25–30 leading directors of original work; 3) the compilation of ideas for a "theatre for children's bible", and 4) the compilation of an ASSITEJ Picture Book as presented at the Haifa Meeting in 1998.

- **C5 – Congress Commission:** Anderson stated that because of budget restraints the Congress could only be in English. There was little money for simultaneous translation. They decided to fund two professional translators for two other languages, based on the number of delegates speaking that language. "Hosts" would try to provide other languages as needed in various delegations.
- The Festival program was still being finalized. Delegates should arrive on 10 June, and the opening ceremonies would be on 11 June, and include the Honorary Presidents' Award. The closing ceremony would be on 18 June with delegates leaving the next day.
- ASSITEJ/Int'l would be asked for 2,000 US$ to fund particular projects, similar to the Newspaper at Rostov.
- **C7 – Finance and Statutes Commission:** Oaks reported that 13 Centers had not paid their dues since 1995. The EC decided he should send them all a letter saying they are no longer members. If they paid the 1999 dues, they would be reinstated. Those countries were: Bulgaria, Iraq, Kenya, Kirgizstan, Madagascar, Mongolia, New Zealand, Philippines, Portugal, Thailand, Uganda, Ukraine, and Uzbekistan. He was also to send a letter to all centers that they must have paid their 1999 dues, or they would have no vote. He agreed to present his Report as an Operating Budget, not a list of expenditures. Also, in the future the Operating Budget should be presented at every meeting!

Report on the General Assembly Preparation: FitzGerald noted that his Presidential Report would cover the excellent accomplishments in the Working Program. The Commissions had worked very well. After discussion the EC decided to base interpretation on the 1+1 principle now in the Constitution. FitzGerald would draw up a Working Program for 1999–2002 from the minutes of meetings in the past three years. To date there had been no nominations for Treasurer. One Center had a Secretary in mind; two members were thinking of nominating for President if their countries were elected to the EC. All applications must be in by 10 March.

Future Congress Sites: Both Japan and Korea were considering holding the 2002 Congress.

Honorary Memberships: The Committee had unanimously recommended Michael Ramløse as an Honorary Member, and he had agreed to have his name presented to the General Assembly.

Miscellaneous:

- Kagawa announced an All Asia Festival from 19 July to 6 August 1999 in Japan. There would be a Festival and symposium also.
- Kim Woo Ok reported he was organizing a seminar in Okinawa to examine the place of tradition in contemporary theatre for young people. FitzGerald urged EC members to attend these festivals.
- MacLean proposed that ASSITEJ produce a document supporting abolition of "child soldiers and child Laborers". Since that was within the Constitution, the EC accepted her offer to write a motion to take to the General Assembly.
- V. Ireland reported on *Action for Children's Arts* as a growing organization, with their first conference in March, sponsored by British Telecom who could become permanent sponsors.
- Schneider asked whether the ASSITEJ Archives should be open to the public, and they agreed to take that question to the General Assembly.
- Elisabeth Kabasa (Zimbabwe) thanked the EC for the valuable opportunity to share ideas with other professionals. She hoped that ASSITEJ/Zimbabwe in the future would be able to organize a Regional ASSITEJ Meeting in Africa.

President FitzGerald closed the meeting with many thanks to all concerned, remarking how much excellent work had been done, and then announced the final meeting of the current EC would take place at 9 am on 11 June 1999 in Tromsø, Norway.

1999
XIIIth WORLD CONGRESS OF ASSITEJ
Tromsø, Norway/10-19 June 1999[50]

Congress/Tromsø, Norway/11-18 June 1999 – Tromsø Harbor

President Harold Oaks (USA)

(left to right) Harold Oaks, Michael Ramløse, Ima Jean Oaks. Courtesy of Harold Oaks.

Delegates at the Tromsø, Norway Congress 1999 (left to right) Vicky Ireland (UK), unidentified blond woman, Nat Eek (USA), Ann Shaw (USA). Courtesy of Vicky Ireland.

View of Tromsø

The Opening Ceremony

Presiding:
President Michael FitzGerald (Australia)

After various presentations and entertainments for all the delegates, the Honorary President's Award was made. FitzGerald introduced Nat Eek, Honorary President of ASSITEJ, who had created and funded the Award.

Honorary Presidents Award for 1999. In his presentation Eek stated that the Award was to an individual artist or theatrical company for sustained artistic excellence during the past three years (1996–1999). He thanked the Award Committee for its outstanding work in reaching a decision. Members of the Committee were Michael Ramløse (Denmark), Galya Kolosova (Russia), Kim Woo Ok (Korea), and Vicky Ireland (UK).

He then announced that the Arena Theatre of Australia was the winner of the 1999 Honorary Presidents Award of ASSITEJ, and presented Rose Myers, Artistic Director, with the prize of 5,000 US$, an engraved goblet, a bottle of champagne, and a citation. Myers gave a speech of thanks and spoke of the work of the Arena Theatre.

Eek then gave an Honorable Mention Citation to play director Eva Bergman of Unga Klara Theatre from Sweden, who was runner-up. Six other finalists were introduced and presented with Citations: Guti Fraga, Director (Brazil); Rolf Lydahl, Director (Sweden); Mikri Porta Theatre (Greece); Halina Machulska,

Director (Poland); Theater Spilkischte (Switzerland); and Childsplay Inc. (USA).

FitzGerald closed the ceremonies by thanking Eek for his donation of this "valuable and remarkable" award, which he said was "unique among international arts associations".

The General Assembly

Present:
President Michael FitzGerald (Australia), VP Helge Andersen (Norway), VP Tisa Chifunyise (Zimbabwe), VP Marjorie MacLean (Canada), Executive Officer Niclas Malmcrona (Sweden), Treasurer Harold Oaks (USA).

National Centers present: Australia, Austria, Bolivia, Brazil, Canada, Chile, Croatia, the Czech Republic, Denmark, Estonia, Finland, Germany, Hungary, Iran, Israel, Italy, Japan, Korea, Netherlands, New Zealand, Norway, Peru, Poland, Spain, Sri Lanka, Sweden, Switzerland, Turkey, Uganda, UK, USA, Venezuela, Zimbabwe.

Corresponding Center: India.
Observers: Latvia, Palestine, Portugal.
Proxies: Belgium, France, Georgia, Greece, Iceland, Ireland, Russia.
Executive Assistant: Rebecca Brinch (Sweden).

Helge Andersen, President of ASSITEJ/Norway, welcomed all the delegates to Tromsø for the General Assembly and Congress. On behalf of the Norwegian Center he gave his sincere wishes for a successful event. Andersen also read a message of greetings from Dr. Ilse Rodenberg, Honorary President of ASSITEJ, wishing them "success and good outcomes".

President Michael FitzGerald welcomed all the delegates, and introduced the members of the EC who were present. He then thanked the EC and the Commissions for their hard work during the past three years. He gave special thanks to Niclas Malmcrona for taking over as Executive Officer for Ulli Plichta (Austria) after her sudden resignation in April 1998, having served for only one year and five months. He commended Malmcrona at that difficult time who had worked very hard and efficiently to see that the work was done. He also mentioned receiving apologies from EC members Judit Benedek (Sweden) and Jacqueline Russo (Venezuela) for not being able to attend the Congress. He then proceeded to give his Report.

The Voting Commission: On the recommendation of the EC, the General Assembly approved the following members to serve as the Voting Commission, whose duty it was to count all the ballots during the elections and report the results to the Executive Officer/Secretary General for his announcement. Members approved the following Commission: Eckhardt Mittelstädt (Germany), Vicky Ireland (UK), Annette Riis Poulsen (Denmark), and Kim Woo Ok (Korea).

The Executive Officer then announced there were 42 Centers who had the right to vote, and that the total number of eligible votes came to 124, making a simple majority of 63.

Minutes: The General Assembly approved unanimously the Minutes from the General Assembly at the Rostov-on-Don Congress in 1996.

Executive Officer's Report: The Report of the activities of the EC for the past 3 years was presented by Malmcrona. There being no questions, the Report was accepted unanimously.

Financial Report: Treasurer Harold Oaks (USA) presented his Report for the past three years, which had been distributed in advance dated July 1999. There had been exceptional expenditures in connection with the replacement of the Secretary General in 1998. Oaks reported that with this expense subtracted, income and expenses would come close to balancing.

On a question from Pete Belcher (Austria), Oaks explained that ASSITEJ was not in debt. The current balance was 38,645.84 US$, while the 1996 balance had been 45,500 US$. Ann Shaw (USA) asked about the expenses for the Honorary Presidents Award, and Oaks replied that the only ASSITEJ expense was for 550 US$ to bring the Jury to the meeting in London, and the shipping of materials to the Archives in Frankfurt.

As of 1999, 48 National Centers had paid their dues, with 4 Centers excused from payment. The total income for the period was 26,189.22 US$ while the total expenditures were $48,097.60 US$, making a deficit of 21,908.38 US$. ASSITEJ continued to be subsidized primarily from the wealthier Centers.

The Treasurer's Report was adopted unanimously.

ASSITEJ/Int'l Membership Survey: The final results of this Survey were presented by the Chair of the Artistic Commission, Marjorie MacLean (Canada). She stated that this was the first time in the history of ASSITEJ that the membership was asked for opinions. Many of the questions asked were compiled from matters raised at previous congresses. They received more answers than they anticipated. A total of 29 Centers had responded. A preliminary abstract of the report was part of the EC Members' packet for the Harare Meeting in 1998.

The Committee had distributed 1,500 surveys with 122 returned, a return of 8%. Professional survey firms consider anything beyond a 3% response guarantees accuracy! 95 responses were from individual members and 23 from representatives of individual centers. 29 different countries were represented:

2 from Africa, 4 from Eastern and Central Europe, 1 from the Middle East, 4 from the Pacific Region, 6 from the Americas, and 12 from Western Europe. A total of 55 questions were asked and responded to. In part, here are some of the interesting answers:

Membership Survey Questions:

(Questions are in Bold Italics, answers in regular print, and missing numbers are questions and responses that are individual personal responses not germane to this Summary.)

1. ***Benefits?*** Access to an int'l network and new information about theatre
2. ***Provided adequately well? What?*** Access to a professional network; new information; new ideas for creation; info on annual meetings, congresses, and Festivals
3. ***Image in 1998?*** An organization with worldwide membership (91%) and relevant to contemporary theatre (64%)
5. ***Relevance to your work?*** Very relevant (46%)
10. ***Most important issues?*** Communication; government support; ability of worldwide members to participate; artistic development
11. ***What should ASSITEJ concentrate on?*** Communication with members; then links with education; then artistic development
12. ***Communication materials?*** Int'l directory; newsletter; int'l website
13. ***Are materials distributed quickly?*** Yes (46%); No (54%) Why? Lack of staff!
14. ***Best form of communication?*** Email (47%); Mail (30%); FAX (21%). ***Access to the internet?*** Yes (56%); No (44%)
15. ***What are ASSITEJ's most important roles?*** Promoting children's theatre to public and government (52%), and information exchange (24%)

National Center Survey Questions

1. ***Subsidized?*** Yes (50%); No (50%)
3. ***How?*** Government funding (49.3%); Membership fees (32%); Other (14%)
4. ***Where does funding come from?*** Government (54%); Membership dues (32%); Ticket sales (26%).
6. ***Do you produce Festivals?*** Yes (59%); No (41%)
7. ***What is your Centers most important activity?*** Sending out information (30%); Awards (23%); Member services (18%)
9. ***Is there cooperation among members and non-members?*** Some (48%); Good (36%)
10. ***Is government funding accessible?*** None (19%); Some (31%); Generally available (50%)
11. ***Does the government favor children's theatre?*** Yes (65%); No (36%)
13. ***3 most important groups to support your theatre?*** Directors/

dramaturges (33%); administrators (31%); actors (21%); **Others?** Writers (17%)

14. ***Do your members earn their primary incomes in the theatre?*** Yes (83%); No (17%)

General Questions to both groups

1. ***What kinds of theatre for young people are produced in your country?*** Solely; dramatic content (49.2%); drama with some educational content (31.7%); educational with some dramatic content (16.3%)

2. ***What is your format?*** Drama (22.9%); drama w/music (19.8%); puppetry (17.6%); comedy (15.9%)

3. ***How many professional theatres for children in your country?*** Ranged from 5 to 300. Median range was 100–200 companies

4. ***Performed by whom?*** Actors with professional actors (59.6%); actors with no professional training (31.5%); children (9.3%)

5. ***Is children's theatre increasing or decreasing in your country?*** Increasing (46%); staying the same (35%); decreasing (18%)

6. ***Where are plays performed?*** Proscenium theatres (46%); School Auditoriums (29%); festivals (17%)

7. ***Does your center commission new plays or co-productions?*** Yes (42%); No (58%)

8. ***What of the following is predominant script form?*** Original scripts (54%); adaptation of books (34%); group devised plays (12%)

9. ***What theatre style is most prevalent?*** Myth & fairy tales (26%); theatre investigating creativity and social ideas (23%); issue based theatre (18%)

10. ***What age children do you most perform to?*** Age 6–9 (61%); age 13 & older (20%); age 10–12 (13%); age 3–5 (7%)

11. ***In production what are your two most important concerns?*** Artistic quality (46%); social context (18%)

12. ***Do newspaper critics write reviews of your productions?*** Sometimes (80%); never (15%); regularly (6%)

19. ***Do you think the content and type of production now created in your country is changing?*** Yes (74%); No (26%)

Personal

2. ***Are you male or female?*** Male (57%); Female (43%)

3. ***What is your main job in the theatre?*** Administrator (21%); Director (20%); Actor (10%); Artistic Director

From these responses the Committee extracted 15 primary recommendations. The Committee hoped that the Members would continue to ask and answer questions during the next 3-year term.

MacLean concluded that if this were done correctly, ASSITEJ would take its proper place as a prominent and efficient Association. She charged the delegates that if they accepted these results, they must feel committed to them. In the discussion that followed, the following points were made:

- Ivica Šimič (Croatia) – praised the hard work, noting its adoption could give a clear picture of what ASSITEJ had achieved during the past nine years. He urged the EC to adopt its recommendations, and pursue them aggressively.
- Judy Potter (Australia) – endorsed its acceptance, Reminding the delegates that they were responsible to see that their individual countries pursued its recommendations.
- Somalatha Suasinghe (Sri Lanka) – stressed the need for the delegates to hear the concerns of the different voices within ASSITEJ.
- Myriam Reàtegui (Peru) – found the document of importance but too technical in its specificity. She urged the EC in responding to include suggestions from other cultures.
- Wolfgang Schneider (Germany) – felt some countries had sent many replies and some none. He recommended a setting up of 3 working groups to consider these 3 possibilities:

    1. to discuss the artistic circumstances
    2. to promote the idea of theatre for children all over the world
    3. to develop the Association

He encouraged the delegates to look specifically at the differences among countries, which the Survey had shown, in order to move the Association forward more progressively. He urged delegates to commit themselves and their Centers to assisting the EC during the next three years.

- Luca Radaelli (Italy) – found the Survey useful, and urged that "quality" should still be the core value of the Association, keeping in mind that theatre can deal with very complex social problems.
- Hagit Rehavi Nikolayevsky (Israel) – said the Survey was clear and sharp, and would give the organization a strong image. It would also be a good starting point to encourage more members to join with their national centers.
- Vicky Ireland (UK) – found the Survey extremely useful for presentation to governments. She recognized the need for much work to be done from this point on, and to bring the results to the next Congress. She

also offered help from Jeremy Turner (Wales) in relation to questions of minority audiences.
- Tisa Chifunyise (Zimbabwe) – expressed her gratitude for the hard work of the Committee. She was pleased to see the links to education, and felt the Survey could serve every country well.
- Jan Skotnicki (Poland) – cautioned against the dangers with all information and communication by forgetting the need for imagination and its impact on the child.
- Annette Riis Poulsen (Denmark) – commented that the current discussion had proved the success of the Survey. She urged all Centers to start working on the recommendations.
- Lou Westbury (Australia) – recommended that the EC find ways of distributing computers to Centers which could not afford them.
- Kim van der Boon (Netherlands) – praised the formidable job done by the Committee, and that it would put pressure on the EC to follow it up. She said that everyone wished to reach children with artistic work, and the Survey offered the opportunity to be practical and start working.
- Harold Oaks (USA) – stated that all the recommendations of the Survey should be discussed, addressed, and commissioned. This would allow the Association to reach out to countries with conditions very different from our own.

FitzGerald closed the discussion by stating that it was now the responsibility of the EC to create a strategy to achieve the concerns of the Survey and the discussion. He called for the vote. The Survey was adopted: Yes – 41, No – 0, Abstained – 3.

Languages: The EC recommended that English become the Working Language of the Association. There were no comments or questions. The recommendation was unanimously accepted.

ASSITEJ World Day: FitzGerald asked the Assembly to discuss the proposal that ASSITEJ establish its own World Theatre Day. He commented that UNESCO already had International Children's Day on the 3rd Monday in October, so it seemed sensible to select the same day. It was suggested that the EC do further research, and with the membership's approval establish an ASSITEJ World Theatre Day in October, starting in 2000. A vote was called for, and the proposal was adopted with its amendment: Yes – 41, No – 0, Abstention – 1.

ASSITEJ/Int'l Charter "Magna Charta": Schneider explained that the statement was intended for the members to use in their work for the promotion of theatre for young people. In the discussion they recommended changing the 22nd line of the Charter as follows: "ASSITEJ/Int'l is a political advocate for the promotion of theatre for children and young people in principle and practice. " FitzGerald called for the vote, and the Charter was approved unanimously. V. Ireland recommended listing the names of the Centers in support of the Charter.

ASSITEJ Archives in Frankfurt, Germany: Schneider stated that the Archives are the cultural memory of the Association, and they contain 2,000 books on children's theatre, more than 3,000 plays for children from around the world, 1,000 copies of video tapes from theatre productions, and over 30,000 articles and photos. He asked that the Centers support the Archives by sending in appropriate materials. FitzGerald stressed that ASSITEJ was indebted to Germany of its admirable creation of the ASSITEJ/Int'l Archives.

Working Program for 1999–2002: FitzGerald asked the Assembly to bring up further questions or proposals to the draft for the Working Program for 1999–2002 as outlined by the EC. It would be the responsibility of the EC to organize and consolidate these materials, even though it seemed an insurmountable task.

In the discussion that followed: Chifunyise asked that special support be given to the African countries; Maria Luiza Monteiro (Brazil) asked that the Program should have extra emphasis on theatre dealing with underprivileged children in all cultures; Jürgen Flügge (Germany) urged the Centers to use the tools available with the ASSITEJ World Theatre Festivals and the ASSITEJ World Project; and Suasinghe suggested holding the EC meetings in countries whose representatives have difficulty in attending the various meetings. It would also allow the EC to see and encourage the work being done in those countries.

FitzGerald called for a vote, and the Working Program for 1999–2002 was adopted unanimously.

Dues for 2000–2002: Treasurer Oaks proposed that the current dues of 100 US$, with encouragement to pay more up to 500 US$, be continued. The Corresponding Members dues would remain at 50 US$. FitzGerald stated that they intended to ask the Assembly in 2002 to raise the minimum dues to 150 or 250 US$. These conditions would be considered before the next Congress in 2002. The proposal was accepted unanimously.

The Budget for 1999–2000 was also accepted unanimously.

Selection of the Congress Site for 2002: FitzGerald was pleased to announce that there were two proposals for the site of the 2002 Congress: Canada and Korea.

Marjorie MacLean and Rémi Boucher (Canada) proposed to hold the next congress jointly in Vancouver, BC and Montreal, Quebec. The Congress would take place in May 2002. The joint Vancouver/Montreal Congress would combine the English and French aspects of Canada. There are festivals in both places, with staffs and office facilities to cope with the arrangements. There would be good prospects for obtaining governmental support, if plans were started immediately.

Kim Woo Ok (Korea) stated it was time for ASSITEJ to venture into new areas of the world, as well as having a Congress organized in a new way. A new government had just been elected, and seemed willing to spend money on children and good cultural programs. Chances of support seemed good. Also, the Japanese Center was willing to help and support the Congress if Korea would take on the financial responsibility.

FitzGerald called for the vote, and the results were: 71 votes for Korea, and 47 votes for Canada. Korea was selected to host the 2002 ASSITEJ World Congress. In accepting Kim said the Congress would only be possible if the money could be secured.

Presentation of the Candidates for the EC for 1999–2002: Each of the candidates was asked to present themselves to the General Assembly, in order to identify themselves and their backgrounds to all the delegates. The next day the elections were held.

The Elections:

The Secretary General reminded the delegates that a total of 121 votes could be cast, since Iran with 3 votes was absent. 61 votes would constitute a majority for election. A total of 13 Centers had nominated themselves to be elected to the EC. Fifteen (15) was the maximum number who could serve on the EC, and all places were filled. The votes were as follows:

Secretary General: Niclas Malmcrona: elected unanimously with 121 votes.
  Treasurer: Vicky Ireland: Yes – 109; No – 6; Abstentions – 9.
  Executive Committee: Those elected were:

		Rank Order
Australia (Lou Westbury)	85 votes	8
Canada (Rémi Boucher)	80 votes	9
Croatia (Ivica Šimić)	92 votes	5
Germany (Wolfgang Schneider)	95 votes	2
Israel (Hagit Rehavi Nikolayevsky)	72 votes	13
Japan (Yoshishige Kagawa)	91 votes	6
Korea (Kim Woo Ok)	94 votes	3
Netherlands (Kim van der Boon)	99 votes	1
Norway (Helge Andersen)	73 votes	12
Poland (Jan Skotnicki)	76 votes	10

Sweden (Niclas Malmcrona)	Already elected	
Switzerland (Peter Rinderknecht)	76 votes	11
USA (Harold Oaks)	87 votes	7
UK (Vicky Ireland)	Already elected	
Zimbabwe (Tisa Chifunyise)	94 votes	4

The President: The EC retired and returned with the name of Wolfgang Schneider for President. However, Schneider stated that he had withheld his nomination so that at least one of the three major offices was from outside Europe. Since Denmark and the UK were already elected, Schneider nominated Harold Oaks (USA) for the Presidency.

The vote was: Harold Oaks: Yes – 92; No – 18; Abstain – 14.

The Vice Presidents: The EC retired again, and there were 4 nominations for the Vice-President.

Wolfgang Schneider (Germany)	113 votes, Elected
Tisa Chifunyise (Zimbabwe)	40 votes, Not elected
Lou Westbury (Australia)	42 votes, Not elected
Kim Woo Ok (Korea)	60 votes, Not elected

The EC retired and returned with 3 names for the remaining 2 Vice-Presidents. The votes were:

Kim van der Boon (Netherlands)	80 votes, Elected
Kim Woo Ok (Korea)	74 votes, Elected
Tisa Chifunyise (Zimbabwe)	72 votes, Not elected

This made Schneider, van der Boon, and Kim Woo Ok the new Vice-Presidents. This concluded the elections.

The Tromsø Declaration: MacLean had drafted a letter of the Declaration from the Minister of Foreign Affairs in Canada Lloyd Axworthy. MacLean explained that the Declaration asserted the right of all children to live without war and child labor. She felt that it was important to have such a statement endorsed by ASSITEJ on the national and international level.

Two amendments were added: "The Tromsø Declaration is against any sort of exploitation, abuse, and violence that can lead to physical, psychological, and social harm that may impair the integral growth of the child".

Then at the end of the last paragraph: "The members of ASSITEJ/Int'l will also actively work towards the implementation of the rights of children and young people in the world through theatre arts".

FitzGerald asked the Assembly to endorse the letter with the proposed amendments, which they did unanimously. (See Appendix L)

Honorary Member of ASSITEJ: On the recommendation of the EC, the title of Honorary Member of ASSITEJ was to be conferred on Michael Ramløse (Denmark), the previous Secretary General. President FitzGerald spoke on behalf of the EC regarding Ramløse's extraordinary service to theatre for children. His talents as a creative administrator while he served ASSITEJ as Secretary General, his sense of fairness and quality combined with his ability to inform, include, and involve the world, all had earned him the right to be named an Honorary member of ASSITEJ. After additional verbal endorsements, Michael Ramløse was made an Honorary Member of ASSITEJ by a unanimous vote.

Miscellaneous:

- **Tisa Chifunyise and Elisabeth Kabasa** (Zimbabwe) reported on a Conference held in Harare in May 1999. Eleven countries took part, and the participants agreed to work together, and to find ways to cooperate with similar organizations in Africa. It was hoped that some of the participating countries would join ASSITEJ/Int'l.
- **Vicky Ireland** gave a report on a new organization formed to promote arts for children. 60 people came together from across UK to discover ways to support the arts. They are beginning to work together, and collectively they are hoping to have a stronger voice.
- **Katariina Metsälampi** (Finland) spoke of "The Bravo Project" in Helsinki in 2000. Nine cultural capitals are networking, and in 2000 there will be performances in all nine locations.
- **Bjarne Thanning** (Denmark) reported on work done by ASSINET, which has a Home Page with general information about ASSITEJ, its newsletter, information about the EC, a list of members, the festival guide, etc. There is also a chat room. Thanning urged all members to use the ASSINET, and to offer suggestions for improvement and expansion.
- **Rosie Belton** (New Zealand) asked the EC to protest against children all over the world becoming victims of the "media". She suggested something like The Tromsø Declaration.
- **President FitzGerald** had received a Fax from the Center in Georgia indicating they are reorganizing 3 national theatres into a single one, at the request of their government. Money is extremely short, and they have appealed to ASSITEJ for support.
- **Myriam Reàtegui** (Peru) informed them that they had not nominated anyone for the EC because of lack of money.

The New Executive Committee Meeting/Wednesday 16 June 1999
Present:
President Harold Oaks (USA), VP Wolfgang Schneider (Germany), VP Kim Woo Ok (Korea), VP Kim van der Boon (the Netherlands), Sec. Gen. Niclas Malmcrona (Sweden), Treasurer Vicky Ireland (UK).

Members: Lou Westbury (Australia), Rémi Boucher (Canada), Ivica Šimić (Croatia), Yoshishige Kagawa (Japan), Helge Andersen (Norway), Jan Skotnicki (Poland), Peter Rinderknecht (Switzerland), Tisa Chifunyise (Zimbabwe).
Member absent: Hagit Rehavi Nikolayevski (Israel).
Executive Assistant: Rebecca Brinch (Sweden)

In their meeting after the General Assembly was adjourned, the EC made the following decisions: They narrowed the Commissions to four and appointed the following persons to them:

- **C1 & C5 – Congress & Advocacy**: Kim and Boucher (Co-Chairs), Kagawa.
- **C2 & C4 – Publication and Communication**: Malmcrona (Chair), Westbury, Chifunyise, Thanning (Counselor), Mittelstädt (Counselor).
- **C3 – Artistic Commission**: Schneider (Chair), van der Boon, Nikolayevski, Rinderknecht, V. Ireland, Skotnicki, and Šimić.
- **C7 – New Commission: responsible for Finance**, planning, statutes, fund-raising, and membership: Oaks (Chair), Andersen, V. Ireland, Jackson Ndawula, Luiza Monteiro.

They co-opted the following members: Luiza Monteiro (Brazil), and Jackson Ndawula (Uganda). **Counselors:** Marjorie MacLean on Survey (Canada), Eckhardt Mittelstädt on Publications (Germany), Bjarne Thanning on Website (Denmark), and Galya Kolosova on Planning and Fundraising (Russia).[51]

Kim Woo Ok will report on the next possible congress in Seoul, Korea in 2002 at the next EC meeting.

Future Meetings:
- Robyn Flatt of the Dallas Children's Theatre in Dallas, Texas, USA invited the EC to meet there on 11-13 February 2000. The EC accepted the invitation to go to Dallas.
- Other possibilities offered were: Zimbabwe in late July 2000; Venezuela in October–November 2001; and perhaps Croatia and Korea.

Miscellaneous:
- Malmcrona urged the centers to buy copies of Annual 98/99 together with the next mailing, and then to distribute them to members of their centers.
- Oaks presented the idea of center and country partnerships. The EC accepted the idea, and the following teams were chosen: Canada–France;

UK–Spain, France; Poland–Lithuania; Sweden–Latvia; Croatia–Slovenia, Romania; Korea–Asian countries; Australia–Singapore; Netherlands–Brazil; Zimbabwe–Kenya, Angola; Japan, Asian countries; Germany–Russia, Turkey, Italy; Norway–India; USA–Venezuela; Brazil–Uruguay; and Uganda–Kenya, Rwanda.

The meeting was then adjourned.

Closing Session:

The new President Harold Oaks thanked ASSITEJ/Norway and especially Helge Andersen for their fine organization of the Congress coupled with a wonderful Festival. Oaks also gave warm thanks to the outgoing members and the counselors of the EC for their dedicated work. He also complemented the Voting Commission on their work during the Assembly, and gave a special thanks to Niclas Malmcrona for his efficient good work as Secretary General.

In closing Vicky Ireland on behalf of the Assembly and the EC thanked Past President Michael FitzGerald for his outstanding contributions to ASSITEJ/Int'l.

The World of 2000 (The Millennium)

People around the world prepared for 1 January 2000, and the dawn of a new century and millennium, despite the fact that the next millennium did not commence officially until 1 January 2001![52] In spite of fears of terrorist attacks, there were jubilant celebrations around the world.

In the USA the November 2000 election of George W. Bush over Al Gore verged on scandal, when neither had a majority, and the outcome hinged on a recount and charges of voting irregularity in the state of Florida where Bush's brother was Governor. Finally, Bush was declared the winner.

The President of South Korea, Kim Dae Jung, and the President of North Korea, Kim Jong II, both whose nations were officially at war, met for the first time in a summit in June, with both promising to work towards *unification*. Kim Dae Jung had won the 2000 Nobel Peace Prize for his efforts.

Russian President Boris Yeltsin resigned, and named his prime minister, Vladimir Putin, to serve as Acting President, who was then elected as President 3 months later in 2000.

The Mideast peace process made strides with Israel ending its 22-year occupation of southern Lebanon, but further talks collapsed in disagreement.

A total of 23.3 million Harry Potter books, written by British author J. K. Rowling, were sold in the USA in 2000.

The previous year a Special Pulitzer Prize in Music was given to jazz musician Edward Kennedy "Duke" Ellington.

The top TV series, interestingly enough, was titled *Survivor II*.

Les Miserables (France), *The Phantom of the Opera* (UK), and *The Lion King* (USA) continued as the top three musicals.

2000
EXECUTIVE COMMITTEE MEETING OF ASSITEJ[53]
Dallas, Texas, USA/11-13 February 2000

Present:
President Harold Oaks (USA), VP Wolfgang Schneider (Germany), VP Kim van der Boon (Netherlands), VP Kim Woo Ok (Korea), Sec. Gen. Niclas Malmcrona (Sweden), Treasurer Vicky Ireland (UK).

Members present: Lou Westbury (Australia), Luiza Monteiro (Brazil), Rémi Boucher (Canada), Ivica Šimić (Croatia), Yoshishige Kagawa (Japan), Helge Andersen (Norway), Jan Skotnicki (Poland), Peter Rinderknecht (Switzerland), Elizabeth Kabasa (Zimbabwe).

Counselors: Bjarne Thanning (Denmark), Galya Kolosova (Russia), Eckhardt Mittelstädt (Germany).

Members absent: Marjorie MacLean (Canada), Hagit Rehavi Nikolayevsky (Israel), Jackson Ndawula (Uganda), Tisa Chifunyise (Zimbabwe).

Executive Assistant: Anastasia Kozak (Canada).

View of Dallas, Texas, USA.

Members of the EC at their meeting in Dallas, Texas, USA in February 2000. Courtesy of the Dallas Children's Theatre.

Production seen at the EC Meeting.

The Island of the Skog by Steven Kellogg, adapted by Linda Dougherty. (Performers left to right) Dennis W. Vincent, Clay Houston, John Harrison Coffman, Karen Rice-Williams, Kristi Cardwell, Karl Schaffer, and Linda Daugherty. Production by the Dallas Children's Theatre. Courtesy of Harold Oaks.

President Harold Oaks welcomed the EC, and expressed his thanks to the Dallas Children's Theatre, Robyn Flatt – Executive Director, for hosting the meeting.

Bureau Meeting/10 February 2000

Oaks announced that at the Bureau meeting the evening before, the following items were discussed:
- Budget for 1999–2002
- Attendance at the meetings
- Agenda and adjustments

EC Meeting/11 February 2000/9:15 am–1:15 pm; 2:30–4:00 pm
EC Meeting/12 February 2000/1:30–4:30 pm
EC Meeting/13 February 2000/9:00 am–12 noon

The EC approved the Agenda as presented by Oaks.

Minutes: The Minutes of the EC meeting in Tromsø, Norway on 16 June 1999 were adopted unanimously as distributed.

New Business: Malmcrona pointed out that the enclosure with the Tromsø Minutes discussed ideas for preparing any future ASSITEJ Congress, which in turn would be helpful to the organizers of the Korean Congress in 2002. Oaks presented his President's Report, and distributed a letter from Nikolayevsky (Israel) with a report from that country.

In the **Secretary General's Report**, Malmcrona indicated that Center contacts were difficult, but those that replied were mentioned in the Newsletter.

New Centers: Malmcrona contracted **Zambia** through the efforts of **Zimbabwe**, and they are very interested in ASSITEJ. Oaks commented that he and Malmcrona would be traveling into Africa in July, and hopefully they would meet with representatives of Zambia.

Elizabeth Kabasa (Zimbabwe) presented a report on the situation in Africa. **Malawi, Lesotho, South Africa,** and **Zambia** were all in the process of forming national centers, and **Mauritius** had been accepted as a new center.

Malaysia was accepted as a Corresponding Center. Malmcrona reported on his visit to **Latvia** in January, recommended that they be accepted to Full Membership, which the EC approved.

Financial Report: V. Ireland reported a total income for 1999–2002 to date as 26,200 US$. Expenditures as equal to that amount. Dues notices had been sent, and contact had been made in Congo, Mexico, Bulgaria, and China. Oaks commented that the centers should at least write to explain their situation.

Partnerships: There had been a Symposium in Okinawa where Japan and Korea had presented information about ASSITEJ. Norway reported on the Nordic Project with India. V. Ireland had received a French book listing all theatres for children and young people in that country. She next planned to travel to Spain. Monteiro reported no contact with Uruguay. Šimić reported things were now easier in Croatia and Slovenia; Montenegro and Serbia were planning a Festival for Youth this year. There was no contact with Albania and Bosnia-Herzegovina. Ndawula had meetings in Kenya and Angola. Westbury reported that Singapore is now to have a Children's Festival in its own right. Kagawa reported the Asian Symposium a great success where 12 Asian countries met. Schneider reported on the Swiss, Austrian, and German ASSITEJ meeting in Austria, and the huge success of the German-Russian collaboration in Ekaterinburg. The Nordic Centers were planning a Nordic-Latvian Theatre Festival for next year. Oaks commended all for their robust activities.

UNESCO Application: No news as usual.

Commissions: The Commissions had been restructured, members appointed, and charges redefined.

- **C2 – Communication and Publication: Niclas Malmcrona (Chair), Lou Westbury, Tisa Chifunyise, Luiza Monteiro, Jackson Ndawula; (Counselors) Bjarne Thanning, Eckhardt Mittelstädt.**
  a. Website: make it easier to navigate, include information about the

upcoming Congress, announce its new activities, establish a Chat Room, add photos of the EC and résumés

b. Newsletter: more informal and interesting, create a Bulletin Board for individual members

c. Redesign the Brochure

d. Distribute a World Day packet

e. Create an ASSITEJ e-mail list

f. Mittelstädt announced the next Annual would report on 10 Festivals around the world, report on the Archives, documentation on the 1999 Congress, bibliography, internet vs. hard copy.

There was discussion on switching the Annual to the Internet, but they decided to keep the same format for the next issue.

- **C3 – Artistic Commission: Wolfgang Schneider (Chair), Kim van der Boon, Hagit Rehavi Nikolayevsky, Peter Rinderknecht, Jan Skotnicki, Ivica Šimić, Rémi Boucher, Vicki Ireland.**

Schneider reported that their discussion centered on how modern dance affected the theatrical language for children and young people. They concluded that "dance theatre" should be developed, and belongs in theatre for young people.

- **C5 – Congress Commission: Kim Woo Ok (Chair), Yoshishige Kagawa, Helge Andersen, Niclas Malmcrona, Galya Kolosova (Counselor).**

Kim Woo Ok asked for letters of support to his government for the 2002 Congress. Boucher offered his help, since Canada was interested in hosting the 2005 Congress. Kim would consider 1) changing the word "new" to "experimental" in the naming of the Theme; 2) since it is being held in Asia, it should be different from any of the previous ones; 3) the 2 Symposium Topics should be combined into one (*Tradition, its Use and Abuse* and *New Theatre for Children and Youth*); discuss how to screen performances.

- **C7 – Finance and Statutes Commission: Harold Oaks (Chair), Vicky Ireland, Niclas Malmcrona, Helge Andersen, (Counselor) Marjorie MacLean.**

A new Commission was being formed and it would meet at the next EC Meeting.

Future Meeting Sites: The next EC Meeting was decided to be in Rio de Janeiro, Brazil from 8-10 December 2000. Also, since they had received invitations, both for the same year, they selected Japan for July 2001 and Zimbabwe for

July 2002. Šimić announced that Croatia would be happy to host the EC on any years following these.

Oaks closed the meeting by distributing the City of Dallas' Proclamation, and he thanked the Dallas Children's Theatre for their good work in organizing the EC Meeting. A special thanks was given to Robyn Flatt, Executive Director of the theatre, and she was presented a gift by Niclas Malmcrona on behalf of ASSITEJ/Int'l.

Performances: On the evening of 11 February the EC saw the Dallas Children's Theatre production of *Roll of Thunder, Hear My Cry*. In the afternoon of 13 February they attended a performance of *If You Give a Moose a Muffin*.

2000
EXECUTIVE COMMITTEE MEETING OF ASSITEJ[54]
Harare, Zimbabwe, Africa/8-11 December 2000

Present:
President Harold Oaks (USA), VP Wolfgang Schneider (Germany), VP Kim Woo Ok (Korea), Sec. Gen. Niclas Malmcrona (Sweden).

Members: Lou Westbury (Australia), Luiza Monteiro (Brazil), Rémi Boucher (Canada), Ivica Šimić (Croatia), Hagit Rehavi Nikolayevsky (Israel), Yoshishige Kagawa (Japan), Helge Andersen (Norway), Peter Rinderknecht (Switzerland), Tisa Chifunyise (Zimbabwe).

Counselors: Peter Manscher (Denmark)/Deputy for Bjarne Thanning, Jackson Nduwala (Uganda).

Members absent: Kim van der Boon (Netherlands), Jan Skotnicki (Poland), Vicky Ireland (UK).

Counselors absent: Marjorie MacLean (Canada), Eckhardt Mittelstädt (Germany), Galya Kolosova (Russia).

Observers: Ricky Gitahi (Kenya), Gertrude Kamkwatira (Malawi), Henry Favory (Mauritius), Manuela Soeiro (Mozambique), Vincent Mwasango (Namibia), Sifiso Mabaso (South Africa), Mpho Melepo (South Africa), Helen Nordenson (Sweden), Maswati Dludlu (Swaziland), Philemon Mwasanga (Tanzania), Cheela Chilila (Zambia), Elizabeth Kabasa (Zimbabwe).

Executive Assistant: Alison Turner (Canada).

Members of the EC and their hosts at the EC Meeting in Zimbabwe, Africa, December 2000.

President Oaks welcomed the EC, and commended all the others present, thanking them for their attendance. Malmcrona also extended his welcome to the EC.

Oaks reported that the Bureau had met the previous day, reviewed, and approved the Agenda with a few amendments.

The EC proceeded to approve the Agenda, and to adopted the Minutes of the Dallas EC Meeting in February 2000 with three minor corrections.

Presidential Report: Oaks presented his Report outlining his activities since the last meeting. He and Malmcrona had attended Festivals in Helsinki, Washington DC, Magdeburg, Zagreb, and Hwange. He announced the resignation of Marjorie MacLean as Counselor in order to pursue a Degree in Law. He urged all centers to get e-mail, web access, and establish a web page to increase communication.

Schneider followed this with his Vice-President's Report, which included his attendance at the UNIMA World Congress in Germany, where he tried to establish stronger links between UNIMA and ASSITEJ; where Oaks, Malmcrona, and Schneider attended the One Theatre World–One Vision meeting in Washington, DC, a well-attended Congress with many discussions among the playwrights attending; and Schneider's attendance at a festival in Uzbekistan for one week where he was impressed by their high quality of performance and production at their March Festival.

Malmcrona presented his Secretary General's Report where he thanked the Nordic countries for their financial support, to SIDA and the Swedish Institute for their help and contributions, and to the Canadian Department of Foreign Affairs and International Trade for their internship program (YIIP), courtesy of MacLean's efforts. His Report had been sent to all the ASSITEJ Centers.

Theatre for Children and Young People World Day – March 20: Malmcrona announced that an information package had been sent to all centers, with a very positive response. Westbury (Australia) suggested that centers contribute photos of their activities. Boucher (Canada) commented that he would have liked a French translation of the Information Package. Malmcrona responded that Maurice Yendt (France) had submitted French translations, which would be posted on the ASSITEJ Website.

Schneider thanked Malmcrona for the assembling of all the World Day materials. Ndawula (Uganda) also complemented Malmcrona saying that they were making much use of the materials, and had invited colleagues from Rwanda to celebrate the event with them in Uganda.

There was considerable discussion about the conflict in dates between

World Theatre Day (March 27) and Theatre for Children and Youth World Day (March 20).

News of Centers and Non-Member Countries: Malmcrona had attended the ITI Congress in Marseilles, France, and that Oaks, Schneider, and he had met with their new President, and then at the UNIMA Congress in Magdeburg, they had met with the UNIMA Secretary General and hosted an ASSITEJ reception for the UNIMA delegates.

Ndawula commended Malmcrona for his contributions to their work in Uganda, and Malmcrona reported on his travels in July to Uganda, Zambia, and Zimbabwe, where he met with representatives from 11 southern African countries.

New Centers: Malmcrona invited the representatives from countries applying for membership who were attending the EC Meeting to make any additional comments which they felt would be appropriate before the EC made their decisions. The following comments were noted:

- South Africa: deferred the decision until the next EC meeting.
- Namibia, Kenya, Mozambique, and Zambia were accepted to Full Membership.
- Tunisia was accepted as a Corresponding Member.
- Tanzania's membership was changed from Corresponding member status to Full Member status.

Financial Report: A report was handed out, and Oaks confirmed the fact that ASSITEJ had more income than expenditures recently, and was in good financial shape. The accounts were well balanced, and the Budget for the Secretarial General's expenses would be available at the next EC meeting, but they did not affect the ASSITEJ/Int'l Budget.

Reports on the Partnership System:

- **Sweden & Baltic Countries:** Malmcrona reported that some Board Members of ASSITEJ/Sweden had been to Latvia and Lithuania, meeting with other practitioners and conducting workshops.
- **USA & Venezuela:** Oaks reported lack of contacts with Venezuela, but things were moving forward with Mexico.
- **Norway & India:** Andersen reported that Denmark and India had been working together a great deal, so Norway was ready for a new partner.
- **Korea:** Kim stated that Korea does not have an official partner, but they have been successful with an Asian Meeting in Japan, and want to hold

another in 2001 in Seoul, which would include 12 members from Asia. He mentioned that contacts are difficult, but hoped that these meetings would provide more contacts with each other.
- **Brazil & Uruguay:** Monteiro reported no response from Uruguay, but they had had contacts with Bolivia, Argentina, Venezuela, and Mexico.
- **Japan:** Kagawa reported on their meeting with Korea, and the Philippines, Thailand, and Singapore had attended as Observers, but there had been little progress.
- **Uganda, Rwanda, & Kenya:** Ndawula reported that he had made several trips to Kenya, and Ricky Githai (Kenya) commented that Ndawula had mobilized them into becoming interested in ASSITEJ. Ndawula had also gone to Rwanda twice, and feels they are ready to apply for membership by the next EC Meeting.
- **Germany & Italy:** Schneider gave Malmcrona a list of the German membership, but regrettably had been unsuccessful in meeting with their Italian colleagues.
- **Germany, Austria, & Switzerland:** These three countries had a meeting in October in Vienna, where Schneider presented, as Editor, a book about "Children's and Young People's Theatre in Austria".
- **Germany & Sweden:** ASSITEJ/Germany with Judit Benedek (Sweden) is compiling a book in German about Swedish theatre for young people. Germany had also recently given a prize to a young Swedish playwright.
- **Germany & Israel:** Schneider reported on meeting with members of ASSITEJ/Israel while visiting there.
- **Germany & Russia:** Schneider had had several meetings at various Russian festivals during the past year.
- **Croatia & Slovenia:** Šimić reported that had been much communication between the two, and they had decided to working together on children's theatre festivals in order to establish such a movement in Slovenia. While some partnerships had caused problems, he felt that partnerships must be mutually beneficial between countries that have a natural interest in each other.
- **Denmark & India:** Denmark is trying to raise money for Arun Agnihotri in India so he can build a theatre venue for middle class children in order to raise their social awareness and consciousness.
- **Australia & Singapore:** Westbury attended the ACT 3 Festival in Singapore, and noted that they are exploring ways to improve both quality and professionalism in their children's theater work.

- **Australia & India:** Westbury had received a letter from a Bombay company that wants to do a Children's festival.

Report on Zimbabwe Meeting: Tisa Chifunyise reported on the successful meetings in Hwange, Zimbabwe, and written Minutes are available through the Secretariat.

News of Counselors: Peter Manscher (Denmark) had replaced Bjarne Thanning on the EC. Marjorie MacLean (Canada) had resigned as Counselor.

UNESCO Membership: In the continuing saga of ASSITEJ Membership in UNESCO, Malmcrona had written them after the Dallas EC Meeting, but had yet to hear from them. There was a brief discussion.

Commission Reports:

- **C2&C4 – Communication & Publications:** Schneider described the contents of the upcoming Annual, reminded centers of the deadline of December 2000.

Changes in the ASSITEJ Brochure would include simplification and modification of the language use; it will direct people to the Website; and there was considerable discussion about using other languages.

Efforts would be made to make the Web-site simple for any machine to use, and easy to read.

The Newsletter: people were not responding to its deadline; upcoming issues will have a theme, giving people an idea of what to submit; centers should notify the Secretariat whether they want the print or digital version; a note will indicate that people are free to copy and distribute the newsletter at will.

Members were reminded to continue submitting all their information to the German Archives in Frankfort.

- **C3 – Artistic Commission:** Schneider asked for proposals that would develop the artistic aims of new members through concrete initiatives; "How to Define Quality?" was part of the Commission's concern; a letter was to be sent to the Seoul Congress proposing 3 Workshops; the creation of a discussion atmosphere during the Congress; and the selection process of a performances to discuss.

On 1-4 November 2001 there will be a conference in Zurich, Switzerland on the topic "How to study theatre for children and young people?" A questionnaire to seek interesting seminar leaders and keynote speakers will be sent out.

- **C5 – Congress Report:** Kim (Korea) read through the current plans of the 2002 Congress in Seoul, Korea. They had the following concerns:
  Some countries were worried about making the application deadline.
  Since the performers were not to be paid for performing at the Festival 1)

ASSITEJ would not be taken seriously; 2) performers "on the fringe" would feel that their attendance was not worth the personal expense if not paid; 3) the EC needs to address the issue at the next EC Meeting.

The program was too large to allow time to see and discuss the performances. Kim felt it was not a problem.

The desire for performance from every continent put special pressures on African and Latin American countries because of the costs.

The theme "Newness" was an equivalent to "technology", and was a resource not available to all countries.

It was felt that more pressure was being put on Korea than any previous Congress. The Report was accepted and the following changes were to be made: 1) the theme should be re-phrased; 2) Oaks and Malmcrona would be visiting Seoul in the first half of 2001; and 3) companies would be selected on the basis of "experimentation" in their work.

- **C7 – Finance & Statutes:** Slovakia, Sri Lanka, Latvia, India, and Mexico were excused from paying their dues for 2000. The Secretary General was instructed to tell them that they would have to pay their dues for 2001. Also letters will be sent to those centers who owe dues at this time.

Honorary President's Award: After having discussed the Jury selection with Nat Eek (USA Sponsor), Malmcrona proposed a Jury of 5 persons – 3 from the EC, plus 2 others. He suggested Michael FitzGerald (Australia) as Chair of the Jury, plus Helge Andersen (Norway), Tisa Chifunyise (Zimbabwe), and Wolfgang Schneider (Germany) as the EC representatives, and Yohei Hijikata (Japan) as the fifth member. After a discussion expressing concern that there were no women nor young members in the Jury, President Oaks called for a vote. The Jury as presented was endorsed: Yes – 11, No – 1, Abstention – 1.

Honorary Membership: Malmcrona stated the criteria, and Schneider recommended that the EC endorse Orna Porat (Israel) as an Honorary Member. While in Israel, Schneider had met with her. He stated she is very popular in Israel, and well known in ASSITEJ/Int'l, and she has been largely responsible for ASSITEJ/Israel's governmental support.

Oaks proposed that her name be presented to the General Assembly for endorsement as an Honorary Member.

World Project: Schneider requested that the International Director's Seminar for Children's and Young People's Theatre being held on 14-19 June 2001 in Nuremberg, Germany be endorsed as an ASSITEJ World Project. The proposal was unanimously endorsed.

Future Meetings: The EC selected Tokyo, Japan on 19-24 July 2001 as the place and date of the next EC meeting. Members making presentations at that meeting were asked to have their papers finished by the end of May, and to limit their presentations to 15 minutes.

Format of EC Meetings: Schneider had received a letter from Jan Skotnicki (Poland) for discussion re: the content and form of the EC Meetings. Skotnicki asked: What is ASSITEJ? What does it do? Why the traveling, the Commissions, and the Congresses? What result is its goal? How could ASSITEJ have more status and authority to enable it to support projects that in turn support the goals of ASSITEJ? (See Appendix N)

Schneider felt his letter should be taken seriously, and in turn change some of ASSITEJ's procedures and structures. Open discussions need to be developed. The letter should be used to inspire ideas to be discussed at the next EC Meeting.

Malmcrona presented an amendment to the Requirements for Hosting an EC Meeting which was adopted 1-5 December 1993:

- The Hosting Center should be in close contact with the Secretariat during the planning phase of the Meeting. The EC needs time for the meeting, but appreciates the opportunities to attend performances.
- The Host should also include opportunities to meet with other theater people of the host country.
- EC members (the Bureau in particular) will be happy to attend Press Conferences and any other media coverage.
- If notified before hand, the President and the Secretary General are happy to meet with authorities (e. g. Ministers of Culture, mayors, representatives of arts councils, etc.) on the invitation of the host country.
- In co-operation with the Host Center, the Secretary General will work out the time schedule of the meetings.
- The Host Center is requested to minimize travel time between hotel/meeting venues/theaters/restaurants etc.

The EC unanimously endorsed this amendment.

Oaks commended and thanked their Zimbabwean colleagues for the Harare Meeting, and for the excellent work they did in organizing the meetings. He also expressed ASSITEJ's gratitude to SIDA for their support, and to Helen Nordenson for her very welcome attendance.

The meeting was adjourned.

A HISTORIC PERSPECTIVE

For the next few years many of the relationships between ASSITEJ countries reflected their attitudes towards the wars in Afghanistan and Iraq.

In 1989 the Soviet Union, which had attempted to bring peace to the country, withdrew their occupying troops from Afghanistan, but a period of unrest continued after the Soviet troops had left. The 1990–1991 Persian Gulf War, originally between Iraq and Kuwait, had escalated to involve the USA. On 7 October 1991 the combined forces of the USA, the UK, Australia, France and others began an invasion of Afghanistan. The various countries' need for oil also undoubtedly entered into the motivation for the invasion.

As a direct result of the attack on and destruction of the World Trade Center in New York City on 11 September 2001, the USA began an attack on Iraq on 19 March 2003 which toppled the reign of Saddam Hussein under the mistaken guise of seeking "weapons of mass destruction", but the war continued for at least ten more years. The USA began its troop removal in December of 2012.

In many of the ensuing meetings and congresses of ASSITEJ/Int'l anti-war feelings strongly surfaced, and the leadership of ASSITEJ attempted to ameliorate the suffering of the children of Iraq by fund raising. The countries responsible for the invasions were silently condemned, and were disciplined sometimes by minimizing or ignoring their contributions.

2001
EXECUTIVE COMMITTEE MEETING OF ASSITEJ[55]
Tokyo, Japan/19-24 July 2001

Present:
President Harold Oaks (USA), VP Wolfgang Schneider (Germany), VP Kim Woo Ok (Korea), VP Kim van der Boon (Netherlands), Sec. Gen. Niclas Malmcrona (Sweden), Treasurer Vicky Ireland (UK).

Members: Lou Westbury (Australia), Rémi Boucher (Canada), Ivica Šimić (Croatia), Hagit Rehavi Nikolayevsky (Israel), Yoshishige Kagawa (Japan), Helge Andersen (Norway), Jan Skotnicki (Poland), Tisa Chifunyise (Zimbabwe).

Counselor: Eckhardt Mittelstädt (Germany).

Members absent: Luiza Monteiro (Brazil), Peter Rinderknecht (Switzerland), Jackson Ndawula (Uganda).

Counselors absent: Peter Manscher (Denmark), Galya Kolosova (Russia).

Invited: Michael FitzGerald (Australia) as Honorary President's Award Jury Member and Chair.

Executive Assistant: Alison Turner (Canada).

View of Tokyo, Japan, July 2001.

Tokyo EC Meeting: (left to right) Lou Westbury (Australia), Wolfgang Schneider (Germany), Harold Oaks (USA), Niclas Malmcrona (Sweden), Vicky Ireland (UK), Helge Andersen (Norway), Ivica Šimić (Croatia), Eckhart Mittelstädt (Germany).

Members of the Japan Center of ASSITEJ with President Harold Oaks.

The Bureau (left to right): Helge Andersen (Norway), Wolfgang Schneider (Germany), and Harold Oaks (USA)

Yoshishige Kagawa, Wolfgang Schneider, Asaji Fujita at the Tokyo EC Meeting. Courtesy of Wolfgang Schneider.

Kabuki Performance in Tokyo.

Same Kabuki Performance in Tokyo.

Same Kabuki Performance in Tokyo.

President Harold Oaks opened the meeting extending the EC's gratitude to ASSITEJ/Japan for their efforts and generosity.

Bureau Meeting

Oaks reported that there were no changes or additions to be made to the Agenda as a result of the Bureau Meeting. Van der Boon requested that Jan Skotnicki's letter (mentioned in the Minutes of the Harare EC meeting) be added to the Agenda. This was done, and the Agenda was adopted.

Executive Committee Meeting

The Minutes from the Harare, Zimbabwe EC meeting were accepted with only a minor change, and no extra business arose from the Minutes. Kim Woo Ok noted that there were 81 member centers, not 18 as indicated in the Minutes.

Oaks presented his **President's Report**. As part of his Report there was discussion about the relationship of ASSITEJ/France and the International Association. To date there had been little contact with Maurice Yendt. Oaks had written him a letter and was "...optimistic that this letter is a positive step towards the participation and presence of ASSITEJ/France". Oaks had hoped that Yendt would come to the 2002 Seoul Congress. Later Oaks told Eek that both Secretary General Malmcrona and he had visited Yendt in Lyon urging him to renew his participation, but nothing came of it.

Secretary General Malmcrona reported as follows:

- The ASSITEJ Website would soon have a new format.
- Finland would no longer be contributing to the funding of the Secretariat. Sweden will cover the remaining amount. When queried he stated that the finances were under control, and a report will be submitted to Vicki Ireland, Treasurer of ASSITEJ.
- The Secretariat had been in contact with numerous countries, organizations, and individuals concerning ASSITEJ, specifically: Nepal, Columbia, Indonesia, Bangladesh, and Armenia to mention a few.
- Cameroon and Lithuania had submitted applications for membership, and both were endorsed for full membership.

Financial Report: Treasurer Vicki Ireland requested all EC members to contact those centers who had not sent in their dues, and were in arrears, despite her correspondence, telephone calls, and e-mails.

New ASSITEJ Annual: Schneider reported that each Center would receive two copies. Additional ones could be ordered through the Website. Prices were 10 US$ per copy with lower costs if more were ordered. He also urged members to let their members know of the availability of the Annual.

Partnership System Report:

- **Scandinavia & the Baltic Countries:** The last Nordic Festival for Children in Falun and Borlänge in Sweden invited representatives from the Baltic countries. Malmcrona reported that there has been growth and development there in the last ten years, to the point that they should become separate centers in ASSITEJ.
- **USA & Venezuela:** Oaks report little contact, and asked for assistance. Schneider suggested that ASSITEJ/Int'l could assist in establishing South American contacts.
- **Korea:** Kim Woo Ok had recently visited China for a meeting through a man he met at a festival in Sweden, and Kim felt this was a positive step towards getting Chinese participation in the 2002 Seoul Congress.
- **Japan & Asian Countries:** No news.
- **Germany & Switzerland:** The two centers have organized a conference together, and there was a festival in May in Berlin, and one in Baden in the middle of May.
- **Germany & Russia:** Jürgen Flügge, a former member of the EC, was

working with members in Rostov-on-Don. An October meeting is planned for many artistic participants which hopes to produce a joint-publication. They are also planning a joint festival between Berlin and St. Petersburg.
- **Germany & Uzbekistan:** Members of Dresden and Tashkent have initiated their own collaborations, and ASSITEJ/Int'l is letting the artists work together as a result of their own initiatives.
- **Croatia & Slovenia:** These two centers are collaborating on the 2002 Milk Tooth Festival. While there is currently only one theatre for children in Slovenia, ASSITEJ/Croatia is involved in connecting Zagreb and Ljubljana.
- **Australia:** Members are considering the possibilities of a Pacific Rim Festival and an Indian Rim Festival.
- **The Netherlands:** Kim van der Boon and Louiza Monteiro have arranged for Van der Boon to do a workshop in Brazil.
- **Israel:** Because of financial straights, many projects are on hold. There is a possibility of a partnership between Tel Aviv and Los Angeles, USA.
- **Zimbabwe:** Non-ASSITEJ affiliated countries met at a Festival in Zimbabwe in 1-3 August 2001. As a continuation of the Harare meeting, Sweden is working with people in Southern Africa to organize another meeting.
- **Canada:** Two weeks ago representatives of all the children's theatre festivals in Canada met, and approved a proposal to host the ASSITEJ Congress in Montreal in 2005. They plan to meet again at the Seoul Congress in 2002. Meanwhile Rémi Boucher has met with many ASSITEJ people throughout Europe, some of whom will be invited to the Montreal Congress in 2005.

Report on Meeting in Seoul, Korea in March 2001: An important meeting of the Asian countries was held in Seoul in May 2001. The theme discussed was "What is the importance of tradition to the theatre for children and young people in your country? How has tradition been utilized in the theatre for children and young people in your country?"

The meeting also gave the attendees the opportunity to celebrate the first World Theatre Day for Children and Young People. Countries attending were Korea, Japan, the Philippines, Thailand, Singapore, Malaysia, Indonesia, and Sri Lanka. Because of communication difficulties four of the twelve invited nations were not able to attend: Vietnam, Brunei, India, and China.

At the meeting Kim urged them to attend and participate in the Seoul

Congress in 2002, and he hoped that there would be a continuation of the Asian meetings.

World Theatre Day for Children and Young People: This first World Theatre Day was important, and many of the countries celebrated it extensively.

- **Zimbabwe:** Chinfunyise reported celebrations in Harare, Zimbabwe on 18 and 20 March consisting of a morning procession with singing, dancing, and drumming that carried into the afternoon.
- **Latvia:** Latvia organized a Festival around World Theatre Day.
- **Norway:** Oslo gave a free performance with a good audience turnout, but little publicity.
- **Croatia:** Croatia had distributed the World Day package, and its letters were read before performances, and there was a TV interview. There was considerable discussion because of its approximation to International Theatre Day.
- **Germany:** Celebrations were held on 27 May. There was a special meeting of German companies, plus a puppet theatre performance, reception, and press conference in Stuttgart. Its Mayor presented a concept for a new children's theatre for 2002, with a new playhouse in 2003.
- **USA:** There were numerous celebrations throughout the country, and the Press Packages were a great help.
- **UK:** All theatres were made aware of the event, and there were celebrations in London, Northern England, and Wales. In London 320 children released celebratory balloons!
- **Holland:** This country already has a National Youth Theatre Day in October, and all performances throughout the country are free at that time.
- **Canada:** All companies funded by the National Council on the Arts received a copy of the promotional letter written by Suzanne Osten in both French and English.
- **Poland:** The World Day Package was distributed to all theatres in Poland, and there were a variety of celebrations and press coverages. The positive response over the entire country was an unexpected success!

There was considerable discussion on the annual date, and it was decided that 20 March would be the official date, but that countries were free to celebrate it when they wished. Skotnicki stressed the importance of the promotional letter written by someone known to everyone everywhere!

However, Malmcrona stressed that budget limitations would prevent the distribution of a Package next year. He also asked for names of possible letter writers for the next year, a proposal that was forwarded to the Artistic Commission.

UNESCO Membership Report: Malmcrona reported that UNESCO was interested in a formal relationship with ASSITEJ, but several years of an informal relationship were necessary. Malmcrona had written a letter seeking further information, but had yet to receive a reply. Schneider commented that membership was essentially a matter of status for ASSITEJ.

Honorary President's Award: FitzGerald presented the jury's report for the 2002 Award. The jury had concluded that all nominations were of the highest quality. The Jury recommended that the Award be given to Suzanne Osten (Swedish playwright). Oaks asked that FitzGerald prepare a report of their recommendations for the EC members in general, and specifically for the Artistic Commission.

Honorary Membership: Oaks reported that Ann Shaw (USA), a former member of the EC and a Vice-President, had been nominated for Honorary Membership on a unanimous recommendation of the Board of ASSITEJ/USA. Shaw's nomination was approved, and it was to be forwarded to the General Assembly for action at the 2002 Seoul Congress.

Miscellaneous Discussions:

Fees & Festivals: There was considerable discussion related to whether to pay the artists who perform at the Congresses. The following points were made:

- Zimbabwe pays their performers, but it would be better not to do so.
- Making payment as a requirement would discourage some countries from offering to host events.
- Not paying would seriously limit the content of the festivals, while limiting a company's international artistic exposure.
- If performers were not paid for their performance, they should be paid for "out-of-pocket" expenses, which might be more than the fee!
- Since ASSITEJ is an international association, payment should be regarded as a political statement of "quality"!
- The EC can only recommend that the performers be paid.
- Van der Boon felt that Oaks should have prepared a Working Paper, with background information and possibilities to solve the issue, in order to introduce the discussion at this meeting. Oaks ended the discussion stating that the matter would be taken up by the Finance & Statutes Commissions, and that a sub-committee may be established to resolve the issue.

ASSITEJ Catalog of Scripts in English: The ensuing discussion proposed that V. Ireland and Tonie Reekie (Scotland) work together on a proposal to bring to the next EC Meeting.

Future Congress Decisions: The discussion centered around whether a General Assembly could decide on Congress locations six years in advance. The Constitution has made no limits. Boucher felt deciding on two congresses in advance would allow for artistic projects to move forward, and better funding be found. Rémi also stated that Canada was interested in hosting the 2005 Congress. Oaks suggested that the Secretariat survey the centers for a recommendation, which was approved.

Commission Reports:

- **C2&C4 – Communication & Publication Commission:** Malmcrona announced a new layout for the ASSITEJ Website, and asked for ideas and requested changes. A new brochure will be ready soon and each center will receive 100 copies. It will be in six languages. The new Annual is ready, and they should encourage people to buy it. Centers need to submit more information for the Newsletter.
- **C3 – Artistic Commission:** The Zurich Conference is their most important project at the moment. The Commission had decided to ask Peter Brook first, and Volker Ludwig second, to write the letter for the 2001 World Day. They also recommended a proposal for a forum/seminar to be held at the Seoul Congress in 2002. They decided on setting one day aside in the General Assembly for such a forum.

  There was considerable discussion of their Report. The extra meetings are a financial drain on its members. The Artistic Commission is the only one to meet separately. Why is this necessary? Oaks concluded the session stating that the travel issues need to be clarified for the participants.
- **C5 – Congress Commission:** Kim reported that the Seoul Congress had selected plays from Germany, Belgium, and Canada to appear at the 2002 Congress. He also distributed brochures. Of the Asian nations Japan, China, Sri Lanka, and the Philippines had been invited to perform. He also asked for proposals of Workshops and Seminars. Also, the International Association of Theatre Critics had submitted a proposal for a Seminar at the Seoul Congress.
- **C7 – Finance & Statutes Commission:** The Artistic Commission had requested 6,000 US$ to support the Conference on the Study of Theatre

in Zurich, Switzerland. The EC approved increasing their budget to 3,000 US$. As a result of this precedent and the ensuing discussion, Oaks asked if a procedure should be designed for requesting funds in the future? The vote was: Yes – 9; No – 3; and Abstain – 2.

Future EC Meeting: The next EC Meeting was proposed for the end of February 2002 in Brazil. Malmcrona said he would travel to Rio de Janeiro in September to meet with members of ASSITEJ/Brazil and discuss the organization of the meeting. He also said there were other offers, and if Brazil canceled he would try to organize a meeting in Stockholm in February.

Oaks closed the meeting by thanking ASSITEJ/Japan for their hosting, and for their generosity during its time in Tokyo. He added a special thank you for the excellent Kabuki theatre performance, and the meeting was officially closed.

2002
EXECUTIVE COMMITTEE MEETING OF ASSITEJ[56]
Rio de Janeiro, Brazil, South America/1-7 March 2002

Present:
President Harold Oaks (USA), VP Wolfgang Schneider (Germany), VP Kim Woo Ok (Korea), Sec. Gen. Niclas Malmcrona (Sweden), and Treasurer Vicky Ireland (UK).

Members: Luiza Monteiro (Brazil), Rémi Boucher (Canada), Ivica Šimić (Croatia), Yoshishige Kagawa (Japan), Helge Andersen (Norway), Jan Skotnicki (Poland), Peter Rinderknecht (Switzerland), Jackson Ndawula (Uganda), Tisa Chifunyise (Zimbabwe).

Counselors: Peter Manscher (Denmark), Eckhardt Mittelstädt (Germany) Galya Kolosova (Russia).

Members absent: Lou Westbury (Australia), Hagit Rehavi Nikolayevsky (Israel), Kim van der Boon (Netherlands).

Observers: Martha Cañete (Argentina), Sergio Rio Hennings (Bolivia).

Executive Assistant: Rebecca Brinch (Sweden).

Rio de Janeiro, Brazil, March 2002.

Eckhart Mittelstädt (Germany), Ivica Šimić (Croatia), Wolfgang Schneider (Germany), Peter Rinderknect (Switzerland), and Jan Skotnicki (Poland). Courtesy of Wolfgang Schneider.

Municipal Theatre

Performance at EC Meeting

Performance at EC Meeting

Bureau Meeting

President Oaks opened the meeting by thanking ASSITEJ/Brazil for hosting the EC Meeting. He then reported that there were no changes or additions to be made to the Agenda from the Bureau Meeting.

The Minutes from the Harare, Zimbabwe EC Meeting were adopted unanimously.

President's Report: In his brief report, Oaks in addition to thanking ASSITEJ/Brazil, he thanked the Nordic countries for their continued support of the Secretariat, and also Malmcrona for the excellent work he was doing as the ASSITEJ Secretary General.

General Secretary's Report: Malmcrona handed out copies of his preliminary Report for 1999–2002, which will be presented to the General Assembly at the 2002 Korean Congress.

He had recently been to Rio de Janeiro in September 2001, and noted their good organization for the future EC Meeting there. In November 2001 he was in Cameroon and was impressed by their artistic work. He also report that SIDA (Swedish International Development Agency) had granted him funding for "Strengthening children's and young people's theatre in Southern and Eastern Africa" during 2002. The total sum was approximately 100,000 US$. In Durban, South Africa in February 2002 he met with representatives of 12 African countries, and helped them prepare a regional workshop, which will take place in Kampala, Uganda, in October or November 2001 with 25–30 participants from the region. While there he underlined the importance of their belonging to ASSITEJ. While "on his way" to Durban, he also visited Swaziland, conferring with theatre artists and representatives of ASSITEJ/Swaziland.

He closed his report saying that the Website has been updated, and needs to be used by more of the ASSITEJ Centers.

Members of the EC enthusiastically thanked Malmcrona for his excellent work, Chinfunyise especially on behalf of the African countries.

Membership Applications: While Bangladesh had submitted an application, more information was needed. Malmcrona recommended accepting Nepal's application for a Corresponding Membership, which the EC accepted. Based on his visit, Malmcrona also recommended that Swaziland be accepted as a Full Member, which was done.

Other Reports: Malmcrona reported that a letter had been sent to Peter Brook and a package of materials on World Theatre Day for Children and Young People. He noted that this ASSITEJ Day is being more and more recognized.

He also handed out copies of the new brochure and the ASSITEJ Festival Guide for 2002. He also handed out papers from ASSITEJ/Japan regarding their seminars in July 2001. All these materials could also be found on the ASSITEJ Website.

Financial Report: Treasurer V. Ireland presented a preliminary report that will be passed out at the Seoul congress. She continued to express concern over those centers that have not submitted their dues. There was a brief discussion raised by Schneider on why wealthy centers did not pay higher dues than others.

Report on the Zurich Conference: Schneider reported it a success, and that 120 people had attended it. Both formats and solutions had been discussed. The Secretariat has published a report on the conference in Newsletter No. 13, and there will be a further discussion at the Seoul Congress in 2002. The EC thanked Switzerland for hosting this important event.

Both Bolivia and Argentina as observers presented reports on their respective county's activities in youth theatre. An Argentinean theatre group will perform at the Seoul Congress.

ASSITEJ/France's Concerns: A letter had been sent to the Secretariat from the French Center expressing major concern about theatre for and by children and young people, and in turn professional quality. Oaks and Malmcrona had drafted a letter in response, which they distributed to the EC for comments. Malmcrona stated that the Constitution in Chapter II, Article IV is clear that membership is to consist of *adult* members of the theatre, and supporting organizations and people interested in theatre for children and young people.

A discussion ensued dealing with professionalism and quality in working with theatre for young people. Schneider commented that the variety of work being done by the different ASSITEJ Centers is a known fact, and a discussion of that variety needs to be developed.

Oaks proposed that he and Malmcrona redo the draft of the letter to take in the comments made in the discussion by the members of the EC. This proposal was endorsed by the EC.

XIVth World Congress of ASSITEJ in Seoul, Korea in 2002: Malmcrona reported that the General Assembly would take place at the Sungkyun University from 23-26 July 2002. During this time the Artistic Commission will have organized a Forum Session on 24 July. He also reminded the EC of their meeting prior to the first meeting of the General Assembly. Then the new EC would also meet after the last General Assembly and Election.

After 20 April the Secretariat would distribute the final information (Agenda, Forum, General Assembly, etc.) to all Centers. The Website would also be constantly updated.

The membership fee will remain as is. The new Treasurer will be asked to work out a new fee proposal to present to the Congress in 2002. The EC endorsed this concept.

Kim Woo Ok distributed a new brochure on the Seoul Congress. 10 copies will be sent to each Center. A new and Final Program will be distributed at the General Assembly. He also urged the EC to select performances they wished to see as soon as possible. Performances and workshops must be selected in advance. A Registration Form could be found in the back of the brochure. It could also be down-loaded from the Korean Website.

All performances were to be played for two days, but because the requirements of a small audience, the Swedish and German plays would be presented for three days. Four performances from Seoul would be announced at the end of May.

Upon inquiry Malmcrona said any request for exemption from the Registration Fee of 100 US$ had to be addressed to the Secretariat.

The President and Secretary General of ITI had been invited to attend the General Assembly. Schneider requested that the President and Secretary General of the International Board of Books for Young People (IBBY) be invited. It was decided that Malmcrona would write accordingly. Boucher asked to include a Canadian Party on 24 July, which was happily scheduled.

Oaks expressed the gratitude of the EC and himself for Kim's excellent work.

Working Program: The Bureau and Malmcrona were to work out a draft of the Working Program for 2002–2005. This draft will be presented to the EC for consideration, and then to the General Assembly for approval.

EC Candidates for 2002–2005: No applications for the Secretariat had been received. However, Malmcrona declared he would continue as Secretary General if the Nordic countries could continue their support. Klaus Eggert (Denmark) will run for election as the new Treasurer.

Many of the out-going EC members have declared that they will not seek re-election. Malmcrona reported that so far he had received nominations from Finland, UK, Latvia, Poland, Zambia, and Zimbabwe.

2005 Congress: Rémi Boucher announced that Montreal, Canada would apply to host the XVth World Congress in 2005. Malmcrona reported that Aberystwyth, Wales, UK would probably be applying also.

Honorary Memberships: Michael FitzGerald (Australia) was nominated to be named Honorary President of ASSITEJ. Yoshishige Kagawa presented a letter nominating Kazuto Kurihara (Japan) as an Honorary Member. Malmcrona proposed that Rose-Marie Moudoués be nominated for Honorary Membership. All three nominations were approved, and their names were to be forwarded to the General Assembly for election.

Future Congresses: Malmcrona presented the results of a survey over the site selection of future congresses. Only 15 centers replied, and of those 12 voted to select only the next congress' site at each General Assembly, not two sites in advance. The EC accepted this recommendation.

Commission Reports:

- **C2&C4 – Communication & Publication Commission:** Every center had received two copies of the Annual. Additional copies can be ordered through the Website. Schneider handed out copies of the new brochure, and more can be ordered. Only a few Annuals had been sold, so Mittelstädt asked for contributions to help distribute more. Malmcrona also pointed out that a recent survey of the membership proved that a single language was no problem for the centers, especially considering the appalling costs of translation and printing. The ultimate solution of financing the Annual will be discussed at the next EC meeting and then forwarded to the General Assembly.
- **C3 – Artistic Commission:** The Minutes of their recent meeting will be sent to all members of the Commission for comments, and then to the Secretariat. The final Report will be presented at the General Assembly in Seoul Korea.

There was discussion on the need for more discussions on the performances seen at the Meetings and Congresses, and a wish for more exchanges, less programming, and more seminars.

Schneider presented the final program of the Forum organized by the Artistic Commission to take place in Seoul on July 24th. Titled "Artistic Development of Theater for Children and Young People in the World" the Forum would include four subjects:

> 1. What is the impact of Modern Dance on the Artistic Development of Theater for Children and Young People in the World?" Introducers will be Kim van der Boon and Rémi Boucher.
> 2. "What is the Impact of Theater with Puppets and Objects on the Artistic Development of Theater for Children and Young People?" Introducers will be Ivica Šimić and Peter Rinderknecht.
> 3. "How to Study Theater for Children and Young People?" Introducers will be Wolfgang Schneider and Hagit Rehavi Nikolayevsky.
> 4. "Theater Arts and the Educational System: In Harmony or Conflict?" Introducers will be Vicky Ireland and Hagit Rehavi Nikolayevsky.

Schneider asked for 4 members from the EC to act as moderators. Skotnicki would be the timekeeper on the 3rd Forum. Other timekeepers will be appointed later.

Peter Manscher (Denmark), the Website Manager, pointed out that on the Website, one could search centers, view and download seminar papers, copy the Festival Guide, get copies of past meeting Minutes, among other things. The number of usages is constantly increasing as is the number of centers using it.

- **C7 – Finance & Statute Commission:** Malmcrona showed that the average membership fee paid for 1999 was 215 US$, while the average for 2001 was 232 US$. Oaks and Malmcrona recommended that they keep the current system for the next three years (2003-2005), and that the new Treasurer be asked to work out a new system to present to the General Assembly at the Seoul, Korea Congress in 2002.

Future EC Meetings: Šimić proposed Zagreb, Croatia as the site for a Meeting at the end of October, during the Milk Tooth festival of 22-27 October. The EC accepted this proposal. Brazil submitted a proposal for hosting an EC Meeting in Blumenau, Brazil at the end of August 2003. Denmark proposed hosting a Congress in Helsingør in connection with their festival.

Miscellaneous: Monteiro proposed the writing of a letter in the name of ASSITEJ asserting the right of children to live without poverty, war, and child labor. She wanted it written with assistance from other centers, and present it to the General Assembly. Malmcrona suggested that ASSITEJ/Brazil draft such a letter, and to present it to the EC via e-mail for consideration. This proposal was endorsed. Malmcrona then said the deadline would be 20 April in order to be on the Agenda of the General Assembly.

Šimić reported on the World Interplay Meeting in Townsville, Australia. He also commented on the need to endorse V. Ireland's concerns on script exchange, that ITI has a similar project, and suggested that the two organizations combine their efforts.

There being no further business, the meeting was adjourned, with thanks again to ASSITEJ/Brazil for their support.

2002
XIVth INTERNATIONAL CONGRESS OF ASSITEJ
Seoul, Korea/20-28 July 2002[57]

The Executive Committee Meeting/21 July 2002[58]
Held during the Congress, prior to the opening of the General Assembly.

Present:
President Harold Oaks (USA), VP Wolfgang Schneider (Germany), VP Kim Woo Ok (Korea), VP Kim van der Boon (Netherlands), Sec. Gen. Niclas Malmcrona (Sweden), Treasurer Vicky Ireland (UK).

Members: Lou Westbury (Australia), Luiza Monteiro (Brazil), Rémi Boucher (Canada), Ivica Šimić (Croatia), Hagit Rehavi Nikolayevski (Israel), Yoshishige Kagawa (Japan), Helge Andersen (Norway), Jan Skotnicki (Poland), Peter Rinderknecht (Switzerland), Jackson Ndawula (Uganda), Elisabeth Kabasa (Zimbabwe) representing Tisa Chifunyise.

Counselors: Eckhardt Mittelstädt (Germany), Galya Kolosova (Russia).
Counselor absent: Peter Manscher (Denmark).

Executive Assistant: Rebecca Brinch (Sweden).

ASSITEJ Congress at Seoul, Korea, July 2002

Ann Shaw, Wolfgang Schneider, and Orna Porat celebrating ASSITEJ's 40th Birthday. Courtesy of Wolfgang Schneider.

Three ASSITEJ Presidents: Michael FitzGerald, Wolfgang Schneider, and Harold Oaks at ASSITEJ's 40th Anniversary at the Seoul Congress in 2002. Courtesy of Wolfgang Schneider.

Delegate from China and Wolfgang Schneider at the Seoul Congress.

View of the General Assembly

A celebratory cake cutting (left to right): Kim Woo Ok, Harold Oaks, Shinji Ishizaka (Sec. Genl. ASSITEJ/Japan), Niclas Malmcrona, Yasuaki Yamazaki.

Four Presidents of ASSITEJ: (left to right) Nat Eek, Adolf Shapiro, Michael FitzGerald, and Harold Oaks

Outgoing EC Members: (left to right) Harold Oaks (USA), Helge Andersen (Norway), Lou Westbury (Australia), Vicky Ireland (UK), Yoshishige Kagawa (Japan), Jackson Ndawula (Uganda), Interpreter, Jan Skotnicki (Poland), Galya Kolosova (Russia), Eckhardt Mittelstädt (Germany), (at table) Niclas Malmcrona (Sweden) and Rebecca Brinch (Sweden), (at podium) New President Wolfgang Schneider (Germany).

President Oaks welcomed the EC, and thanked Kim Woo Ok and ASSITEJ/Korea for hosting the World Congress in Seoul.

The Agenda was approved, as were the Minutes from the EC Meeting in Rio de Janeiro.

New Centers: Since the Brazil Meeting, Bangladesh had sent in more information, and Malmcrona recommended that it be accepted as a Full Member.

Benin, West Africa had submitted an application for membership, and on Malmcrona's recommendation, it was approved.

South Africa had submitted an application for membership, and on Malmcrona's recommendation, it was also approved.

Old Business: Malmcrona reported problems in raising the needed funds from the Nordic countries to support the Secretariat for the next 3-year period. However, he stated that the funds raised so far would be sufficient for a new 3-year period.

Andersen stressed the need to start raising funds for the Secretariat for 2005–2008, and recommended it be put on the Working Program Agenda for the next EC.

The list of those dues-paying centers that were approved to vote in the General Assembly would be presented to that body when they first met.

The General Assembly: The EC divided the Agenda for the General Assembly into 3 parts among 3 days, and stressed that the Forum on the 3rd day was open to the public.

- **Candidates for Secretary General and Treasurer:** Malmcrona noted that the EC could give its recommendation to the General Assembly for these offices. Unanimously the EC decided to recommend Niclas Malmcrona as Secretary General and Klaus Eggert as Treasurer.
- **Candidates for the EC:** Malmcrona recommended that Israel, Japan, and Turkey should be added to the nominations for the EC, even though their applications had arrived after the deadline. The EC also decided to review the Constitution to clarify these guidelines. This decision resulted in the appointment of a special Voting Commission.
- **Budget:** Malmcrona recommended that they keep the current budget to be presented to the General Assembly. Then he also recommended that the new EC draft a new budget. The EC approved his recommendations.
- **Voting Commission:** The EC recommended that the General Assembly appoint the following people to a special Voting Commission: Michael Ramløse (Denmark) as Chair; Elisabeth Kabasa (Zimbabwe), Niclas Malmcrona (Sweden), Luiza Monteiro (Brazil), Wolfgang Schneider (Germany), and Rémi Boucher (Canada). This Commission's responsibility was to review and codify the current voting procedures.
- **Honorary Members:** Rose-Marie Moudoués (France) was nominated as an Honorary Member of ASSITEJ, and the EC approved the nomination and forwarded it to the General Assembly for election.

Miscellaneous: V. Ireland reported that there would be a meeting between the British Guild of Writers and ASSITEJ/UK regarding the circulation of scripts. Their joint recommendation will be presented at the next EC meeting.

Oaks announced that Volume VII of "Outstanding Plays for Young Audiences" would be handed out during the General Assembly by ASSITEJ/USA.

Mittelstädt announced that the ASSITEJ/Int'l archives are now on the Internet, and one could view all documents and reports in the Archives. Guidelines for articles and reports to be published on the Website will have to be decided upon.

Van der Boon invited the EC to their International Theatre for Children and Young People's meeting in the Netherlands 23-26 October 2003.

President Oaks officially closed the EC Meeting.

General Assembly/23, 24, and 26 July 2002
President Harold Oaks (USA), VP Wolfgang Schneider (Germany), VP Kim Woo Ok (Korea), VP Kim van der Boon (Netherlands), Sec. Gen. Niclas Malmcrona (Sweden), Treasurer Vicky Ireland (UK).

The Secretary General commented that it was the most countries that had ever attended an ASSITEJ Congress. By region those countries were: Europe: 19; Africa: 7; South and East Asia/Australia/Pacific: 6; North and South America: 3; and Mideast/Central Asia: 2; a grand total of 37 Full Membership countries and 1 country as a Corresponding Center.

The countries represented were: Australia, Austria, Belgium, Brazil, Cameroon, Canada, China, Croatia, Czech Republic, Denmark, Estonia, Finland, Germany, UK, Hungary, Israel, Japan, Kenya, Korea, Latvia, Lithuania, Malaysia (corresponding member), Namibia, Netherlands, Norway, Philippines, Poland, Russia, Sri Lanka, Sweden, Switzerland, Tanzania, Turkey, Uganda, USA, Vietnam, Zambia, and Zimbabwe.

Countries represented by proxies were: Bolivia, France, Georgia, Greece, Iceland, Ireland, Italy, Peru, and Slovenia.

There were three delegates from each country as well as visitors with the delegates. Of the approximately 1,000 total at the Congress, there were 700 from abroad and 300 from Korea. Truly the largest Congress of ASSITEJ to date, and remarkably well organized and executed.[59]

Kim Woo Ok, President of ASSITEJ/Korea welcomed all the delegates to Seoul, Korea, and gave his sincere wishes for a successful event. President Harold Oaks (USA) welcomed all the delegates, and thanked ASSITEJ/Korea for hosting the meeting and ASSITEJ/Japan for assisting. Oaks then read a letter of greetings form Honorary President Ilse Rodenberg (Germany) wishing for "success and good outcomes". Secretary General Niclas Malmcrona (Sweden) expressed his thanks to all centers for coming, and gave a short introduction of each of the EC members present.

Nomination of Voting Commission: This Voting Commission had acted as Tellers at all elections. Their chief function was to verify those Centers with Rights to Vote, and Proxies, and in turn count the ballots and certify the accuracy of the vote. On the recommendation of the EC the General Assembly elected the Voting Commission as follows: Michael Ramløse (Denmark), Eckhardt Mittelstädt (Germany), Robyn Flatt (USA), and Kim van der Boon (Netherlands).

They verified a total of 38 centers with the right to vote, and noted that the total number of votes that could be cast as 139. This made a simple majority of 70 votes.

The following proxies were identified: Iceland to Sweden; Ireland to the UK; Slovenia to Croatia; France to Belgium; Georgia to Russia; Italy to the Netherlands; Bolivia to Brazil; Peru to Canada; and Greece to Germany. The current Constitution only allows one proxy to be given to each center (Art. IX, No. 3).

Approval of Minutes: The General Assembly approved the Minutes as distributed of the last meeting of the General Assembly in 1999 at the Tromsø, Norway World Congress.

EC Report: President Oaks reported, thanking the EC for their hard and efficient work during the past three years. He also expressed his gratitude to the Nordic countries for their financial support of the Secretariat for the past three years. At the same time he thanked Malmcrona for hard work as Secretary General.

Oaks mentioned the seminars organized by the Artistic Commission, and how they have contributed to the work of ASSITEJ/Int'l. He also noted the work in the development of the Website and the Internet, as assisting contacts among all the Centers. He closed his Report with four suggestions:

1. The importance of seeking different ways to fund the Secretariat during the next three years.
2. Old centers need to encourage and offer assistance from the older established centers. They must reach out internationally and nationally. ASSITEJ must develop a global perspective.
3. They must support each other in the political changes, citing Sweden's exchanges with the African countries.
4. Countries must be more responsible in paying their dues.

Secretary General's Report: Malmcrona thanked the membership for their support during the past three years. He also expressed delight that EC Meetings had been in different places around the world, and thanked those Centers for hosting the meetings, at the same time mentioning the seminars/symposia held in Tokyo and Rio de Janeiro during the EC Meetings. He also thanked ASSITEJ/ Germany for organizing and hosting similar events. Furthermore, he expressed his gratitude for the African members attending the Congress, and stressed the need to help take care of these 15 new Centers who had joined ASSITEJ in the last three years.

Malmcrona announced that the Secretariat had only one full-time employee, but that he could be contacted by e-mail at any time. He presented job descriptions for the EC and copies of the Constitution of ASSITEJ. Since several points needed to be clarified, he requested that a commission be appointed for this purpose. He also requested that each EC member have a deputy so that if he or she could not come, the deputy would come instead.

He further reported that there are usually four EC meetings held during each three-year term, approximately 10 to 12 months between them.

- **C2&C4 – Communication & Publication Committee Report:** Malmcrona (Chair) presented the new ASSITEJ brochure. He also mentioned that the World Theatre for Children and Young People Day was being widely recognized, and 2 packages of promotion had been sent to all Centers. The Festival Guide can now be down-loaded from the Website, as well as the ASSITEJ Newsletter.
- **C3 – Artistic Commission Report:** No report.
- **C7 – Financial & Statute Commission Report:** No report.

Site of the 2005 World Congress: There were a total of three invitations sent to the Secretariat from centers which proposed to host the 2005 World Congress: Aberystwyth, Wales, UK; Adelaide, Australia; and Montreal, Canada.

Jeremy Turner (UK) presented the invitation from UK, which was one of the original founding members of ASSITEJ, and has never hosted a World Congress. The proposed Congress would take place in Aberystwyth, Wales, a seaside town on the west of the UK, in June 2005. It offers excellent facilities and people can get everywhere easily by foot and car, or public transport. The University of Wales Aberystwyth is only 10 minutes from the town center, and has excellent facilities for the General Assembly. Aberystwyth has a variety of performance venues. There would be a festival at the same time, and funding is supported by the Assembly Government of Wales, the art council of Wales, and others.

Judy Potter presented the invitation from Adelaide, Australia, which was proposed for the month of March 2005 in Adelaide, a time of early fall. The global concept is important, and Australia has a rare blend of cultures from Asia and the Pacific. Adelaide is known for its children's festivals, and has partnerships over the world. They would offer a multicultural theme, have large and small performances, and different forms of the arts. They have excellent facilities and the necessary funds to support a world congress, as well as the festival.

Rémi Boucher presented the invitation from Canada. The Congress would take place in May 2005 in Montreal, Quebec, Canada. Montreal blends European charm with North American modernity. It features a wealth of cultural and sports activities, and international and world-class gatherings year round. Their hosting the Congress would be featuring: 1) the General Assembly and all its components;

2) a performing arts festival at the same time; 3) a colloquium focusing on major issues of the time; and 4) an exposition available to all ASSITEJ Centers for sharing artistic and theatrical traditions. It has the necessary funding, the support of the Prime Minister of Canada, the Minster of Canadian Heritage, and the Minister of State for International Relationships among others. Their facilities are excellent.

The General Assembly voted as follows: Aberystwyth, Wales: For – 48; Adelaide, Australia: For – 9; and Montreal, Canada: For – 82. Montreal, Canada was elected as the site of the 2005 Congress of ASSITEJ.

The Elections/26 July 2002

Candidates for Election:

Secretary General – Niclas Malmcrona (Sweden).

Treasurer – Klaus Eggert (Denmark).

Executive Committee – Australia (Tony Mack); Austria (Stephan Rabl); Brazil (Luiza Monteiro); Canada (Rémi Boucher); Croatia (Ivica Šimić); Denmark (Klaus Eggert); Finland (Katariina Metsälampi); Germany (Wolfgang Schneider); UK (Jeremy Turner); Israel (Hagit Rehavi Nikolayevski); Japan (Yuriko Kobayashi); Korea (Kim Woo Ok); Latvia (Lauris Gundars); Peru (Myriam Reàtegui); Poland (Jan Skotnicki); Russia (Mikhail Bartenev); Sweden (Niclas Malmcrona); Switzerland (Peter Rinderknecht); Turkey (Tülin Sağlam); Uganda (Jackson Ndawula); USA (Kim Peter Kovac); Zambia (Cheela Chilala); Zimbabwe (Elisabeth Kabasa).

The Elections: The President reminded the delegates that a total of 139 votes could be cast with 70 votes constituting a majority. The votes were as follows:

Secretary General: Niclas Malmcrona: Yes – 136; No – 1; Abstain – 2.
Treasurer: Klaus Eggert: Yes – 123; No – 9; Abstain – 7.
Executive Committee: Those elected were:

		Rank Order
Australia (Tony Mack)	80 votes	12
Austria (Stephan Rabl)	86 votes	7
Brazil (Luiza Monteiro)	101 votes	3
Canada (Rémi Boucher)	100 votes	5
Croatia (Ivica Šimić)	97 votes	6
Denmark (Klaus Eggert)	Already elected	
Germany (Wolfgang Schneider)	124 votes	1
UK (Jeremy Turner)	86 votes	8
Israel (Hagit Rehavi Nikolayevski)	85 votes	10
Japan (Yuriko Kobayashi)	117 votes	2
Korea (Kim Woo Ok)	86 votes	9
Russia (Mikhail Bartenev)	81 votes	11
Sweden (Niclas Malmcrona)	Already elected	
Switzerland (Peter Rinderknecht)	101 votes	4

Those not elected were:60

Finland (Katariina Metsälampi)	67 votes
Latvia (Lauris Gundars)	56 votes
Peru (Myriam Reàtegui)	11 votes
Poland (Jan Skotnicki)	59 votes
Turkey (Tülin Sağlam)	68 votes
Uganda (Jackson Ndawula)	66 votes
USA (Kim Peter Kovac)	69 votes
Zambia (Cheela Chilala)	69 votes

The President: The EC retired and then returned with their nomination for President: Wolfgang Schneider. The vote was: Yes – 112; No – 26; 1 – Absent.

The Vice-Presidents: The EC retired again and returned with four nominations for the Vice-Presidents. The vote was:

Tony Mack (Australia)	95 votes
Luiza Monteiro (Brazil)	102 votes
Rémi Boucher (Canada)	89 votes
Hagit Rehavi Nikolayevski (Israel)	70 votes (not elected)

This concluded the elections.

Honorary Members: The following members had been nominated for Honorary Membership by the EC. The General Assembly elected all of them for that honor.

Honorary President: Michael FitzGerald (Australia)
Member of Honor: Rose-Marie Moudoués (France)
Member of Honor: Orna Porat (Israel)
Member of Honor: Kazuto Kurihara (Japan)
Member of Honor: Ann Shaw (USA)

Miscellaneous: The following members who had died since the last Congress in Tromsø in 1999 were honored with a moment of silence: Penny Bernard (UK); Maria Clara Machado (Brazil); Hans Snoek (Netherlands); and Ray Nüsselein (Denmark).

The remaining items of business consisted of open invitations to various festivals and meetings, announcements of seminars, publications, and personal awards received.

President Schneider closed the Assembly thanking Oaks for his hard work as President during the past three years, another thank you to ASSITEJ/Korea for their excellent Congress and outstanding Festival, to Kim Woo Ok for making it all possible, and special thanks to Niclas Malmcrona for his excellent work.

He thanked the outgoing EC and their counselors for their hard work, and finally the Centers and their delegates for their appearance and their support. He declared the Assembly adjourned.

Performances

While the Congress went on, delegates were able to see 30 performances from Argentina, Australia, China, Belgium, Denmark, Japan, Korea, Philippines, Sri Lanka, Spain, Sweden, UK.

The most successful and popular ones were: a two-person *Hamlet* from Denmark, *The Brave Tin Soldier* from Germany, *Tai-Yo* from Belgium, *It Feels Like Mad* from Sweden, *The Happy Bird* from China, *Tiger Hunt in Mount Kumgang* from Japan, and *The Dwarf Who Loved Snow White* from Korea.

Oaks[61] also cited the Danish *Hamlet*, as well as "*...Walking the Tightrope* which dealt with the death of a grandparent from England, *Tiger Hunt in Mount Kumgang* which was a puppet and live action piece with outstanding innovation and imagination, and *It Feels Like Mad* – a delicacy from Sweden for very young children that was sensitive and lovely."

For the first time delegates were treated to a spectacular production from China – *The Happy Bird*. "It was easily the most lavish of the whole festival – elaborate scenery and costumes and a very large company...having won a prize from the Chinese Propaganda Department in 2001. It told us much about the attitudes and current approaches to...theatre in China."[62] Despite its overwhelming production values, to some of the delegates it seemed dated and "old-fashioned" in approach.

The New Executive Committee Meeting/27 July 2002[63]

Present:
President Wolfgang Schneider (Germany), VP Luiza Montiero (Brazil), VP Rémi Boucher (Canada), VP Tony Mack (Australia), Sec. Gen. Niclas Malmcrona (Sweden), Treasurer Klaus Eggert (Denmark).

Members: Stephen Rabl (Austria), Ivica Šimić (Croatia), Hagit Rehavi-Nikolayevski (Israel), Seini Shimada (Japan) representing Yuriko Kobayashi, Kim Woo Ok (Korea), Mikhail Bartenev (Russia), Peter Rinderknecht (Switzerland), Jeremy Turner (UK).

Executive Assistant: Rebecca Brinch (Sweden).

President Schneider opened the meeting welcoming the members of the new EC. The first item of business was the adoption of the meeting's Agenda.

Secretary General's Report: Malmcrona discussed the new Secretariat in Sweden. There was only one staff member in addition to himself, but he could always be reached by email, and he encouraged all members to visit him when in Stockholm.

He handed out job-descriptions of the EC, copies of the current ASSITEJ Constitution, and requested a committee be formed to codify the Constitution.

He asked all members to fill out informational forms, which he had handed out. They were to be returned to the Secretariat.

He also commented that the Constitution required each EC member to appoint a Deputy to attend the meetings, if the elected member could not. He added that there would be four EC meetings during the next three year term, and they would always receive notice three months ahead of time.

Schneider requested that a list of addresses be produced as soon as possible, and that he would welcome any EC members who might be traveling through Germany.

Commissions: Schneider presented a draft for a Working Program for 2002–2005, which included 22 different guidelines. He proposed that he and the Malmcrona go through that draft, and prepare a paper with suggestions for the Commissions and the Working Program for the EC Meeting in Zagreb in October. He also recognized the need for forums for discussions between meetings, and the need for more regional meetings such as that in Harare, Zimbabwe.

Malmcrona reminded the EC that the Zagreb Meeting would need to establish the Working Program and the Budget for the next term; the two would have to be inter-connected. Schneider and Malmcrona were to prepare these working papers, and to send them to the EC in advance of the meeting.

Co-option of EC Members: The EC had to decide if they were to co-opt a member from the list of candidates for election, as had been done previously. Schneider and others felt strongly that a member from Africa must be co-opted as a full voting member of the EC. The Africans were asked to make a choice, but they refused asking the EC to make that choice. Schneider suggested that if the EC chose to select an additional co-option that member should come from a country other than Europe, since there were already 6 European nations elected. Also a woman would be desirable since 11 of the current members were men, and only 3 women!

There was considerable discussion, and Schneider proposed that they co-opt one member from the African countries. This was passed unanimously. The question of co-opting a second member was postponed to the Zagreb Meeting.

Counselors: Schneider proposed having 3–4 Counselors, including another one from the African countries. Monteiro proposed Katarina Metsälampi (Finland), Tülim Sağlam (Turkey), and Lauris Gundars (Latvia). Nikolayevski proposed Kim Peter Kovac (USA).

Schneider closed the discussion by stating they would finalize these decisions at the Zagreb Meeting: 1) Selecting counselors and another co-option at that meeting; 2) Selecting another Counselor from the African countries; and 3) Naming Eckhardt Mittelstädt as a Counselor now. Schneider's recommendations were approved.

Future EC Meetings: Schneider announced that the next EC Meeting would be in Zagreb, Croatia on 22-27 October 2002.

Malmcrona reported on possible invitations from Denmark and Brazil during 2003. He would contact these centers for further information to be presented at the Zagreb Meeting.

Miscellaneous: Šimič asked the EC to consider giving financial support for the Zagreb Meeting. This question was deferred to Schneider, Malmcrona, and Eggert for consideration.

Schneider thanked Kim Woo Ok and ASSITEJ/Korea for "their kindness and generosity" during their stay in Seoul. He also announced that a letter would be sent on behalf of the EC to all outgoing members, thanking them for their hard work during the last term. Monteiro read letters of congratulations from ASSITEJ/Brazil and ASSITEJ/Bolivia to the new members of the EC.

Schneider officially closed the meeting.

The Status of ASSITEJ as of August 2002

As of 29 August 2002 following the Korean Meeting, the following Centers were listed as active:

Argentina	Cyprus
Australia	Czech Republic
Austria	Denmark
Belgium	Estonia
Australia	France
Bangladesh	Finland
Belgium	Georgia
Benin	Germany
Bolivia	Greece
Brazil	Hungary
Cameroon	Iceland
Canada	Iran
Chile	Ireland
China	Israel
Croatia	Italy
Cuba	Japan

Kenya	Uganda
Korea	Ukraine
Latvia	United Kingdom
Lithuania	United States
Mexico	Uruguay
Mozambique	Uzbekistan
Namibia	Venezuela
Netherlands	Vietnam
New Zealand	Zambia
Nicaragua	Zimbabwe
Norway	
Peru	
Philippines	
Poland	**Corresponding Centers:**
Romania	
Russia	Angola
Slovakia	Congo
Slovenia	India
South Africa	Madagascar
Spain	Malaysia
Sri Lanka	Nepal
Swaziland	Singapore
Sweden	Thailand
Switzerland	Tunisia
Tanzania	
Turkey	

This meant that ASSITEJ/Int'l in 2002 had 68 Full Centers and 9 Corresponding Centers for a total of 77 National Centers.

A SUMMARY OF 1997 – May 2002

1997

In doing research during the year and a half that Ulli Plichta was Secretary General, it became obvious to the authors that the exchange of information was seriously lacking. In some cases Minutes were hard to find and sketchy, so they had to be reconstructed through the haphazard means of comparing correspondence. It was appalling to find such chaos after the precision of Secretary General Ramløse. This part of the history of ASSITEJ was primarily reconstructed from the accurate and voluminous correspondence and records of FitzGerald and Oaks.

In the August 1997 Peruvian EC Meeting the Board was confronted with the growing problem of the conflict between Plichta and the Austrian Center, which in turn endangered the function of the new Secretariat. However, there seemed to be attempted communication between the Secretariat and the Centers, but everyone seemed to be suffering from lack of funding. However, according to the Treasurer there were sufficient funds in reserves to cover any deficit. The new Logo was put in place, and is still used to this day. Zvjezdana Ladika was nominated to be an Honorary Member of ASSITEJ. Keeping the current Austrian situation in mind, they accepted the future meeting dates in Biel, Switzerland in October 1997 and possibly Haifa, Israel in May 1998.

In Biel the deteriorating Austrian situation overshadowed the meeting. Michael Ramløse and Ann Shaw both were recommended to receive Honorary Membership. There was considerable discussion over problems of funding theatre for young people in all countries, and ended with Schneider proposing the writing of a Magna Carta for Children which was to be investigated.

1998

The main problem the EC had to confront in 1998 was the conflicts between the Secretary General and the Austrian Center. The Center disliked her management style and lack of accountability. Accordingly they had withheld the government funds granted to support the ASSITEJ/Austria Center, and following the Biel, Switzerland Meeting in 1997 things were at a complete standstill, despite many efforts at reconciliation. In addition reports and mailings to the ASSITEJ Membership were arriving late or non-existent, the Secretariat was in the home of Plichta, and details were left unattended.

At the April 1998 EC Meeting in Haifa, Israel Plichta tendered her resignation to the EC as Secretary General of ASSITEJ/Int'l without comment. Prior to that meeting the Bureau had thoroughly discussed the problems involved, and in turn made the following recommendations to the EC:

1. To pay 15,500 US$ for expenses and traveling costs from 1 January 1998 to 30 April 1998, conditional on verification by the Treasurer and the President;
2. To establish a "Confidential File" of all pertinent documents of the controversy, which any Members of ASSITEJ can examine while in the presence of either the President or the Treasurer. The file must remain in the ASSITEJ Archives;
3. The President will write the appropriate Austrian authorities reporting the situation, and the satisfactory work done by Ulli Plichta. Also, in accord with the Austrian State Contract with UNESCO, ASSITEJ will ask the Austrian government for reimbursement of 15,500 US$ which they had guaranteed for the Secretary General for the full 3-year term;
4. To accept the resignation of Ulli Plichta.

The EC voted For – 5, Against – 1, Abstention – 2, Absences – 2 on the first recommendation to pay expenses, etc. Then those present voted unanimously For – Numbers 2, 3, and 4.

There was considerably discussion following the vote related to the hiring of a new Secretary General. President FitzGerald recommended that in the future a candidate must 1) present a letter of support from the candidate's National Center, and 2) a letter guaranteeing financial support from the government, the Center, or appropriate organization for the term of that office.

The EC then made a formal offer to Niclas Malmcrona to become ASSITEJ/ Int'l's Executive Officer until the election of a new Secretary General at the 1999 Tromsø Congress. His acceptance was greeted with acclamation and many thanks.

On a note of completion, President FitzGerald received an e-mail of tragic explanation from Henri Brugat of ASSITEJ/Austria dtd 15 January 1999 nine months after Plichta's resignation. It said in part:[64] "I am very sad about these troubles with Ulli. I have lost a friend....I very slowly began to realize that Ulli had trapped herself in a web of half-truths and assertions which I truly think she persuaded herself to believe in...Eventually I began to feel that Ulli was developing a persecution complex..."[When he tried to persuade her to seek help, she presented herself as being a victim of 'mobbing'!] "As I [Brugat] began to realize that I could do very little (apart from being attacked from both sides!) I gave up and resigned from the [Austrian] board."

Brugat continued: "Since this [current] board was elected there have been no further quarrels, ASSITEJ [Austria] work has been conscientiously carried out, cordial contact has been made to those companies which resigned their membership, and we have enjoyed two wonderful meetings…I have no idea what has become of her."

1999

It's astonishing how many times Niclas Malmcrona came to the rescue of ASSITEJ/Int'l. He first began his involvement in 1990 working as Media Officer at the Stockholm World Congress of ASSITEJ/Int'l, and that same year he was elected to the ASSITEJ/Sweden Board where he has served as Treasurer and then as Vice-Chairman.

He was asked to step in as Executive Secretary of ASSITEJ/Int'l immediately after Ulli Plichta resigned in 1998, and then he was elected Secretary General in 1999 at the Tromsø Congress. He served a total of three terms in that position. After he stepped out of those shoes, he went on to help lead his National Center.

Every time he took over the reins of leadership he brought organization, efficiency, intimate knowledge of the electronic processes, knowledge of many languages, and a great deal of persuasive charm.

After two years of turmoil under Plichta, ASSITEJ/Int'l with the Secretariat in Sweden resumed its forward direction under the stewardship of Executive Officer Niclas Malmcrona. It was house-cleaning time at the London EC Meeting in February, and it was all business—no Festival!

There was now considerable unrest in the Artistic Commission. Its Chair, Maurice Yendt (France), had missed their last four meetings, and he was concerned that ASSITEJ was violating the intent of the Constitution.

The new ASSITEJ web-site was up and running, and over the next decade plus, its usefulness in maintaining communication among the centers and potential members and just readers had been immeasurable. The German Center revealed the new *ASSITEJ Annual 1998/1999*, the first of many biennial editions which became an important publication and showcase which promoted the Association with excellent information in a handsome contemporary format.

The ASSITEJ Congress in Tromsø, Norway was not only a true breath of fresh air, but a clearing of the skies of despondency. The accompanying Festival showed many examples of true artistry in theatre for young people, while the deliberations in the General Assembly moved the Association forward once more. FitzGerald and Malmcrona had made a strong leadership team.

Perhaps the most important accomplishment was the presentation of the results of the ASSITEJ Membership Survey by Marjorie MacLean. For the first time in its 34-year history, ASSITEJ/Int'l now had an honest picture of its membership, their personal and professional data, their opinions, and their hopes for the future. It had been a mammoth undertaking, but a wondrous success. The General Assembly accepted the Report and immediately began implementing the 15 primary recommendations. (See the Minutes from the XIIIth World Congress in Tromsø, Norway/10-19 June 1999).

In the elections 13 Centers were elected, and the Bureau became Harold Oaks (President), Wolfgang Schneider, Kim van der Boon, and Kim Woo Ok (Vice-Presidents), Niclas Malmcrona (Secretary General), and Vicky Ireland (Treasurer).

At the Tromsø Congress at 2 am several of us were viewing the "midnight sun" from on top of a mountain overlooking the city. With no return transportation available, Ivica Šimić, the Croatian delegate, announced that he had a cell phone and would call to get a cab for all of us. After our effusive thanks, he placed the call on his Cell Phone and then slyly commented "Of course the cab is coming from Sarajevo!"

2000

Following the Tromsø Congress in 1999, there was considerable interest and action in Africa. Oaks and Malmcrona would be traveling in Africa in July. Zimbabwe had presented a report on Malawi, Lesotho, South Africa, and Zambia who were all in the process of forming centers.

Oaks, Schneider, and Malmcrona continued to be world travelers on behalf of ASSITEJ. They would visit the Congress site in Seoul in 2001, Kim Woo Ok noted that performing companies would be selected on the basis of "experimentation" in their work. Meanwhile the partnership system among the various national centers proved to be very successful, with the stronger centers providing support and advice to the newer and smaller centers.

Orna Porat (Israel) was recommended to be appointed as an Honorary Member, and Tokyo was selected as the site for the next EC meeting in July 2001. Jan Skotnicki (Poland) had sent a letter questioning ASSITEJ's long range goals and future, which was taken seriously and formed the basis for discussions in the next several meetings. (See Appendix N)

2001

As one reads the minutes of these various meetings, one is conscious of the incredible amount of cooperation and collaboration that was going on between the various international centers, focusing on joint festivals and meetings, and joint-artistic ventures.

The correspondence with UNESCO began in 1966 when Moudoués was Secretary General. Now in 2001 its recognition of ASSITEJ was still being pursued, 36 years later! To the writers this recognition is a further waste of time, although the lure of recognition and possible funding from UNESCO to this day is a dangling carrot!

Apparently because of the defeat of Moudoués as Secretary General in 1990, Yendt in a pout and a fit of loyalty to the "old regime" had decided to limit his and France's participation in ASSITEJ/Int'l. Unfortunately he was also Chair of the Artistic Committee.

From the beginning of the establishment of ASSITEJ in 1965, the French Center had opposed any and all theatre companies as members which utilized children as actors, apparently because of some appallingly mediocre children's performing companies in France and Europe.

This difference of opinion had prevented "creative dramatics" from ever becoming part of ASSITEJ, as well as companies casting children as actors and performers. The logic behind this distinction lay in the belief that child performers were incapable of high quality and believability in performance.

The European companies traditionally had been composed of adult actors, albeit some in their late teens or early 20's. In the former Soviet Union small adult actors, called *travesti*, had been professionally trained to perform children's roles in plays. However, many western companies had used children in children's roles, and of course film and television had always used "natural" or professionally trained child actors.

ASSITEJ came of age at the 1987 ASSITEJ Congress in Adelaide, Australia when several productions utilized child actors, including a specially written and professionally designed and directed production which opened the Congress.

Now it seemed time in 2001 to challenge that presumption of 36 years ago. Especially since many of the new members from Australia, Asia, and Africa had companies that had children as performers. Excluding these people from membership would seriously prevent ASSITEJ from truly becoming a "world" association.

In Seoul in May 2001 there was an important meeting of Asian countries. 12 had been invited and 8 attended: Korea, Japan, the Philippines, Thailand, Singapore, Malaysia, Indonesia, and Sri Lanka. Kim Woo Ok urged all of them to attend the Congress in Seoul in 2002.

The world of ASSITEJ was expanding in the East.

2002

At the Rio de Janeiro EC Meeting in March, in anticipation of the Seoul Congress that year, there was the usual request for programming more artistic discussions. After almost every Congress in its critique, there were requests for more artistic discussions and in turn critiques and/or discussions on the productions seen.

On a historic note, at the 1972 Congress in Canada and the USA, 3 professional newspaper and magazine critics presented "live" their reviews of all five of the featured productions: 1 Russian, 1 Romanian, and 3 USA. There was always a lively question and answer period at the end of each critique, and this obviated the need for any delegate to be the first to voice an unpopular or negative opinion unless he or she chose to do so. It must be remembered that this was still the time of "the cold war" and delegations were closely watched as to what they said. While Congresses are now much more open and less polarized, the use of such critics might open discussions much wider.

In Malmcrona's Report to the EC he announced that SIDA had granted him funding in the amount of 100,000 US$ to "...strengthen youth theatre in Southern and Eastern Africa." An incredible financial boost to ASSITEJ/Int'l!

At this Rio de Janeiro Meeting there was considerable discussion on the French concern of using young people as performers, which to them was neither "professional nor artistic"! Oaks and Malmcrona would draft a reply, but it was the opening wedge to further discussion on using young people professionally, which many of the African and Asian nations did!

The Seoul Congress was the second, after Australia, to take in the far east, and accordingly it was the largest ASSITEJ Congress to date, with 700 delegates from abroad, and 300 from Korea! It was remarkably well organized and executed.

No applications for the Secretariat had been received, and Malmcrona stated that he would continue as Secretary General if the Nordic Centers could continue their financial support. Klaus Eggert would run for election as the new Treasurer.

Three Centers had proposed to host the 2005 World Congress: Aberystwyth, Wales, UK; Adelaide, Australia; and Montreal, Canada. The General Assembly chose Montreal.

The Honorary Presidents Award was presented to Suzanne Osten, the Swedish playwright and director.

In the elections at the Congress, the USA Center was not returned to the EC. This was the first time that the USA was not so represented since the founding of ASSITEJ in 1965, but a total of nine nominated countries were not elected. Only 14 seats on the EC were filled by the election, despite the fact that 17 seats were available! Four of the defeated countries lost by only one to three votes! Those were Turkey, USA, Zambia, and Zimbabwe. The remaining five were obviously out of the running.

Kovac wrote to Eek[65] that 23 centers had nominated themselves to be elected to the new EC. This pool included 5 candidates from Africa. The counting of the ballots took 2-3 hours because of the large number of candidates and the fact that the votes were so close, according to the Voting Commission. Michael Ramløse much later wrote: "Because of the extremely close voting – and the shocking outcome of the election – the Commission made go into a number of recounting using various 'methods'. Hence the extra long time."[66]

Kovac also wrote that "When the vote was announced, my memory is that the room went silent. Certainly there was a huge sense of shock. There were no Africans elected, and there had been African representatives on the EC previously. The intent of the voting in the General Assembly may not have been racist, but it was certainly in result."[67]

In 1999 the entire slate of 17 of the EC had been filled, 15 countries plus the two countries of the Secretary General and the Treasurer. In 2002 a total of 23 centers had nominated themselves, but only 12 countries, plus the Secretary General and the Treasurer, were elected. Three slots remained empty!

According to Kovac[68] after the election of the new Bureau, Schneider, "...a bit white-faced and at a loss for words"...stated that the results of the election could not be ignored, but that the result could not be allowed to stand." ASSITEJ was an organization that represented all the inhabited continents."

Kovac, the new representative of ASSITEJ/USA, was the new man in town. He had just replaced former ASSITEJ/Int'l President Harold Oaks as the USA representative, and was an "unknown" to many of the members of the EC. To many delegates familiarity was very important.

There was considerable correspondence among the Board Members of ASSITEJ/USA regarding their Center's failure to be elected to the EC. The discussion centered around whether to accept being a counselor, rather than wanting a co-option which had not been offered.

FitzGerald wrote Eek "Michael Ramløse told me that Denmark and Norway voted for the USA as he believed the other Nords did. He also told me that the Africans have no idea how to block-vote, and are indeed jealous/envious of each other and vote/not accordingly [and are very competitive in their relations with each other[69]]. Which lays the charge right back into Western Europe."[70]

Ramløse felt that the eastern delegates were also responsible. He wrote much later:[71] Malmcrona and he had both advised the African delegates to limit their candidates to two since they both felt there would be no problem in having two African members on the EC. "And it would be wise not to spread the votes as it might endanger all three candidates." Ultimately the African candidates received a total of 204 votes, which could have easily elected two candidates, but not three. "So unfortunately part of the disaster was "self-inflicted" because of a wrongly conceived strategy and lack of political experience in such matters...." Also the Africans tend to be extremely competitive in their relations with each other.

The USA Delegation was both saddened and infuriated by their not being elected. Some members were for immediate withdrawal from ASSITEJ, but wiser heads prevailed with a "wait and see" attitude. Scot Copeland, President of ASSITEJ/USA, wrote: "...whether Wolfgang [Schneider] deliberately stacked the deck against us or if we were the unintended casualty of his stacking the deck to make sure he was president he still stacked the deck and we were left out."

Copeland continued that Harold Oaks was right when he wrote that "The US Center for ASSITEJ should not... EVER... manipulate the process, even to counter the manipulations of others. We can politic, we can lobby, but we best advocate...democracy by insisting on it...even to our own detriment. Should we be asked to proxy, then fine, but we should not solicit proxies."[72][73]

Kovac commented on Copland's letter that "It's important to note that the forces of Euro-Centrism are not just Wolfgang."[74]

The upshot of all the discussions and the emails was that the USA should "suck it up" and accept with honor whatever post might be offered—either as a co-option or a counselor. Kovac put it rather wryly "Sometimes you're the windshield, sometimes you're the bug."[75]

The day following the election at the Congress the EC met and co-opted Cheela Chilala (Zambia) which gave him and Africa a vote. Also, according to Kovac and others when queried, this meeting was very contentious. Several wanted Kovac co-opted also, but Jeremy Turner (UK) stated that he would resign if the EC selected another "Caucasian male."

At the next EC meeting in Zagreb, Croatia in October 2002, they were still unable to achieve consensus on co-option, so they appointed the following three people as Counselors: Tülin Sağlam (Turkey), Jackson Ndawula (Uganda), and Kim Peter Kovac (USA). This temporarily resolved the exclusions which the elections had created. Clearly this election had proved to be one of the most political and contentious in the history of ASSITEJ/Int'l.

In the arts in the USA *Friends* was the top series on television, and Yann Martel's novel *Life of Pi* was a Best Seller, a remarkable story of a youth and a tiger cast adrift together in the ocean in a sailboat, which also had won the British Man Booker Prize. The novel was later made into an Oscar winning movie by Chinese Director Ang Lee in 2012.

PART VIII

BUILDING THE FUTURE

2002
EXECUTIVE COMMITTEE MEETING OF ASSITEJ
Zagreb, Croatia, Europe/22-27 October 2002.[76]

Present:
President Wolfgang Schneider (Germany), VP Luiza Monteiro (Brazil), VP Tony Mack (Australia), Sec. Gen. Niclas Malmcrona (Sweden), Treasurer Klaus Eggert (Denmark).

Members: Stephan Rabl (Austria), Ivica Šimić (Croatia), Hagit Rehavi Nikolayevski (Israel), Yuriko Kobayashi (Japan), Kim Woo Ok (Korea), Mikhail Bartenev (Russia), Jeremy Turner (UK), Cheela Chilala (Zambia).

Counselors: Eckhardt Mittelstädt (Germany), Tülin Sağlam (Turkey).

Members absent: Rémi Boucher (Canada), Peter Rinderknecht (Switzerland).

Executive Assistant: Rebecca Brinch (Sweden).

View of Zagreb, Croatia

Ima Jean Oaks, Zvjezdana Ladika, Harold Oaks. Courtesy of Harold Oaks.

Ivica Šimić, Ima Jean Oaks, Harold Oaks.

Newly elected President Wolfgang Schneider welcomed the EC, and expressed the EC's gratitude to Ivica Šimić and ASSITEJ/Croatia for organizing the meeting. He continued emphasizing that the new EC must increase in numbers, and must find ways to communicate with all national centers.

Ivica Šimić welcomed the EC to Zagreb, and gave his best wishes to them for a successful meeting and enjoyable stay.

Bureau Report: Schneider reported that Malmcrona, Mittelstädt, and he had met a few weeks before this meeting to discuss how to move forward in co-opting new members, and made a draft proposal for Working Groups, based on that passed by the General Assembly.

Co-Options: Malmcrona reported that the African delegation had asked the EC to choose a delegate for co-option on behalf of them. Malmcrona had e-mailed the EC for recommendations, and they had chosen Cheela Chilala (Zambia). Schneider asked for a vote of approval co-opting him as a full voting member of the EC. Chilala was accepted unanimously.

Minutes of the Seoul Congress: In the discussion on the Minutes they requested clarification on the need for the EC to represent as wide a world as possible. They felt one person should be co-opted to represent the USA, that Kim Peter Kovac should be elected as a Counselor, and that Denmark, Wales, and Brazil all had offered to host future EC Meetings.

Report of Secretary General: Malmcrona announced that Newsletter No. 32 had been sent to all centers, since it reported on the Seoul Congress. The ASSITEJ Website had been updated with the new EC profiles, and asked that any corrections be sent to him.

EC Member Luiza Monteiro asked for a letter of support in that they were in danger of losing their ASSITEJ/Brazil office, and Malmcrona had sent such a letter. He had visited with Schneider; Šimić (whose work impressed him very much) will visit a creative workshop organized by ASSITEJ/Uganda and supported by the Swedish International Development Agency; and then he will also visit Rwanda and Kenya. He also hoped to get information about the centers in Bangladesh and India.

The Seoul Congress: Schneider commended Kim Woo Ok and ASSITEJ/Korea for the excellent Congress, and asked Kim to add any remarks he might have. Kim commented that they had strived to have performances that used technology and tradition in new ways. Also, they had received excellent feedback, indicating that the Congress had been a great success. There had been some complaints about the large number of Korean performances. Kobayashi stated that ASSITEJ/Japan was more than satisfied with the Congress and the Festival, and that Kim and his Center had been extremely cooperative.

Schneider asked all the EC Members to send him articles, reports, photos, in order to document the Congress. The Members told him that there were reports and newspaper articles in the following countries: Russia, Zambia, Denmark,

Australia, Brazil, Israel, UK, and Germany. Nikolayevski noted that there was less tradition and more similarities from country to country. Monteiro found the Forums very important, and felt the theme of "cultural identity" needed to be explored further.

The session closed with the President reminding them to send him their articles, etc.

The Following Meeting:

Working Plan – 2002–2005: Schneider opened the discussion by proposing Working Groups instead of Commissions. This nomenclature would link Working Groups with the Working Plan. He also proposed that they all did not have to be working at the same time. He suggested the following WGs:

- No. 1 – Policy
- No. 2 – Networking
- No. 4 – Information
- No. 6 – Catalog of Scripts

Malmcrona suggested the following be added to the list
- No. 7 – Constitution, dues, fund-raising

After the discussion Schneider moved to close the discussion, set up WGs (not Commissions) as follows:

- **WG1** – Policy (adding promoting Centers with their governments on a regular basis)
- **WG2** – Networking
- **WG3** – Artistic
- **WG4** – Information
- **WG5** – Congress
- **WG6** – Catalog of Scripts
- **WG7** – Constitution, dues, and fund-raising

This was endorsed unanimously by the EC with the recommended changes.

Forming of the Working Groups: The President and the Secretary General proposed the following working groups and members:

- **WG1** – Policy – Niclas Malmcrona (Chair), Luiza Monteiro, Kim Woo Ok
- **WG2** – Networking – Wolfgang Schneider (Chair), Ivica Šimić, Yuriko Kobayashi, Stephan Rabl

- **WG4** – Information – Tony Mack (Chair), Klaus Eggert, Eckhardt Mittelstädt (Counselor)
- **WG5** – Archives – Luiza Monteiro (Chair)
- **WG6** – Catalog of Scripts – Jeremy Turner (Chair), Cheela Chilala, Mikhail Bartenev, Hagit Rehavi Nikolayevski
- **WG7** – Constitution, dues, fund-raising – Klaus Eggert (Chair), Niclas Malmcrona, Stephan Rabl

In the discussion that followed, Malmcrona presented a verbal report for Group No. 1; Schneider, a written report for Group No. 2; Mack, a verbal report for Group No. 4; Turner, a verbal report for Group No. 6. All of the Reports were approved.

Turner stressed the need for more practical and artistic activities be added to Group No. 2. They discussed partnerships between centers as a possible solution, but that decision was tabled until the next EC meeting.

Under No. 4 Malmcrona and Eggert recommended that they would see about distributing a Center Address List to *all* members of the Association.

The EC endorsed all the Reports.

Budget for 2002–2005: Eggert presented the Treasurer's Report, which included the ASSITEJ Dues Payment List, the ASSITEJ Accounts for 2002–2005, and a proposed Revised Budget for 2002–2005.

He also reported that the ASSITEJ Account in the UK had been closed, and the funds transferred to a new account in Denmark. Letters have been sent to all Centers informing them of their dues status for 2002. Centers paying less than 500 US$ have been asked to consider raising their dues up to the 500 US$. Argentina had asked to be excused from payment for 2000 and 2001, which the EC granted.

Auditors had not been appointed at the 2002 Congress, but according to the Statutes ASSITEJ must have two such auditors appointed. The question was tabled until the next EC Meeting.

Eggert, Schneider, and Malmcrona were appointed to draft a new budget for 2002–2005 to include the Zagreb recommendations, and to present it at the next EC Meeting.

Several members commended new Treasurer Eggert for his hard and efficient work.

World Day 2003 for Young Audiences: Malmcrona proposed that the Secretariat would print postcards to promote the International Theatre for Children and Young People World Day. These cards with the ASSITEJ Logo would be sent to the national centers to be used as they wished. The package would include a letter from President Schneider, as well as a letter from a theatre personality. Last year's letter was written by Peter Brook.

The EC approved the proposal, and asked that Malmcrona contact Nelson Mandela to see if he would write this year's letter. If not he, then Wole Soyinka.

ASSITEJ Annual 2002/2003: Mack made a presentation re: a recommendation made by WG2. They had proposed to publish the Annual 2002-2003 in May/June of 2003. There would be changes in the format making it more visually appealing, making each country's contribution more visible, more use of performance and festival photos, and selling of advertising. He proposed that this issue focus on cultural identity and globalization. The EC approved the proposal and its changes. Schneider, Malmcrona, and Eggert were assigned to work out a budget.

Co-option of more Members: The discussion centered on whether to co-opt any more members to the EC or not. They had already co-opted Cheela Chilala (Zambia) at the Seoul Congress. Schneider moved to add *no* new co-options. The EC voted in favor of his motion: Yes – 9 votes; No – 1 vote; Abstentions – 3 votes.

Counselors: The EC appointed three Counselors – Jackson Ndawula (Uganda) giving Africa a second voice, and added him to WG2; Tülin Sağlam (Turkey) which gave the Mideast a voice for the first time, and added her to WG6; and Kim Peter Kovac (USA) which gave North America another voice, and added him to WG1.

Future EC Meetings: Malmcrona announced that he had received three proposals to host the next EC Meeting: 1)Aberystwyth, Wales, UK in March 2003; 2) Blumenau, Brazil in September 2003; and 3) Zaanstadt, Netherlands, October 2003. The EC voted unanimously to have the next EC meeting in Aberystwyth, Wales, UK on 25-30 March 2003. The meeting would coincide with "Agor Drysau/ Opening Doors", the Wales International Festival of Theatre for Young Audiences. Malmcrona then commented that the next EC Meeting after Wales would have to be sited out of Europe, preferably in the Asian region, and he added that he would try to present them with a long range listing of future meetings.

In closing the Meetings, President Schneider thanked all the EC Members for coming to Zagreb, and expressed his gratitude to Ivica Šimić and ASSITEJ/ Croatia for all their efforts and generosity.

INTERIM FALLOUT/2002

The decisions to co-opt an African, and appoint three counselors (Turkey, Uganda, and the USA) to the EC ended the election controversy, and fortunately helped ASSITEJ get back to its chosen task.

However, there was continued correspondence among the members of ASSITEJ/USA and some of the international delegates. Of particular interest was the correspondence between Kovac (President, ASSITEJ/USA) and Ann Shaw (ASSITEJ Member of Honor/USA). In part she wrote him giving her evaluation of the election results, and he in turn responded.[77]

Shaw: "I feel certain that these things are the major reasons we lost [the election]:

- Wolfgang Schneider was 'getting back at us' for his failure to win the presidency in Tromsø in 1999. (He is or will try to get back at the Scandinavians for this, too. They FOUGHT for Harold [Oaks as President] because they wanted an honest man whom they could trust.)
- Wolfgang feels the main purpose of ASSITEJ is to raise the artistic standard of theatre for young audiences and although he wouldn't say he thinks we have a ways to go in that regard; he sees us (USA) as another one of those countries who thinks ASSITEJ should be open to all countries and their theatre traditions should be respected, nay valued by other members.
- Wolfgang feels Central Europe has the highest concentration of countries DOING FINE THEATRE, SO CENTRAL EUROPE SHOULD CONTROL ASSITEJ AND SET THE EXAMPLE FOR THE INEXPERIENCED AND UNENLIGHTENED.
- The German Center has lots of money and can host "enlightening" forums and festivals at no cost to those invited except travel. (That cost is minimal for most Europeans and he can supply transportation as well for some. Israel is one center which has received travel assistance from the German Center since the days of the GDR.)"

Kovac: "I prefer to think that instead of "getting back at us", what happened is that they gathered all their troops, but the gathering of the troops eliminated the USA and Africa and was because of the latter—let's be frank—a racist and colonialist result.

- However, I had conversations with Niclas and all three new Vice-Presidents following the meeting of the new EC and here's what I learned and here

are some comments: The EC as a whole was in shock and unable to act much at their meeting the next morning.
- One African (to be chosen by the African delegates) was co-opted [Chilala] and one will be added as a counselor [Nduwula]. [Schneider's assistant Eckhardt Mittelstädt was also added as a counselor.]
- All three Vice-Presidents (Tony Mack, Luiza Monteiro, and Rémi Boucher) told me that the three of them had made a strong case to the EC that they needed the USA on the EC, and my skills and attitude in particular.
- The EC decided to wait until the meeting in Zagreb to add the last co-opt spot and one more counselor.
- If I were offered a position on the EC by co-option I would accept. I don't know if it would be good for the USA to accept a counselor position if one were offered.
- My one small encounter with Wolfgang was that he sort of shook his head and said "One vote!"
- I think the EC, and the Congress as a whole, were shocked because, in effect, the whole election system needs to be changed radically.
- It's very good, in an odd sort of way, I think, that no Africans were voted on – It's significantly more shocking than if one had made it, and it may force the organization to make changes.
- The best thing I said following the result was when I stood with Jackson and Elizabeth and Cheela, the three Africans who also lost, and said "I'm very proud to be a loser with you three." [78]

Kovac's final comment was "I think that some serious changes need to be made in the voting procedures or this is going to happen again. I know we don't want to get into quotas, but a way has to be found to build in diversity within the governing structure."

On 1 January 2002 the biggest currency exchange in the world began with 12 European countries trading their currencies for the new Euro.

Queen Elizabeth II celebrated her Golden Anniversary (50th) on the British throne.

A Beautiful Mind, a film based on the story of mathematical genius John Nash who struggles through life with schizophrenia but nonetheless wins a Nobel Prize, was named Best Picture by the Oscars, while Halle Berry became the first African-American woman to win the Oscar for Best Actress.

In 2003 the top grossing film was *Finding Nemo*, the animated hunt for a very small fish, filled with terror and triumph. A notable best-selling book was *The Kite Runner* by Khaled Hosseini. *CSI* was the top rated TV series in the USA.

2003
EXECUTIVE COMMITTEE MEETING OF ASSITEJ
Aberystwyth, Wales, UK/25-30 March 2003[79]

Present:
President Wolfgang Schneider (Germany), VP Luiza Monteiro (Brazil), VP Rémi Boucher (Canada), VP Tony Mack (Australia), Sec. Gen. Niclas Malmcrona (Sweden), Treasurer Klaus Eggert (Denmark).
    Members: Stephan Rabl (Austria), Ivica Šimić (Croatia), Yuriko Kobayashi (Japan), Kim Woo Ok (Korea), Peter Rinderknecht (Switzerland), Jeremy Turner (UK), Cheela Chilala (Zambia).
    Counselors: Eckhardt Mittelstädt (Germany), Tülin Sağlam (Turkey), Kim Peter Kovac (USA).
    Members absent: Hagit Rehavi Nikolayevski (Israel), Mikhail Bartenev (Russia), Jackson Ndawula (Uganda).
    Executive Assistant: Louise Landin (Sweden).

Aberystwyth, Wales

Wolfgang Schneider welcomes the EC to Wales. All photos courtesy of Wolfgang Schneider.

Members of the EC in disguise at the EC Meeting in Wales in March 2003.

The EC Members revealed: (Front row), Peter Rinderknect, Yuriko Kobayashi, Stephan Rabl, Niclas Malmcrona, (behind him) Kim Peter Kovac, Tülin Sağlam, (behind her) Kim Woo Ok, Luiza Monteiro, (behind her to the right) Rémi Boucher; (second row) Cheela Chilala (w/ mask), Eckhardt Mittelstädt, Ivica Šimić, Wolfgang Schneider, Jeremy Turner, Tony Mack, Klaus Eggert, Louise Landin.

The EC at their meeting.

President Schneider opened the meeting extending the gratitude of the EC to Jeremy Turner and the UK for organizing the meeting. He especially welcomed the new Counselors: Tülin Sağlam (Turkey) and Kim Peter Kovac (USA). Lastly he welcomed all, and expressed hopes for new ideas which would further the future work of ASSITEJ/Int'l. Importantly he commented upon the meeting being held in a time of war [Iraq/USA], and the need to communicate, not with weapons, but with the spirit and the mind.

Turner welcomed the Members and wished them a successful meeting and an enjoyable visit at the AGOR DRYSAU – OPENING DOORS Festival in Wales. He stressed that the EC should put emphasis on the EC initiative to exchange scripts. He also asked that they give advice to the Welsh Arts Council re: "their preparations to create a central bureau for young audiences in Wales".

The Agenda: No Bureau Meeting had been held prior to this meeting. Eggert and Šimić requested that the Iraq War be put on the Agenda as Item # 7e. The Agenda was revised and adopted. Then they approved the Minutes from the Zagreb EC Meeting.

- Approval of the Minutes from the Zagreb EC Meeting
- Report of the Secretary General
- President's Report
- Treasurer's Report
- Report from other EC members
- Report on *International Theatre for Children and Young People World Day 2003*
- Discussion and work on the Working Groups
- Reports from the Working Groups
- Items from the Working Group Reports
- Budget 2001–2005
- Future location of the General Secretariat (from 2005)
- Future EC Meetings
- New Business
- Adjournment

Secretary General's Report: Malmcrona stated that his Report will be posted on the ASSITEJ Website. He emphasized his work with meetings and workshops in South Africa and Uganda.

A new ASSITEJ Festival Guide had been printed but Malmcrona emphasized the need for accurate information meeting the deadlines.

The new ASSITEJ Website (www.assitej.org) is accessible in 7 languages, and is an excellent source of information. He has received many contacts wanting more information on ASSITEJ.

Finally he reported on his visit to the festival in Gijón, Spain, and future trips to China, North Korea, and the USA in the next two months.

Re: contacts with non-members

- **Serbia:** No contact possibly due to the recent assassination of their Prime Minister, and their current state of emergency.
- **Senegal:** Schneider added that Senegal had to establish a national center before there could be any further consideration.
- **Taiwan:** wants extensive contact with practitioners of theatre for young audiences. Re: the possibility of Taiwan becoming a member, Malmcrona was in touch with the UN. It would be difficult for ASSITEJ to endorse Taiwan with China a member of the UN. Turner questioned the importance of abiding by UN guidelines. Both Schneider and Malmcrona will consider the possibility of future co-operation with Taiwan.
- **India:** Chilala reported on a visit to Bangladesh, and raised the question of raising India to Full Membership. Since India is so large, Malmcrona felt that the establishment of a national center was paramount to becoming a Full Member.

There had been the following Membership applications:

- **Macedonia:** Šimić pointed out that the group applying represented a very small portion of their theatres for young people. Before accepting their application, they should encourage their creation of a national center and then apply for membership. Both Šimić and Sağlam offered to contact them and encourage the creation of such a center. The EC decided not to accept them as a member at the time.
- **Jordan:** Malmcrona recommended that the EC accept Jordan as a Full Member, since it was important to have new members from this part of the world. Kovac stated that their theatre was worthy of international recognition. Chilala agreed and said it would encourage countries in North Africa to apply for membership. The EC endorsed Jordan for Full Membership.

Malmcrona's Report closed with a discussion on the ongoing war in Iraq. Eggert expressed a wish that ASSITEJ would make a statement against that ongoing war. Turner and Šimić supported the suggestion. Turner reminded the EC that the war was started on 20 March 2003, the Theatre for Children World Day. Šimić further stated that ASSITEJ should concentrate on helping artists in children's theatre in Iraq. Sağlam mentioned the help Turkey received from national centers after their earthquake. Schneider urged the members to come up with ideas to help the children and the producing theatres after the war. Chilala stated that ASSITEJ should consider what actions it should take in a future, similar situation. Schneider closed the discussion saying that ASSITEJ needed to be more sensitive to this kind of situation, but there was no resolution.

President's Report: Schneider reported on his activities since the Zagreb meeting. In November 2002 he attended a conference at the University of Hildesheim where the topic of integrating theatre for children and youth into the school system was discussed. In May of 2003 the University established a Professorship in Theory and Practice of Theatre for Children and Youth, the first in Germany.

The German and Russian Centers have met establishing communication between artists working in the field of youth theatre. Their next meeting will be in Berlin in May 2003.

He had made a number of speeches as the President of ASSITEJ, attended a symposium in Israel at the University of Tel Aviv, and gave a speech in Russia.

Treasurer's Report: Eggert presented his report explaining that differences in figures were due to the instability of the rate of exchange. While there had been only minor expense, he asked that the WGs plan their future budget requests so they could be included in the overall budget.

So far only 16 Centers had paid their dues. Mack remarked that several centers had not paid their dues in years, and that the EC should consider expelling them. Schneider suggested sending this issue to WG7 for recommendations.

He thanked Eggert for his excellent work.

Reports from the Working Groups: Five of the seven WGs presented reports on their achievements.

WG1 – Policy

Honorary Presidents' Award: This group proposed several changes in the criteria of the Honorary President's Award. The criteria will now clearly state that the Candidates have to be new or emerging artists working in new ways. The EC approved this. They also felt the EC must find more candidates, and should promote the Award by flyers to all centers. Nominations must be submitted to the EC by January 2004, for the Prize of 5,000 US$ to be presented at the opening of the Congress in Canada in 2005.

Theatres of the World – ASSITEJ World Project: This group recommended two designations: *Festivals* (ASSITEJ global festival) and *Projects* (ASSITEJ global projects/seminars). Criteria required would be: 1) at least five (5) countries would participate, and 2) the event must have a duration of at least five (5) days. Boucher suggested changing "global" to "international" since that word was more recognizable. The EC accepted these two designations: *ASSITEJ/Int'l Festival* and *ASSITEJ/Int'l Project.*

In the discussion that followed it was suggested that an EC member attend as an "official" representative, but that choice would be up to the organizers, and such attendance would not be a criterion. Malmcrona asked the Treasurer for funding for a flyer to be sent to all organizers to promote these ASSITEJ designations.

International Theatre for Children and Young People World Day 2004: Malmcrona proposed the mailing of postcards to the centers to remind them of the event, and centers could order the number of cards they could use. He also suggested that a Logo be designed for that Day to be used as needed. Sağlam said the Turkish Center had made good use of the postcards issued that year. Monteiro suggested the printing of Bookmarks also. The EC approved these suggestions.

Finally the EC decided that for the World Day 2004 to ask Augusto Boal, and if not him then Gabriel Garcia Marquez, to write the Important Person Letter which apprised people and organizations of this world event. Malmcrona felt it would be of importance to have someone from South America write such a letter.

ASSITEJ on the War Issue: The WG proposed that ASSITEJ feature a Bulletin Board on their Website where artists could post their thoughts and feelings about the War in Iraq. If done, ASSITEJ very clearly must state that the opinions expressed were not those of the Association. This way ASSITEJ could offer an opportunity for the free exchange of thoughts. This concept was endorsed by the EC, as well as a written statement from the group. All members of the EC who were present signed off on the statement. Copies were to be sent to all centers as well as to the governments of the USA, UK, Australia, Denmark, and Turkey. It was to be posted on the ASSITEJ Website.

The WG also proposed that a delegation of volunteers from the EC primarily be prepared to go to Iraq as soon as possible when the war was over. Its intention was to establish contact with the artists in Iraq and help rebuild the structure of the theatre. Malmcrona stated that preparations for the proposed trip should be initiated right away, so it would be ready to leave as soon as possible.

WG2 – Networking:

Partnership System: Schneider reported on their Partnership System whose object was to integrate all ASSITEJ Members in the international work. At the moment up to one-fifth (1/5) of the centers are "ghost centers", ones that are run by a single member and to which no other members belong. Kim Woo Ok told of his difficulties in networking with China, Japan, and Korea, revealing how difficult it was to start but it ended up with great rewards. The EC determined that the Partnership System would remain in force.

Theatre Art & the Educational System: The Group proposed organizing three one-day conferences on the issue of "studies of theatre for children and young people". Their purpose would be to promote theatre art in educational programs. They proposed the following timetable: Conference # 1: 2003, autumn; Conference # 2: 2004, during an EC meeting; and Conference # 3: 2005, as part of the World Congress in Montreal, Canada. The opinions and ideas from each meeting would be followed up by the next meeting. Three topics were suggested: *Practice Models; Theatre for children as an Education Program;* and *Promotion Guidelines of Good Partnerships.* The EC endorsed the Proposal and the Topics.

Rabl suggested that Conference # 1 be held at the Vienna Festival (24-27 September 2003) in Austria. Apparently no decision was made.

WG4 – Information:

The ASSITEJ Annual: Mittelstädt reported that the Group recommended that the Annual be financed partly by a pre-sales system. They had now received 675 orders from 13 different centers.

Mack showed the EC proposals for a new cover design and one was selected with silver letters, which would make production costs much cheaper.

Mack thanked Kim Woo Ok for his information on the festival in Korea in 2002, and asked the EC to send him photos for the Annual, which would come out in July of 2003. Mittelstädt asked Malmcrona to submit information on the results of the General Assembly at the Seoul Congress in 2002.

The EC endorsed the work of Group No. 4.

WG6 – Catalog of Scripts:

Database of Scripts: Turner reported that the Group proposed creating a central, international database of scripts. The EC should invite each Center to submit synopses for two of the country's best plays. Each center would have to appoint at least two (2) people for the choosing process. Criteria included were: 1) plays must be aimed at audiences of children and young people; and 2) the plays must have been already produced, be widely relevant, and be adaptable to other cultures and languages. The WG has also drawn up a list of what information is required from each of the Centers. Boucher stated that the information must be in English, as well as other languages. The deadline for submitting synopses was November 2003. ASSITEJ would not be responsible for copywriting issues.

Hopefully, by the spring of 2004, the Database will be added to the ASSITEJ Website, and would contain 150 synopses. By the Montreal Congress in 2005, the scripts should be accessible to all Centers. This archival process should be repeated every EC term. The EC endorsed the proposal.

WG 7 – Constitution, Subscription, & Fundraising:

As Treasurer, Eggert stated that 10 Centers have long since failed to pay their dues and had not asked to be excused from payment: Angola, Congo, Cyprus, Mexico, and Nicaragua since 1998 have never paid nor asked to be excused from payment. Since 1999 Chile, Cuba, Ukraine, and Venezuela have never paid nor asked to be excused from payment.

The Group proposed excusing them from payment up to the year 2002. Eggert also proposed that the Secretary General send a letter to each of these Centers, stating that unless they pay this year's dues by 1 September 2003 or ask to be excused from payment, that Center will be expelled automatically. The EC endorsed these proposals and Malmcrona agreed to write the letters.

Eggert also proposed that the EC urge all Centers that can afford to pay more than the minimum fee of 100 US$ to do so, which was endorsed. He also proposed that the Secretary General ask ASSITEJ/Finland to appoint a person to audit the ASSITEJ Treasurer's accounts. This was also endorsed. Then the Auditor for 2005–2008 can be elected by the General Assembly at the Congress in Montreal in 2005.

Constitutional Changes: Eggert stated that since the Constitution requires the election of 2 Auditors, that statement needs to be revised. Also, the Group has commenced a review of the Constitution for proposals of additional changes.

Budget 2001–2005:

Eggert reported that the WG's asked for 29,500 US$ be added to the Budget. Total expenses for the period up to the next Congress in 2005 will be at 40,500 US$. Estimated income for the years from 2003 onwards was 19,000 US$. Malmcrona also reminded the EC that as of July 2005, the Secretariat will no longer be subsidized by ASSITEJ/Sweden. He also questioned who would fund the Secretariat for the 4-month period if the Congress was moved from May to September.

Eggert then proposed that 15,000 US$ be added to the Secretariat's Budget as a contingency. The EC consented to the proposal, and then unanimously adopted the changed budget.

Location of the Next Secretariat:
As Secretary General Malmcrona stated that he will be resigning that position as of the Montreal Congress in 2005, and he felt that position needs to be changed over time. Consequently, the EC must find a new location for the Secretariat as well as a candidate for the Secretary General. He indicated that he and the Nordic Centers will try to assist the EC in every way to find the new location and the Secretary General.

Rabl suggested that the candidates for Secretary General should be on the Agenda within the year, so that he/she can prepare and get funding from his/her country.

Schneider said that this will be referred to WG7, and then thanked Niclas Malmcrona for his excellent work as Secretary General.

Future EC Meetings:
After considerable discussion related to the costs to the members of the EC in attending the meetings, the EC decided that there would be six (6) EC meetings between 2002 and 2005.

Rabl invited the EC to hold its next meeting during the Vienna Festival from 24-28 September 2003, and the EC accepted Rabl's offer.

Malmcrona then presented the following future proposals that had been received by the Secretariat:

- **China** (April 2004): Their Center proposed holding the EC meeting in Beijing. Malmcrona said he would meet with them in April of 2003 for discussion, and Schneider asked the EC to consider this date.
- **Brazil** (September 2004): Schneider stated that ASSITEJ would benefit by holding an EC meeting in a continent other than Europe.
- **South Africa** (September 2004): Schneider reported that this EC meeting would be during the World Congress of the IBBY (International Board on Books for Young People) being held in Cape Town, South Africa. Chilala added that there is considerable interest among the African countries in having an ASSITEJ/Int'l EC meeting in Africa again.
- **Spain** (February 2005): Malmcrona, who had attended a festival in Gijón, stated that ASSITEJ/Spain wished to participate more in the work of ASSITEJ, and Monteiro pointed out that Latin America was interested in attending an EC meeting held in a Spanish-speaking country.
- **Australia** (March 2005): Mack reported that Australia wished to host an EC meeting at this date, and he would look into the possibilities.

The EC approved the next meeting in Austria, and endorsed the proposed plan for future EC meetings.

Miscellaneous:

- Schneider reported meeting with Manfred Bailhardt (current President of ITI) that it would be fruitful for ASSITEJ and ITI to cooperate. Schneider had invited Bailhardt to attend the next meeting of ASSITEJ/Germany, and in turn Bailhardt had invited the EC Members to attend the next ITI Meeting in Mexico in March 2004.
- Rabl said he would like ASSITEJ to become involved in establishing an international network for dance for and by children and young people. Such a network would build a knowledge base on dance, and new ideas would arise from such a network. He asked the EC to support such a network, and the EC consented to the proposal.
- Rinderknecht wished for more discussion of the performances seen at these meetings. He suggested a forum for such reflections be part of the Agenda, and both Boucher and Schneider agreed to such future discussions.
- Mack asked for fewer performances in the future, since there was much work to be done. Schneider agreed to one or two performances per day.

There being no further business, Schneider thanked Turner, the Arad Goch Theatre Company, and the members of the EC for their fruitful meeting, the good discussions, and an enjoyable festival experience.

The meeting was adjourned.

2003
EXECUTIVE COMMITTEE MEETING OF ASSITEJ
Vienna, Austria, Europe/23-28 September 2003[80]

Present:
President Wolfgang Schneider (Germany), VP Tony Mack (Australia), VP Rémi Boucher (Canada), Sec. Gen. Niclas Malmcrona (Sweden), Treasurer Klaus Eggert (Denmark).

Members: Stephan Rabl (Austria), Ivica Šimić (Croatia), Hagit Rehavi Nikolayevski (Israel), Yuriko Kobayashi (Japan), Mikhail Bartenev (Russia), Jeremy Turner (UK), Cheela Chilala (Zambia).

Counselors: Eckhardt Mittelstädt (Germany), Tülin Sağlam (Turkey), Jackson Ndawula (Uganda), and Kim Peter Kovac (USA).

Members absent: Luiza Monteiro (Brazil), Kim Woo Ok (Korea), Peter Rinderknecht (Switzerland).

Executive Assistant: Peter Manscher (Denmark).

Vienna, Austria.

Wolfgang Schneider opened the meeting expressing the EC's gratitude to Stephan Rabl and ASSITEJ/Austria for hosting and organizing the meeting.

Rabl welcomed everyone to Vienna, and informed them of the Festival and the special arrangements: meetings, speeches, performances, the International Peace Act, Peace Sand Action, Children's Paintings exhibition, etc. There would be 76 international guests present at the different events. Schneider reminded the EC of the importance to keep focus on their agenda, despite the tight programming.

Report of the Bureau Meeting: Schneider, Eggert, Malmcrona, and Boucher had discussed the Agenda, and had set up the daily organization. As requested at the Wales EC meeting, a meeting with some of the artists from the Festival would take place on Sept. 26.

Agenda: The Agenda was approved with the removal of 2 items, and Schneider recommended some slight changes in the WGs based on the absence of some of the members. The EC adopted the Agenda as revised. The Minutes of the Wales Meeting were accepted as distributed.

Secretary General's Report:

- **Newsletters:**

During 2003 two Newsletters were sent out to the membership as printed copies, by e-mail, and posted on the Website. A third one will be posted in December. Schneider asked about the Mailing List, and Malmcrona said it went to Centers, e-mailed to 2,000 addresses, and to a number of relevant organizations. He asked all EC Members to send him the e-mail addresses of members in their respective countries.

- **Festival Guide:**

The Festival guide for 2003 was completed in February, and printed copies went to all Centers and other organizations. It was also posted on the Website, and a new lay-out for the next issue is under way.

- **Iraq Statement:**

The statement approved at the Wales Meeting was sent to the governments of the USA, the UK, Denmark, Spain, and Turkey. A formal answer was received from the UK later. It was also sent to all ASSITEJ Centers, and posted on the ASSITEJ Website.

- **New Designations:**

The EC had approved the granting of the official titles – *ASSITEJ/Int'l Festival* and *ASSITEJ/Int'l Project* to such worthy projects as came from the Centers. The title ASSITEJ/Int'l Festival had been granted to two festivals: The CaraVan

– InternationalChildren's Theatre Biennial in West Zealand, Denmark on 17-24 August 2003, and the Theatre Festival for Children and Young People in St. Petersburg, Russia on 18-25 October 2003.

- **Zimbabwe Center:**

This Center was extremely important when establishing the network for the South African countries. The network has enlarged, the situation has changed, and support is now channeled through the Secretariat. Schneider commended Malmcrona on his handling of the project.

- **Contacts with Centers:**

Netherlands: The Center seems no longer to exist. Monteiro has attempted to make contact. Schneider suggested they contact Dennis Meyer from the Netherlands, who was attending the Austrian Festival.

India: Malmcrona informed the EC that former contacts no longer existed. He will work on establishing new contacts.

Taiwan: A festival was organized in Taipei which Kim Woo Ok attended. Schneider had also received correspondence from a theatre in Taipei. Malmcrona will continue the communication.

Macedonia: Šimić had been in contact with Nelko Nelkovski in Skopje, and believes he should continue to find out if their artists there would be interested in establishing a Center. Malmcrona noted that it could only be a Corresponding Center, because of their small number of professional theatres. Šimić was told to continue contact to determine their interest. He also felt it important to include artists and theatres from the Albanian minority. The matter was postponed until the next EC Meeting.

- **Membership Applications:**

Serbia-Montenegro: After many contacts, a Serbia-Montenegro ASSITEJ Center has been founded. Šimić recommended full membership, which the EC endorsed.

Mauritius: Malmcrona reported since Mauritius is a small country with few theatres, it can only become a Corresponding Member. However, he has been in close contact, and will attend a workshop and a meeting in November 2003. The EC accepted them as a Corresponding Member.

Armenia: This country is already a member of ITI, and in their application they stated they have five (5) professional theatres working with theatre for children and young people, and their Center seems well organized. The EC approved Armenia as a Full Member of ASSITEJ.

Rwanda: Malmcrona explained that Rwanda had met the conditions for a Corresponding Center. He with Jackson Ndawula had visited Rwanda in 2002, and met with representatives in Kigali and Butare. Hope Azeda in turn was invited to a festival and a meeting in Sweden, another meeting in Sweden, and a symposium in Denmark. She had also participated in a regional African ASSITEJ meeting in Nairobi in June 2003.

The EC endorsed Rwanda as a Corresponding Center.

Centers Behind in their Dues: The National Centers in Angola, Congo, Cyprus, Mexico, Nicaragua, Chile, Cuba, UK, Uruguay, and Venezuela had been contacted as requested. Malmcrona recommended expelling Chile, Congo, Cuba, Nicaragua, Uruguay, and Venezuela for not having paid their dues, and for not answering the letter sent to them in April regarding their non-payments. Malmcrona reminded the EC of their decision at the Wales Meeting.

The Centers in Angola, Cyprus, UK, and Mexico had been in contact, so they remained as members. Accordingly, the EC expelled Chile, Congo, Cuba, Nicaragua, Uruguay, and Venezuela.

President's Report: Visits: President Schneider had visited the Danish Children's Theatre Festival in Kolding; the Kinder und Jugend Theatertreffen in Berlin, Germany; the Rainbow Festival in St. Petersburg, Russia; the International Directors Seminar in Hanover, Germany; the Prague Quadrennial on Stage Design in the Czech Republic; and the Danish Children's Theatre Festival in Horsens, Denmark. **Publications:** There were a total of four: "Theater for Children and Young People in Austria"; "Theatre for Children and Young People in Sweden"; a publication on Russian Theatre; and the ASSITEJ Yearbook. **Projects:** Schneider was to visit Teheran, Iran with a delegation from the German Foreign Ministry.

Treasurer's Report: Eggert presented the Report, and discussed certain items. When Mack asked for a financial overview, Eggert reported that the Balance to date was 31,120 US$, and if the Budget remained as projected, they would end up with a Balance of 7,001 US$.

The Situation in Iraq: Malmcrona had been in contact with Lina Attel of ASSITEJ/Jordan in Amman to find out how ASSITEJ could distribute children's school books to Iraq. The books would be bought with contributions from the ASSITEJ Centers. He informed the EC that Lina Attel would attend the EC Meeting and share her experiences.

Malmcrona asked the EC for the authority to continue the work for Iraq together with Kim Peter Kovac (USA) and Lina Attel (Jordan), and if necessary find others ways of support.

The EC endorsed his suggestion.

Report from the Working Groups:

- **WG1 – Policy** did not meet
- **WG2 – Networking** – Wolfgang Schneider, Ivica Šimić, Yuriko Kobayashi, and Jackson Ndawula:

The WG suggested hosting meetings with representatives from regions that ASSITEJ/Int'l needed in the organization.

They recommended the continuing of workshops of *Education of Teachers in the field of Theatre for Children and Young People*, conducted by people with experience in that work.

Schneider and Malmcrona will attempt another contact with UNESCO at their November meeting in Paris in hopes of being accepted as a part of the UNESCO Network. Jackson Ndawula will participate in the UNESCO General Assembly.

- **WG3 – Congress** – Kim Peter Kovac, Rémi Boucher, and Niclas Malmcrona:

The WG is working on closer contacts with Latin American countries to find performances from there. They will try to gather as many contacts as possible during 2004.

At the 2005 Congress in Montreal they hope to have 40 performances: 10 Canadian, 10 from the Americas, and 20 from the rest of the world.

A book-fair is planned in connection with the Congress.

There will be organized celebrations, since 2005 celebrates the 40th Anniversary of ASSITEJ!

Boucher argued to change the dates of the next Congress from May to the end of September, because it would be the start of a new theatre season, it would give them more time to fundraise, and more time to prepare the program. There were many festivals in Canada in May, and this would prevent many from attending the Congress. He recommended the dates of 23 September-3 October 2005.

In the succeeding animated discussion Eggert reminded the EC that May had been chosen at the Korean Congress in 2002, and all centers had agreed. Chilala emphasized the importance of choosing dates in relation to choosing shows to perform. Rabl added it was important to promote the Festival now in order to plan ahead. Nikolayevski asked the organizers to respect religious feasts and traditions. Kovac added that a desirable artistic goal would be to have as many continents represented as possible.

Ultimately the EC approved the new dates as 23 September to 3 October 2005, with the General Assembly Meetings during 23-29 September 2005.

- **WG4 – Information** – Tony Mack, Klaus Eggert, and Eckhardt Mittelstädt: They reported that the ASSITEJ Annual had changed its name to the ASSITEJ Yearbook. The number of advance orders, together with the grant of 4,500 US$, would balance the production costs.

  A photo-archive will be established in Australia and Denmark.

  They would like a feed-back from the Membership at the next EC Meeting.

  The WG will undertake a survey of the membership to see if they are satisfied with the information provided by the ASSITEJ Website.

- **WG5 – Archives** did not meet.

- **WG6 – Scripts Catalog** – Jeremy Turner, Hagit Rehavi Nikolayevski, Cheela Chilala, Tülin Sağlam, and Mikhail Bartenev:

  Turner expressed his satisfaction with the catalog draft on the Website, but suggested reducing it to save on costs. He suggested limiting each Center to a maximum of 8 scripts, but to recognize that some centers with cultural differences may have to do it differently.The WG's next step was to finish the Catalog work, and turn it over to the Secretary General. They hoped to be finished in September 2004. Links to other networks would be included in the final product.

Future EC Meetings:

- **Beijing, China:** Malmcrona reported that he had received no confirmation from Beijing. Kim Woo Ok said he would check up on their invitation. Malmcrona suggested that if they did not confirm their invitation, the EC could consider Spain or Jordan.

- **Cape Town, South Africa:** Schneider and Malmcrona had met with Peter Schneck (President of the International Board of Books for Young People – IBBY) to consider an EC meeting in Cape Town at the same time of an IBBY Congress. Malmcrona was directed to write a formal letter to IBBY with the proposals of cooperation. They would aim for a meeting of the EC in Cape Town in September 2004. This would also be discussed at the next regional African ASSITEJ Meeting in November 2003.

- **Spain and Australia:** ASSITEJ/Australia offered to host an EC Meeting in Adelaide on 7-12 March 2005. Mack expressed concern over European dominance in working methods, ways of thinking, and meeting places. Malmcrona stated that all meetings in 1999–2002 were held outside Europe, but the EC is always dependent on invitations. He added that Spain had responded positively to the EC's request for an invitation from them, especially since they had been inactive for some time. Kovac invited Mack to work with him on developing a network in the region.

The EC accepted the invitation from Australia, and decided to work on the other possibilities in 2004.

Adjournment:

President Schneider thanked Stephan Rabl for hosting their meeting, and for presenting an interesting Festival program. He also thanked the EC Members for their attendance, stating that it had been a fruitful meeting with good discussions. The meeting was adjourned.

2004
EXECUTIVE COMMITTEE MEETING OF ASSITEJ
Amman, Jordan, MidEast/13-17 April 2004[81]

Present:
President Wolfgang Schneider (Germany), VP Rémi Boucher (Canada), VP Tony Mack (Australia), Sec. Gen. Niclas Malmcrona (Sweden), Treasurer Klaus Eggert (Denmark).

Members: Stephan Rabl (Austria), Ivica Šimić (Croatia), Yuriko Kobayashi (Japan), Kim Woo Ok (Korea), Peter Rinderknecht (Switzerland), Jeremy Turner (UK), Cheela Chilala (Zambia).

Counselors: Eckhardt Mittelstädt (Germany), Tülin Sağlam (Turkey), Kim Peter Kovac (USA).

Members absent: Luiza Monteiro (Brazil), Hagit Rehavi Nikolayevski (Israel), Mikhail Bartenev (Russia).

Counselor absent: Jackson Ndawula (Uganda).

Executive Assistant: Louise Landin (Sweden).

Amman, Jordan

Members of the EC at their Amman, Jordan meeting in April 2004. (Front row) Eckhardt Mittelstädt, Jeremy Turner, Niclas Malmcrona, (far right) Rémi Boucher, Ivica Šimić; (back row-left to right) Louise Landin, Wolfgang Schneider, Peter Rinderknecht, Klaus Eggert, Cheela Chilala, Kim Peter Kovac. Courtesy of Jeremy Turner.

Wolfgang Schneider, Jeremy Turner, and Cheela Chilala at the EC Meeting in Amman, Jordan. Courtesy of Wolfgang Schneider.

President Schneider opened the Meeting, and extending his thanks to Lina Attel Batayneh and ASSITEJ/Jordan for organizing the meeting. He also welcomed the EC, and expressed his wish for a productive meeting.

Lina Attel Batayneh welcomed everyone to Amman, informed them about the ongoing Amman International Theater Festival, and the special arrangements made for them, including a ceremonial visit with HRH Princess Wijdan Ali. She also thanked Kovac and Malmcrona for assisting the Jordanian Center in preparing the meeting.

The Bureau Meeting

The meeting dealt with the following issues:

- **The Working Plan** needs to be reviewed during this meeting.
- Some items of the Working Plan approved at the Seoul Congress need to be evaluated.
- A printed copy of the Treasurer's Report will now be sent to the EC members in advance of their meetings.

Minutes of the Vienna Meeting: The Minutes were approved as distributed.

Secretary General's Report:

- **Newsletter:** In 2003 Nos. 33, 34, and 35 were written and sent to all Centers in printed copies as well as by e-mail, plus being posted on the Website.
- **Festival Guide:** This was updated in February, posted on the Website and distributed to all Centers and relevant organizations.
- **World Day Package:** The World Day 2004 package was sent to all Centers on a CD, and was posted on the Website. There was little feedback as to whether it was used or not.
- **Beijing, China:** Malmcrona updated the EC on the cancellation of the Meeting that was to be in Beijing, but which was held in Amman, Jordan instead. The new Beijing facility was not ready in time. Kim Woo Ok was informed that the facilities would be ready by the end of April 2005, and will be the site of their International Children's Theatre Festival. This could be an opportunity to have an EC Meeting in China. Malmcrona said he would keep it in mind.
- **Funding of the Secretariat:** The funding for the Secretariat is now provided entirely by the Swedish National Council of Cultural Affairs.

Malmcrona expressed optimism regarding fund-raising for 2005 to support the Secretariat.

News from the Centers:

- Malmcrona announced that the **Italian Center** had now been re-established.
- **Macedonia** had applied for membership, but had been denied. Eggert said that Macedonia qualifies for a Corresponding Center. However, Šimić remarked that those applying have ignored the Albanian theatre companies, which constitute a 30% minority in Macedonia. This is not in accord with the principles of ASSITEJ. Turner agreed. Malmcrona said a decision is difficult when the EC has more information on the country's theatre activities than those applying.

  Šimić had been corresponding with Mr. Nelko Nelkovski, the corresponding applicant, and in the letter Nelkowski asked that Šimić be removed from the EC discussions about their application. Boucher asked if it was in the best interest of ASSITEJ to have an applicant make such a comment. Mittelstädt agreed, but proposed that Macedonia be accepted as a Corresponding Center, but to notify Nelkovski that his behavior was unacceptable to the EC. Chilala added that the Center should be informed that decisions on applications are made by the EC, not Malmcrona and Šimić. There was a visit to the Center before any decision was made.
- **Nigeria:** Malmcrona recommended that the Nigerian Center be given Full Membership. He had been in contact with the applicant, and urged how important the presence of Nigeria was to ASSITEJ.

  In the discussion that followed there was concern about how much information an application can supply. Chilala pointed out that Nigeria had a strong culture and a large population, and is an important presence in ASSITEJ. Eggert urged the new membership, wishing that ASSITEJ would be more positive about accepting new memberships. Schneider suggested inviting the Nigerian Center to the EC Cape town meeting. The EC accepted Nigeria to Full Membership.
- **Albania:** Malmcrona met the Albanian representatives in Sweden, and based on their application, he recommended Albania for Full Membership. Šimić added that considering the political situation, it would be important to have an Albanian presence in ASSITEJ. The EC approved them for Full Membership.

- **India:** Malmcrona had had extensive correspondence with them on establishing a national center. He would be visiting the country in November 2004, and recommended them for Full Membership. Kim Woo Ok added that he would invite India to attend the Asian Theatre Festival for Young Audiences in Seoul, Korea on 17-21 July 2004.
- **Botswana:** An application had yet to be received, but Malmcrona hoped for more information when he visited Africa in June.

The President's Report:

- **Travels and Visits:** Schneider visited Teheran, Iran in October with a delegation from the German Foreign Ministry. He met with local artists, and found their theatre for young people well organized. ASSITEJ must continue its efforts to establish a Center in Iran.
- In November and December he was in Bahia, Brazil helping prepare a World Cultural Forum. In March 2004 he opened the EPOS-Festival, had a meeting with European story tellers, and gave a lecture on *Children's Theatre in Africa* at the University of Hildesheim. He visited Nuremberg, Germany in February for the Panoptical Festival. In a visit to Lichtenstein he found a well organized theatre for young audiences.
- **Projects:** Schneider attended the ITI General Assembly and Congress in Mexico in early June. While there he observed that performances in children's theatre were offered daily. He then proposed that Boucher be appointed the official representative of ASSITEJ/Int'l to the ITI Congress, which the EC approved.
- **Miscellaneous:** Schneider had two books published in 2003: "Theatre for Children and Young People in Russia" (with Gerd Taube), and "Theatre for Children in Sweden". He was also elected as a member of the German Center of ITI, re-elected as Chair of ASSITEJ/Germany, as well as elected to the Committee for Culture in the German Parliament.

The EC accepted his Report.

Treasurer's Report: Eggert announced that the current balance was 31,120 US$, and if the Budget held, the final Balance would be 9,212 US$. He also reported that ASSITEJ/Finland had agreed to audit the ASSITEJ accounts.

He pointed out continuing problems related to the paying of dues by the national centers, along with their failure to ask to be excused from payment. The paying of dues proved a national center's interest in participating in the activities of ASSITEJ, and the least they could do was ask to be excused from payment.

He also asked for advice on how to deal with centers that paid their dues at the last minute so they could vote in the immediate Congress. He recommended that such a center be required to pay 300 US$ between congresses, and that this amount must be paid at least six (6) months prior to the Congress. The EC referred the matter to the WG7 – Statute/Constitutional.

Malmcrona closed the discussion announcing that the Budget would probably have to be adjusted, since the EC was to pay for their upcoming meeting in Cape Town. He would provide more information after his visit in June.

Schneider commended Eggert for his excellent work, and the EC approved his Report.

The Situation in Iraq: In January Malmcrona met with Iraqi theatre workers, and they informed him that Iraqi theatres needed equipment and human resources. They would also like to organize a theatre festival.

Because of the continuing war, the EC did not plan any immediate visits to Iraq. However, the EC was continuing to collect money for the benefit of the children and their theatre in Iraq. So far ASSITEJ had raised almost 4,000 US$, Korea and the USA having made the largest contributions.[82] Malmcrona also stated that it was important to present many small contributions from a large number of countries, rather than a large sum from a few countries. He also proposed that the EC set up a WG to deal specifically with the Iraqi situation.

The EC created a WG of Malmcrona, Kovac, and Turner assisted by Lina Attel Batayneh, and then accepted Malmcrona's Report on Iraq.[83]

Correspondence with ASSITEJ/Argentina: Malmcrona handled out copies of a letter received from Martha Cañete and Liliana Comelio urging the EC to:

- Support Latin-American centers by being present at their seminars and conferences;
- Integrate the Latin-American centers more in the ASSITEJ network;
- Investigate the possibilities of national centers receiving scholarships/ grants;
- Promote ASSITEJ activities in all Latin-American centers;
- Promote support for and respect towards all national centers;
- Support activities that generate a stronger unity between centers; and
- Investigate the possibility of at least one person in the EC, who stays permanently in Central or South America [This was no criticism of Luiza Monteiro, but she did not live in the area on a continuous basis].

There was considerable discussion over the importance of Latin American contacts, but Malmcrona pointed out their lack of correspondence, even though he wrote to them in Spanish. Turner pointed out that all centers had accepted English as the Working Language of ASSITEJ. Schneider noted that some of the region's centers clearly felt left out, and he felt it was necessary for ASSITEJ to make an effort to have them feel a part of ASSITEJ/Int'l. He added that EC Members should try to visit festivals in those regions.

Malmcrona agreed, but he has received only a few such invitations. He plans to make a tour of Latin America in preparation for the next Congress. Boucher added that the Website for the Congress will present information in four (4) languages: English, French, Spanish and Portuguese.

The EC decided to have the WG1 – Policy draft a letter to ASSITEJ/Argentina informing them of their discussion.

World Cultural Forum: Mr. Kofi Annan, UN Secretary General, will be opening the Forum in São Paolo, Brazil from 29 June-3 July. Malmcrona handed copies of a letter from Monteiro suggesting that the forum would provide the EC with the opportunity to make multiple contacts on behalf of ASSITEJ. She also pointed out many regions do not have subsidies for travel.

Schneider hoped the Forum would strengthen the connections between UNESCO and the regional Centers as well its artists. ASSITEJ would provide organizers of the Forum with a list of artists to invite.

Reports of the Working Groups:
WG1 – Policy: Malmcrona reported the following:

- **ASSITEJ/Int'l Projects & Festivals:** The WG reviewed the criteria and felt no changes were needed. However, the letter sent to applicants needed better information, and they demanded better reports from the festivals and projects. These reports should be kept in the Archives in Frankfurt.
- **Use of the name ASSITEJ:** All centers should use the title **ASSITEJ/Country** or in a subtitle **The national center of ASSITEJ.**
- **Honorary President's Award:** The WG recommended the following jury for selection of the Awardee: Klaus Eggert (Denmark) as Chair; Yuriko Kobayashi (Japan); Ivica Šimić (Croatia) – all from the EC; plus Rosemary Myers (Australia) and Etoudi Zeyang (Cameroon). They also proposed Sergio Rios Hennings (Bolivia) as a substitute if either of the two outside appointees could not participate.

Malmcrona clarified some details: The Award of 5,000 US$ is provided by former ASSITEJ President Nat Eek. Also the 3,000 US$ listed in the Budget was to be used for travel expenses for the jury.

WG2 – Networking: Schneider reported as follows:

- The WG would give centers a list of examples of what has been done.
- The WG discussed how, and by whom the name ASSITEJ should be used. Kovac volunteered to have the name Trade Marked. However, upon investigation Kovac found it to be too expensive and impractical, since it had to be done legally and, other than the European Union, done country by country.[84]
- For the Cape Town meeting, the WG proposed a Seminar to integrate the work of ASSITEJ and IBBY. Also a Workshop was proposed to deal with the process of transforming books for children and young people into theatrical form. Workshop leaders were to be: Chilala and Rinderknecht from the EC, Director Hagit Rehavi Nicolayevski, and from outside Henning Mankell (Sweden), and a representative of IBBY.
- Several items of the Seoul Congress' Working Plan were evaluated:

    1. Members were able to meet more frequently by ASSITEJ organizing symposia and meetings.
    2. ASSITEJ had been communicating with USESCO on several levels, and some progress seemed to being made.
    3. The WG felt the partnership system was a successful way to improve communication. Turner stated that EC members needed to co-ordinate their contacts with the Centers, to clarify who was speaking about what and to whom.
    4. Constant reporting of contacts/visits should be made to the Secretariat, and updated every two weeks, and then a list could be distributed to the EC.
    All the Networking WG proposals were approved by the EC.

WG4 – Information: Boucher reported the following on the upcoming Montreal Congress:

- He handed out copies of a brochure and asked all centers to use it to promote the Congress. The Congress Website was <www. montreal-2005. com>, which could also be reached from www.assitej.org.

- Financing was well on its way.
- Seminars and Workshops were being planned in cooperation with local theatre schools as well as the University of Quebec with its program for theatre and film-animation. Boucher asked the EC to provide him with any information on other events that could be held at the Congress. Companies wishing to perform could apply on the Website—the deadline "to be announced." Mack liked the idea of integrating film for young audiences into the program. Schneider stated that the program should also celebrate the 40th Anniversary of ASSITEJ.
- Malmcrona noted that an ASSITEJ Congress required a minimum of two languages to be provided. Boucher proposed English, French, and Spanish. The EC accepted his language proposal. However, the current Brochure said four languages, so Boucher would look into it. Schneider, Malmcrona, and Boucher were to meet in Montreal in November to prepare the Congress.
- The WG will make a survey to evaluate the usefulness of the Website. The Survey will ask about usefulness, what information is wanted, and what ways can they improve the Website.
- The WG felt that the festivals should promote ASSITEJ/Int'l more. A flyer, or banner, could provide festival visitors with information on ASSITEJ. Costs would need to be investigated.
- The ASSITEJ Yearbook showed sales last year exceeded expectations. Mack credited Mittelstädt's successful pre-sale strategy. They had also received great praise for the visual information, the articles, and the overall layout of the yearbook. There was discussion about "too plain" a cover. The WG asked for suggestions. There was need for a change in Title, so changing to Volume Numbering was recommended. Lastly the WG proposed that the Yearbook present different themes.
- There were two alternative dates for the publication of the next Yearbook:
    1. Before the 2005 Congress in Montreal
    2. After the Congress in September

There was considerable discussion over the two possibilities. If it were published after the Congress, it would be immediately out-dated and of little value. If it were published before the Congress, which was the most advantageous solution, there was no money in the Budget for publication. The selling of advertising was the only means of raising the publication money. Schneider accepted the idea of publishing before the Congress, and would investigate the selling of advertising to pay for it.

The publication date was postponed until the next EC Meeting, but Mack and Schneider would start collecting materials for a "before" publication, and the WG was to survey the membership to find out if there was an interest in advertising among the Centers. Schneider thanked Mack his excellent work.

WG6 – Scripts Catalog: Turner requested that the EC urge Centers to submit the forms, and the EC agreed to contact the Centers during June and July. The WG hopes to launch a Script Catalog Website in September before the EC Meeting in Cape Town. Malmcrona added that the countries represented on the EC at the very least should be submitting scripts.

WG7 – Constitution: The WG reported that they had found there were many contradictory details and wording in the current Constitution, and requested that the EC make a proposal at the Congress for some technical re-writing of the Constitution. They would present a more complete list of the details at the next meeting. The EC accepted their Report.

Future EC Meetings:

- **Cape Town, South Africa:** The approved dates were 2-7 September 2004. Arrival on 2 September, departure on 7 September, with a site-seeing day at personal expense on 8 September. The EC will pay for accommodations. The Secretariat will organize the program, and the meeting will be in connection with the Congress of IBBY.
- **Adelaide, Australia:** The EC Meeting was scheduled for 14-19 March 2005, and Mack will provide more detailed information later.

Miscellaneous:

- Šimić reminded the EC to visit the UNIMA Congress in Croatia in June, and Kim Woo Ok would be attending.
- Malmcrona reminded the EC to plan a visit to the African Theatre Festival in Cameroon on 9-14 November 2004.

Schneider expressed his gratitude to the EC for all their hard work, and adjourned the Meeting.

2004
EXECUTIVE COMMITTEE MEETING OF ASSITEJ
Cape Town, South Africa, Africa/2-8 September 2004[85]

Present:
President Wolfgang Schneider (Germany), VP Luiza Monteiro (Brazil), Sec. Gen. Niclas Malmcrona (Sweden).
Members: Stephan Rabl (Austria), Ivica Šimić (Croatia), Hagit Rehavi Nikolayevski (Israel), Yuriko Kobayashi (Japan), Kim Woo Ok (Korea), Mikhail Bartenev (Russia), Peter Rinderknecht (Switzerland), Cheela Chilala (Zambia).
Counselors: Tülin Sağlam (Turkey), Jackson Ndawula (Uganda), Kim Peter Kovac (USA).
Members absent: Tony Mack (Australia), Rémi Boucher (Canada), Klaus Eggert (Denmark), Jeremy Turner (UK).
Counselor absent: Eckhardt Mittelstädt (Germany).
Executive Assistant: Louise Landin (Sweden).

Cape Town, South Africa

Members of the EC at their meeting in Cape Town, South Africa in September 2004.
Courtesy of Wolfgang Schneider.

President Schneider opened the meeting, welcoming the EC members, wished for success, and thanked Malmcrona for organizing the program. Malmcrona expressed the hope that the performances would provide the EC with interesting insights on some of the African styles of theatre for children and youth. Between sessions the EC would be meeting with ASSITEJ Representatives from southern and eastern Africa.

Schneider called for a minute's silence to honor former ASSITEJ members who had recently died: Zvjezdana Ladika (Croatia), Zinovy Korogodsky (Russia), Lowell Swortzell (USA), and Tisa Chifunyise (Zimbabwe).

Schneider said that no Bureau Meeting was held, the Agenda was reviewed, and the Minutes of the Amman Meeting were approved with one minor addition.

Report of the Secretary General: Malmcrona reported on his activities since April 2004.

- **Newsletters:** Newsletter No. 36 had been distributed to all Centers in a printed version as well as by e-mail.
- **Travels and Visits:** Malmcrona visited a festival in Denmark, met with Web-master, and the Nordic Council of Ministers. Along with ASSITEJ/Sweden and ASSITEJ/Mozambique he organized a playwrights workshop as part of the African regional networking project. With Cheela Chilala (Zambia), Frederick Philander (Namibia), and Brenda Toko (South Africa) visited Cape Town in June in preparation for the EC Meeting. Future travels were to include Latvia for the Nordic Baltic Festival, and High Fest in Armenia, a new member of ASSITEJ.
- **ASSITEJ Int'l Festival & Projects:** Approved the following Festivals: *Seoul Performing Arts Festivals for Young Audiences and the Asian Theatre Festival for Young Audiences* – 17-25 July 2004 in South Korea; *Bank*

273

of Scotland Children's Int'l Theatre Festival – 5 May-2 June 2004 in Scotland; *Festival Africain de Théâtre pour l'Enfance et la Jeunesse* on 9-14 November 2004 in Yaoundé, Cameroon; and *Milk Tooth – The 4th Int'l Festival for Children and Young People* on 19-23 October 2004 in Zagreb. Under Projects: *"Welcome to the European Union"*, and A Network for Children's and Young People's Theatre at "Triangel" – the Children's and Young People's Festival in Konstanz, Germany on 13-20 June 2004.

- **New Secretariat:** Mack informed the EC through Malmcrona that he should be able to let them know as to whether he and Australia would be able to stand as a candidate for the office of Secretary General and to host the Secretariat in 2005.
- **Center Correspondence:**

    1. Argentina: At the request of the WG1 – Policy, a letter has been sent to ASSITEJ/Argentina acknowledging their concern for more ASSITEJ promotion in Central and South America. No reply yet.

    2. New Zealand: A letter from Rosie Bolton of ASSITEJ/New Zealand indicated that they are intent on reviving their connections, and would be present at the Montreal Congress. Malmcrona hoped to visit their Center during the EC Meeting in Australia.

    3. Albania: In a letter from Elvira Diamonti and Shkelzen Tuzi of ASSITEJ/Albania, they asked for an ASSITEJ representative to come to a workshop they planned to present in November 2004. They also thanked Šimić for assisting them in establishing their Center.

    4. Peru: Myriam Reàtegui of ASSITEJ/Peru wrote regretting that her Center was not able to finance a presence at the World Cultural Forum in Brazil, but they are striving to strength their Center. She also invited President Schneider to meet in Lima in March 2005 for discussion on ASSITEJ's Latin American presence.

    5. Venezuela: Malmcrona reported that apparently their Center had been re-established, and he had asked them to submit a new application for membership.

    6. Macedonia: A new application had been submitted, signed by professional theatre companies, which fulfilled the criteria for a Full Membership. The EC accepted Macedonia to Full Membership in ASSITEJ.

    7. Botswana: Malmcrona and Bernt Höglund of ASSITEJ/Sweden recently met with representatives from Botswana at their capital Gaborone. While they have a small population, they do provide theatre for young audiences. Becoming a member of ASSITEJ would facilitate their work and give status to them with their government. Chilala agreed, and hoped that such a co-operation would have a beneficial effect within the field of youth theatre in Africa. Malmcrona recommended them as a Corresponding Center, and the EC approved their application.

8. Others: Malmcrona reported on a Partnership Project between the ASSITEJ Centers of Jordan, Denmark, and Sweden. Kovac offered to add his contacts with Algeria and Israel.

Discussion on the Secretary General's Report centered on non-English-speaking Centers. Chilala said he often encourages French-speaking centers to establish contacts with France or French Canada. Schneider closed the discussion suggesting that while preparing the Congress, the EC should address strategies for expanding the global work of ASSITEJ.

The EC accepted the Report of Secretary General.

Report of the President:
- **Travels and Visits:** President Schneider visited the "Welcome to the European Union" Conference in Konstanz, Germany hosted by "Triangel", which welcomed ten new members. In Holon, Israel, he attended the opening ceremony of the "Mediatheque", whose facilities will provide workshops on the production of youth theatre as well as a library of children's books. The building will be the new location of ASSITEJ/Israel. In Stuttgart, Germany he visited the opening ceremony of the "Junges Ensemble", whose establishment Peter Rinderknecht stated will have a dynamic effect on children's theatre throughout the region. In Cork, Ireland Schneider gave a lecture on Arts and Education at the Annual Meeting of the European Network of Arts Organizations for Children and Young People. Finally, in St. Petersburg, Russia he gave a lecture on theatre for children at their annual Conference of the International Federation for Theatre Research.
- **Miscellaneous:** Schneider handed out copies of an article by Ian Herbert, President of the International Association of Theatre Critics, which described ITI as an organization in a state of crisis, while commending them for launching a Website which provides international information on world theatre. The next ITI Congress will be in the Philippines in May 2006. Schneider stated that it would be important for ASSITEJ and the EC to take part in that Congress in order to strengthen the work and reputation of ASSITEJ/Int'l.

The EC accepted the Report of the President.

Treasurer's Report: In Klaus Eggert's printed Report which Malmcrona handed out, Eggert had noted that the majority of the Centers had yet to pay their dues. Malmcrona again reminded the EC that only those who had paid their dues could vote at the next Congress. Dues amounted to 300 US$ and must be paid by March 2005. A letter will be sent to all Centers to remind them of these facts. Eggert also had altered the Budget to finance the Cape Town Meeting. The EC accepted the Treasurer's Report with the Budget changes.

World Cultural Forum & Festivals: Monteiro reported on the UNESCO World Cultural Forum held in São Paolo, Brazil, which had been successful for the future work of theatre for young audiences in Latin America. She had made contacts with representatives from ASSITEJ/Spain and ASSITEJ/Mozambique, and she was particularly grateful that Schneider and Joachim Bernauer, Latin American Cultural Director of the Goethe Institute, were present.

Festivals in Asia:

- Kim Woo Ok reported on the Asian Theatre Festival in Beijing, China in July 2004 with participants from China, Japan, Korea, Malaysia, Nepal, and Taiwan. Their next Festival will be in late May 2005.
- He also reported on the Taipei Festival of August 2004, which was Taiwan's fifth children's theatre festival. Audiences of 300,000 attended the Festival, which offered outdoor performances from Beijing, Hong Kong, Seoul, Shanghai, and Taipei. Next year they have plans for a networking project in Asia. Malmcrona reminded the EC of their discussions about accepting Taiwan as a member. Schneider recommended that because of political complications, ASSITEJ should consider accepting Taiwan as a Corresponding Member. However, Schneider emphasized that ASSITEJ must not be influenced by political issues.

The Cape Town Seminar with IBBY: During the seminar Schneider urged the EC to come up with ideas for new experiences in the fields of the arts for young people. Kovac commented that young people were tending to read books rather than go to the theatre. He recommended that ASSITEJ/Int'l consider urging more theatrical adaptations of books to bring young audiences into the theatre. He also felt that it would be interesting to see different adaptations of the same book.

The Situation in Iraq: Malmcrona reported that no further action could be taken until the situation stabilized, but he handed out copies of a list of donations made by the Centers. Ndawula suggested the EC set up these as unrestricted funds for severe conflict areas anywhere in the world, and Kovac agreed. However, the setting up for any such fund would call for a thorough investigation into the Constitution of ASSITEJ, and as such could not be resolved at the moment. However, Malmcrona promised to look into the possibility.

Reports of the Working Groups:

WG1 – Policy: Malmcrona reported the following:

- ASSITEJ/Denmark proposed to organize a Children's Theatre Relay for World Day 2005. The costs would be covered by the Secretariat, and the work would be carried out by those two groups. They also proposed that the World Day Message should be an Asian. Yuriko Kobayashi recommended Kensaburo Oe, the Japanese recipient of the Nobel Prize. Kim Woo Ok recommended Kim Dae Joong of Korea, recipient of the Nobel Peace Prize. Malmcrona also suggested that the EC come up with a design for a symbolic "torch" for the Theatre Relay.
- The WG proposed that the Honorary President's Award should be given at the ASSITEJ Birthday party at the Montreal Congress. Kovac was asked to discuss this with Ann Shaw and Nat Eek, and the EC approved the proposal.

WG2 – Networking: The WG proposed the following:

- Networking within ASSITEJ should reflect the regional meetings of the Association. Further contacts should be made with Asia. They should form a WG to establish a Network in Latin America, and Monteiro, Kovac, Boucher, and Malmcrona were to meet to make such a proposal at the next EC Meeting.
- The WG recommended further contacts with ITI, and ASSITEJ/Int'l should have a presence at the ITI Congress in the Philippines in 2006. Schneider stated that further contacts would give ASSITEJ a chance to take part in theatre seminars, discussions about theatre systems, etc. Also, many ASSITEJ Centers are already members of ITI.
- Šimić informed the EC that the ITI Int'l Playwright's Forum has invited ASSITEJ to join them in their Int'l Playwriting Competition 2006, under playwrights writing "plays for the young". The Award would be named jointly between ITI and ASSITEJ.

- The EC appointed Šimić, Rinderknecht, and Malmcrona to establish further contacts with ITI. Šimić would represent ASSITEJ in the playwriting competition, Malmcrona would examine possible financial issues, and the WG would discuss criteria for the competition.
- The WG proposed: At the Montreal Congress a Forum take place that could include: how to create/transfer plays from literature; the relationship between theatre and schools; and discussions on the institutionalization of children's theatre. Rabl added that another topic would be "new models of theatre houses". The WG also proposed that the Congress should offer a special location and time each day for playwrights, and perhaps to have them read short selections from their plays. The Catalog of Scripts could be promoted at this time. Malmcrona urged the WG to check with Boucher to see if there would be space in the schedule, and then report to the EC.
- Also, the following was announced for the Montreal Congress: the International Association of Theatre Critics would meet parallel to the ASSITEJ Congress. Schneider also mentioned that the EC of the International Federation for Theatre Research will be meeting in Montreal at this same time.
- The WG also proposed that Rinderknecht produce an experimental play based on the worst possible way to communicate with a young audience, and its aim would be to start discussion on quality in theatre for youth. Monteiro felt it was a risky venture since different cultures had different values, with corresponding differences in what constituted quality.
- Mack stated that the next Yearbook depends on funds being made available during the current term of the EC. Schneider also reported the following regarding the Yearbook: the layout was in progress; the content will reflect the 80 member centers; and the Yearbook will have 2–3 different themes. The WG had proposed that funding would come from pre-sales and 10 pages of advertisements. The proposed charges were: Full Page – 600 US$; Half Page – 350 US$, and Quarter Page – 200 US$. Mack and Eggert were to discuss this recommendation. For presales Kovac suggested that there be a checking box in the Congress Application that says "I wish to receive the Yearbook for the amount of 10 US$."

The EC approved the various proposals as required.

WG6 – Catalog of Scripts:

- At the request of the **WG–6** Malmcrona was to send e-mails to all Centers urging their submission of scripts. If the budget allowed, a Brochure would be issued informing the Centers of the Catalog of Scripts and the Web-catalog, which will be launched soon. Kovac added that the USA Center would contribute with their Catalog of Best Plays. The EC approved the Report.

WG7 – Archives:

- Schneider proposed that the EC form a WG of Monteiro, Mittelstädt, and Schneider to meet in Frankfurt to investigate how to make the Archives more accessible and how to collect more material. Monteiro noted that the Archives lacked artistic material, and primarily consisted of protocols, etc. The EC accepted their Report.

Future Meetings of the EC:

- **Adelaide, Australia:** The EC Meeting had been confirmed for 7-12 of March 2005. Arrival will be on 6 March, and departure on 12 March. Mack will contact individual Members to see if they could attend meetings with Australian theatre companies on 14 and 15 of March.
- **Meetings for 2005–2008:** Malmcrona stated it was most important to have the new EC Meeting as soon as possible after the Congress. Possible alternate locations were Denmark, Spain, or the UK. The EC should look for further possibilities. To facilitate the work of the Secretariat, the EC should be sure that all future meetings be organized by the Center at the site.

Miscellaneous:

- ASSITEJ/Spain had been asked to translate the Secretary General's Report from English into Spanish. Kovac offered his assistance, since his Center had many members who were fluent in Spanish, depending on the quantities of material needing translation.
- For a future project within ASSITEJ, Monteiro suggested linking Brazilian theatre groups that work in the field of health education (e.g. AIDS

campaigns) with African theatre companies. She also suggested a tour in Latin America to strengthen the name and work of ASSITEJ.
- Rabl wished to make a presentation at the next meeting on how to promote the work of ASSITEJ. Kovac offered his assistance, since his Center was discussing the same matter.

Schneider thanked all the participating EC Members for their good work, and adjourned the meeting.

2005
EXECUTIVE COMMITTEE MEETING OF ASSITEJ
Adelaide, Australia/6-12 March 2005

Present:
President Wolfgang Schneider (Germany), VP Rémi Boucher (Canada), VP Luiza Monteiro (Brazil), VP Tony Mack (Australia), Sec. Gen. Niclas Malmcrona (Sweden), Treasurer Klaus Eggert (Denmark).
Members: Stephan Rabl (Austria), Ivica Šimić (Croatia), Nava Bik/Deputy (Israel), Yuriko Kobayashi (Japan), Kim Woo Ok (Korea), Cheela Chilala (Zambia).
Counselors: Eckhardt Mittelstädt (Germany), Tülin Sağlam (Turkey), Jackson Ndawula (Uganda), Kim Peter Kovac (USA).
Members absent: Hagit Rehavi Nikolayevski (Israel), Mikhail Bartenev (Russia), Peter Rinderknecht (Switzerland), Jeremy Turner (UK).
Executive Assistant: Louise Landin (Sweden).

Adelaide, Australia

President Schneider opened the meeting, welcoming the EC members, and wished for success of the meeting.

Schneider said that no Bureau meeting had been held, the Agenda was reviewed, and the Minutes of the Cape Town Meeting were approved with two small additions.

Secretary General's Report: Malmcrona reported on the following activities:

- **World Day:** The EC had asked Nobel Prize Winner Kim Dae Joong to write the World Day Message for 2004, but he declined. Accordingly Playwright and Artistic Director Volker Ludwig (Germany) was asked to write it. Malmcrona felt in the future that young practitioners within the field of youth theatre should be asked to write the messages. This would invigorate the entire process.
- **Festival Guide:** Since the response had been poor, Malmcrona asked all members to supply him with updated information.
- **Iraqi Statement:** Malmcrona with Lina Attel have decided to approach a cultural center in Baghdad, which has close contacts with France.
- **Catalog of Scripts:** Malmcrona had reminded all Centers to be sending their scripts forward. The Website for "Catalog of Scripts" was officially launched in December 2004, presenting 46 scripts from 8 countries.
- **Co-operation with ITI:** Malmcrona thanked Šimić for his extensive work in communicating with ITI, since ASSITEJ and ITI were co-sponsoring the International Playwriting Competition 2006. In turn Šimić thanked Rinderknecht, Henry Favory, and Chair Lia Caravias for their work.
- **Travels and Visits:** Malmcrona listed the following: a trip to Jordan, Syria, and Lebanon as part of the ASSITEJ Partnership; Syria and Lebanon plan to apply for membership; Syrian theatre is supported by the government, while theatre in Lebanon relies on the support of commercial interests.
- **Argentinean Decision:** In October Malmcrona had received numerous e-mails from South American theatres regarding a Festival in Cordova, to which they had been invited by ASSITEJ/Argentina. The Festival never took place, the companies found themselves stranded at the location, without money or a place to stay. The office of ASSITEJ/Argentina could not be reached. Their conduct had obviously damaged the reputation of ASSITEJ/Int'l.

Malmcrona e-mailed the EC, and the Bureau recommended expelling ASSITEJ/Argentina from ASSITEJ/Int'l. By letter Malmcrona informed the Argentinean Center of their expulsion, which they could appeal to the General Assembly. He also wrote the theatre companies involved explaining and regretting the appalling situation.

The EC unanimously approved the decision.

- **Contacts with Centers:** Malmcrona reported on good communication with the Centers via Newsletters and the celebration of World Day 2005. Mittelstädt reported that the ASSITEJ Centers of Belgium, France, Portugal, and Spain all expressed great interest in taking part in the international work of ASSITEJ.
- **Contacts with Non-Member Countries:** Malmcrona said he hoped soon to get applications for membership from Chile and Uruguay, and added that the EC would be able to endorse new members in Montreal, at its last meeting before the Congress.
- **Membership Applications:** The Secretariat had received an application for a new membership from ATINA (The Argentinean International Theatre Association), and according to Malmcrona they had fulfilled the requirements for a full membership, and had expressed interest previously on several occasions. He recommended their acceptance accordingly. He also recommended the acceptance of the Lichtenstein application. The EC approved Full Memberships for both Centers. There were now a total of 78 National Centers.
- **World Day Relay:** The Relay was postponed until 2006, which would give the Secretariat sufficient time for preparation.

Honorary President's Award: Eggert reported on the decision of the Jury (Eggert, Kobayashi, Šimić, Etoudi Zeyang, and Rosemary Myers). There were five (5) Nominees: Kim Woo Ok (Korea), Zeal Theatre (Australia), Peter Brosius (USA), János Nóvak (Hungary), and Haluk Yuce (Turkey). The recipients would be announced by Honorary President Eek at the ASSITEJ 40th Anniversary Party at the Montreal Congress. All Centers will be informed of the five Nominees. The recipients' names would only be announced at the ceremony.

The Jury wished for the future of the Award to be discussed at the General Assembly. Eggert suggested that perhaps the Award could be replaced by an "International Award", recognizing theatre practitioners/administrators who spread their work for young people at an international level. Kovac commented that it is important to award and encourage persons who broaden their work beyond regional/national boundaries. The Jury was also disappointed in the low number of Nominees. They were also concerned about the quantity and quality of supporting materials which varied greatly, which complicated the process of fair evaluation. The Jury felt there needed to be stricter guidelines. Malmcrona agreed, adding that the EC needs to discuss this. Schneider thanked the Jury for its work, and the Zeal Theatre and Dr. Kim Woo Ok split the Award at the Montreal Congress.

President's Report: President Schneider handed out a copy of his Report since the last meeting in September, along with written versions of the speeches he gave during 2004.

Treasurer's Report: Eggert provided copies of the 2002–2005 Budget to all EC Members.

- The Budget has no more money to spend this term, and all fees for 2005 will go into accounts for the new EC.
- Each center needs to have paid 300 US$ since the last Congress in order to vote. 1 July is the deadline. After that Eggert will give the EC an updated list of those countries who have yet to pay their dues.
- Eggert asked the EC how to treat centers who paid the full fee, but only 84 US$ reached the Treasurer as a result of bank charges. He recommended accepting it as full payment since that was the Center's intent. The EC agreed. He also urged that the EC consider whether a higher membership fee and/or a currency fee should be charged. This decision should be made by the General Assembly.
- **Uganda Request:** Uganda had requested that it be excused from paying its dues for 2004 and 2005, due to severe financial restrictions in its country. Eggert recommended to the EC that this be granted. Approving this request would still give them the right to vote. Malmcrona opposed this, and asked to postpone the decision so that he could discuss it both with Chilala and Ndawula, and at the upcoming regional meeting in Zambia in June. The EC agreed with Malmcrona's request.
- **Budget for 2005–2008:** Eggert wished to present a Preliminary Budget for 2005–2008 to the General Assembly. Schneider felt he should just present the Budget Expenditures for 2002–2005. The new EC could draw up a Budget after establishing the Working Plan for 2005–2008. The EC decided to have Eggert present an estimate of expenditures for the next term to the General Assembly.
- **Auditor:** Eggert reminded the EC of the need to appoint an Auditor of the Accounts for approval by the General Assembly.

- **Fund-raising & Marketing:** Malmcrona stated that the EC must solve how to fund the Secretariat for the next term. Since 1990 the Secretariat had been granted 500,000 US$ from the Nordic countries. In the discussion that followed Eggert recommended that ASSITEJ raise money strictly on regional/national levels. Kovac suggested that there must be international granting agencies. Malmcrona said that the EC should set up a WG to deal with fund-raising and marketing. The EC approved this suggestion.
- **Yearbook:** Mack noted with the drop in the currency rate there would be an extra 1,800 US$ available to print and market the Yearbook.

This closed the Treasurer's Report and Schneider thanked Eggert for his excellent work with the Accounts.

New Voting System: Malmcrona presented Michael Ramløse's suggestions for a new voting system for the next Congress, copies of which had been sent to all EC members. The proposal tended to speed up the process and make it more reliable, but would not require a constitutional change. [That would not come until 2011 in the Copenhagen/Malmö Congress.] The EC formed a WG of Mittelstädt, Malmcrona, and Ramløse to peruse the proposal, and then make a decision before the General Assembly meets.

Essentially they were trying to eliminate the possibility of future results similar to the vote taken in Seoul, Korea in 2002, which eliminated all the African candidates and the USA. The European dominance was obvious, but the organization lacked diversity. Kovac pointed out the problem of achieving diversity without imposing quotas, but no one seemed to want to change the current procedure. All decisions according to the Constitution were made by a simple majority, and this was not to be changed.

The Future Secretariat: Malmcrona stated that the most effective solution was to out-source the routine work of the Secretariat, such as Guides, Translations, Catalog of Scripts, etc. Kovac suggested separating the routine chores for a staff to handle, letting the Secretary General concentrate on networking and creating and maintaining contacts for the benefit of ASSITEJ.

Boucher suggested setting up the Main Office in Montreal, for which the city would provide the funding as well as the staff. The EC would present Montreal with a 3-year plan for the Office and work out the details. Eggert suggested that such an office should also take over the accounts. Kovac and Schneider agreed.

Schneider felt it was important to maintain the Secretariat's current professionalism, as well as having a Secretary General skilled in Networking. He noted that ASSITEJ/Int'l had indeed been fortunate to have a Full-time Secretary General financed by the Nordic countries and the National Council of Cultural Affairs of Sweden.

The EC asked Malmcrona to stand for the position of Secretary General if no other candidate came forward. Boucher was to investigate the possibility of moving the Head Office to Montreal.

The Montreal Congress – 2005: Boucher reported as follows:
- The Congress would run from 20-26 September 2005. Delegates were to arrive on the 19th, and the EC would meet on the 20th. The General Assembly would meet on the 26th; Forums were to be held on the 23rd; the Anniversary Party would be held on the 25th. Registration would begin on 22 April. The Website was: www. montreal-2005.com.
- *Les Coups de Théâtre* (the World Festival of the Arts for Young Audiences) would run 20-30 September.

The EC expressed satisfaction with the arrangements so far.

The Working Groups:

WG2 – Networking: At the Congress EC members would present topics on 1) how to create dramatic literature; 2) how to develop partnerships between theatre arts and the educational system; and 3) how to organize Festivals and set up Theatre Centers. Theatre Criticism would be a joint venture with AICT, and Creating Dramatic Literature would be a joint venture with IBBY. All the Forums would be in the round, in order to allow everyone to participate, and would be limited to 50 persons. If there was a larger enrollment, the Forum would be split up into two sections. Boucher set a deadline of 15 April to receive names of participants, chair persons, and topics, since the Congress Website would be launched on 22 April.

WG4 – Information: Mack reported that the Yearbook will be included in the Registration Fee for the Congress, The projected income for the Yearbook was 12,930 US$, with a safety margin of 3,000 US$.

- **Timeline:** Collecting material should be finished by May. A first Draft would be done 1 July; printing would take place in August; and the Yearbook would be finished around 8 September, just 2 weeks before the Congress.
- **Content:** The Yearbook would feature articles on playwriting; the art of creating dramatic literature; theatre arts in the educational system; and directing for young audiences. The 40th Anniversary would be

acknowledged: the past in a timeline, the present focusing on regional co-operation, and the future with articles on young directors and writers, and how ASSITEJ can support practitioners in the field. Schneider urged the EC to supply photos for as much visual information as possible.
- **Printing and Design:** The WG had discussed the possibility of printing the Yearbook in the USA, in order to save freight costs, and allow them to print more photos in color. Kovac was to explore the possibilities in the USA, and Boucher, in Canada, and Šimić in Croatia. Mittelstädt will investigate costs of color printing.

WG 5 – Archives: Monteiro suggested that the Archives should be digitalized to make them more accessible. She stated that equipment, such as scanners, computers, and software, were already available in the German Archives. Costs were estimated at 2,000 Euros, but there was nothing in the Budget for this so far. She also felt it needed to be started *before* the Montreal Congress. In the discussion that followed, the EC decided on a Budget of 1,000 US$ within the current EC term in order to start the project of digitalization. Schneider thanked Monteiro for her Report, and urged the EC to ask the Centers to supply the Archives with documentation which he could bring to the Congress, or by their sending materials directly to the Frankfurt Archives.

WG 7 – Constitution: The WG–7, consisting of Eggert, Kovac, Malmcrona, Monteiro, and Turner, handed out copies of the proposed changes. Kovac noted that the changes were mostly of a technical nature, and not essential to the content. This should be noted and stated accordingly when the changes are mailed out to the Members three (3) months prior to the Meeting of the General Assembly at the Montreal Congress. The EC approved the changes.

Reports: Malmcrona reminded the EC of his need for short written Reports on the activities of their centers, which could be presented to the General Assembly, with a 1 June deadline.

Honorary Titles: Malmcrona reminded everyone that nominations for the titles of Honorary President and Member of Honor need to be sent to the Secretary General, who will then forward them to the General Assembly. Each nomination must first be endorsed by the EC at its last meeting before the General Assembly.

Future EC Meetings: EC meetings before and after the Congress would be held in Montreal, and Malmcrona stated that the new EC should hold its second meeting no later than January 2006. The following options and dates were presented:

- São Paolo, Brazil in early 2006
- Graz, Austria, February 2006
- Linz, Austria, June 2006
- Burca, Turkey, October 2006
- Vienna, Austria, February 2007
- Seoul, Korea, July 2007

No decision on acceptance was made.

Miscellaneous: Boucher noted that the South American Theme at the Festival in conjunction with the Congress was an important step in bringing South American artists closer to and into ASSITEJ.

Schneider thanked everyone for their participation, and especially thanked host Tony Mack for providing an agreeable site, and a friendly atmosphere for their deliberations. The meeting was adjourned.

Performances: The productions were part of the Come Out Festival, one of three large Australian Festivals of youth theatre.

Quality of the productions was high according to Kovac.[87] "High points included: *Emily Loves to Bounce* from Patch Theater; *Where is the Green Sheep?* from Windmill Theater; and a truly wacky and wonderful solo performer who calls herself Madam Lark and does bird-whistles and vocal interpretations of graphic designs and peoples' 'hair' which was really charming for both children and adults.

"The delegates were also able to see the Bangarra Aboriginal Dance Company on an outdoor stage that was "quite wonderful".

2005
XVth WORLD CONGRESS OF ASSITEJ/Montreal, Quebec, Canada/20-30 September 2005[88]

Montreal, Canada. Site of the XVth World Congress of ASSITEJ, Montreal, Canada, September 2005. All photos courtesy of Megan Ann Rasmussen (USA – Past President TYA/USA).

Members of the EC at the Congress: (left to right): Wolfgang Schneider (Germany) President of ASSITEJ; Niclas Malmcrona (Sweden) Secretary General; Rémi Boucher (Canada) Vice-President; Klaus Eggert (Denmark) Treasurer; Yuriko Kobayashi (Japan); Ivica Šimić (Croatia); Cheela Chilala (Zambia); János Nóvak (Hungary); Kim Peter Kovac (USA) Counselor; Tülin Sağlam (Turkey) Counselor; Tony Mack (Australia) Vice-President; Kim Woo Ok (Korea).

Host Rémi Boucher (Canada) welcoming the delegates to the Congress. XVth World Congress, Montreal, Canada, September 2005.

(left to right) Officials Louise Landin (Executive Secretary – Sweden), Niclas Malmcrona (Secretary General of ASSITEJ – Sweden), and Wolfgang Schneider (President/ASSITEJ/Int'l) on stage. XVth World Congress, Montreal, Canada, September 2005.

Kim Peter Kovac (USA). XVth World Congress, Montreal, Canada, September 2005.

Paper Puppets in performance, XVth World Congress, Montreal, Canada, September 2005.

Nat Eek (Honorary President of ASSITEJ) presenting the Honorary Presidents Award of ASSITEJ and a bottle of champagne to the Artistic Director of the Zeal Theatre (Australia) at the XVth World Congress, Montreal, Canada, September 2005.

(Left to right) Nat Eek (Honorary President of ASSITEJ), Wolfgang Schneider (President of ASSITEJ) presenting the Honorary Presidents Award of ASSITEJ to Kim Woo OK (Korea) with Niclas Mamcrona applauding at the XVth World Congress, Montreal, Canada, September 2005.

Wolfgang Schneider (Germany – President ASSITEJ/ Int'l), Hope Azeda (Rwanda), and Michael Ramløse (Denmark – Honorary Member of ASSITEJ). XVth World Congress, Montreal, Canada, September 2005.

(Left to right) Ann Shaw (USA), Joyce Doolittle (Canada), Fumie Naiki (President of ASSITEJ/ Japan) and his interpreter, Maurice Yendt (France), Wolfgang Schneider, all presenters and speakers at the 40th Birthday Party of ASSITEJ/Int'l. XVth World Congress, Montreal, Canada, September 2005.

Members of the African National Centers wishing ASSITEJ a Happy Birthday. (Left to right) Cheela Chilala, Hope Azeda, David Ndjavera (Namibia), Onkemetse Clark (Botswana), Jackson Ndawula, Etoundi Zeyang. XVth World Congress, Montreal, Canada, September 2005.

An aborigine guest making fire as part of Australia's presentation for their hosting of the 16th Congress in Adelaide, Australia in 2008. XVth World Congress, Montreal, Canada, September 2005.

(Left to right): Megan Ann Rasmussen (USA), Klaus Eggert (Denmark – Treasurer/ASSITEJ), Mrs. Anette Eggert. XVth World Congress, Montreal, Canada, September 2005. Courtesy of Megan Ann Rasmussen (USA – Past President TYA/USA).

Nat Eek (USA – Honorary President/ASSITEJ/Int'l), Erik Eek (his son and co-host). XVth World Congress, Montreal, Canada, September 2005.

Ann Shaw (USA – Honorary Member of ASSITEJ) performing at the 40th Birthday Party of ASSITEJ. XVth World Congress, Montreal, Canada, September 2005.

Wolfgang Schneider (Germany – President, ASSITEJ/Int'l) blowing out the candles on ASSITEJ's 40th Anniversary cake. XVth World Congress, Montreal, Canada, September 2005.

Most of the delegates arrived on Monday 19 September 2005, and upon registration were given copies of the entire program in French and English, lists of all the registered participants, tickets, name tags, a narrative of the plots of the plays to be seen, and many informational brochures – all printed in the two (2) official languages. The graphics were beautifully coordinated and printed.

The Congress and the Festival of the Arts were well organized, and the strong presence of the festival of plays was evident in the many posters throughout the city, including giant, lighted displays in the Metro stations.[89]

The Opening Ceremonies:

The next day Tuesday, the Opening Ceremonies were held at 7:00 pm in the Théâtre du Nouveau Monde. Dr. Wolfgang Schneider, President of ASSITEJ Int'l, greeted the delegates, followed by various welcoming speeches.

At the opening ceremony[90] a minister from Quebec (or from Canada as a whole), while giving a speech to the assembly, made an insulting joke about the USA's cultural policy. This was totally inappropriate for a number of reasons, including that 75 or so USA delegates were paying to be there.

"The next day I [Kovac] made a verbal formal complaint to Rémi Boucher's Managing/Executive Director...He was shocked and apologized on behalf of the Congress organizing group. Over the next couple of weeks, he and I tried to figure out the best way to handle this – he spoke with some people in that minister's office, I spoke with some other Canadians not involved with the Congress. We decided sending a letter to this minister would not really do any good, so we dropped it."

The evening concluded with a performance of *Pour Ceux Qui Croient Que La Terre Est Ronde* (Quebec).

The EC Meeting/Monday 19 September 2005
Present:
President Wolfgang Schneider (Germany), VP Luiza Montiero (Brazil), VP Rémi Boucher (Canada), VP Tony Mack (Australia), Sec. Gen. Niclas Malmcrona (Sweden), Treasurer Klaus Eggert (Denmark).
Members: Stephan Rabl (Austria), Ivica Šimić (Croatia), Hagit Rehavi Nikolayevski (Israel), Yuriko Kobayashi (Japan), Kim Woo Ok (Korea), Mikhail Bartenev (Russia), Peter Rinderknecht (Switzerland), Jeremy Turner (UK), Cheela Chilala (Zambia).
Counselors: Eckhardt Mittelstädt (Germany), Tülin Sağlam (Turkey), Jackson Ndawula (Uganda), Kim Peter Kovac (USA).

The current EC met from 9 am–12 m at the Hyatt Hotel where they were housed.

The Agenda for this first meeting consisted primarily of setting the Agenda and a listing of items of business for all the meetings of the General Assembly at the Montreal Congress.

The 1st Meeting of the General Assembly/Wednesday 21 September 2005

Present:

President Wolfgang Schneider (Germany), VP Luiza Montiero (Brazil), VP Rémi Boucher (Canada), VP Tony Mack (Australia), Sec. Gen. Niclas Malmcrona (Sweden), Treasurer Klaus Eggert (Denmark).

A total of forty-one (41) countries attended with twenty-four (24) National Centers of ASSITEJ represented. Paul Harman (UK) estimated that 500 people from over 50 countries attended.

Countries attending: Argentina, Australia, Austria, Belgium, Botswana, Brazil, Cameroon, Canada, Croatia, Czech Republic, Denmark, Estonia, Finland, France, Germany, Hungary, Iceland, India, Iran, Ireland, Israel, Italy, Japan, Korea, Lichtenstein, Lithuania, Mexico, Namibia, New Zealand, Norway, Russia, Rwanda, Serbia and Montenegro, Spain, Switzerland, Turkey, Uganda, UK, Uruguay, USA, Zambia.

By proxy: Benin, Cyprus, Jordan, Latvia, and Nepal.

President Schneider welcomed the delegates, and he was followed by brief remarks and Congress updates from Rémi Boucher, President of ASSITEJ/Canada and planner of the Congress and Festival. Schneider then immediately proceeded to the Agenda, as printed and distributed from the Secretariat for the delegates to bring with them to the Congress.

. **Voting Commission:** The first item of business was the appointment and approval of the three (3) members of the Voting Commission. They were Michael Ramløse (Denmark), Eckhardt Mittelstädt (Germany), and Marina Medkova (Sec. Gen. of ASSITEJ/Russia). This was quickly followed by the verification of the Centers present with voting rights, and the naming of proxies. No center could have more than two (2) proxies. It was announced that there were a total of 147 votes, making 74 the majority for election.

Approval of Minutes: The Minutes of the World Congress in Seoul, Korea in 2002, which had been distributed in June 2005, were approved as distributed with only one minor correction.

Presidential Report: Schneider presented his President's Report, followed by that of the Secretary General.

Secretary General's Report: Highlights of the Report of Secretary General Malmcrona included the following:

- The Swedish government and several of its councils are the main financial support of ASSITEJ/Int'l. At the moment this amounts to 145,000 plus in Euros. This funding will end in 2007, and the Association must come up with other sources of income in order to survive in the future.
- Nineteen (19) membership applications had been received and approved during the 3-year period between Congresses. The original Argentinean Center had been expelled, and a new and different one accepted. Six (6) centers had been expelled for lack of dues payment, but Uruguay had been reinstated. A stricter policy of payment of dues had been communicated to all centers and was now in force.
- A statement urging all involved governments to end the war in Iraq by political means had been approved and distributed by the EC in 2004, and 8,683 US$ had been collected for the future benefit of children and children's theatre in Iraq.
- An impressive total of 49 international visits to centers and festivals was made by the Secretary General during the past three (3) years.

Treasurer's Report: Klaus Eggert presented the Treasurer's Report.

Changes in Statutes: Kim Peter Kovac (USA) presented the proposed changes to the Constitution made by WG7. He stated most of the changes were for clarification and codification, and after a short discussion all the changes were approved.

Funding: The session closed with a short but solemn discussion chaired by Malmcrona on the serious need to address immediately the problem and solution to the funding of the international organization. The meeting was adjourned for lunch.

The 2nd Meeting of the General Assembly/Thursday 22 September 2005

President Schneider opened the meeting and presided. The session primarily dealt with items brought up by individual centers.

- Latin American forum
- Political concerns – Israel
- Sensitive issues in children's theatre
- Working program for 2005–2008
- Change in subscriptions
- Budget for 2006–2008

- Acceptance of the ASSITEJ/Australia's offer to host the World Congress in 2008. Tony Mack indicated that it would be held during the first week in May in Adelaide in 2008, which would be in their wintertime which is quite balmy. Aberystwyth, Wales, UK had withdrawn their invitation to host the 2008 Congress because of lack of funding.

The session concluded with the individual presentations of each of the candidates for election to the EC which would take place the next day. Those twenty-three who had been nominated were: Argentina, Australia, Austria, Brazil, Cameroon, Canada, Croatia, Finland, Germany, Israel, Japan, Kenya, Korea, Rwanda, Serbia and Montenegro, Spain, Switzerland, Turkey, Uganda, UK, USA, Zambia, and Zimbabwe.

The International Forums of Friday, 23 September 2005

Friday was devoted to six Forums for the delegates that had been created by the WG2–Networking. Delegates could attend those Forums which interested them the most. The Forums and their topics were as follows:

- Forum A – Adapting literature into theatre
- Forum B – How to build relationships between theatre arts and the educational system
- Forum C – How to expand the scope of criticism of theatre for young audiences
- Forum D – The new role of theatre houses
- Forum E – How to profile an artistic directorship of festivals
- Forum F – How to network in theatre for young audiences

The 40th Anniversary Celebratory Party on Friday, 23 September 2005

At 9 pm at the Théâtre du Nouveau Monde, ASSITEJ/Int'l celebrated its 40 years of continuous existence and service to the world of theatre for young people. President Wolfgang Schneider presided, welcomed all the delegates, introduced Secretary General Niclas Malmcrona, who in turn introduced Nat Eek to present the Honorary Presidents Award.[91]

Honorary Presidents Award: The members of this year's Jury were: Klaus Eggert, Chair (Denmark); Yuriko Kobayashi (Japan); Ivica Šimić (Croatia); Rosemary Myers (Australia); and Etoundi Zeyang (Cameroon).

There were a total of five nominations: Janos Novak – Composer & Director, ASSITEJ/Hungary; Peter C. Brosius – Artistic Director of the Children's Theatre Company of Minneapolis, Minnesota, USA; Haluk Yuce – Artistic Director,

Tiyatro Tempo, Ankara, Turkey; plus the two Awardees. The jury selected The Zeal Theatre of Redhead, New South Wales, Australia for "their Artistic Practice particularly in the creation of contemporary work that speaks powerfully to and with young audiences. The Jury commended the substantial international influence this work has exerted over the past three years."; and Dr. Kim Woo Ok, President of ASSITEJ/Korea for "his contribution to extending international dialogue surrounding the creation of performance for young audiences; in particular for his important work in nurturing Asian networks." Each received a check for 2,500.00 US$, plus a bottle of champagne for an appropriate celebration.

The Party: Following the Award, President Schneider showed a TV biography and a filmed live interview with Dr. Ilse Rodenberg (Germany), ASSITEJ President from 1978–1987, who was celebrating her 99th birthday. It was an excellent presentation, a delightful interview, and showed many scenes from her theatre years with the Theater der Freundschaft in Berlin.

After this viewing, Schneider had asked five members of the early history of ASSITEJ to briefly describe an anecdote from their many memories. The panelists were Maurice Yendt (France), Yuriko Kobayashi (Japan), Joyce Doolittle (Canada), and Ann Shaw (USA). The anecdotes were well received, and Shaw delighted the audience with her memories and impersonations of Dr. Rodenberg and Natalia Sats (Honored Artist USSR).

Several groups then made congratulatory presentations and songs, a special poem written for the occasion, Schneider brought forth a birthday cake, and the entire crowd sang Happy Birthday to ASSITEJ on its 40th Birthday.

The Elections of Sunday, 25 September 2005

President Schneider opened the General Assembly for the elections.

Candidates for Election:

Secretary General – Niclas Malmcrona (Sweden).

Treasurer – Klaus Eggert (Denmark).

Executive Committee – Argentina (Maria Inés Falconi) Australia (Tony Mack); Austria (Stephan Rabl); Croatia (Ivica Šimić), Germany (Wolfgang Schneider), Finland (Katariina Metsälampi), Israel (Razi Amitai), Japan (Yuriko Kobayashi), Korea (Young-Ai Choi), Rwanda (Hope Azeda), Switzerland (Peter Rinderknecht), Turkey (Tülin Sağlam), UK (Jeremy Turner), USA (Kim Peter Kovac).

The Elections: The President reminded the delegates that a total of 147 votes could be cast with 74 votes constituting a majority for election. The votes were as follows:

Secretary General: Niclas Malmcrona: Yes – 128; No – 6; Abstain – 3.
Treasurer: Klaus Eggert: Yes – 134; No – 4; Abstain – 4.
Executive Committee: Those elected were: 92

		Rank Order
Argentina (Maria Inés Falconi)	123 votes	4
Australia (Tony Mack)	128 votes	3
Austria (Stephan Rabl)	85 votes	14
Croatia (Ivica Šimić)	120 votes	5
Denmark (Klaus Eggert)	Treasurer	Already seated
Germany (Wolfgang Schneider)	142 votes	1
Finland (Katariina Metsälampi)	87 votes	11
Israel (Razi Amitai)	108 votes	7
Japan (Yuriko Kobayashi)	130 votes	2
Korea (Young-Ai Choi)	91 votes	9
Rwanda (Hope Azeda)	89 votes	10
Sweden (Niclas Malmcrona)	Secy-Gen'l	Already seated
Switzerland (Peter Rinderknecht)	85 votes	15
Turkey (Tülin Sağlam)	86 votes	12
UK (Jeremy Turner)	100 votes	8
USA (Kim Peter Kovac)	110 votes	6
Zambia (Cheela Chilala)	87 votes	13

The President: The new EC retired and returned with their nomination for President: Wolfgang Schneider. The vote was: Yes – 143; No – 3; Invalid – 1

The Vice Presidents: The new EC retired again and returned with five nominations for the Vice Presidents. The vote was:

Tony Mack (Australia)	114 votes
Yuriko Kobayashi (Japan)	115 votes
Jeremy Turner (UK)	43 votes, Not elected
Kim Peter Kovac (USA)	57 votes, Not elected
Cheela Chilala (Zambia)	87 votes

Schneider thanked the Assembly for his election and asked for the support of all the National Centers in his work. He also thanked the members of the old EC for their excellent past work and support.

Performances: While the Congress convened the delegates were able to see 68 performances of 25 plays. Performances continued through the following week with 9 new plays opening during that time, and the Festival concluded on Saturday 1 October. There was a total of 34 plays from 13 countries presented: Argentina, Bolivia, Brazil, Canada, Denmark, France (3), Israel, Japan, Mexico (2), Peru, Quebec (18), Spain, and USA. It was disappointing that there were no more plays from English-speaking Canada.[94]

Among the plays seen during the Congress, some of the most admired were: *Desert Dream* (Quebec), *Bekkanko-Oni* (Japan), *The Story of Charly and Violet* (Argentina), *The Little Matchgirl* (Denmark), *Baba Yaga* (Quebec), *Quijote* (Spain), and *Pequeñas Historias* (Peru).

One Quebec company, Theatre Le Clou, translated their production, *Au Moment de sa Disparition* into English as *Desert Dream*, which was impressive and moving. For audiences of 14 or older, it used multi-media technology, but depended on fine acting and an eloquent script for its emotional power. Mental illness, brotherly love, and spirituality were explored to create a compelling story.

Bekkoni-Oni was a striking retelling of a famous Japanese folk tale of a gentle blind girl and an ogre, which had echoes of *Beauty and the Beast* for western audiences. It featured a simple, but elegant setting of fabric panels, spectacular costumes, and masks. Featuring eight actors and four musicians, it was one of the largest casts in the Festival, which included many solo and two person companies.[95]

Quijote from Spain was performed by two puppet masters in full view of the audience, with candlelight and other simple theatrical techniques used brilliantly to animate Quijote's and Sancho Panza's adventures.[96]

Harmonie (Quebec) was probably the most elaborate and expensive production, with giant rod puppets manipulated by eight puppeteers, too loud music and dialogue amplification, excellent multiple special effects of projections and films, but a simple environmental message repeated too many times.

The opening production of the Congress *Pour Ceux Qui Croient Que La Terre Est Ronde* (Quebec) seen by all the delegates proved to be wordy and dull without any immediate translation. It went on much too long, with only two characters – Christopher Columbus and a deck hand, a single set of a ship's bow, and little action beyond the raising and the lowering of the ship's sails. This along with productions of *Bashir Lazhar* (Quebec) and *Lettres d'Amour* (France) proved to be poor choices for an international Congress, since they relied solely on the vocabulary and nuances of the French language.[97]

The New EC Meeting of 26 September 2005
Present:
President Wolfgang Schneider (Germany), VP Yuriko Kobayashi (Japan), VP Tony Mack (Australia), VP Cheela Chilala (Zambia), Sec. Gen. Niclas Malmcrona (Sweden), Treasurer Klaus Eggert (Denmark).

Members: Maria Inés Falcóni (Argentina), Stephan Rabl (Austria), Ivica Šimić (Croatia), Katariina Metsälampi (Finland), Razi Amitai (Israel), Young-Ai Choi (Korea), Hope Azeda (Rwanda), Peter Rinderknecht (Switzerland),

Tülin Sağlam (Turkey), Jeremy Turner (UK), Kim Peter Kovac (USA).
Counselor: Eckhardt Mittelstädt.
Executive Assistant: Louise Landin (Sweden)

On Monday, 26 September many of the delegates departed, while others stayed on to attend more days at the Festival. A meeting of the new EC was held on Monday from 9am to 12m at the Hyatt Regency Hotel. The Agenda covered the following items and decisions:

- Opening
- Review of the Agenda
- Report of the Secretariat
- Commissions – Working Program
- Co-option of EC Members
- Counselors
- Future EC Meetings
- Miscellaneous
- Closing

President Schneider opened the meeting welcoming the newly elected members of the EC: Falconi, Metsälampi, Amitai, Young Ai Choi, Azeda, and Sağlam.

Secretariat Report: Malmcrona handed out job descriptions for EC members, and asked them to keep in touch always. He introduced Barbro Frambäck, Chair of ASSITEJ/Sweden, who thanked ASSITEJ/Int'l for entrusting ASSITEJ/Sweden with the General Secretariat for another term. Tony Mack expressed the EC's gratitude towards Sweden and the Nordic countries for their impressive financial support.

Working Program: The following Working Plan for the next three years (2005–2008) was adopted by the General Assembly on Saturday, 24 September.

ASSITEJ/International
Working Plan 2005–2008

Drafted by Working Party at the Montreal Congress on 24 September 2005

The Working Party recommends the following: The goal of the working plan is the artistic development and promotion of theatre for children and young people, and therefore Congress directs the Executive Committee (EC) to carry out the following tasks, under such Working Groups as the EC considers appropriateSecure stable funding for the General Secretariat.

1. Review the current subscription system.
Increase income by identifying and develop new income sources.(Examples: fundraising, ASSITEJ supporter scheme).
2. Review Festival Guide.
Further develop ASSITEJ Awards, especially the Honorary President's Award, including clarification of the guidelines, and increasing participation.
6. Actively support the next generation of practitioners in the field of theatre for children and young people and their involvement within ASSITEJ.
7. Improve communication to, from, and between ASSITEJ Centers, with an emphasis on translation of ASSITEJ material.
8. Expand and develop the ASSITEJ Website. (Example: Create 'resource areas' with information, links to Websites, links to practitioners, on topics such as conflict resolution, theatre criticism, and work for very young children.
9. Continue to develop and expand the script database and ASSITEJ archives.
10. Actively assist in the creation of new national centers and regional networks, and in the development of existing centers and regional networks.
11. Produce and distribute the ASSITEJ Book.
12. Promote the World Children's Theatre Day; ASSITEJ/Int'l Projects; ASSITEJ/Int'l Festivals; Honorary Membership.
13. Produce and distribute the ASSITEJ Newsletter.
14. Investigate dormant and gatekeeper centers, and assist in making them active and inclusive.
15. Organize EC meetings, review current procedures (including actively co-ordinating with the Congress organizer), and report on outcomes to ASSITEJ members.
16. Seek connections with parallel organizations such as UNESCO, UNIMA, ITI, FIRT, IATC, as well as theatre education organizations.

17. Increase the visibility of ASSITEJ both within member nations as well as internationally through increased public relations activity. (Example: the EC creates a PowerPoint presentation with information about ASSITEJ on DVD).
18. Develop research on the cultural environment of contemporary children and young people (Examples: theatergoing trends; how audiences respond to theatre; and what is the influence of mass media).

Commissions: Schneider proposed five (5) Commissions to carry out the Working Program for the next three years:

- **Congress:** Tony Mack (Chair), Young Ai Choi, Hope Azeda. Responsible for Items: # 6, 15, 18.
- **Playwriting:** Cheela Chilala (Chair), Jeremy Turner, Peter Rinderknecht, Tülin Sağlam. Responsible for Item: # 9.
- **Public Relations:** Wolfgang Schneider (Chair), Razi Amitai, Ivica Šimić, Stefan Rabl. Responsible for Items: # 4, 8, 11, 12, 13, 17.
- **Networking:** Yuriko Kobayashi (Chair), María Inés Falconi, Katariina Metsälampi. Responsible for Items: # 6, 7, 10, 14.
- **Future of ASSITEJ:** Niclas Malmcrona (Chair), Klaus Eggert, Kim Peter Kovac. Responsible for Items: # 1, 2, 3, 5, 10, 14, 16.

There was considerable discussion and many recommendations were made for changes. The EC postponed the decisions on the Commissions until the next meeting.

Co-option: There were no recommendations since the EC already had its Statutory limit of 17 Members.

Counselor: The EC unanimously appointed Eckhardt Mittelstädt as Counselor for the next term.

Future EC Meetings: The EC first approved holding their next meeting in Frankfurt am Main, Germany on 2-6 December 2005. They then approved holding two meetings per year, and the following options were suggested:

- February 2006: Graz, Austria
- June 2006: Linz, Austria
- 31 May-5 June, 2006: Manila, the Philippines (during ITI Congress)
- September 2006: Warsaw, Poland
- Any time: Holon, Israel
- May/June 2007: Lusaka, Zambia

- July 2007: Seoul, Korea
- July 2007: Šibenik, Croatia
- October 2007: Bursa, Turkey

Next EC Meeting: Carlos de Urquiza of ASSITEJ/Argentina presented his invitation for the next EC Meeting. While the Center could not afford to accommodate the EC, costs would be very affordable, and the meeting would be held in conjunction with a meeting between Latin American Centers, during the Atina International Festival.

The EC approved holding the meeting in Buenos Aires, Argentina on 16-22 October 2006. They postponed any decisions on other dates and places until their next meeting.

President Schneider thanked everyone for their participation and closed the meeting.

2005
EXECUTIVE COMMITTEE MEETING OF ASSITEJ
Frankfurt am Main, Germany, Europe/2-6 December 2005

Present:
President Wolfgang Schneider (Germany), VP Tony Mack (Australia), VP Yuriko Kobayashi (Japan), VP Cheela Chilala (Zambia), Secretary General Niclas Malmcrona (Sweden), Treasurer Klaus Eggert (Denmark).

Members: María Inés Falconi (Argentina), Stephan Rabl (Austria), Nora Krstulovic/Deputy for Ivica Šimić (Croatia), Katariina Metsälampi (Finland), Razi Amitai (Israel), Young Ai Choi (Korea), Hope Azeda (Rwanda), Peter Rinderknecht (Switzerland), Tülin Sağlam (Turkey), Jeremy Turner (UK), Roger Bedard/Deputy for Kim Peter Kovac (USA).

Counselors: Eckhardt Mittelstädt (Germany).

Executive Assistant: Louise Landin (Sweden).

Frankfurt, Germany.

Cheeli Chilala, (partially hidden) Yuriko Kobayashi, Wolfgang Schneider, (partially hidden) Gordon Vajen, Young Ai Choi, (partially hidden) Eckhardt Mittelstädt, Dirk Fröse, Hope Azeda at the EC Meeting in Frankfurt, Germany. Courtesy of Wolfgang Schneider.

Nat Eek, Niklas Malmcrona, and Wolfgang Schneider at the EC Meeting in Frankfurt, Germany in December, 2005. Courtesy of Wolfgang Schneider.

Members and guests at the EC Meeting in Frankfurt, Germany in December 2005: (front row) Representative of ASSITEJ/Croatia/Deputy of Ivica Šimić, Stephan Rabl, Yuriko Kobayashi, (behind her) Hope Azeda, Niclas Malmcrona, Tülim Sağlam, (behind her) Eckhardt Mittelstädt, Maria Inés Falconi, (behind her) Cheela Chilala, Young Ai Choi, (behind her) Nat Eek, Roger Bedard/Deputy of Kim Peter Kovac, (behind him) Erik Eek, Wolfgang Schneider; (top row) Tony Mack, Klaus Eggert, Peter Rinderknecht, Razi Amitai.
Courtesy of Wolfgang Schneider.

The following Agenda was approved for the EC Meeting at Frankfurt am Main:[98]

- Opening
- Opening words by the host (Germany)
- Apologies
- (Report of the Bureau Meeting)
- Review of the Agenda
- Adoption of the Minutes of the Montreal Meeting
- Report from the General Secretariat
- Reflections from the Montreal Congress and performing Arts Festival
- Report from EC members (3 minutes)
- Working Plan 2005–2008, continued discussion
- Working Groups (WG's) 2005–2008, continued discussion
- Work Working Groups
- Report from the Working Groups

- Budget 2005–2008
- International Theatre for Children and Young People World Day 2006
- Counselors
- Coming EC Meetings
- Any other business
- Closing

On the invitation of the EC, Nat Eek (USA) and his son Erik met with the EC during this December Meeting. Under miscellaneous business at the end of the Agenda, they were to present a Revision of the Rules and Regulations for the Honorary President's Award. Both the EC and the Eeks as donors had previously agreed that such revisions were needed.

Working with Klaus Eggert (Denmark) during the Meeting, the Eeks revised the Rules and Regulations. The Eeks then presented this Revision to the EC, which they and Eggert had agreed upon. Below are listed the major changes that were presented:

- The name of the Award is to be changed to "The ASSITEJ Award For Artistic Excellence."
- It is "to recognize artists in the profession of theatre for children and young people in the national centers of ASSITEJ".
- It is to be presented every three years at the ASSITEJ World Congress of the time.
- It is to be given to an individual creative artist or theater company that has achieved remarkable artistic excellence in the previous three years.
- Only the creative work of the previous three years can be considered for the Award.
- The Award is to be in the amount of 5,000 US$, donated by Nat Eek and his family, in honor of his wife—Patricia Fulton Eek.
- The Secretariat and the EC are to handle the details of selection: choice of the jury, the time schedule, the solicitation of nominations, etc. A budget item to accomplish this will be part of the tri-annual ASSITEJ Budget.
- Changes to these Rules and Regulations must be made in consultation and through agreement between ASSITEJ/Int'l and the financial donor.

After discussion and the review of the changes, the EC unanimously approved the revisions. They are still in effect as of this time – 2014. (See Appendix I)

A SUMMARY OF 2003–2005

2003

At the time of the 2002 Congress in Seoul, Korea, the USA was at an undeclared war with Afghanistan since October 2001. Then the USA had suffered immeasurably from the attack on the twin towers in New York City on 11 September 2001. Despite the world-wide sympathy for the USA as a result of that attack, President George W. Bush had squandered that goodwill by starting another war, against Iraq this time, on 20 March 2003 in a futile search for "weapons of mass destruction". It was not surprising that the USA was in "ill-favor" in ASSITEJ/Int'l as well as around the world!

Kovac recently commented as follows:[99] "A very important insight into how this EC wished to operate came when Niclas Malmcrona, Klaus Eggert, and myself were drafting the anti-Iraq war statement the EC was to sign. I volunteered for this task because I have good English-language writing skills. We went back and forth about whether or not the statement should or should not directly condemn the action of the United States. At one point, when the sentiment of our small group seemed to be leaning this way, I said to Niclas words to the effect of 'I'm happy to continue to help write this statement as the EC wishes it be written, and if it's too radical or anti-US, I just don't have to sign it, the rest of you can.' And Niclas said words to the effect of 'No, we must have a statement that all of us can agree on and you need to be a part of it.' From that moment I knew that I and the other counselors would be treated as equals. Though we technically did not have a vote, that really didn't matter. My memory is that all the actions taken by the EC were done by consensus – it seemed like we very seldom had formal votes."

At the Zagreb EC meeting in October 2002, for the first time Wolfgang Schneider took over the reins as President of ASSITEJ/Int'l following his election in Seoul in May. Cheela Chilala (Zambia) was co-opted with vote to sit on the EC representing the African members of ASSITEJ. Malmcrona had e-mailed the new members of the EC, and this was their recommendation. It also passed a resolution that there would be no more co-options in this term. At the same time Turkey, Uganda, and the USA were added as Counselors. The healing process was beginning.

A major accomplishment was at this Zagreb Meeting with the EC's approval of President Schneider's recommendation to change the Commission titles to Working Groups, and adding a seventh one. This new titling would dove-tail in with the concept of Working Plans, whose use by now had moved the business of ASSITEJ forward remarkably well and efficiently.

The new Working Groups (WG) were as follows: WG1 – Policy; WG2 – Networking; WG3 – Artistic; WG4 – Information; WG5 – Archives; WG6 – Catalog of Scripts; and the "new" WG7 – Constitution, dues, and fund-raising.

The ASSITEJ Funds had now been transferred to Denmark, the home of its Treasurer – Klaus Eggert. A new budget was to be drafted and presented at the next EC Meeting. Vigorous letters had been sent to all the members regarding the importance of paying their dues promptly, both past and current.

World Theatre Day for Young Audiences was now a reality, and many countries held celebrations accordingly.

The EC voted unanimously to have the next EC meeting in Aberystwyth, Wales, UK, on 25-30 March 2003. The meeting would coincide with "Agor Drysau/ Opening Doors", the Wales International Festival of Theatre for Young Audiences. Of particular interest was the fact that Malmcrona stated that the next EC meeting after Wales must be located away from Europe, and preferably in an Asian location.

The status of the world had changed immeasurably with the invasion of Iraq by the USA with some UN support in 20 March 2003. Schneider opened the Welch Meeting after welcoming the members and thanking their host, by commenting that the meeting was being held at a time of war, and they had "... the need to communicate, not with weapons, but with the spirit and the mind."

It was also interesting to note that Schneider did not use the Bureau to set the Agenda, but had the EC do it at the beginning of the Meeting. This approach would eventually enable the membership to eliminate the Bureau and its use from the Constitution by an amendment in 2011.

Both the Secretary General's Report and the President's Report are remarkable in their foreign travel. Both of them visited many countries, seeing festivals, meeting with members, and encouraging the establishment of new centers. They had rigorous schedules, excellent funding, and used their visits to great effect.

" Malmcrona and Schneider, especially, worked very hard on diversity during 2002–2005, and the result was a diverse EC elected in 2005. I cannot speak more highly of the organization's work at diversity—it is to be highly commended."[100]

At the same time Treasurer Eggert was tightening the screws, and urged that non-dues-paying centers needed to be expelled, since the funding of ASSITEJ was very limited.

There was a major change in the criteria for the Honorary President's Award. The new criteria now clearly stated "... that the Candidates have to be new or emerging artists working in new ways." The EC also felt there needed to be more nominations as well as more promotion.

After Malmcrona's Report there was considerable discussion about ASSITEJ making a statement re: the recent declaration of war in Iraq. The comments centered on what ASSITEJ could do to help the children and the artists, but nothing was resolved at first. Later when the Working Groups made their reports, the WG1 on Policy suggested an electronic Bulletin Board where members could post their thoughts on the war, as long as the thoughts were identified as individual, not ASSITEJ policy. This was endorsed by the EC, along with a statement that was sent to all centers and the governments most involved.

Interestingly it was proposed to establish a group of volunteers that would go to Iraq as soon as the war was over to help the artists and to rebuild the theatres. Malmcrona, who was most concerned about the war, promised to start the Bulletin Board right away. Tragically, it would be nine years before the USA troops would begin to leave Iraq in 2011.

WG6 on Scripts proposed creating a central database of script information. Hopefully the Database would be added to the ASSITEJ Web-site by the spring of 2004.

WG7 on Finances zeroed in on non-dues-paying centers, and Eggert proposed that they be given a deadline of 1 September 2003 for payment or a request to be excused from payment. The EC endorsed this recommendation.

Payment of dues had always been a problem for some countries with tight currency, but there was no excuse for their not having written asking for an exemption. Eggert was doing his job well!

From the very beginning there had always been non-paying centers. Moudoués as Secretary General had always urged their inclusion, as ITI did, since it was better to have them in the organization than outside it, especially if ASSITEJ was to be worldwide. However, the lack of writing to be excused from payment, while possibly embarrassing to the country, was inexcusable. The Secretariat always granted these exemptions.

Of major concern was the search for a new Secretary General (Malmcrona had announced his resignation as of the 2005 Congress) and along with that they would need a new site for the Secretariat. Malmcrona promised that the Nordic Centers would help in every way they could.

The EC decided there would be 6 EC Meetings in the new term (2002–2005). They promptly accepted Austria's offer of hosting them in Vienna from 24-28 September 2003, and noted five later proposals, but took no action on them.

In September 2003 ASSITEJ/Austria proposed a full schedule, and there were 76 international guests in attendance at the concurrent Festival, along with the EC Meeting. As requested at the Wales EC Meeting, there was a meeting with the artists on 26 September.

The Iraq War Statement had been sent to all centers and the designated governments as requested at the Wales EC. It also had been posted at over 2,000 email addresses, and relevant organizations. A formal response was received from the UK later.

On a positive note, Malmcrona, Kovac, and Lina Attel of ASSITEJ/Jordan were working together to find ways of distributing books to children in Iraq, the monies being contributed by ASSITEJ Centers.

Of particular interest was the EC approving the granting of official titles (*ASSITEJ/Int'l Festival* and *ASSITEJ/Int'l Project*). Prior to this Meeting, the International Festival title had been granted primarily to the RITEJ Festival in Lyon, France. This now opened these two titles to all the centers who would make appropriate applications. Not only would this spread the name of ASSITEJ, but indicate a high level of quality and commitment at the Festival or the Project.

Malmcrona had done an excellent job of correspondence with the national centers, and now he presented Serbia-Montenegro and Armenia for Full Membership, and Mauritius and Rwanda for Corresponding Membership. All were approved as members.

Importantly, of the ten centers that were behind in their dues payments, all had been contacted by the Treasurer, and four had been in contact to remain as members. The remaining six were expelled from ASSITEJ for lack of payment and response.

In an accurate Financial Report, Treasurer Eggert reported a balance to date of 31,120 US$. If the Budget remained as projected, they would end up with a positive balance of 7,001 US$. Unfortunately this was only possible because of the high level of subsidy provided by the Nordic Centers.

Once again ASSITEJ would attempt to contact UNESCO at their November Meeting in Paris in hopes of being accepted as a part of their Network.

WG3 in charge of the Montreal Congress reported to be working closely with South America, and hoped to get performances from there. They also hoped to have 40 performances: 10 Canadian, 10 from the Americas, and 20 from the rest of the world. The 40th Anniversary of ASSITEJ would be well celebrated! At the request of Boucher the dates of the Congress were changed from May to 23 September-3 October 2005.

The EC accepted the invitation from Australia to hold their next meeting in Adelaide on 7-12 March 2005. Malmcrona noted that all the EC meetings from 1999-2002 had been held outside Europe! However selection of a meeting site was always dependent on what invitations were received. They also decided to consider the invitations from Beijing, China; Cape Town, South Africa; and Spain in the future.

2004

The April EC Meeting was held in Jordan, not in China, since the Beijing facility was not ready in time, and would not be ready until April 2005. This Jordan meeting concentrated primarily on "old business". Malmcrona announced that the Secretariat was now completely funded by the Swedish National Council of Cultural Affairs, and he had good hopes for the future funding of ASSITEJ.

New Centers were accepted: Italy as a re-established one; Nigeria, India, and Albania to Full Membership; but the application from Botswana was still to be received.

Treasurer Eggert announced a balance of 31,120 US$, with a final balance of 9,212 US$ if the Budget held. Also, ASSITEJ/Finland had agreed to audit the accounts, since the General Assembly in Korea had failed to make such an appointment. More importantly, Eggert asked the EC to impose a requirement that any center in arrears would have to pay 300 US$ six months in advance in order to have a vote at the next General Assembly. The legality of such an assessment was referred to WG7.

Regarding the lack of dues payments, embarrassment may have been a partial motive for the lack of default requests. Also, in many cases, the Center was a one person center.

With the war in Iraq still going on, the EC planned no immediate visits. However, ASSITEJ had raised over 2,000 US$ so far, and Malmcrona recommended the creation of a Working Group for the Iraq situation, but no action was taken.

There was considerable discussion on the importance of Latin American contacts, but Malmcrona reported their lack of correspondence, even when he wrote them in Spanish. He planned to make a tour of South America before the Canadian Congress, and Boucher stated that the Congress Web-site would be in four languages: English, French, Spanish, and Portuguese!

All the WG's reported real progress, and many valuable decisions had been made (see the Minutes of the Jordan EC Meeting).

The EC selected Cape Town, South Africa as their next meeting site on 2-7 September 2004, with the EC paying for the accommodations. This was a real boon to the South Africans, since they had been prohibited from membership as long as *apartheid* was still in place. As a result of their open elections, they were now being welcomed into the affairs of the world.

Malmcrona opened the September EC Meeting in Cape Town, South Africa by expressing the hope that "...the performances would provide the EC with interesting insights on some of the African styles of theatre for children and youth."

The most important announcement was that Tony Mack (Australia) would let them know soon if he would be able to be a candidate for the Secretary General and move the Secretariat to his country.

They approved the use of the title *ASSITEJ Festival* to four international festivals, and the title *ASSITEJ Project* to one.

Both Schneider and Malmcrona reported on their constant travels and contacts made on behalf of ASSITEJ. Their efforts were truly impressive.

Malmcrona reported that there could be no further action on the War in Iraq until the situation stabilized. Uganda suggested that the funds collected so far be used as unrestricted funds for severe conflict areas around the world. Malmcrona promised to look into the legality of this possibility.

All the WG's presented impressive lists of activities and goals achieved.

The EC confirmed that the next meeting would be held in Adelaide, Australia on 7-12 March 2005, the last meeting prior to the Montreal Congress. Malmcrona stated that the new EC should make site decisions as soon as possible after the elections in Montreal. He listed three possible future sites for EC meetings: Denmark, Spain, and the UK.

Niclas Malmcrona was a remarkable envoy for ASSITEJ in his constant travels and his concentration on getting new memberships, especially from the countries in Asia and Africa. He never denied the need for the presence of professional companies and people, but he recognized that different countries in the world had a wide variety of theatrical cultures, and they must be included in the Association.

Like Malmcrona, Wolfgang Schneider traveled a great deal on behalf of ASSITEJ, making the Association better known, and spreading the word of its activities. The two of them made an excellent team in promoting the interests of ASSITEJ.

2005

In the March EC Meeting in Adelaide, Australia, President Schneider noted that no Bureau Meeting had been held to approve the Agenda. Increasingly, the use of the Bureau Meeting prior to the EC meeting was being abandoned, much to the relief of all.

Prior to 1990, the Bureau meetings had been misused by not just setting the Agenda (its original purpose), but in many cases making decisions to be approved by the EC when it met later. Since this had made the EC much less responsible for the running of ASSITEJ affairs, while making the Bureau the more powerful decision maker, it made ASSITEJ less responsive to the needs of the membership, and was in a sense being managed only by six people. At the Congress in 2011 amendments to the Constitution eliminated the Bureau in its entirety.

The Secretary General's major concern in his Report was of an abandoned South American Children's Theatre Festival in Cordova, Argentina supposedly sponsored by ASSITEJ/Argentina that left performing companies stranded at that location, without money and no place to stay. ASSITEJ/Argentina could not be reached. The EC informed Malmcrona to expel ASSITEJ/Argentina from the Association, which he immediately did, informing all concerned of that decision.

In discussing new centers Malmcrona hoped soon to get applications from Chile and Uruguay, and the EC could endorse them at the Montreal Congress. However, this contradicted their decision to require a payment of 300 US$ three months before the congress for a center to have a vote in the elections. This was never resolved, but the vote went on! He also recommended the acceptance of the Argentinean International Theatre Association as well as Lichtenstein for Full Membership. The EC approved. ASSITEJ/Int'l now consisted of 78 National Centers!

Eggert reported on the results of the Honorary President's Award. Five nominations had been received, and the Jury had elected to split the 5,000 US$ prize in two, and to give an Award of 2,500 US$ to the Zeal Theater of Australia and to Dr. Kim Woo Ok (Korea). Eek, the donor of the Award, initially contested the splitting of the Award and the fact that one recipient, though more than worthy, was not a new emerging artist. However, the Jury's recommendations held. In turn Eek met with President Schneider, and they agreed to meet at the EC Meeting in December 2005 in Frankfurt, Germany to codify the terms of the Award in the future in order to avoid these disagreements. (See EC Meeting in Frankfurt (Main) Germany, December 2005).

Under the Treasurer's Report it was interesting to note that only 84 US$ reached the ASSITEJ Treasury with each center paying 125 US$, the rest going for bank fees! Eggert recommended that these lesser amounts be accepted as payment in full, which the EC approved. The EC also decided to have the Treasurer present an estimate of expenditures for the next three-year term to the General Assembly.

The EC also appointed Malmcrona, Ramløse, and Mittelstädt as a committee of three to peruse the New Voting System proposal by Michael Ramløse, in hopes that it would be used in Montreal. Copies had been sent to all centers.

The fate of ASSITEJ rested on two decisions: who would run for Secretary General, and where would be the site of the future Secretariat. Schneider said that its current professional style of management must be maintained. Malmcrona mentioned that much of the Secretariat work could be out-sourced. The EC asked Malmcrona to continue temporarily, if no other candidate emerged for his office. Boucher was to determine if the Secretariat could be set up in Montreal, with that city helping with the funding. No other decision was reached.

Boucher reported briefly on the Montreal Congress, which was scheduled from 20-26 September 2005, with the Old EC meeting that first day. The General Assembly would start meeting on 21 September, and the ASSITEJ 40th Anniversary party would be on 25 September.

When discussing future EC meeting dates, Malmcrona stated that the 2nd EC Meeting of the new term must be held no later than January 2006. The following sites were possibilities for meetings: São Paulo, Brazil; Graz, Austria; Linz, Austria; Burca, Turkey; Vienna, Austria; or Seoul, Korea. No decision was made.

The XVth World Congress of ASSITEJ was held in Montreal, Quebec, Canada from 20-30 September 2005. 24 National Centers were present, with a total of 41 countries participating. The entire program was printed in English and French, beautifully coordinated and printed. The first EC Meeting primarily set the Agenda, with the General Assembly opening on 21 September.

The proposed Agenda had been printed and distributed to all the centers prior to the Congress meeting, and members were told to bring these copies with them. This kind of preparation and organization was in stark contrast to materials available in the 60's, which consisted of an Agenda, several mimeographed pages of a financial report, and possible position papers. In those days the rest of the Congress was all verbal and droning verbosity with an occasional flash of artistic brilliance and fervid emotion.

Starting with Ramløse as Secretary General and FitzGerald as President, the EC Members worked continually and hard at their meetings. While time was given for them to see many performances and attend major receptions, the majority of the time was spent on the business of ASSITEJ, and the Working Groups were really working!

In the General Assembly the first item of business was the appointment and approval of Michael Ramløse (Denmark), Eckhardt Mittelstädt (Germany), and

Adolph Shapiro (Russia) as the Voting Commission. It was announced that there were a total of 147 votes, making 74 the majority for election.

The Assembly accepted the invitation from Australia to hold the XVIth World Congress in Adelaide, Australia in 2008. The UK had had to withdraw their invitation because of a lack of funding.

Twenty-four (24) countries had nominated themselves as candidates for election to the EC, with a total of 17 seats available on the EC.

The General Assembly first overwhelmingly approved both Niclas Malmcrona as Secretary General and Klaus Eggert as Treasurer. Thus Sweden and Denmark took two of the seats.

The following countries were then elected to fill the remaining 15 seats: Argentina, Australia, Austria, Croatia, Germany, Finland, Israel, Japan, Korea, Rwanda, Switzerland, Turkey, UK, USA, and Zambia. Not elected were: Brazil, Cameroon, Canada, Serbia and Montenegro, Spain, Uganda, and Zimbabwe.

From among these, the following members were elected to the Bureau: President – Wolfgang Schneider; Vice-Presidents – Yuri Kobayashi, Tony Mack, and Cheela Chilala.

The 40th Anniversary Celebration proved to be a spectacular production with President Schneider showing a TV biography and personal interview with Past President and Honorary President Dr. Ilse Rodenberg. Five members, including the President, gave delightful personal anecdotes and insights, and a 40th Anniversary Birthday Cake was enjoyed by all.

As part of the adjoining Festival, 13 countries presented a total of 34 plays. Altogether it was a successful Congress, and opened the doors to a very productive next three years. However, it was interesting to note that Rémi Boucher (Canada) was specifically not returned to the EC after hosting the Congress. Informal comments passed on to the authors indicated that the EC and the membership felt that he had not lived up to the promises that he had made in putting the Congress together. He was more interested in supporting the French Canadian part of the Festival, and consequently gave it most of his attention.

In 2002 in his Report to the ASSITEJ/USA Board Kovac had commented on the defeat of the USA and Zambia in the election at the Korean Congress of 2002. The USA had had a representative on the EC since the creation of ASSITEJ/Int'l, and Africa had had a representative on the EC for 10 years. "... one could interpret the results as a combination of Euro-centrism and good-old-boy networking."[101] It also could easily have been a result of "white ballots" that went too far. At the time there was also considerable anti-USA sentiment because of the threatening war.

Kovac wrote "...there continued to be anti-USA sentiment because of the Iraq war – it may have been true in 2002, it certainly was true in 2005 and 2008 elections. Though I was perceived (I believe) as a hard worker from the national cultural center and an advocate for diversity, Tony Mack at one point suggested that I lost 10–15 votes in elections because of Anti-US sentiment." [102]

Some vindication had come in the Montreal elections when the USA was re-elected to the EC and ranked 7 out of a possible 17. Through his dedicated activity, Kovac and his Center were back in the good graces of ASSITEJ.

The XVth Congress had been an unqualified success in terms of the efficient dispatch of its business and of its election. Schneider had proved himself to be a well organized, responsible leader with vision, grace and consideration, and a good deal of personal charm. After the manipulated debacle of the elections at the World Congress in Korea in 2002, it was wonderful to see the President and the Secretary General deal with diversity with such fairness and aplomb. According to one delegate, the new EC as elected consisted primarily of individuals who had proved to be solid, responsible workers, and who would carry forth the work of the organization with energy.

Also, there was a shakeup among the African centers, with those newly elected who were good workers, rather than just sitting delegates.

In the past the elections were often controversial. While there was some minor politicking, the elections ran smoothly, despite a lengthy counting of the first balloting for the EC. The full complement of national centers had been elected, and the new EC would be able to consider co-option and appointment of counselors, if any.

The final tally showed the following six continents represented: North America – 1; South America – 1; Europe – 8; Mideast – 2; Asia – 2; Africa – 2; Australia – 1. ASSITEJ had truly become a world organization. In addition, the EC now consisted of 10 men and 7 women, in contrast to the male-dominated early years of the EC.

The World of 2005

The War in Iraq continued into its third year since its inception in March 2003. Some 138,000 U. S. troops remained in Iraq, where 1500 had been killed, 15,000 wounded, and 26,500 civilians had been killed since the beginning of the war. A new Constitution for Iraq was approved in October 2005. However, Iraq had its first democratic election in January, and Interim Prime Minister Iyad Allawi called the elections "a victory over terrorism" and the beginning of a new national dialogue.

In the first extremist suicide bombings in Western Europe, 56 people were killed in the London subway, with 700 injured. In Bali, Indonesia 3 suicide bombers killed 20 others.

In September Israel completed its evacuation of the Gaza Strip, and handed over control to the Palestinian Authority. It had been held by Israel since the 1967 Six-Day War.

After 2 years of negotiations North Korea agreed in principle to abandon its nuclear weapons program, and planned to rejoin the Nuclear Nonproliferation Treaty and allow inspection of its facilities. Meanwhile Iran continued to pursue its own controversial nuclear program.

The Kyoto Protocol for the reduction of greenhouse gases took effect 16 February for the 141 nations who had agreed collectively to reduce emissions of heat-trapping gases, believed to contribute to global warming. Regrettably the USA did not ratify the treaty.

In April Pope John Paul II died, and Cardinal Joseph Ratzinger was elected to the papacy and took the name Benedict XVI. He was 78 years old.

In the USA in August 2005 Hurricane Katrina devastated three Gulf States (Mississippi, Alabama, and Louisiana), forcing the evacuation of the city of New Orleans. $62.4 billion in Federal funds were appropriated to the victims.[103]

In Germany Angela Merkel, leader of the Christian Democratic Union (CDU), became the first woman Chancellor of that country. She was from the former German Democratic Republic (GDR).

The Nobel Peace Prize went to Egyptian diplomat Mohamed El Baradei and the International Atomic Energy Agency (IAEA) which he headed "for their efforts to prevent nuclear energy from being used for military purposes and to ensure that nuclear energy for peaceful purposes is used in the safest possible way."

Astronomers at the California Institute of Technology reported that an object they had discovered in 2003 was 3 times as far away as Pluto, and should be classified as the 10th solar system planet based on its size and motion. Much later Pluto was declared a planet no longer.

Titanic (1997) was the All-time Top-Grossing American Movie. *Doubt* by John Patrick Shanley won the Tony Award as the best play of the season in the USA.

The Bureau (2005–2008)
At the XVth World Congress in Montreal, Canada the following Bureau was elected:
President: Wolfgang Schneider (Germany)
Vice-Presidents: Yuriko Kobayashi (Japan)
　Tony Mack (Australia)
　Cheela Chilala (Zambia)
Secretary General: Niclas Malmcrona
Treasurer: Klaus Eggert (Denmark)

The Bureau (2008–2011)
At the XVIth World Congress in Adelaide, Australia the following Bureau was elected:
President: Wolfgang Schneider (Germany)
Vice-Presidents: María Inés Falconi (Argentina)
　Young Ai Choi (Korea)
　Kim Peter Kovac (USA)
Secretary General: Ivica Šimić (Croatia)
Treasurer: Yvette Hardie (South Africa)

The Officers (2011–2014)
[**Amendments to the Constitution in 2011 eliminated the term Bureau entirely.**]
At the XVIIth World Congress in Copenhagen, Denmark/Malmö, Sweden the following officers were elected:

President: Yvette Hardie (South Africa)
Vice-Presidents: Maria Inés Falconi (Argentina)
　Stephan Fischer-Fels (Germany)
　Kim Peter Kovac (USA)
Secretary General: Ivica Šimić (Croatia)
Treasurer: Noel Jordan (Australia)

A LEADERSHIP EVALUATION by Nat Eek

From its very beginning in 1965 to its continued existence now almost fifty years later ASSITEJ has almost always been blessed with strong leadership, especially at times of crisis.

Gerald Tyler (UK) was one of the first visionaries. As a dedicated leader and teacher of Theatre in Education, he had traveled many times to Europe with his equally dedicated wife Emily, and had established contact with many of the leaders in theatre for young people on both sides of the Iron Curtain. Vladimir Adamek (Czechoslovakia) was a close friend, who produced high quality artistic theatre for young people with as little political message as possible.

The Tylers, along with other dedicated artists, began talking over several years about a professional association of workers in theatre for young people. But it was Gerald Tyler who took the first step forward in 1964 by having a conference in London bringing everyone together for the first time. When 30 workers from the Soviet Union showed up without warning at that conference, Tyler knew they were on their way.

In June 1965 in Paris ASSITEJ was born, Tyler was elected its first president, and for two terms with charming determination and persuasion he helped the fledging association stand on study feet and begin to grow at a time when the Cold War dominated the political arena. But ASSITEJ was almost equally divided between East and West.

When Tyler released the reins of leadership to incoming President Konstantin Shakh-Azizov (USSR) in 1968, there was no question that ASSITEJ would continue, although dominated by European members. In 1966 Gerald Tyler was named an Honorary President of ASSITEJ/Int'l.

The second most important and successful leader was **Rose-Marie Moudoués** (**France**) who was elected as ASSITEJ/Int'l's first Secretary General in 1965. As a dedicated leftist she saw that the leadership and membership remained half and half, east and west, by astutely managing the correspondence and admittance applications. However, most importantly she made her home at 98 Boulevard Kellermann the new Secretariat, giving the fledging association a home, an address, and a correspondent at little cost to ASSITEJ, which had very little money from its dues.

For 25 years she maintained a political presence and international visibility while new national centers were added. And all this was done with great charm and *politesse* as an unpaid volunteer. In 2002 Rose-Marie Moudoués was named an Honorary Member of ASSITEJ/Int'l.

Because of visa problems in getting from east to west, the third great leader **Dr. Ilse Rodenberg** (**GDR**) could not attend the Constitutional Conference in Paris in 1965. But as host of ASSITEJ's first EC Meeting in February 1966 in Berlin (GDR), she immediately established a strong presence. She was elected President of ASSITEJ/Int'l for the first time in 1978, and presided through three 3-year terms, an unbeatable record. During that time she traveled extensively for ASSITEJ, making her presence known and helping new centers form. She established a voluminous correspondence. Although many of her missions were political, she remained dedicated to theatre for young people, and her own Theater der Freundschaft in East Berlin was strong, highly artistic, and professional.

In 1990 the General Assembly in Stockholm in a landmark election chose **Michael Ramløse** (**Denmark**) to replace Moudoués as Secretary General. Supported financially by his own Center and the Nordic Ministries of Culture, Ramløse was able to bring the Secretariat and ASSITEJ/Int'l into the 21st Century, with modern equipment, rapid communication, addition of new centers, an excellent staff, especially Else Marie Mandøe, great personal charm, an awesome sense of equal treatment, and a far-reaching eye that wanted ASSITEJ to become truly international, not just Eurocentric. He traveled extensively, and eventually he made ASSITEJ/Int'l a truly professional association of artists, managers, and educators in the field of theatre for young people. His dedicated organizational sense helped make the Havana, Cuba and the Rostov-on-Don, Russia Congresses the successes they were.

In his two terms over six years he succeeded admirably, and has continued to this day to be involved in ASSITEJ internationally. At the same time as a professional and much admired playwright and producer, he was able to carry on with his life as a theatrical artist to great acclaim. In his lighter moments he was also a delightful pianist. In 1999 Michael Ramløse was named an Honorary Member of ASSITEJ/Int'l.

In 1993 **Michael FitzGerald** (**Australia**) was elected President and served for two terms. He and Secretary General Ramløse became an energetic formidable duo. Over the next three years (1993–1996) they communicated by FAX every Friday, bringing up to date knowledge on the current actions and reactions of the Association.

Along with Ramløse, FitzGerald traveled extensively, even though he was always having to scrape and beg for travel funds. He hosted the first World Congress of ASSITEJ to go beyond the confines of Europe and North America in Adelaide, Australia in 1987. He established English as the Working Language of the Association; he conceived of and supported along with Marjorie Maclean (Canada) the first

ASSITEJ Membership Questionnaire which categorized the members and centers of ASSITEJ/Int'l, as well as codifying its various missions and goals.

He had an eye for keeping the discussions centered on the topic at hand, and established Working Groups and Long Range Goals for each three-year term. In 2000 he was named an Honorary President of ASSITEJ/Int'l.

When **Niclas Malmcrona (Sweden)** in 1998 became Executive Officer and then Secretary General for two terms, he quickly established himself as another great leader. He had formidable financial support from the Nordic Centers as well as the Nordic Foundations, and he used that funding to enlarge ASSITEJ/Int'l's influence around the world. At the Secretariat he kept communication open with all the centers, while traveling extensively in Africa, South America, and the Middle East on behalf of ASSITEJ/Int'l, urging the establishment of new centers, bringing individuals and countries into the Association.

He treated all centers and members with courtesy, dispatch, and fairness, never losing his eye-contact with the greater goals of ASSITEJ. His determination and expertise allowed ASSITEJ to enlarge its membership to beyond 80 national centers.

With support from SIDA (the Swedish International Development Cooperation Agency) he together with many African countries established and managed an African ASSITEJ Network which brought various African countries into ASSITEJ.

Through his many personal contacts and persuasive abilities, he with the help of his colleagues was able to raise considerable amounts of money from Nordic Ministries and Nordic Foundations to support ASSITEJ/Int'l as well as himself. He earned every dollar he received.

In 2008 for his excellent extended service to ASSITEJ/Int'l he was made an Honorary Member of ASSITEJ.

Like Ramløse and FitzGerald, Malmcrona teamed up with **Harold Oaks (USA)** to move ASSITEJ farther into the global "new world" of theatre. Oaks began his leadership as Treasurer of the Association in 1993, and served two terms known for financial and up-to-date accuracy. He became President for one term in 1999 at the Tromsø Congress. As Treasurer he solidified the constant presentation of accurate Financial Reports, kept accurate account of all funds, reported the Centers in arrears recommending their expulsion if they received no communication requesting an exception.

As President he solidified the changes made by the FitzGerald administration, concentrating on the General Assembly approved Working Plan. With Secretary General Malmcrona, he traveled extensively promoting ASSITEJ/Int'l, especially in Africa, South America, and the Middle East. He presided at the

Korean Congress in 2002 turning the gavel over to incoming President Wolfgang Schneider.

In 2002 he was named an Honorary President of ASSITEJ/Int'l.

Wolfgang Schneider (Germany) proved to be formidable in his personal charm, sense of decorum, sense of humor, and corporate size! Most importantly, along with Malmcrona he proved through three terms to be an incredibly well traveled President. He attended many international Festivals by himself, establishing an ASSITEJ presence around the world. He established the ASSITEJ/Int'l Archives in Frankfurt (Main), Germany, which gave a perpetual home to all those records. He established the publication of the ASSITEJ Annual. Schneider and Malmcrona were constant in their correspondence.

Financially supported by the German Center and the Nordic Centers and Sweden, the two of them made a dynamic duo on the ASSITEJ/Int'l scene, and increased the number of centers, and saw that all six continents were visited. The number of new national centers increased accordingly. When Schneider stepped down as President, the ceremony and reception in Copenhagen/Malmö in 2011 was a true love feast. He also duplicated, through his own leadership, Ilse Rodenberg's 3 terms as President.

In 2008 Schneider was named an Honorary President of ASSITEJ/Int'l.

To this author, these eight have been the major past leaders of ASSITEJ, and I have had the privilege of serving them all. All are Honorary Presidents or Honorary Members of ASSITEJ. They are the ones who have kept their eyes on the stars with love of theatre for young people in their hearts. ASSITEJ has been extremely fortunate in having such strong and visionary leaders. May that strength in leadership continue as ASSITEJ moves towards its 50th Anniversary, and well beyond.

Lastly, two newcomers should be mentioned. **Kim Woo Ok (Korea)** not only organized and drove the 2002 World Congress in Seoul to a high level of achievement, but through his dedication, hard work, and leadership he opened up the Pacific Rim and Asian countries to ASSITEJ, helped create new National Centers, and helped make us a truly "international" association.

Since his election as Secretary General **Ivica Šimić (Croatia)** has proved to be a conscientious and thorough communicator, and has made the channels of information open and up to date, keeping ASSITEJ/Int'l active through his efforts and his computer. Final judgment awaits him whenever he decides to step down, but that will have to be of someone else's writing.

The torch of "high-level leadership" continues to be passed to willing and able hands!

The World of ASSITEJ in 2014

Perhaps the most appropriate way to conclude this three volume *History of ASSITEJ* is with a summary of the accomplishments made at the XVIIth World Congress in Copenhagen, Denmark/Malmö, Sweden in May 2011. At that Congress itself, major changes were voted in to the Constitution making it more all-inclusive and world-wide.

Also, as of that World Congress, ASSITEJ/Int'l celebrated a continuous history of existence for 46 years. Its Secretariat had been located in four countries: France, Denmark, Sweden, and Croatia. Its eleven presidents had come from seven countries: Australia, Czechoslovakia, Germany, Russia, South Africa, the UK, and the USA.

It had held 17 Congresses and 63 EC Meetings in 31 countries and in all 6 continents, averaging 2 meetings a year. The 32 countries visited were: Australia, Austria, Brazil, Bulgaria, Canada, Croatia, Cuba, Czech Republic, Denmark, France, Germany, Hungary, Italy, Japan, Jordan, Kenya, Korea, the Netherlands, Norway, Peru, Poland, Romania, Russia, Slovakia, South Africa, Spain, Sweden, the UK, the USA, Venezuela, Yugoslavia, and Zimbabwe.

During those 46 years the members on the EC had come from 46 different countries and all 6 continents, which were:

- **North America:** Canada, Cuba, Mexico, the USA;
- **South America:** Argentina, Brazil, Peru, Venezuela;
- **Europe:** Austria, Belgium, Bulgaria, Croatia, Czech Republic (Czechoslovakia before 1991), Denmark, Finland, France, Germany, Hungary, Iceland, Italy, the Netherlands, Norway, Poland, Portugal, Romania, Russia, Serbia, Slovakia, Spain, Sweden, Switzerland, UK, and Yugoslavia (before 1991);
- **Africa:** Kenya, Rwanda, South Africa, Uganda, Zambia, Zimbabwe;
- **Asia – Mid-East:** Israel, Jordan, Turkey;
- **Asia – Far East:** India, Japan, Korea;
- **Australia**

ASSITEJ had truly become "a world-class organization."

CONCLUSION

This is being written in March of 2014, nine years after the date that the authors chose as their concluding year in their writing of the first forty years of the existence of ASSITEJ/Int'l. During the most recent six years the Association was saved from a severe shortage of maintenance funds by electing Ivica Šimić (Croatia) as their new Secretary General, and by a generous financial subsidy from his government. At the same time the EC launched a serious fund raising drive, created Friends of ASSITEJ with donations of 500 US$ or more, as well as conscientiously monitoring expenditures.

However, the existence of ASSITEJ still relies heavily on its members and their countries paying their own expenses, and by the various meetings being subsidized by the governments of the countries in which the current meeting is being held. Some money may be raised by the publication of this History, but according to Klaus Eggert as Treasurer in 2005, a minimum of 60,000 US$ is required annually to support the organization. Since that time much more of the work of the organization has been done by volunteer labor, and publication and correspondence costs have been strongly supported by individual national centers. It is doubtful that the Association will ever become financially self-sufficient, but its membership feels so strongly about the need for its existence that it will undoubtedly continue to survive.

The authors have been fortunate to have had at least one of them in attendance at all the World Congresses from 1965 to 2011, as well as many of the EC Meetings. We hope this history will prove to be a balanced eye-witness basis for many of the events which shaped the international association, but it will be up to future members, witnesses, and scholars to continue the history of ASSITEJ/International, and perhaps to add additional material to this one.

Our Authors:

Nat Eek

Ann Shaw

Katherine Krzys

Kim Peter Kovac

APPENDIX A.
Volume III.
LIST OF OFFICERS AND HONORARY MEMBERS.

Presidents of ASSITEJ

1965 – 1968	Gerald Tyler (Great Britain)	– 2 terms
1968 – 1972	Konstantin Shakh-Azizov (USSR)	– 2 terms
1972 – 1975	Nat Eek (USA)	– 1 term
1975 – 1978	Vladimir Adamek (Czechoslovakia)	– 1 term
1978 – 1987	Ilse Rodenberg (German Democratic Republic)	– 3 terms
1987 – 1990	Hildegard Bergfeld (Federal Republic of Germany)	– 1 term
1990 – 1993	Adolph Shapiro (USSR/Russia)	– 1 term
1993 – 1999	Michael FitzGerald (Australia)	– 2 terms
1999 – 2002	Harold Oaks (USA)	– 1 term
2002 – 2011	Wolfgang Schneider (Germany)	– 3 terms
2011 – 2014	Yvette Hardie (South Africa)	– 1 term

Vice-Presidents

1965 – 1968
  Vladimir Adamek (Czechoslovakia) – 2 terms
  Konstantin Shakh-Azizov (USSR) – 2 terms
1968 – 1972
  Vladimir Adamek (Czechoslovakia) – 2 terms
  Nat Eek (USA) – 2 terms
  Ilse Rodenberg (GDR) – 2 terms
1972 – 1975
  Vladimir Adamek (Czechoslovakia) – 1 term
  Ilse Rodenberg (GDR) – 3 terms
  Joyce Doolittle (Canada) – 1 term
1975 – 1978
  Ilse Rodenberg (GDR) – 1 term
  Joyce Doolittle (Canada) – 2 terms
  Maria Sunyer (Spain) – 1 term
1978 – 1981
  Joyce Doolittle (Canada) – 3 terms (resigned in 1978)
  Maria Sunyer (Spain) – 2 terms
  Natalya Sats (USSR) – 1 term
1981 – 1984
  Ann M. Shaw (USA) – 1 term
  Maria Sunyer (Spain) – 3 terms
  Eddy Socorro (Cuba) –1 term
1984 – 1987
  Ann M. Shaw (USA) – 2 terms
  Eddy Socorro (Cuba) – 2 terms
  Nena Stenius (Finland) – 1 term
1987 – 1990
  Mårten Harrie (Sweden) – 1 term

          Maria Navarro (Spain) – 1 term
          Eddy Socorro (Cuba) – 3 terms
1990 – 1993
          Michael FitzGerald (Australia) – 1 term
          Harold Oaks (USA) – 1 term
          Eddy Socorro (Cuba) – 4 terms
1993 – 1996
          Marjorie MacLean (Canada) – 1 term
          Eddy Socorro (Cuba) – 5 terms
          Maurice Yendt (France) – 1 term
1996 – 1999
          Marjorie MacLean (Canada) – 2 terms
          Helge Andersen (Norway) – 1 term
          Tisa Chinfunyise (Zimbabwe) – 1 term
1999 – 2002
          Wolfgang Schneider (Germany) – 1 term
          Kim van der Boon (Netherlands) – 1 term
          Kim Woo Ok (Korea) – 1 term
2002 – 2005
          Luiza Monteiro (Brazil) – 1 term
          Tony Mack (Australia) – 1 term
          Rémi Boucher (Canada) – 1 term
2005 – 2008
          Yuriko Kobayashi (Japan) – 1 term
          Tony Mack (Australia) – 2 terms
          Cheela Chilala (Zambia) – 1 term
2008 – 2011
          Maria Ines Falconi (Argentina) – 1 term
          Choi Young Ai (Korea) – 1 term
          Kim Peter Kovac (USA) – 1 term
2011 – 2014
          Maria Inés Falconi (Argentina) – 2 terms
          Stephan Fischer-Fels (Germany) – 1 term
          Kim Peter Kovac (USA) – 2 terms

Secretary Generals
1965 – 1990	Rose-Marie Moudoués (France) – 25 years
1991 – 1996	Michael Ramløse (Denmark) – 2 terms
1997 – 1998	Ullide Plichta (Austria) – 1 year, 5 months
1998 – 2008	Niclas Malmcrona (Sweden) – 1 year, 3 terms
2008 – 2014	Ivica Šimić (Croatia) – 2 terms

Treasurers
1965 – 1968	José Géal (Belgium) – 3 years
1968 – 1972	Ion Kojar (Romania) – 4 years
1972 – 1987	Ion Lucian (Romania) – 15 years
1987 – 1993	Paul Harman (UK) – 6 years
1993 – 1999	Harold Oaks (USA) – 6 years

1999 – 2002   Vicki Ireland (UK) – 3 years
2002 – 2008   Klaus Eggert (Sweden) – 6 years
2008 – 2011   Yvette Hardie (South Africa) – 3 years
2011 – 2014   Noel Jordan (Australia) – 3 years

Honorary Presidents
As of 1966   Gerald Tyler (Great Britain)
As of 1972   Konstantin Shakh-Azizov (USSR)
As of 1981   Vladimir Adamek (Czechoslovakia)
As of 1984   Nat Eek (USA)[104][105]
As of 1988   Ilse Rodenberg (Germany)
As of 2000   Michael FitzGerald (Australia)
As of 2008   Harold R. Oaks (USA)
As of 2008   Wolfgang Schneider (Germany)

Honorary Members
As of 1975
    Leon Chancerel (France)
    Alexander Bryantsev (USSR)
    Charlotte Chorpenning (USA)
    Mila Milanova (Czechoslovakia)
    Victor Ion Popa (Romania)
As of 1978
    Caryl Jenner (Great Britain)
    Hans Rodenberg (GDR)
    Sara Spencer (USA)
As of 1981
    Kaoru Ota-Ai (Japan) – posthumously
    Hans Snoek (Netherlands)
As of 1987
    Maria Nieves Sunyer y Roig (Spain)
As of 1996
    Zvjezdana Ladika (Croatia)
As of 1999
    Michael Ramløse (Denmark)
As of 2002
    Kazuto Kurihara (Japan)
    Rose-Marie Moudoués (France)
    Orna Porat (Israel)
    Ann M. Shaw (USA)
As of 2008
    Kim Woo Ok (Korea)
    Galina Kolosova (Russia)
    Niclas Malmcrona (Sweden)
    Maurice Yendt (France)
As of 2011
    Paul Harman (UK)

APPENDIX B
Volume III
BIOGRAPHIES OF THE ASSITEJ LEADERS (1965–2005)

All names are listed. However, for those leaders not active during 1991–2005, their biographies can be found in Vol. I and/or II.

Vladimir Adamek (Czechoslovakia) I, 294 & II, 297.
Dr. Adamek died 20 March 1990.

Razi Amitai (Israel)[106]
Dr. Razi Amitai studied theater at Seminar at the Hakibbutzim College of Education. In 1976 he founded the Community Theater of Beit Shemesh, and then traveled to the United States to continue his studies. He completed his doctorate in Theater at the Graduate Center of The City University of New York.

Upon his return to Israel in 1982, he founded and ran the Theater Group in Kiryat Gat for three years. In 1985 he joined the team that founded the School of the Arts in Tel Aviv. There he taught and headed the Drama Department for five years.

In 1986 Amitai was appointed Educational Director of the Orna Porat Theater for Children and Youth. In 1991, he was appointed Artistic and General Director of that theater. During the time of his tenure in this position, the Theater became the leading theater in Israel offering performances for young audiences.

From 1997 to 2004 he was appointed Artistic and General Director of the Municipal theater of Beer Sheva where he directed several plays.

In 2001 he joined the team that founded Mediatheque—the new cultural center of Holon. He wrote the program and served as chief advisor for the establishment of the Theater. In 2004 he was appointed CEO and the Artistic Director of Mediatheque—which includes the Central Library—and founded a new repertory theater—The Theater Center for Young People.

Throughout his career Amitai has been involved in theater education in a variety of fields. He taught at Seminar Hakibbutsim College of Education, Tel Aviv University, the College of Management, the Beit Tsvi School of Theater Arts, and in the Yoram Levinstein Acting Studio. He has also served as an academic advisor who has given hundreds of lectures, seminars, and continuing education courses for teachers and educators on the subject of the theater in Israel and abroad.

He was a Board Member and Chair of ASSITEJ/Israel. After he became a member of ASSITEJ/Int'l, he was elected to the Executive Committee from 2005 to 2011. He is also a member of the Theater Committee of the Israeli Council for Culture and the Arts.

Currently Amitai is the Artistic and General Director of the Inbal Dance Theater at the Suzan Dallal Center in Tel Aviv.

Helge Andersen (Norway) II, 297 & III
Helge Andersen received his Doctor of Drama from the University of Oslo. He was a dramaturge/producer at the Department of Drama at the Norwegian Broadcasting Corporation, where he has worked with radio drama for children and young people for ten years.

He was a member of the Norwegian Playwrights Society (Norske Dramatikers Forbund). He wrote plays for professional puppet theatres in Norway and for radio.

He also worked as a theatre critic at the largest morning newspaper in Norway "Aftenposten", mainly on children's theatre and literature. He wrote two books for children.

Helge Andersen died on 1 January 2013.

Hope Azeda (Rwanda)

At the EC Meeting in September 2003 Hope Azeda was first recognized for her work in creating an ASSITEJ Center. At that meeting the Secretary General Niclas Malmcrona recommended that Rwanda be accepted as a Corresponding Center.

Malmcrona with Jackson Ndawula had visited Rwanda in 2002, and met with representatives in Kigali and Butare. Hope Azeda in turn had been invited to a festival and a meeting in Sweden, another meeting in Sweden, and a symposium in Denmark. She had also participated in a regional African ASSITEJ meeting in Nairobi in June 2003.

Subsequently Azeda was elected to the EC for the three-year term 2005–2008 at the Montreal Congress in 2005.

Mikhail Bartenev (Russia)[107]

Mikhail Bartenev was born in 1953 in Moscow. He graduated from the Moscow State Architecture Institute. He began his working life as an architect, designing several buildings in Moscow. Later he turned to the arts, and is a renowned playwright and film scriptwriter.

In 1986 he wrote his first play for children entitled *Ivan, the Fool*. Since then he has written more than 30 plays, mainly for children and young people. They have been produced in more than 400 theatres in Russia, CIS (Commonwealth of Independent States)[108], the Netherlands, Germany, Denmark, Latvia, Poland, and Greece.

He is the author as well as a participant in a number of international theatre projects such as "Magic House", "European Stories from the Schoolyard", and others.

In 1991 a Festival entitled "Plays by Mikhail Bartenev at the Puppet Theatres of Russia" was held in Nizhniy Novgorod.

In 1996 he received one of the Honorary President Awards of ASSITEJ at the Rostov-on-Don Congress. Then in 1997 he was nominated from Russia for the International Hans Christian Andersen Prize.

He was elected to the EC of ASSITEJ/Int'l, and served one term from 2002–2005 as the delegate from Russia.

During his extensive career he has won many other awards and prizes. He was a prize-winner for the Best Play for Children in a competition sponsored by the "Contemporary Playwriting" Magazine. He was a winner of the National Prize "Musical Heart of the Theatre" for his nomination as Best Playwright.

Bartenev was nominated and also the winner of the prize for his script *Three Whales* as "the Best Script for a TV Series". He was also Winner of the National Prize "Musical Heart of the Theatre" as the Best Playwright for his adaptation in script form of "Dandelion Wine", the novel by USA writer Ray Bradbury.

Judit Benedek (Sweden)[109]

Judit Benedek received her Bachelor of Arts degree as an actress from Statens Scenskola (1971–73). She worked as an actress for ten years before she became a theatre director.

She has directed over 50 plays in various theatres in Sweden, among them Riksteatern, Stockholm's Stadsteater, and the Royal Dramatic Theatre (Dramaten). Since 2004 she has also been presenting and directing Swedish playwrights in her native country Hungary. She has mainly worked with children and young people's theatre.

Benedek received the Stig Dagerman Prize 2011 for her theatre co-production between Sweden (Teater De Vill) and Hungary (Kolibri Theatre) on a project for children and young people on changing the attitude towards the "gypsy people".

She has been a member of the ASSITEJ/Sweden Board since 1990, and was elected President for 1993–2000. She was elected to the EC of ASSITEJ/Int'l for a three year term (1996–1999) at the Rostov-on-Don Congress. She attended the EC Meetings in Haifa, Israel in April 1998, London in February 1999, and the XIIIth World Congress in Tromsø, Norway in June 1999.

Hildegard Bergfeld (FGR) II, 298.

Benito Biotto (Italy) I & II, 298.

Andrew Kingsnorth Bleby (Australia) II, 298.

Rémi Boucher (Canada)

Rémi Boucher was elected to the EC at the XIVth World Congress in Seoul, Korea in July 2002. At that Congress his offer of holding the 2005 Congress in Montreal, Canada was accepted, and accordingly he was voted onto the EC, as well as being elected Third Vice-President for the three-year term of 2002–2005. He was not re-elected at the Montreal Congress in 2005, and no longer represented ASSITEJ/Canada.

Joao Luiz Brites (Portugal) II, 299.

Léon Chancerel (France) I, 295.

Tisa Chifunyise (Zimbabwe)

Tisa Chifunyise was first elected to the EC at the Rostov-on-Don, Russia Congress in 1996, and was listed as the 2nd Vice-President. She was elected to another three-year term at the Tromsø, Norway Congress, and served from 1999–2002.

Cheela F. K. Chilala, PhD (Zambia)[110]

Dr. Cheela F. K. Chilala was born in Lusaka, the capital of Zambia, on 2 January 1965. He graduated with a Bachelor of Arts degree from the University of Zambia (UNZA) in 1988, and then graduated with an Master of Arts degree from the same University in 2006. In 2011, he received a Doctor of Philosophy in Literature degree from the University of Zambia with his thesis focused on the cultural factor in the semiotics of contemporary African drama.

Chilala first became involved in the work of ASSITEJ in 1997 when he participated in the formation of the Zambian National Center of the Association. He was the first National Secretary of the Center before becoming its President in 2001, a position he still holds. He played a key role in the development and consolidation of the Center during those early stages. In that period he represented the National Center of Zambia at numerous ASSITEJ events in the African region and beyond.

Chilala has also been instrumental in developing and strengthening the African network of ASSITEJ centers. In 2007 he was voted the first Chair of the African network of ASSITEJ, known as the African Children and Youth Theatre Arena (ACYTA). He has made a number of presentations on children's theatre at various ASSITEJ seminars.

Chilala was one of two Africans co-opted by the EC of ASSITEJ/Int'l after the XIVth World Congress in Seoul, Korea, in 2002. In 2005 at the XVth World Congress in Montreal, Canada, he was elected to the EC and voted one of the three Vice Presidents of ASSITEJ, along with Yuriko Kobayashi of Japan and Tony Mack of Australia. He stepped down at the XVIth World Congress in Adelaide, Australia in 2008.

However, at that same Congress Chilala was elected to sit on the Board of ITYARN (International Theatre for Young Audiences Research Network). He was re-elected to that board at the XVIIth World Congress in Copenhagen/ Malmö in 2011.

At present he teaches literature, drama, and theatre at the University of Zambia, Great East Road Campus, and also manages the University's Creative Arts Center, which is involved in the promotion of various forms of art including theatre for young audiences. He is a poet and playwright with several national and international awards to his credit. One of his plays for children, *Kalulundi Mulimi* (The Hare and the Farmer), is an adaptation of a Zambian narrative tale, that toured Finnish schools and theatres in 2007. Some of his articles have been published in the ASSITEJ Yearbook.

Ian Cojar (Romania) I, 297.

Orlin Corey (USA) I, 297.

Elisabeth Cozona (Switzerland) II, 300.

Ljubiša Djokič (Yugoslavia) I, 298.

Joyce Doolittle (Canada) I, 298 & II, 300.

Nat Eek (USA) I, 299, II, 301, & III.
Nathaniel Sisson Eek was born on 16 October 1927 in Maryville, Missouri, USA. He obtained his degrees from the University of Chicago (PhB), Northwestern University (BS, MA), and Ohio State University (PhD). He taught theatre arts, children's theatre, art administration, and directed plays at the University of Kansas, Michigan State University, and the University of Oklahoma. He was Director of the School of Drama at the University of Oklahoma from 1962–1975, and then Dean of the College of Fine Arts from 1975–1991. He retired from the University of Oklahoma in 1993, and was named Regents Professor Emeritus of Drama and Dean Emeritus of Fine Arts.

He was the USA representative at the Founding Congress of ASSITEJ in Paris, France in

1965, and served on the Executive Committee from 1965–1975 at which time he retired from active participation in the international Association.

He was the USA representative to ASSITEJ, was twice elected as Vice President from 1968–1972, and was elected President serving from 1972–75. In 1984 he was made an Honorary President of ASSITEJ. From 1988–1994 he was producer and director of the professional Southwest Repertory Theatre in Santa Fe, New Mexico.

During his career he directed over 100 plays, musicals, operas, and did the *mise en scène* of several ballets. He was a Board Member of the American Theatre Association, President of their national Children's Theatre Association, and President of the International Association of Fine Arts Deans. He was named a Fellow of the American Theatre in 1985.

He continues to be active in his professional associations, and began the writing of The History of ASSITEJ in 2002. With the publication of Vol.3 The History of ASSITES was completed in 2014. He currently lives in Santa Fe, New Mexico, USA.

Klaus Eggert (Denmark)[111]

Klaus Eggert was born in 1947, and received his MA from the University of Copenhagen (Political Science and Russian Language) in 1975.

From 1985 to 1995 he was a Member and Administrator of the collective management of Baggård Teatret (The Backyard Theatre) which was one of the leading free theatre companies in Denmark. After the re-organizing of the structure of Baggård Teatret, he became its Managing Director and later Chair of the Board of the theatre.

He left his position at Baggård Teatret in 1995 to become a free-lance administrator/producer/managing director/and board member of several theatres, festivals, and other cultural projects.

The aim of his "back-stage" work has been to establish the best possible circumstances for the artists to focus on their artistic work, and not to have to deal with the basic administrative procedures or problems of their theatre.

He has worked for and with Teater Rio Rose, Hans Rønne's TEATRET, Odense Internationale Musikteater, Bruthalia Teatret, Rialto Teatret, Dacapo Teatret, Paraplyteatret, as well as others.

From 2006–2007 Eggert involved himself in theatre organizations in Denmark, including ASSITEJ/Denmark, where he became a member of the Board, and later Vice-President. His first participation in ASSITEJ/Int'l was at the Xth World Congress in Stockholm, Sweden, and since then he has attended all the Congresses. In Seoul, Korea in 2002 he was elected Treasurer and a Member of the EC. In Montreal, Canada at the XVth World Congress he was re-elected as Treasurer from 2005–2008.

Eggert's major contribution to ASSITEJ has been to establish a reliable, consistent, and transparent "system" of the finances of ASSITEJ/Int'l . As Treasurer he was able to provide a consistent but flexible collection of Membership Fees, with day-to-day administration and management of the expenses, and with regular Financial Reports, which include "easy to understand" updated budgets and overviews of the finances. In turn he presents these to the EC and to the General Assembly at each Congress.

Eggert attended the XVIIth World Congress of ASSITEJ in Copenhagen/Malmö as auditor of the ASSITEJ/Int'l accounts, and as a volunteer.

Egmont Elschner (FGR) II, 301.

John English (Great Britain) II, 301.

Maria Inés Falconi (Argentina).
Maria Inés Falconi was first elected to the EC for a three-year term at the XVth World Congress in Montreal, Canada in 2005, and served from 2005–2008. She was re-elected for two additional terms (2008–2011 and 2011–14), serving as Vice-President in 2011–2014.

Michael FitzGerald (Australia) II, 302 & III. [112]
Michael FitzGerald was born in Hobart, Tasmania on the third of October in 1936. After obtaining a BA and a Diploma of Education from the University of Tasmania in 1957, FitzGerald was a High School Teacher of English, Modern History and Social Studies for some years. Both at University and during these teaching years, FitzGerald was an actor in Tasmania in the professional/amateur theatre movement (Pro/Am) then flourishing across Australia. He won a number of Awards in both acting and later directing. In his teaching he used the new methods of drama-in- education. These early experiences shaped FitzGerald's commitment to the place of theatre in the education and the cultural development of children and young people.

In the 1960's and 70's FitzGerald lived in different countries in Europe and the Middle East where he was a Teacher of English as a Foreign Language (TEFL). Later he settled in London and obtained a Post Graduate Diploma in TEFL. At this time, he continued to use drama-in-education methods in his work as well as involving companies and artists in the then burgeoning theatre-in-education movement, particularly in Great Britain.

Upon his return to Australia in 1975, FitzGerald became an arts administrator and bureaucrat at the Australia Council, the Australian Federal Government's Arts Advisory and Funding Body. He joined the Theatre Board as the Youth/Puppetry Project Officer, and over the ten years became its Senior Project Officer and finally Director. This period was a major time in the development of a distinct Australian theatre culture which saw the establishment of major theatre companies across the country. These included Australia's first theatre-in-education companies. FitzGerald was a significant supporter of this development.

In 1985 FitzGerald was appointed Director of the IXth ASSITEJ World Congress and General Assembly which was held in Adelaide in 1987. Also in 1985 he became Australia's representative on the ASSITEJ Executive Committee, and attended his first meeting in Šibenik, Yugoslavia that year. In 1990 he became a Vice President of ASSITEJ, and in 1993 he was elected President. He was re-elected President in 1996, and held this office for a total of six years.

Concurrently with his ASSITEJ work and after the Adelaide Congress, he became Artistic Director of the Come Out Festival, Australia's premier youth arts festival, until 1991. He then became Director of Youth Performing Arts Australia (YPAA) and ASSITEJ Australia until his retirement in 1999. Since his retirement he has continued his involvement as a youth arts consultant.

Throughout his working life, FitzGerald has been a prime force in the promotion and development of theatre for children and young people at national and international levels. In 1989 FitzGerald was appointed as a Member of the Order of Australia (AM) for services to youth arts and arts administration.

In 1994 he was presented with The Frannie Arts for Young Audiences Award for his outstanding contribution in the field of arts for Young Audiences from The Canadian Institute of the Arts for Young Audiences, Vancouver, B.C.

In 2002 he was made an Honorary President of ASSITEJ/Int'l in recognition of his extraordinary work as President of ASSITEJ/Int'l (1993-1999) and in the service of theatre for children and young people.

Jürgen Flügge (Germany) II, 303 & III.

Jürgen Flügge was born in 1944 in Darmstadt, Germany.

From 1967-1972 he studied Theatre Science and Literature in Munich. From 1972-1977 he was the Dramaturge in Frankfurt (TAT, Schauspielehaus), Munich (Theater der Jugend), and Stuttgart (Staatstheater).

From 1976-1979 he was a member of the group "Rote Grütze" in Berlin; Director, Dramaturge, and co-author of "Was heisst hier Liebe".

As of 1980 he was Director of the Theater der Jugend in Munich, Art-Director of the festivals "Schauspiele 1985/86" and 'Schauspiele 88 "Theatre of the World".

Since 1989 he was Director of "Württembergische Landesbühne Esslingen".

From 1993-1994 he was General Director of the state theater at Braunschweig.

He has directed various plays for children and young people as well as adults. He was Chairman of ASSITEJ/Germany, and served three terms on the EC (1990-1999).

Jean-Yves Gaudrault (Canada) II, 303.

Victor Georgiev (Bulgaria) I, 303 & II, 304.

Hanswalter Gossmann (FRG) I, 300.

Paul Harman (Great Britain) II, 304 & III.[113]

Paul Harman was born in 1940. After four years at Birmingham University acting such parts as Laertes in *Hamlet* and Lucky in *Waiting for Godot*, he gave up studying Russian and started work as a professional actor in 1963. However, playing small character parts in the standard repertory of the time did not entirely satisfy his desire to make theatre accessible to everyone and to be of some social usefulness. By 1966 he joined the pioneering Theatre in Education (TIE) team at Belgrade Theatre, Coventry, and with them he began a 42-year career creating and directing over 100 plays for young audiences.

After similar TIE experiments in Liverpool with the Everyman Theatre, he founded and became Artistic Director of Merseyside Young People's Theatre (now Fuse Theatre) from 1978 to 1989. There he commissioned Willy Russell to write the original version of a play about the English class system, and later the highly successful musical, *Blood Brothers*.

From 1994 to his retirement in 2008 he was Artistic Director of the Cleveland Theatre Company (CTC) in Darlington, North East England, creating a repertoire of plays from improvising with actors, from new commissions, and from international sources, such as Germany, Holland, and Canada. About 250 performances are given each year, mostly in schools in the region.

CTC received invitations to take productions to nine countries during that time, and for some years there was also a successful program of theatre events for young people in museums as well as open air productions of Shakespeare in local parks with the region's resident professional actors.

Since 1994 he has, as part of the company's annual program, directed the annual Takeoff Festival of professional theatre for young audiences to celebrate the best of Great Britain theatre for young audiences, as well as to introduce them to overseas companies with ideas new to the Great Britain.

He has directed plays in Poland and Russia, and translated plays from both French and German. He is currently performing with Sylvie Bloch of the French company Pointure 23 in C(H) AT, a bilingual play for children about the one thousand year old love-hate relationship between France and England.

Because of his service to the Great Britain Center of ASSITEJ, he was named Honorary Life President in 2006. He served ASSITEJ as International Treasurer from 1990–1993, and was elected again to the Executive Committee for 2008–2011.

As Chairman of TYA/Great Britain Center of ASSITEJ in recent years he has compiled a Guide to Great Britain Theatre for Young Audiences, commissioned a new Website and edited regular newsletters.

At the XVIIth World Congress in Copenhagen/Malmö in 2011 he was made an Honorary Member of ASSITEJ, and in that same month was also elected as a local Councilor for the town of Darlington, UK.

Mårten Harrie (Sweden) II, 305 & III[114]

Mårten Harrie received his high school diploma in 1961. As a youth he performed in theatre during the holidays at the Arena Theatre in Stockholm. After high school he practiced as a technician and Assistant Director at the Malmö Statsteater.

He studied further at Axel Witzansky's Theatre Acting School in Stockholm, with additional courses at Dramatiska Institute in Stockholm. He has had theatrical experiences at many theatres in Sweden, as well as Swedish Radio, Television, and Film.

He is a professional actor, director, playwright, technician, and dramaturge. He has directed about 80 plays for children and youth, 10 plays for theatre, and 5 scripts for film.

He has worked in the theatre for over 25 years, and for 14 years has been a Producer and Director for the Children and Youth Theatre Group at Östgötateatern in Norrköping.

He has been a member of ASSITEJ/Sweden since it was started in 1980, both as a Vice-President and President. He served as a member of the Executive Committee of ASSITEJ from 1987–1993.

Shaun Hennessey (Great Britain) II, 305.

Yohei Hijikata (Japan) II, 305 & III.

Yohei Hijikata was born in Japan in 1927. His father, Yoshi Hijikata, was one of the leaders of the "New Play" movement, which was started around the 1920's to create modern plays in Japan, in contrast to the old style Kabuki theatre. In 1924 he founded with his colleague the Tsukiji Small Theatre in Tokyo as their pilot work, and later his young son Yohei was proud of being a member of its pioneering children's troupe.

Before long, however, Yohei had to spend much of his childhood in Russia and France with his parents who took political asylum away from Japan, which made him a tri-linguist.

Through the 1950's, he worked to develop youth cultural movements in Japan. In 1966 he joined Theatre Seinen Gekijo to work in translating and producing various foreign plays for young people, such as E. Schwarz's *Dragon* and *The Naked King*. He later became this theatre's Chief Producer, and continuing in that position until 1997. He was then nominated as Advisor to the Theatre.

In 1983 he was elected to the Executive Committee of ASSITEJ/Japan, and in 1990 became a member of the Executive Committee of ASSITEJ/Int'l , remaining in that position until 1996, a total of two terms.

In 1998 he received the Art & Culture Award Chevalier from the French Ministry of Culture for his lifelong service in the field of youth theatre.

He died of cancer on 21 January 2010 at the age of 82.

Vicky Ireland (Great Britain), II, 306, & III.[115]

Vicky Ireland was trained at the Central School of Speech and Drama, London, where she received her Teaching Diploma in English and Drama. At the University of London she received a Diploma in Dramatic Art.

She is an actress, staging director, playwright, and artistic director. After her training she joined the newly formed Theatre-in-Education team at the Belgrade Theatre. She has worked as an actress all over the UK and on radio and TV, including presenting BBC TV's award-winning schools program *Words and Pictures* for twelve years.

As a playwright she has authored over twelve original plays, as well as adapted works of other authors for the stage, including six books by the celebrated children's writer, Dame Jacqueline Wilson. She has won awards for her work both in radio and television, and received a Writer's Guild of Great Britain nomination for best children's TV series, *Happy Families*.

She wrote and directed original children's productions for five years at Regent's Park Open Air Theatre, and was an international guest director in Russia and Cypress. She has taken productions to the Ukraine, Spain, Singapore, Finland, and the United Arab Emirates, has been a guest speaker in Israel and Hungary, and held drama workshops in the Philippines and Cyprus.

She has taken productions to Great Britain, Ukraine, Spain, Singapore, Finland, and the United Arab Emirates, has been a guest speaker in Israel and Hungary, and held drama workshops in the Philippines and Cyprus.

She has represented the UK at Children's Theatre Festivals in Australia, Sweden, Russia, Cuba, Peru, Israel, Norway, Japan, Poland, Denmark, Brazil, Korea, and Canada.

From 1989–2002 she was Artistic Director of the Polka Theatre for Children where she directed and produced over 60 productions. She commissioned three original plays, all of which won Writer's Guild of Great Britain nominations.

From 1996–2002 she was International Representative of ASSITEJ/UK, and a member of the EXCOM of ASSITEJ. From 1999–2002 she served as the Treasurer of ASSITEJ.

She was a guest of the Japan Foundation and ASSITEJ/Japan to study Children's Theatre and primary education in Tokyo and Osaka, and in 2007 took part in a plenary seminar on Theatre and Education in Okinawa. She is currently Co-Artistic Director with Kumiko Mendl of A Thousand Cranes, using theatre to share Japanese culture with British children. She is also a visiting director at various Drama schools.

She was awarded the Member of the British Empire (M.B.E.) medal in Queen Elizabeth's

Jubilee Birthday Honors list 2002 for her services to children's drama, and in 2008, she was elected a Fellow of the Royal Society for the Arts.

Currently in the UK she is Vice-Chair of Action for Children's Arts; Patron of the Polka Theatre for Children; Vice-Chair of TYA England; a Board member TYA ASSITEJ/UK; and the Producer of TYA/UK's Disability/Inclusivity team.

Caryl Jenner (Great Britain), I, 301.

David Johnston (Great Britain) II, 307.

Inga Juul I, 307 & II, 307.

Yoshishige Kagawa (Japan)[116]

Yoshishige Kagawa was born in 1932 in Japan. He studied at the performing Arts School in Bugeiza. Then after studying Japanese Literature at the Graduate School of Hosei University in Tokyo, he joined the director's section of Theatre Zenshinza in Tokyo. While there he produced and directed many plays for adults and children as well as classic Kabuki.

He received many awards and prizes for his works, such as: the Art Festival Prize by the Japan Agency for Cultural Affairs; the Welfare-Culture Prize by the Japan Welfare Ministry; the Tokyo Municipal Award for Excellent Drama for Young Audiences; and an Award by the Japan Children's Theatre Association.

Two of the most popular plays that he directed were "Sansow Dayu" (Lord Sanshow) and "Obake-chan" (A Goblin).

He was sent as a specialist to study theatre in the United Kingdom by the Japan Agency for Cultural Affairs for three months in 1990.

During his long career as a director, he has been a lecturer at such colleges as: Hosei University, Rikkyo University, and Komazawa University in Tokyo.

He served as Japan's Representative on the EC of ASSITEJ/Int'l for two terms, from 1996-2002.

At present, he is a non-regular staff member of Theatre Zenshinza, an advisor to the Japan Educational Drama Association, and a Board Member of ASSITEJ/Japan.

Kim Woo Ok (Korea) II, 319 & III.[117]

Kim Woo Ok was educated at Yonsei University in Seoul, Korea, and received his BA in English there in 1957. He then received his MA in English at that university in 1963. In 1971 he received his MA in Drama (majoring in Directing) at the University of Washington, Seattle, Washington, USA, and in 1980 he received his PhD in Drama at New York University.

On his return to Korea he became a Professor in the Department of Theatre at the Seoul Institute of the Arts, and served as Artistic Director of the Dong Rang Repertory Company from 1980-1994, one of the most prestigious theatre companies in Korea. In 1985 he founded the Dong Rang Theatre for Young Audiences, the first professional theatre company for the youth in Korea, and has continued in that capacity to the present day (2011).

In 1983 he helped found the Korean National Center for ASSITEJ. In 1991 he became a co-opted EC member of ASSITEJ/Int'l . In 1993 he was elected as an EC Member, serving on it until 2005. While on the EC he served as a Vice-President from 1999-2002. He also served as President of ASSITEJ/Korea twice from 1986-1993 and from 1998-2006.

From 1993–2006 he served as Artistic Director of the Seoul Performing Arts Festival for Young Audiences, and from 1994–2000 he served as Dean of the School of Drama at the Korean National University of Arts in Seoul.

He has directed 5 original plays for youth. The first piece, *The Wandering Stars* (1985), was invited to be performed at the IXth World Congress of ASSITEJ in Adelaide, Australia. The fourth piece, *The Burning Stars* (1987), was invited to be performed at the 2nd All-Japan Performing Arts Festival for Children on Sado Island, Japan in 1991. Other titles he has directed include: *"Light/Liquid/Mist"* (1980), *"Revolutionary Dance"* (1981), *"Double Gothic"*(1982), *"Bicycle"* (1983), *"Dreaming Stars"* (1986), *"The Han River Flows"* (1987), *"Arirang, Arirang"* (1988), *"Nameless Stars"* (1989), *"Lonely Stars"* (1991), *"Arirang"* (1999), and *"Tripitaka Koreana"* (2000). As an actor he has appeared in *"Eight People"* (1972), *"Revolutionary Dance"* (1974), and *"Identity Control"* (1975), all of which were performed in New York City, USA.

He has received the following Awards and Honors: Best Director & Best Production (1980), Best Director (1983), Best Director & Best Production (1985), Best Production (1991), Commendation from the President, Republic of Korea (1997), Medal of Merit from the President, Republic of Korea; the ASSITEJ Award for Artistic Excellence (2005); Commendation from the Ministry of Culture and Tourism; and the Cultural Medal of Merit from the President, Republic of Korea (2006).

He was named an Honorary Member of ASSITEJ/Int'l in 2008.

Ladislav Knižátko (Czechoslovakia) – II, 307.

Yuriko Kobayashi (Japan)[118]

Yuriko Kobayashi is Professor of Child Studies at Tokyo City University in Japan. Previously she was a Visiting Professor at the University of Exeter (Great Britain), and an Academic Visitor at the University of Jordan and its National Performing Arts Center in Jordan.

As a Member of ASSITEJ/Japan she was elected to the EC of ASSITEJ/Int'l for two terms, from 1996–2002. While on the EC she served as a Vice-President, and continues now in Japan as a Member of ASSITEJ/Japan.

Her writing has covered a wide spectrum of issues related to theatre for young audiences, drama/theatre education, and teacher training through drama/theatre.

Her most recent publications include *Theatre Workshop: An Introduction to Drama Education*, which is the first general book on drama education in Japan, and *Applied Drama*, which is the first book in the file *A Case Study of an International Theatre Festival for Young Audiences in Okinawa* (KIJIMUNA FESTA), which is part of the peace building through the arts, a project in conjunction with the Japan Foundation.

Her most recent research is in *Development of a Teacher Training Program for Communication Skills through Drama*, which is supported by a Japanese Government subsidy for Scientific Research.

Galina Kolosova (Russia) – I, 302, II, 308 & III.[119]

Mrs. Galina Kolosova was born on 11 May 1940 in Moscow. She graduated in 1965 from the Moscow State University majoring in the Department of Philology specializing in Romanic and Germanic Languages and Literature. She worked for the Soviet Women's Committee (International Department) till 1969.

In 1970 the Soviet centre of ASSITEJ was formed and she was designated its Executive Secretary, which functioned within the framework of the Theatre Association of USSR (now of Russia) and united 60 professional repertory companies for young spectators all over USSR.

Kolosova also functioned as translator to many delegates at international gatherings, and attended many sessions of the EXCOM and Congresses from 1970 on.

She organized and coordinated the steering committees for the VIII (Moscow) and XII (Rostov-on-Don) World Congresses of ASSITEJ and their corresponding Festivals (1984 and 1996).

Kolosova initiated and coordinated the first in Russia permanent biannual International Festival of Theatre for Children and Young People (MINIFEST) on the base of the Rostov-on-Don Theatre for Young Spectators (1989, 1991, 1993, 1995, and 1996). She started together with the Netherlands counterparts the first in Russia international seminars on management and marketing in theatre (1990, 1991, and 1992). For the XII ASSITEJ Congress she created a special volume of the leading Teatralnaya Zhizn (Theatre Life) magazine dedicated to the problems of survival of theatres for young spectators. Galina left the position of the Executive Secretary of the Russian ASSITEJ centre in 1996.

Since 1980 she has been a translator of many English, American, Canadian, and French plays into Russian, and these translations have been performed in more than 40 cities in Russia and CIS.

From 1996 to 2000, she was a member of the Advisor's Council of Teatralnaya Zhizn Magazine, a member of the "George Soros" Foundation (Open Society Institute) as an expert on cultural programs, a member of the editorial Board of the new Moscow Quarterly Theatre for Children and Young People (affiliated to the Contemporary Playwriting Magazine).

In 1996–2002 she was an Advisor to the EXCOM of ASSITEJ and a jury member for the Honorary President's Award. In 2008 she was named a Member of Honor of ASSITEJ.

For 10 years (2000–2010) Galina Kolosova has been the Projects Coordinator for the prominent Chekhov International Theatre Festival organizing presentation of many outstanding productions from Great Britain, Canada, USA. In 2001 within the framework of this festival she arranged a little international festival of children's theatre productions from various countries. In 2007 she compiled and published a book—a collection of 9 contemporary Canadian plays, translating 6 of them. Of late she has started to translate Russian plays into English in order to promote them in other countries.

In 2012 she was awarded a Diploma of Honor of the Russian Authors' Society for her contribution to the field of professional translation and copyright.

Galina Kolosova is a member of the Russian ASSITEJ Center Board, a member of the Russian Authors' Society, a member of the Theatre Association of Russia.

Kim Peter Kovach[120]

Kim Peter Kovach was born a native of New York City, NY, and he received his MFA in Directing from the University of Texas at Austin, Texas, USA.

Kovac is Producing Director of the Kennedy Center Theater for Young Audiences in Washington, DC, which commissions, produces, and presents new productions for young audiences. At the Center he has served as producer of over fifty new plays, operas, and dances, and co-founded *New Visions/New Voices*, which has assisted in the development of 88 new plays, musicals, and operas from 78 playwrights and 35 composers, working with 57 U.S. and 8 international theater companies.

He was a State Department/Arts America Fellow to Amman, Jordan, teaching a four-week seminar in theatrical design to professional directors and designers. In recent years he has spoken at many international symposia: on Theater for Young Audiences (TYA) and school systems (Vienna, Austria); on international networking (Amman, Jordan and Adelaide, Australia); on playwriting for young audiences (Tokyo and Okinawa City); and on cultural diversity in TYA (Bursa, Turkey, and Adelaide, Australia). He also was invited by the Japanese league of producers of theater for children and young people to conduct a seminar on the international landscape of the field, community engagement, and acting, and was keynote speaker at "TYA: A Gathering" in Cork, Ireland. In the USA, he taught seminars on "Business of New Play Development" and "International TYA" at the University of Central Florida, where he is a Graduate Faculty Scholar, and was recently a guest artist at the University of Texas–Austin.

He first became involved in ASSITEJ in 1986 when he attended the Director's Seminar in East Berlin as the U.S. Representative. Since 2002, he has been on the Executive Committee of ASSITEJ/ Int'l, and is currently serving his second term as Vice-President of ASSITEJ/Int'l. Since 1988, he has been on the Board of TYA/USA, was its President from 2004–2008, and was on the Board of International Performing Arts for Youth (IPAY) from 2010–2013.

In May 2011 he co-founded *"Write Local. Play Global"*, an international network for playwrights for young audiences, which presently has over 500 members in 64 countries.

In 2008, both IPAY and the American Alliance for Theater in Education (AATE) honored him for long-time distinguished service to the field. In May 2013 the Children's Theatre Foundation of America (CTFA) presented him with their highest award, a Medallion for long-time excellence.

Fusako Kurahara (Japan) – II, 309 & III[121]

At the age of 5, Fusako Kurahara was taken to see a traditional *Noh* play by her grandmother, a theatre experience which became a part of her life forever.

She studied English and Psychology (counseling) at the international division of Sophia University. She then taught English at the Kyoritsu Girls' High School in Tokyo for 14 years.

During the 1970's she helped translate a pamphlet "Children's Theatre in Japan" into English, which led her to become involved in the Japanese Center for ASSITEJ.

In 1983 she became the Secretary of ASSITEJ/Japan, and they were visited by a delegation from ASSITEJ/USA, which was their first formal visitation by members from another ASSITEJ Center. This eight person delegation, led by Dr. Ann Shaw as Vice-President of ASSITEJ, had just returned from China in search of a play performance to bring to the New Orleans, Louisiana World's Exposition in the USA in 1984. As a result of this visit Shaw became known to the Japanese Center as their "Shoguness"!

From this beginning ASSITEJ/Japan became very much involved in the affairs of ASSITEJ, developing international theatrical exchange through meetings, festivals, and Congresses, and as a result of their hard work, they were elected to serve on the ASSITEJ Executive Committee, with Kurahara as their translator.

In 1987 at the Adelaide International Congress of ASSITEJ, she saw the plays of David Holman (Great Britain), one was "Small Poppies", and she asked permission to do translations of his plays into Japanese. As a result of his approval many Japanese children have been enjoying his plays. "Small Poppies" performed by Theatre Nakama received the Best Children's Play of the Year Award in 1998, and had been performed 175 times by 2002.

She retired as Secretary of ASSITEJ/Japan in 1997. Currently she is helping the Kijo Picture Book Village on Kyushu Island to invite foreign theatre groups to visit each year. They also hold workshops for children and young people there.

As a result of her teaching, recently one of her students is planning to host a theatre workshop for children in his town, after being a student at her Workshop in Kijo. He is now 21 and interested in the theatre as a profession.

She feels that theatre for young people is blessed work, a joy which makes children happy, which in turn lets those children convey that joy to others "like flying seeds of a dandelion".

Kazuto Kurihara (Japan) II, 309, & III.[122]

Kazuto Kurihara graduated from the Art Division of Nihon University in 1939. He worked as an assistant and an instructor in actor-training at various colleges. While writing, dramatizing, and directing plays for children, he helped establish the Association of Children's Playwrights in 1948. Later this Association became known as the Japan Children's Theatre Association, Inc. In 1958 he became the Association's first President, and remained so until his death in 1994.

In 1955 he was appointed a Judging Committeeman for the Art Festival sponsored by the Governmental Agency for Cultural Affairs. In 1974 this same Agency appointed him a Project Commissioner for its Children's Art Theatre.

In 1979 the Japan Center for ASSITEJ was established, and he became its first President until his death. In 1984 he was elected a Member of the Executive Committee of ASSITEJ/Int'l, and continued in that capacity until 1990. Also, in 1984 he became a member of the Board of Directors for ITI, continuing until 1992.

In 1985 the first all Japan Children's Performing Arts Festival was held on Sado Island. He became Head of the Festival, and chaired the International TYA Symposium with 12 countries attending. As President of ASSITEJ/Japan, he was eager to develop international exchange, especially among Asian countries.

During his presidency the Japan Center held several TYA meetings in Japan with many Asian colleagues attending. In 1988 the first Asian TYA Meeting was held on Sado Island; in 1989 the 1989 Asian TYA Symposium was held in Tokyo and Koufu; in 1991 the Japan-Sea Rim TYA Meeting was held. And in 1993 to facilitate the spread of information, the Asian TYA Newsletter "CURTAINS UP!" was issued by the Japan Center.

After a rich and active life in the theatre, Kurihara died at the age of 83 in 1994.

Zvjezdana Ladika (Croatia) I, 303 & II, 310.

Zvjezdana Ladika was born in Karlovac, Croatia 1921, but moved to Varazdin in her early childhood where she received her secondary-school education. At the University of Zagreb, she completed the studies of the literatures of the nations—the former Yugoslavia, French language and literature, and Russian language and literature.

After graduation, she spent a short time teaching at a secondary school, but resigned in order to study directing at the Film Studio, which she completed in 1950. In addition, she graduated in staging from the Academy of Dramatic Arts in Zagreb.

After her second graduation, she found employment at the Zagreb Theatre for Young People as both a director and theatrical educator. It was there that she staged Shakespeare's *Romeo and Juliet* as her graduation piece. Over the years, she staged more than a hundred performances for and with children and young people at the same theatre.

In the year 1956 she went on a study tour to Prague, and in 1960 to France where theatre for children developed as creative dramatics for children and young people.

With her plays she took part in numerous theatre festivals throughout Europe. Her international theatre exchange also included an exchange with the professional theatre for children and young people in Brno (Prague, Bratislava, Brno, 1956).

Mme. Ladika published a large number of writings on children's dramatic creativity—in her own book *The Child and the Dramatic Art*, and as a co-author of the books *Theatrical Plays; The Child and Creativity; I'm Bored, I Don't Know What to Do*. She published her writings in professional periodicals and publications in Croatia and abroad.

She was a long-standing member of the ASSITEJ Executive Committee, where she left an indelible imprint through her activity and influenced the development of the world's theatre for children and young people. As a result she was named an Honorary Member of ASSITEJ in 1996. She was one of the founders of the Mala Scena Theatre in 1989, where she was active as a director, writer, and head of its drama studio.

Mme. Ladika received numerous rewards for her artistic work, the most important of them being Young Generation in 1972 for direction of the play Tom-cat Genghis Khan and Miki Trasi; an award from the Dramatic Artists' Society for direction in 1984; Dubravko Dujsin Award in 1988 for her long productive theatrical work with children and young people at the Zagreb Theatre for Young People; and the Vladimir Nazor Life Achievement Award.

She died on 17 August 2004 at the age of 82.

Don Raffaello Lavagna (Vatican, Italy) II, 311.

Volker D. Laturell (FGR) II, 311.

Sara Lee Lewis (Canada) II, 312.

Ion Lucian (Romania) I, 304 & II, 313.

When Nat Eek was in Romania in August 2012, he was informed by their tour guide that Ion Lucien had died that summer in June, 2012. Lucien was such a well known theatre artist that the entire country knew of him and greatly mourned his death.

Marián Lucky (Slovakia) II, 313, & III.

Marián Lucky worked for his degree from Comenius University in Bratislava from 1969-1975. Since 1974 he has been working in the theatres for children as a dramaturge and a psychologist. His activity is concentrated on the scientific work—researches in the field of the young audience.

He is tutor to works on the theme of Children's Theatre at the High Academy of the Arts and Philosophical Faculty.

He is an actor, musician, and also the author of several plays for children presented in theatres, on radio broadcasts, and television. He is an organizer of Festivals of Theatres for Children.

Since 1974 he has actively worked for ASSITEJ. In 1988 he became President of the Czechoslovakian Center for ASSITEJ, and has been a member of the EC.

From 1991-1992 he worked in the Ministry of Culture of the Slovak Republic as Vice-Director of the Arts Department. Since November 1992 he has been the dramaturge in Theatre for Children and Deputy Director in the National Theatre Center.

João Luiz (Portugal) II, 314.

Halina Machulska (Poland) II, 314.

Tony Mack (Australia)[123]
Tony Mack was born in Melbourne, Australia in 1958. He began work as an actor in films while still a teenager. He moved to Sydney in 1977 to study acting at the National Institute of Dramatic Art (NIDA). After graduating, he worked professionally as an actor in both Sydney and Melbourne with companies such as Sydney Theatre Company and Melbourne's Playbox Theatre. He acted in TV series such as *Prisoner* and *The Sullivans*, and spent a year in Christchurch, New Zealand at the Court Theatre where he met his wife, Leigh Mangin.

Returning to Australia, Mack settled in Adelaide, working with companies such as State Theatre Company (South Australia), Harvest Theatre, Patch Theatre Company, Stage Company, and Vitalstatistix. Apart from film and television work, Mack also worked extensively in film, video, and radio in the corporate world—performing, narrating, presenting or doing voiceovers for some of Australia's best known corporations.

In the early 1990's, he founded Boulevard Theatre and, as its Artistic Director, toured early childhood theatre throughout South Australia, writing and directing acclaimed shows such as *Try Again Red Riding Hood* and *Next Door*. He trained some of South Australia's finest performing artists at the University of Adelaide, and was Editor of *Lowdown*, Australia's youth performing arts magazine, from 1999-2007.

From 2002-2008 he served as Vice-President of ASSITEJ/Int'l. In that capacity, he promoted and advocated theatre for children and young people in visits to more than 20 countries. He has written articles for publications in the USA, Great Britain, and Japan, and has co-edited, with Wolfgang Schneider, three ASSITEJ Year Books that have been distributed to youth performing arts organizations in up to 81 countries. He was the Australian international representative of Young People and the Arts Australia/ASSITEJ Australia (YPAA) from 2002-2008.

From 2005-2008 he was the Chair of the ASSITEJ Executive Committee's Congress Working Group, and was responsible to the Executive Committee for the successful delivery of the XVIth ASSITEJ World Congress and Performing Arts Festival in Adelaide, Australia. After the Congress, Mack was awarded an Australia Council Fellowship from 2008-2010.

In 2011, Mack co-founded, with Kim Peter Kovac and Deidre Lavrakas, the ASSITEJ playwright network *Write Local, Play Global*. He continues to work as an actor, acting teacher, consultant, and arts journalist.

On Australia Day in 2014 Mack was appointed a Member (AM) of the Order of Australia, one of the country's highest civilian honors, for "significant service to the performing arts, particularly theatre for children and youth."

Marjorie E. MacLean (Canada) II, 315, & III[124]
Marjorie E. MacLean was born in North Vancouver, Canada, March 2, 1953.

She obtained a BA degree in 1977 and a BFA degree in 1979 from the University of British Columbia. She practiced as a professional visual artist while also beginning a career in the performing arts – diverse work that ranged from sewing tutus for the local ballet company, to stage management, to arts administration for an alternative theatre company.

During this period, she was hired as a technician in 1978 for a new concept in presenting Canadian performing arts for children. This was the Vancouver International Children's Festival, an event that became the foremost North American showcase for children's professional theatre, music, and dance. As Artistic Director of the Festival from 1981 to 2000, she presented works that both challenged and entertained, including some commissioned pieces.

In 1992 she was named Festival Producer. She led the Festival as both Artistic Director and Producer until June 2000. She established a national touring circuit for visiting artists from across the world to children's festivals in Canada and the United States, providing significant work and new opportunities for artists, while bringing new ideas about the arts to young audiences in both small and major venues. It was an honor that festivals were established in Edinburgh and Japan that were modeled after the Vancouver Festival.

In 1997 she received a three-year appointment to the Minister of Foreign Affairs' Foreign Policy Advisory Board representing cultural interests. She willingly volunteered her time on many other cultural boards including ASSITEJ. She was head of ASSITEJ/Canada from 1993 until 1999, serving on the International Executive Committee and as International Vice-President (1993–1999) and Chair, Marketing and Communications Commission (1993–1996) as well as Chair, Artistic Commission (1996–1999). While serving in these capacities for ASSITEJ she created and wrote the MacLean Report for President Michael FitzGerald. This excellent report detailed brilliantly the artistic goals and activities of all the national centers of ASSITEJ at that time, and was used as a guide for the working program of ASSITEJ under President FitzGerald.

She returned to school after leaving the Festival in June 2000, and attended the Université de Laval, Québec, and Simon Fraser University in British Columbia where she obtained a teaching degree in Fine Arts (2003), and a Masters degree in Educational Leadership (2006). She also provided consulting services to the Canada Council for the Arts, the National Arts Centre and others, such as the 2010 Olympic Bid Committee (Cultural Division).

She worked in the field of early education as Principal of an independent primary school for oral deaf children, and sat on the Executive Committee of the Federation of Independent Schools of British Columbia. She continued to support the performing arts and practiced as an artist, working in photography and painting.

She died in 2013.

Niclas Malmcrona (Sweden)[125]
Niclas Malmcrona was born on 23 January 1961 in Gothenburg, Sweden's second largest city. He graduated from the University of Gothenburg majoring in Drama, philosophy, and cultural and social science.

From 1985–1987 he worked as a production manager at the Wästswänska Teatern in Uddevalla, moving from there to Stockholm and the TURteatern where he worked as a producer from 1987–1999.

During leaves from TURteatern he worked as Marketing Manager of Parkteatern (1990-1992) in Stockholm, and also as a consultant for Teaterförbundet (the Swedish Union for Theater, Artists, and Media). In addition to his work as producer at TURteatern he also organized a number of children's theatre festivals in Stockholm with Swedish and Nordic participation in the years 1994-2000.

Malmcrona was instrumental in the establishment of *Bibu. se*—the Swedish National Performing Arts Biennial for Children and Youth, and was a member of its Board from its start in 2005 until he resigned in 2009. Since the first Biennial in 2006 until today, he has been a member of the jury selecting performances for the Biennial.

Malmcrona was first involved with ASSITEJ in 1990 working as Media Officer with the 10th ASSITEJ World Congress and Festival in Stockholm, and that same year he was elected to the ASSITEJ/Sweden Board where he has served as Treasurer and currently as Vice-Chairman.

After the resignation of Ulli Plichta as Secretary General of ASSITEJ in 1998, he was asked to be the ASSITEJ Executive Officer, and in turn was elected their Secretary General in 1999 at the XIIIth ASSITEJ World Congress in Tromsø, Norway. He was re-elected twice to that position—at the XIVth World Congress in Seoul, Korea in 2002 and at the XVth World Congress in Montreal, Canada in 2005. Between 1997 and 2008 he attended all the EC Meetings of ASSITEJ/International.

As Secretary General Malmcrona continued the work begun by Michael Ramløse, making the Association more inclusive, more manageable, and more visible internationally. With support from SIDA (the Swedish International Development Cooperation Agency) he together with many African countries established and managed an African ASSITEJ Network which brought various African countries into ASSITEJ. He also organized several cooperative projects in the Baltic countries, Russia, and the Middle East between 2000 and 2008. As Secretary General he traveled extensively, and visited more than 50 foreign countries.

In 2008 for his excellent extended service to ASSITEJ/Int'l he was made an Honorary Member of ASSITEJ.

When Malmö/Copenhagen were selected as the site of the XVIIth World Congress of ASSITEJ, Malmcrona was appointed Secretary General (together with Peter Manscher) for the Swedish/Danish Secretariat.

Malmcrona currently works as General Manager of ASSITEJ/Sweden, and lives in Stockholm with his wife and three sons.

Graziano Melano (Italy)

Graziano Melano was first elected to the EC at the Cuban Congress in 1993. He suceeded Franco Passatore as the Italian representative who had served two terms from 1987 to 1993. Melano served one term (1993-1996).

Katariina Metsälampi (Finland)[126]

Katariina Metsälampi was born in Helsinki in 1958. She received a thorough knowledge of the French language and culture in the French School of Helsinki from Kindergarten to her graduation. She received her MA Degree from the University of Helsinki, majoring in French, Spanish, and Literature. In 1996 she finished a two-year program in Arts Management.

From an early age she has been doing dance as a hobby, later as a second job, both teaching and doing small choreographic works.

Metsälampi has made a long career in the Helsinki City Cultural Office as a Producer, the Director of Cultural House, Festival Producer and Festival Director. Since 2002 she has worked in the Children's Arts Center Annantalo as Manager for dance and theater arts. From 2003–2006 she has been co-coordinating the three-year-long Trans Dance European Culture Program in Finland. She is now the Finnish Coordinator in the Small Size-Big Citizens project, which includes twelve European countries. Its aim is to support and develop performing arts for 0-6- year-olds.

Metsälampi has been on the Board of ASSITEJ/Finland for twenty years, eight of them as Vice-President and President, and then later she was made Honorary President. In March 2011 she resigned from the Board, but continues her work on some projects.

She has participated in the Nordic Centers' Network since 1995. She has represented the Finnish Center in the World Congresses of 1996 at Rostov-on-Don, Russia; 1999 at Tromsø, Norway; 2002 at Seoul, Korea; 2005 at Montreal, Canada; 2008 at Adelaide, Australia; and 2011 at Copenhagen, Denmark/Malmö, Sweden.

She was heading the ASSITEJ World Project named "Bravo!" during the years from 1997–2000. She has been Director of the international theatre festivals BRAVO! 2002 and BRAVO! 2004, both designated as ASSITEJ/Int'l Festivals, as well as the Finnish national HURRAA! Festivals 2003 and 2005.

Metsälampi was elected to the EC at the 2005 Montreal Congress, and served until 2011. During that time she has been working specially to develop the networking in the Association. Together with Maria Inés Falconi she was organizing the 5-year-long ASSITEJ/Int'l World Project: Taboos – How to stage difficult subjects for children and young people! The Project was a research and meeting forum for theater makers in the Latin American countries, Spain, and the Nordic countries.

She has commented "For me ASSITEJ has always been an opportunity. The members are your partners and colleagues. It is good to work together when we have common goals and a child in one's heart."

Zdravko Mitkov (Bulgaria) II, 316.

Penina M'Lama (Tanzania)

Penina M'Lama was elected to the EC in 1993 at the Cuban Congress in Havana and served from 1993–1996. During that time she attended the EC meetings in Frankfurt, Germany (1993), Caracas, Venezuela (1994), Seattle, Washington, USA (1995), and Brisbane, Australia (1996).

Rose-Marie Moudoués (France) I, 305 & II, 316.

Maria Navarro (Spain) II, 317.

Jackson Ndawula(Uganda)

Jackson Ndawula was co-opted to join the newly elected EC at the XIIIth World Congress in Tromsø, Norway in 1999, and was appointed to serve the next three years (1999–2002) as well as to sit on the new Financial Commission. He also attended the EC Meeting in Harare, Zimbabwe in December 2000.

During his time he was very active in many African countries, such as Kenya and Rwanda as well as Uganda, urging them to form national centers. He attended the EC Meeting in Rio de

Janeiro, Brazil in March 2002, and the XIVth World Congress in Seoul, Korea in July 2002 when he went off the EC.

Ottorino Negri (Italy) II, 317.

Hagit Rehavi Nikolayevski (Israel).[127]

Hagit Rehavi Nikolayevski is an award winning playwright, play director, dramaturge, and teacher. She is a graduate of the Theater Department in the Tel Aviv University.

Over her career she has written many plays for children and adults. Some of her well known titles are: *What A Youth, The Girl I love, The Hana's Method, Alifim, Zohara's Shmulik, Uri, A Girl with a Kea, Eliezer the Dreamer, The Alien, Open the Gate, Ephraim's Grandma, A Kiss in the Pocket, Itamar's Love, Stronger Than Superman, Papadakis' Party*, and *The Devil from the 7th Grade*.

In 1981 she received the Harp of David Prize for the best children and youth production with her play *Zohara's Shmulik*. In 1994 she received the Excellency Prize at the Haifa International Festival for children and youth for the monodrama *A Girl with a Kea*, for both its adaptation and its direction.

She served as Artistic Director of the Haifa International Theatre Festival for Children and Youth in 1996.

In 1997 she received the Best Play Prize at the Aco Theatre Festival for her play *Yona-Yona*, both as its playwright and its director.

She served as the General Director and Artistic Director of the Orna Porat National Theatre for children and youth from 1997–2003. She won the Tel Aviv Municipality Rozenblum Prize in 2003 for her contribution to the field of children's theatre.

She has been the Chair of ASSITEJ/Israel, and served on the ASSITEJ/Int'l EC for two terms from 1999–2005.

Critic Yediot Acharonot wrote about her play *Alifim*: "Hagit Rehavi Nikolayevsky managed to weave the different stories into one organic, flowing and pleasant unity. This is a lovely play and an exciting one for the adolescents of today."

Harold R. Oaks (USA), II, 318 & III. [128]

Harold Rasmus Oaks was born in Provo, Utah, 20 June 1936. He completed BA and MA degrees at Brigham Young University and his PhD at the University of Minnesota. As a professor teaching at Brigham Young University, he chaired the Theatre & Film Department for 12 years, was coordinator of the Child Drama Program, and founded the Young Company which toured nationally and internationally (Šibenik, Yugoslavia, and Vienna, Austria in 1983, and Tromsø, Norway ASSITEJ CONGRESS and Festival, 1999).

Oaks directed over 40 productions for young people and adults across the United States. The Church of Jesus Christ of Latter-day Saints commissioned him to write, design & construct puppets, and direct a series of puppet shows for Health Fairs in various countries around the world. These have been translated into over 15 languages, and have been performed in over 25 countries for thousands of young people and adults.

Oaks served ASSITEJ as a member of the Executive Committee (1988–2002), as Treasurer (1993–1999), and as President (1999–2002). He also served on the Board of Directors of the American College Theatre Festival (1974–79); as Treasurer of the American Theatre Association

(1972-73); as President of the Children's Theatre Association of America (1985-86); as President of the American Alliance for Theatre & Education (1987-88); as President of ASSITEJ/USA (1988-95); and served on the Education Advisory Panel (1986-91) of the John F. Kennedy Center for the Performing Arts, Washington, DC.

Oaks has done over 80 workshops and presentations at many locations in the USA as well as in Tonga, Fiji and Western Samoa, Canada, Germany, Poland, Norway, Croatia, Sweden, Japan, Switzerland, and Brazil. He has over one hundred publications and reviews in national and international journals, newsletters and books. He was editor of The ASSITEJ/USA INTERNATIONAL HOT LINE from 1989 to 2001.

He was awarded the Gold Medallion of Excellence from the American College Theatre Festival in 1978, was given a Presidential Citation from the American Alliance for Theatre and Education in 1993, was elected to the College of Fellows of the American Theatre in April 2002, and was awarded a 2004 Medallion for Excellence by the Children's Theatre Foundation of America. He was given the Alumni Distinguished Service Award by Brigham Young University on October 7, 2011.

He retired from Brigham Young University as Associate Dean, College of Fine Arts & Communications in 2002. Following his retirement in 2002, Oaks and his wife, Ima Jean, served in St. Thomas, US Virgin Islands (2002-2004) and on the island of Palawan, the Philippines (2004-2006). There they presented Health Service puppet shows to thousands of young people, delivered wheelchairs, arranged for health care for those with special needs, taught English as a Second Language, helped organize youth activities, and worked with local Church leaders on various projects. They also served in the Europe Area Office of the Church of Jesus Christ of Latter-day Saints in Frankfurt, Germany (2008-2010), helping with country Websites, writing, and directing a short film, as well as other public affairs activities.

He was named an Honorary President of ASSITEJ at the XVIth World Congress in Adelaide, Australia in 2008.

Sozaburo Ochiai (Japan) – II, 319.

Anne van Otterloo (Netherlands).[129]

Anne van Otterloo was born in Geleen in the Netherlands in 1951. She started her university education in 1969, and studied for a year at Leicester University in the Great Britain after achieving her first degree. Back from her year in the Great Britain, she studied Theatre Sciences and graduated at Utrecht University in 1977.

She started her career as an arts-officer concerned with performing arts for the Regional Arts Council of the province Noord-Holland. In 1984 she left the Council and worked 5 years for the Dutch Federation of Artists Associations as performing arts officer. In 1987 she was asked by the board of De Bundeling, Dutch Association of Theatre Companies for Children and Young People, to become their General Secretary. She set up a professional office for this Association and brought new life into the Dutch Center of ASSITEJ. The national budget for theatre for children and young people doubled with the aim to raise the professional level of the companies.

Through the Dutch Center of ASSITEJ she became involved in the international exchange in the field of theatre for children and young people. Her first visit to an ASSITEJ World Congress was in 1990 in Stockholm, Sweden, where Michael Ramløse was elected Secretary General.

She initiated exchange projects with Russia in collaboration with the Russian Center of ASSITEJ, which later resulted in theatre management training programs that were held all over Russia from 1990 until 1998. She was a Counsellor to the EC of ASSITEJ/Int'l from 1993–1996, and worked with Marjory MacLean on proposals for a new ASSITEJ logo with a world image.

She also initiated an artistic exchange between six theatre companies working for children and young people from France, Italy, Germany, Portugal, Belgium and The Netherlands. The idea for this exchange was born during an ASSITEJ Directors meeting in Germany held in 1992.

This exchange resulted in the production *The Right Shoes*, which was performed for children in refugee camps in Croatia in 1994. In that same year she set up the Foundation—Arts and Young People in Europe—in order to develop a Secretariat for the European Network of Art Organisations for Children and Young People, known as EUnetART. She was a founding member of this network, which had its first meeting in 1991 in Bologna, Italy.

During the next five years Anne van Otterloo was the heart of the development of the EUnetART network. As General Secretary she did not only raise funds in Europe and the Netherlands for the Secretariat, but also for several European co-operation projects like *A Myth for Europe*, *Ouch*, *Theatre meets social Reality in Europe*, *The Magic House*, and *Zapping through Wonderland*. As Secretary General of EUnetArt she participated in the meetings of the European Forum of Arts and Heritage (EFAH) and was a member of several of EFAH's working groups. In this capacity she helped to set up a lobby for European Cultural networks with the members of the European Parliament.

In 1999 Anne van Otterloo set up her own consultant business *Annalin, Cultural Enterprise and Advice*, and worked as a freelance professional. From 2002 to 2010 she was engaged in international European cooperation projects as a freelance as well as employed by the Dutch Foundation Kunstenaar & Co. such as *Transmission*, a European pilot project that explores the possibility of increasing the mobility and employability of workers in the performing arts. She helped to set up the postgraduate KIS education program at the Theatre School in Amsterdam for artists who want to broaden their portfolio outside the boundaries of the arts world. She coordinated the Leonardo Transmission Art education program and ran the Equal project "Kunst werk(t) in de tertiaire sector" (Art Works in the Third Sector), which she initiated and developed with her colleagues at Kunstenaars & Co.

Anne van Otterloo was a member of the committee for international affairs of the Dutch National Council for Culture (2001–2005), and a member of the jury for the program Culture 2000 in 2001. She still works as a freelance consultant for her company *Annalin, Culture & Innovation (adaptation in the name)*, and is currently a partner in the Grundtvig learning partnership Teatral.

Franco Passatore (Italy) II, 320.

Luiz Velez Dos Santos Pisco (Portugal) II, 320.

Ullide Plichta (Austria)

Ulli Plichta was a theatre manager and member of the Board of ASSITEJ/Austria when she was elected to a three-year term as Secretary General of ASSITEJ at the XIIth World Congress at Rostov-on-Don in October 1996. As a result of internal management conflicts between her and the Austrian National Center and a subsequent lack of financial support, she resigned that position in April 1998.

Stephan Rabl (Austria)

Stephan Rabl was elected to the EC at the XIVth World Congress in Seoul, Korea in July 2002 as the Austrian representative. Previously Austria had been represented by the newly elected Secretary General Ulli Plichta but who had resigned that position as of April 1998. Because of the situation in the Austrian National Center, they had no representative as an immediate replacement. However, Rabl had taken over the reins of ASSITEJ/Austria, and was elected to the EC for one 3-year term (2002–2005). He chose not to run for re-election. Much later he was appointed as Counselor to the EC for a 3-year term (2011–2014).

Michael Ramløse (Denmark) , II, 321, & III.[130]

Michael Ramløse was born 8 November 1949 in Copenhagen. He graduated in 1976 from the University of Copenhagen, having majored in Russian and German Languages and Literature.

From 1976–1984 he was a member of BANDEN, one of Denmark's leading free theatre companies for children in the city of Odense. Then for three years he worked freelance as a director, playwright, composer, and translator of plays for children. From 1987–1996 he served as head of TEATERCENTRUM, a semi-official office under the Ministry of Culture whose purpose is to promote professional theatre for children. TEATER-CENTRUM is the organizer of the large annual Danish Children's Theatre Festival in April, performing in a new part of the country each year.

In 1983 he was one of the key-persons in re-organizing the Danish Center for ASSITEJ, and as its head made it an all-inclusive organization, taking over from Mme. Inga Juul. His involvement in ASSITEJ led him to be elected as the first new Secretary General of the organization, succeeding Mme. Rose-Marie Moudoués who had served for the twenty-five years since the founding of ASSITEJ in 1965. The national centre became ASSITEJ/DENMARK-TEATERCENTRUM which served as the Secretariat for both the Danish national center and the Secretary General. Ramløse served as Secretary General for two terms, from 1990–1996.

In 1997 he became administrative director of FAIR PLAY, one of Denmark's leading children's theatre companies, and continues in that capacity to this day. In addition he has served as Chair of the Children's Theatres' Association of Denmark, was on the steering committee of "The Playwrights' Greenhouse II and III", as well as Chair of the Regional Theatre Council of West Zealand County. For two years he was director of the international children's theatre festival CARAVANEN.

He has written numerous articles and given key-note speeches on Danish children's theatre in Denmark and abroad. He has received the 25th Anniversary Prize of the Children's Theatre Association; the Cultural Prize of FTF (Denmark's second largest trade union); the Children's Theatre Award of the City of Horsens, and was made an Honorary Member of ASSITEJ in 1999. In Denmark he headed the Committee which created the Celebration of the 100th Anniversary of Hans Christian Andersen.

An author of numerous plays for children, he lists among those most often performed are: *Mum's the Word, The Fifth Commandment, The Earth We Walked On, Our Performance about Sarah,* and *A Word is a Word.* He has translated other plays from English, Swedish, Russian, and German.

As Secretary General of ASSITEJ, he headed the first fully professional Secretariat of the organization, which was financed by a consortium of Ministries of Culture of Denmark, Norway, Finland, Iceland, and Sweden in cooperation with the staff of TEATERCENTRUM. His new approach to the administration of ASSITEJ improved administrative practice and procedures, improved communication among the National Centers, implemented a new subscription system, and most importantly changed ASSITEJ from a Euro-centric organization to a global association, which made it inclusive instead of exclusive, making it more manageable and visible internationally.

Peter Rinderknecht (Switzerland)

Peter Rinderknecht was elected to the EC for a three-year term at the XIIIth World Congress at Tromsø, Norway Congress in 1999. He was re-elected for two additional three-year terms—2002-2005 and 2005-2008. He is known as an excellent actor-director of high-quality plays for children which have been presented at many international festivals.

Ilse Rodenberg, PhD (Germany) I, 307 & II, 322.

Susan Rubes (Canada) II, 323.

Jacqueline Russo (Venezuela)

Jacqueline Russo was elected to the EC for a three-year term at the XIth World Congress in Havana Cuba in February 1993.

Tülin Sağlam, PhD (Turkey)[131]

Dr. Tülin Sağlam was born in 1960 in Ankara, Turkey. She studied theatre at Ankara University, Faculty of Letters Theatre Department. She received her degrees (BA – 1986, MA – 1989, and PhD – 1998) all from the same Department. She specialized in theory and history of theatre. After completing her PhD research on Drama in Education at Manchester University, Department of Drama (1992-1994) in the UK, she also specialized in Drama in Education and Theater for Young Audiences.

Since 1988 she has been a Professor, and is teaching Drama in Education, Theatre for Young Audiences, Criticism, Theory, and History of Theatre. She has been teaching in the same Department since 1988.

Sağlam became involved in ASSITEJ/Turkey in 1990. In 1995 she became the Secretary General of the ASSITEJ/Turkey National Center, and then its President in 1999. She is still the current President of their Center.

She was appointed as a Councilor to the EC for the term of 2002-2005. She was first elected to the ASSITEJ/Int'l EC at their World Congress in Montreal, Canada in 2005 for the 2005-2008 term.

In 2006 she became one of the Founding Members and an EC Member of ITYARN (the International Theatre for Young Audiences Research Network), which is the International Research Network of ASSITEJ/Int'l.

As Head of ASSITEJ/Turkey, she is the Artistic Director of Bursa International Theatre Festival for Children and Young People (from its inception in 1995), and advisor for the International Eskisehir Children's and Youth Theatres Festival which was started in 2006.

Currently she is the Head of Theatre History and Theory sub-Department. She is also the coordinator of the master's program on TYA and Drama since 2001 at Ankara University,

Social Sciences Institute Theatre Department. In addition, she is the Founding Member and Coordinator of Ankara University's Children's University since 2009.

Besides her involvement with ASSITEJ, she is a member of such professional associations as the Turkish Contemporary Drama Association, and the International Association of Theatre Critics (Turkish Branch).

She runs workshops on Drama in Education and TYA for school teachers and professional artists. She has written several articles, has presented papers in Turkey and abroad on TYA, and Turkish Theatre and Drama in Education. She has also written a book for teachers and young people on creating performances using drama as a tool.

Natalia Ilyinichna Sats (USSR) I, 308 & II, 324.[132]

Natalia Sats was born on the 27th of August 1903. Ilya Sats, her father, was a famous composer, and as a young girl she remembered hearing music being played in the next room to her bedroom. She described the music as "...sometimes impetuous, sometimes shimmering like water and magically glimmering as if a fairy had arrived. " It was the music composed by her father to *The Blue Bird* of Maurice Maeterlinck, the famous production by the Moscow Art Theater. Her great love of music for children dates from these early childhood experiences.

By the time she was 15, she was running the Mossovet Theatre in 1918, the first theatre for children that was born of her initiative. People would refer to her as "the Mother of all the theatres for children in the world." The Moscow Theatre for Children, the Moscow Central Theatre for Children, and the Moscow Musical Theatre for Children, named and dedicated to her, were all a result of her efforts, including the first Theatre for Young Spectators in Kazakhstan. In the early 1920's she had become known as an outstanding theatre director, and her productions of *A Little Negro and a Monkey, About Dzyuba, The Golden Key,* and *Seryozha Streitsov* were highly acclaimed by both the press and the public.

On the opera stages of the world she collaborated with conductor Otto Klemperer in productions of Verdi's *Falstaff* at the Crollopera in Berlin, Germany in 1931, and Mozart's *The Marriage of Figaro* at the Teatro Colon in Buenos Aires, Brazil that same year.

Tragically she fell afoul of the governmental authorities, and she was exiled to Siberia soon after. But even in exile she created a theatre in the gulag in which she was imprisoned. In the early 1960's she was rehabilitated under Premier Khrushchev, and began a new life in Moscow. She immediately created a musical theatre for children that had no venue at first, but by 1983 she had succeeded in building the State Musical Theatre for Children in Moscow, which was later named in her honor. After her reappearance, she immediately became involved in ASSITEJ, and during the 1980's she served as head of the USSR National Center and was elected to the Executive Committee of ASSITEJ. During her long career she was given many awards—People's Artist of the USSR, Hero of the Socialist Labor, and a winner of the Lenin and State Prizes of the USSR.

She died on 18 December 1993 at the age of 90.

Wolfgang Schneider (Germany)[133]

Dr. Wolfgang Schneider was born 12 July 1954 in Mainz, Germany. He graduated in 1977 from Johann Wolfgang University of Frankfurt with a Master of Arts in Literature, and started his career as a teacher of German language and political science. He was a photography assistant involved in productions for television, receiving an award at the 1982 International Berlin Film

Festival for his movie *Keine Startbahn West! Eine Region wehrt sich* ("No Runway Number 18! A Region in Rebellion").

In 1984 he completed his PhD in Performing Arts with his dissertation entitled *Kindertheater seit 1968. Neorealistische Entwicklungen* ("Children's Theater since 1968. Neo-realistic developments"). As an Assistant Professor he worked with Klaus Doderer, the founder of the Department for Children's Literature Research at Frankfurt University. While there he organized two conferences about Theater for Young Audiences.

In 1989 he founded the Kinder-und Jugendtheaterzentrum in der Bundesrepublik Deutschland *(Children's and Young People's Theater in the Federal Republic of Germany)* supported by the Federal Ministry for Youth, the state of Hessen, and the city of Frankfurt. When Germany was reunited in 1991 the center continued the work in the former ASSITEJ/GDR office in Berlin. It has had two offices (Frankfurt and Berlin) ever since. That same year Schneider founded the first National Festival for Theater for Young Audiences in Germany, a biennale event with the West Berlin "Grips" Theater and the Theater an der Parkaue (formerly the GDR Theater der Freundschaft/Theater of Friendship). He also established two prizes for Theater for Young Audiences, honoring dramatic literature for young people.

In 1997 he was appointed a Full Professor of Cultural Policy at the University of Hildesheim, where he founded the Department of Cultural Policy in 1998. From 2001–2009 he was Dean of the Faculty for Cultural Studies and Aesthetic Communication. In 2012 he was appointed by the UNESCO in Paris with a professorship as UNESCO Chair in "Cultural Policy for the Arts in Development". He has been Chair of many symposia, lecturer at seminars, and editor of many publications about cultural policy. In his field he is one of the international well-known and highly respected researchers at conferences of the international Scientific Community.

Schneider first became involved in ASSITEJ in 1986 in Munich when he was elected to the Board of ASSITEJ/Germany. He has been serving as President of ASSITEJ/Germany from 1997 onwards. In 1991 with the approval of the EC he established the Archives of ASSITEJ/Int'l in Frankfurt, Germany. He was elected to the EC in Tromsø in 1999. He served first as a Vice-President, and then he was elected President of ASSITEJ/Int'l in 2002 at the Seoul, Korea Congress, and served three terms in that office until 2011. He and former President Ilse Rodenberg (Germany) are the only presidents to have served three terms. In 2011 at the Copenhagen/Malmö World Congress he was appointed Honorary President of ASSITEJ/Int'l.

He has attended seven (7) World Congresses of ASSITEJ, beginning with the one in Havana, Cuba in 1993, and has attended all EC Meetings from 1993–2011, visiting all 6 continents.

For ASSITEJ/Int'l Schneider as Editor presented for the first time in 1996 "The ASSITEJ Annual", the Yearbook about theater for young audiences. This is printed every two years, and he has been assisted by Tony Mack (Australia) and Ivica Šimic (Secretary General of ASSITEJ/Croatia). In 2011 as Editor he created the new magazine for ASSITEJ/Int'l, which was presented at the XVIIth World Congress at Copenhagen/Malmö.

In Germany as a prolific author he has continued to write and publish many articles and books related to theatre for young people, many of which have been published in other languages. He has received many distinguished awards for many of his publications.

He has been President of the European Network of Arts Organizations for Children and Young People, Vice-President of the German Federation for Arts Education, Chair of the Advisory Board for Theater in the State of Lower Saxony, member of the Advisory Board for Theater and

Dance in the Goethe Institute, and is *ad personam* appointed member of the German UNESCO Commission and the International Theater Institute (ITI).

He continues to write and contribute publications on theater for young audiences, theatre education, cultural policy, and theatrical practice.

Konstantin Shakh-Azizov (USSR), I, 309.

Adolf Shapiro (Russia) II, 324 & III.[134]

Adolf Shapiro is a theatre director, playwright, author, and lecturer. He graduated from the Kharkov Theatre Institute where he received his early training. His advanced studies took place at the Theatre Directors' Workshop under the guidance of the legendary teacher and director Maria Knebel, who had studied under Stanislavski and Mikhail Chekhov. After her death Shapiro was appointed to her position to run the Workshop, and he also continued to teach as a professor at the Riga Conservatory. Shapiro's artistic work is based on the Stanislavski Method and further theatrical experiments of Bertold Brecht and other theatre reformers.

He directed his first play at the age of 23, winning great acclaim. At 25 he was designated the Artistic Director of two companies—the Russian and the Latvian ones, operating in two spaces under his leadership. For 30 years he was the driving force behind the Latvian Youth Theatre in Riga.

Shapiro has worked extensively abroad. His productions have been presented in Italy, Yugoslavia, Canada, the USA, Germany, Columbia, Venezuela, Finland, and elsewhere. Among his acclaimed productions are *Peer Gynt* by Ibsen, *Prince of Homberg* by Kleist, *The Last Ones* by Gorky, *Moliere* by Bulgakov, *Who's Afraid of Virginia Woolf?* by Edward Albee, *The Fear and Misery of the Third Reich* by Bertold Brecht, and *Democracy* by Joseph Brodsky. Shapiro's reputation rests strongly on his interpretations of Chekhov, which he has returned to time and time again.

Apart from work at his own theatre, he has directed plays at the Moscow Art Theatre and the Vakhtangov Theatre in Moscow; Bolshoi Drama Theatre in St, Petersburg; the Estonia National Theatre, Noorsooteater, and Linnateater in Tallinn, Estonia; Teatro Comedia Nacional in Managua, Nicaragua; Ateneo de Caracas in Venezuela; Gesher Theatre and Jiddischishpille Theatre in Tel Aviv, Israel; and Teatr Ochoty in Warsaw, Poland. His master teaching has taken him to many countries, and he has an ongoing relationship with the American Repertory Theatre's Institute for Advanced Theatre Studies, and Northern Illinois University's School of Theatre and Dance in the USA.

He has served on the EC of ASSITEJ/Int'l , where he was elected President of ASSITEJ from 1990-1993. At present he is the President of ASSITEJ/Russia, and the Supervisor of the artistic programs of the St. Petersburg Theatre for Young Spectators in that city as well as SAMART (the Theatre for Children and Young People in Samara).

He maintains a partnership with ENSATT, the National Theatre High School in Lyon, France, where he teaches directing and acting.

Shapiro is Honorary Doctor at the Theatre Academy in Tallinn, Estonia, where he conducts classes twice a year. In 2003 he was granted the Order of "Pro Terra Mariana" for his contribution to the development of Estonian culture. In 2006 he was the winner of the International Stanislavski Award for his productions of the classics. He was awarded the Pris d'Or in a unanimous decision of the international jury at the European "Theatre on TV" Festival.

He writes regularly for newspapers and theatre magazines. He has written two books: *Entr'acte I* and *When the Curtain Drops* which are devoted to the subjects of acting and directing, one of which received a literary award. He has also directed the film "The Victorious Woman".

His latest productions include *Moliere* by Bulgakov and *The Cherry Orchard* by Chekhov in Moscow, *Fahrenheit 451* after Ray Bradbury at the Et Cetera Theatre, *Children of the Sun* by Maxim Gorky at the Maly Theatre, and *Lucia di Lammermoor*, the opera by Donizetti at the Stanislavski and Nemirovitch-Danchenko Musical Theatre.

He is currently working on a book about Stanislavski for Vagrius Publishing House.

Ann M. Shaw, EdD (USA) I, 310, II, 324 & III.

Dr. Ann M. Shaw was born on 26 June 1930 in Wilsonville, Nebraska, USA, and was smitten by theatre at the age of 4 when she won First Prize (a silver dollar) in an amateur contest singing and dancing to the song "I'll never say never again, again."

She studied acting and directing at Colorado Woman's College. She received degrees from Northwestern University (BA, MA) in Theatre, and Columbia University (EdD). Her dissertation was considered seminal in creative drama.

Beginning in 1952 she taught creative dramatics in the Evanston, Illinois public schools, and continued her academic career at Western Michigan University, Hunter College, and Teachers College, Columbia University. She retired in 1990 having taught for 22 years at Queens College, City University of New York.

Author of many publications on children's theatre, and on theatre by, with, and for the disabled, her works have been translated into many languages. For the American Theatre Association (ATA) she served on their Board of Directors, key committees, organized two national conferences, and founded their program for the disabled (ATD).

Early professional theatre activities included Head, Wardrobe Department of the Central City Opera (Colorado); Box Office Manager, D'Oyly Carte Opera Co. (Colorado); costume execution of new productions (New York City Opera); and study at the Berghoff Studio, and appeared in several off-Broadway productions.

Shaw's honors include a CTAA Special Citation, Kennedy Center's Outstanding Educator Award, and Northwestern University's Award of Merit, a Medallion from the Children's Theatre Foundation, and ASSITEJ/USA named the Ann M. Shaw Fellowship Awards in her honor.

She attended her first meeting of ASSITEJ at the IVth International Congress in Canada and the USA in 1972 where she programmed the Creative Drama sessions. She was the USA representative to the ASSITEJ Executive Committee from 1978–1987. In 1981 she created the new US Center for ASSITEJ, known as ASSITEJ/USA and was its President until 1987. She initiated the Pacific Rim TYA exchange (1984) and the Mexico-USA Exchange (1985). She directed the World Theatre Festival for Young Audiences and the Symposium at the New Orleans World's Fair (1984).

She was twice elected ASSITEJ/Int'l Vice President, 1981–84 and 1984–87 and served as a USA voting delegate at eight Congresses from Madrid in 1978 through Tromsö in 1999. In 2002 at the XIVth World Congress in Seoul, Korea she was made an Honorary Member of ASSITEJ. She has attended every international Congress from 1972 to 2005, with the exception of the Vth Congress in Berlin, GDR in 1975.

She lives in Santa Fe, New Mexico, USA, and is active in St. Bede's Episcopal Church, and continues to encourage young people pursuing careers in theatre for young audiences.

Dr. Shaw currently lives at El Castillo, a retirement residence in Santa Fe, NM, USA.

Ivica Šimić (Croatia).[135]

Ivica Šimić was born 12 March 1953 in Grizane, Croatia. He graduated in Acting from the Academy of Dramatic Arts, at the University of Zagreb in 1983.

From 1983 to 1989 he was engaged as an actor in the Youth Theatre of Zagreb. In 1989, together with Vitomira Lončar, he founded the Theatre Mala Scena, where he continues to serve as its Artistic Director. At the Theatre Mala Scena he also directs their plays and performs as an actor for audiences of all ages.

The first play he directed professionally was Tom Stoppard's *The Real Thing* in 1989. Since then he has directed more than 50 performances in theatre for young audiences, as well as theatre for adults at the Theatre Mala Scena. He has also served as a guest director in Croatia and abroad.

Šimić works as a director of international projects, such as the Borges project in Manila, the Philippines in 2006, and the *iFdentit Project* for the International Theatre Institute in Madrid, Spain in 2008. He is currently directing *The Patchwork Family Project* in cooperation between European and Asian Theaters in 2011.

He first became a Member of the Executive Committee of ASSITEJ in 1999 representing Croatia at the XIIIth World Congress in Tromsø, Norway in that year. He was elected as Secretary General of ASSITEJ/Int'l in 2008 at the World Congress in Adelaide, Australia, and was re-elected to that office at the XVIIth World Congress in Copenhagen/Malmö in May 2011.

He is the founder of *Theatre Epicentre* (the Theatre Centre for Young Audiences in Central and Southeastern Europe).

Hans Snoek (Netherlands), I, 311.

Patricia Di Benedetto Snyder (USA) II, 325.

Eddy Socorro (Cuba) II, 326, & III.

Eddy Socorro was the Artistic Director of the Teatro Nacional de Guiñol in Havana, Cuba. He is a member of the National Counsel of Scenic Artists. He is a member of the National Union of *Environs* and Artists of Cuba (UNEAC). He was elected President of the Cuban Center for ASSITEJ in 1976.

He was elected to the EC in 1981, and served six terms until 1999, and served as a Vice-President each term. During the time he was on the EC, he hosted its Meeting in 1982 and 1990. In February 1993 he hosted the XIth World Congress of ASSITEJ/Int'l in Havana, Cuba.

Currently, the authors have not been able to contact him since he left his ASSITEJ office in 1999.

Sara Spencer (USA) I, 312.

Nena Stenius (Finland) II, 326.

Maria Nieves Sunyer y Roig (Spain) I, 313, & II, 327.

Pham Thi Thanh (Vietnam)

Pham Thi Thanh was the head of ASSITEJ/Vietnam. She was a member of ASSITEJ/International from 1991 to 1996. As a Vietnam Representative she first attended the EC Meeting in

Lyon, France in December 1991. Pham Thi Thanh was elected to the EC at the Cuban Congress in February 1993. She chose not to run again for election at the Rostov-on-Don, Russia Congress in October 1996.

Kathrin Türks (FGR) II, 327.

Jeremy Turner (Wales, UK).[136]
Jeremy Turner studied theatre at Aberystwyth University before founding his own experimental company "Cwmni Cyfri Tri (CC3)" in 1979. This brought him in touch with much contemporary European work, primarily that of Barba's "Odin Teatret" in Denmark. The Mission of CC3 was to try to define new models for contemporary theatre in the Welsh language—a minority language spoken by 25% of the population of Wales. This led to his interest in theatre for children and young people—an audience unblemished by the ways and conventions of "established" theatre.

In 1989 he became the director of a new company, "Cwmni Teatr Arad Goch", whose mission was to create new work for young audiences to be performed in schools or in regular theatres: www.aradgoch.org.

Turner became aware of ASSITEJ when he was taken by an older colleague, John Prior, to the RITEJ Festival in Lyon, France in 1989. He recognized the value of the organization as a bridge between Wales and other cultures, and soon became involved in establishing a Welsh sub-committee of ASSITEJ/Great Britain (now ASSITEJ/UK). He has been involved in the work of the UK Center of ASSITEJ since that time.

He was invited to give a keynote speech on the importance of theatre for young audiences of minority languages at the ASSITEJ World Congress in Havana, Cuba in 1993, and since then he has attended the following ASSITEJ World Congresses: Tromsø, Norway in 1999, Seoul, Korea in 2002, Montreal, Canada in 2005, and Copenhagen-Malmö in 2011. He was a member of the EC from 2002 to 2008. During that period he hosted a meeting of the EC in Wales in 2003, and chaired the Commission which established the first ASSITEJ on-line data-base of scripts.

In 1996 he established the "AGOR DRYSAU-OPENING DOORS Wales International Festival of Performing Arts for Young Audiences" as an international forum and as a market place for theatre from Wales: www.agordrysau-openingdoors.org. The Festival is now a biennial event, and its success lies in the network of friends and colleagues it has created between Wales and many other countries.

Turner was a member of the Arts Council of Wales' project *"Arts and Young People* Task Force" between 1997 and 2005. He wrote a study of *Participatory Youth Theatre in Wales* in 1996, has written for various publications in Wales, and has taught in a number of universities and schools. He has spoken in conferences in Wales and abroad—especially on the subject of youth culture in minority languages.

Under Turner's leadership "Arad Goch" which started work in a rented office, and which rehearsed in old, damp buildings, has now developed its own production house in Aberystwyth, Wales. It is the only company for young audiences in Wales that owns its own purposely-built facilities, which are being developed as a hub for the company's own work as well as a resource for other artists. "Arad Goch's" work is performed in Welsh and in English, and tours extensively in Wales. Turner has also had his work performed in Ireland, Scotland, Denmark, Sweden, Austria, France, Poland, the USA, Canada, and Singapore.

Jeremy Turner lives near the sea in mid-Wales.

Gerald Tyler (Great Britain) I, 313.

Ivan Voronov (USSR) II, 327.

Maurice Yendt (France) II, 328, & III.[137]

Maurice Yendt was born in Lyon, France on 15 November 1937. He spent his childhood in Brittany, and then in 1951 he pursued his studies in Lyon receiving a Degree in Letters.

In 1960 at the age of 23 he founded the Théâtre des Jeanes Années (TJA) in Lyon. He met in 1968 with Marcel Maréchal of la Compagnie du Cothurne, and together they created the new Théâtre du Huitième. From 1968 to 1980 Yendt created 18 productions, among which were *Le pays du soleil debout* (1969), *Le rossignol et l'oiseau mécanique*, and *La machine à théâtre* (1970), *La marche à l'envers* (1974), all of which were performed at the Festival d'Avignon under the direction of Jean Vilar, and later Paul Puaux.

In 1971 Yendt was named technical advisor in the dramatic arts to the Ministry of Youth and Sports. In 1973 he traveled to Germany to direct *Die Theaterspielmaschine* at the Landtheater Dortmund.

In 1977 with Michel Dieuaide he founded the Rencontres Internationales Théâtre Enfance Jeunesse (RITEJ), which in 1993 became the Biennale du Théâtre Jeunes Publics/Lyon. In 1980 Yendt was named Director of the National Drama Center by the French Minister of Culture. At that time the Théâtre des Jeunes Années (TJA) moved its activities to a new theatre which featured two performance theatres seating 490 and 100 respectively, supported by the City of Lyon and the Ministry of Culture. The Théâtre des Jeunes Années/centre dramatique national became the first permanent French theatre for young audiences.

From 1980 to 2005, Yendt directed 26 plays. Among the most recent were: *Ubu Roi* by Alfred Jarry, *Candide* after Voltaire, *Le pupille veut être tuteur* by Peter Handke, *Pinocchio* from the book of Carlo Collodi and the operatic version by Sergio Menozzi for the National Opera of Lyon, and in 1999 *Ce qui couve derrière la montagne*. These productions had numerous tours in France, and also were performed in Germany, Australia, Belgium, Brazil, Canada, Czechoslovakia, Spain, USA, Italy, Morocco, Portugal, Russia, and Switzerland.

Yendt has written 28 plays, of which 15 were original texts published in France and Belgium Cahiers du Soleil Debout, Actes Sud-Papiers, l'Amandier, Lansman, as well as numerous articles, including an essay *Les ravisseurs d'enfants* (Actes Sud-Papiers). Many of these plays are performed regularly, as well as being translated into other languages and performed abroad. Part of his work has been edited in Germany (Fischer-Verlag et Theater Stück Verlag).

Starting in 1993 Yendt was President of l'Association du Théâtre pour l'Enfance et la Jeunesse (ATEJ). He was an Advisor to the Executive Committee of ASSITEJ from 1981–1993, and Vice-President from 1993–1999.

After the dissolution of TJA in June 2004, he along with Michel Dieuaide became a Co-Artistic Director of la Biennale du Théâtre Jeunes Publics/Lyon. He continues his activities as author and director, most recently directing *The Marriage Proposal* by Anton Chekhov in 2005, and a new play *A Loving History of Theatre* (presented in Lyon in 2007, and in Brussels in 2010). He published in June 2010, a new collection of dramatic reflections entitled *Propos d'avant-scène, instantanés en marge d'un parcours théâtral* (Lansman Editor).

Yendt was awarded the title Chevalier of the Order of Arts and Letters on 20 May 1985. He was appointed an Honorary Member of ASSITEJ/Int'l on 11 May 2008.

Choi Young Ai (Korea) [138]

Choi Young Ai was educated first at Ewha Womans University in Korea. She then received her MA in Theatre from Dongguk University. She completed her graduate education receiving an MA and an MFA from Eastern Michigan University in the USA.

From 1966 to the present day she has been a member of the faculty of the School of Drama at the Korea National University of Arts, attaining the rank of Professor.

From 2005-2011 she served on the EC of ASSITEJ/Int'l for two terms as the Korean representative. She was elected to serve as one of the three Vice Presidents of ASSITEJ/Int'l from 2008-2011. In 2011 she was named Executive Director of the National Theatre Company of Korea.

Among the many productions that she has directed are: *The Stones*, *The Wrestling Season*, and *Cyrano* for the Korea National University of Arts as well as *Giant's Cradle* for their Tour Theatre; and *African Folk Tales* and *Children, Looking for Dreams* for Theatre Sadari.

She received awards for Best Director and Best Play of the Year in Children's Theatre for *African Folk Tales*, and Best Play of the Year in Children's Theatre for *Children, Looking for Dreams*.

She has been involved in the presentation of many Symposia, Seminars, and Forums. As examples these include in 2008 "What Can Arts Do for Child Abuse and Domestic Violence?" in Okinawa; in 2009 "The Values of International Co-Production in Theatre for Young People" in Tokyo; in 2010 "New Development and Trends: Theatre for Young Audiences in Korea" in Hong Kong, "Drama/Theatre for Baby in Korea" at the Baby Drama Festival in Uijeongbu, and "Challenges of Curriculum Development for Training Drama Educators and/or Teaching Artists in Korea" in Taipei; and in 2011 "Youth Culture, Theatre for Young Audiences, and Arts Policy" in Seoul, "Communication Education in Asia" in Okinawa, and "Establishing a Network and Base of Activities for Asian Artists" also in Okinawa.

She has written many articles and publications on theatre for young people: "Audience in TYA: Role and Expectation" (Theatre Forum, Korea National University of Arts, 2006), "Arts Education Module for Community" (Seoul Foundation for Art and Culture, 2007), "Drama and Reading" (The National Library for Children & Young Adults, 2008), "Curriculum Development for Teaching Artists on Aesthetic Experience" (Seoul Foundation for Art and Culture, 2010), "New Vision of Theatre for Young Audiences in Korea" (National Theatre Company of Korea, 2011), and *Dramatic Play in Childhood*, trans. by Y. A. Choi and Y. H. Park (H & S Media, Seoul, Korea).

Her international articles include: "Directing Theatre for Children and Young People in Korea" (The ASSITEJ Book 2004/2005) and "The New Generation of Theatre Companies in Korea" (Theatre for Young Audiences Today, USA, 2007).

APPENDIX C, Volume III
LIST OF WORLD CONGRESSES OF ASSITEJ
(1965–2011)

7-9 June 1965	The Constitutional Conference of ASSITEJ/Paris, France
26-30 May 1966	Ist International Congress of ASSITEJ/Prague, Czechoslovakia
25-31 May 1968	IInd International Congress of ASSITEJ/The Hague, Netherlands
19-24 October 1970	IIIrd International Congress of ASSITEJ/Venice, Italy
14-23 June 1972	IVth International Congress of ASSITEJ/Montreal, Ontario, Canada and Albany, New York, USA
19-26 April 1975	Vth International Congress of ASSITEJ/East Berlin, GDR
10-17 June 1978	VIth International Congress of ASSITEJ/Madrid, Spain
13-20 June 1981	VIIth International Congress of ASSITEJ/Lyons, France
19-27 September 1984	VIIIth International Congress of ASSITEJ/Moscow, USSR
8-16 April 1987	IXth World Congress of ASSITEJ/Adelaide, Australia
19-27 May 1990	Xth World Congress of ASSITEJ/Stockholm, Sweden
22-27 February 1993	XIth World Congress of ASSITEJ/Havana, Cuba
1-8 October 1996	XIIth World Congress of ASSITEJ/Rostov-on-Don, Russia
11-18 June 1999	XIIIth World Congress of ASSITEJ/Tromsö, Norway
20-28 July 2002	XIVth World Congress of ASSITEJ/Seoul, Korea
20-30 Sept 2005	XVth World Congress of ASSITEJ/Montreal, Canada
9-18 May 2008	XVIth World Congress of ASSITEJ/Adelaide, Australia
20-29 May 2011	XVIIth World Congress of ASSITEJ/Copenhagen, Denmark and Malmö, Sweden
23-31 May 2014	XVIIIth World Congress of ASSITEJ/Warsaw, Poland (scheduled)

APPENDIX D
Volume III
LIST OF EXECUTIVE COMMITTEE MEETINGS OF ASSITEJ (1965–2005)

Executive Committee of ASSITEJ Meeting/Berlin, GDR/19-26 February 1966
Executive Committee of ASSITEJ Meeting/Nuremberg, FRG/5-11 March 1967
Executive Committee Meeting of ASSITEJ/Moscow, USSR/1-10 March 1968
Executive Committee Meeting of ASSITEJ/Sophia, Bulgaria/21-31 October 1968
Executive Committee Meeting of ASSITEJ/Šibenik, Yugoslavia/27 June-1 July 1969
Executive Committee Meeting of ASSITEJ/Bucharest, Romania/7-10 June 1970
Bureau Meeting of ASSITEJ/Paris, France/3 May 1971
Executive Committee Meeting of ASSITEJ/Bratislava, Czechoslovakia/17-24 October 1971
Executive Committee Meeting of ASSITEJ/Berlin, Leipzig, & Dresden, GDR/4-11 May 1972
Executive Committee Meeting of ASSITEJ/Dresden, GDR/10 May 1972
Bureau Meeting of ASSITEJ/Bordeaux, France16-21 October 1972
Executive Committee Meeting of ASSITEJ/London, England/11-17 June 1973
Executive Committee Meeting of ASSITEJ/Madrid, Spain/16-22 April 1974
Executive Committee Meeting of ASSITEJ/Zagreb & Karlovac, Yugoslavia/3-9 February 1975
Bureau of ASSITEJ Meeting/Paris, France/13-18 October 1975
Executive Committee of ASSITEJ Meeting/Milan and Rome, Italy/8-16 May 1976
Bureau of ASSITEJ Meeting/Sophia, Bulgaria/4-5 October 1976
Executive Committee Meeting of ASSITEJ/Calgary, Banff, Montreal, and Ottawa, Canada/12-20 May 1977
Bureau of ASSITEJ Meeting/Paris, France/October 1977
Executive Committee of ASSITEJ Meeting/Moscow, USSR/26-30 March 1978
Bureau Meeting of ASSITEJ/Paris, France/October 1978
Bureau Meeting of ASSITEJ/Moscow, USSR/10-13 June 1979
Executive Committee of ASSITEJ Meeting/Šibenik, Yugoslavia/25-28 June 1979
Executive Committee of ASSITEJ Meeting/Washington, DC, USA/ 9-14 April 1980
Bureau Meeting of ASSITEJ/Dortmund, FGR/28-30 November 1980
Executive Committee of ASSITEJ Meeting/Prague, Czechoslovakia/17-20 March 1981
Bureau of ASSITEJ Meeting/Lille, France/11-13 October 1981
Executive Committee of ASSITEJ Meeting/Havana, Cuba/5-11 April 1982
Bureau of ASSITEJ Meeting/Paris, France/12-13 October 1982
Executive Committee of ASSITEJ Meeting/Lisbon, Portugal/28-30 June 1983
Bureau of ASSITEJ Meeting/London, Great Britain/31 October-3 November 1983
Executive Committee of ASSITEJ Meeting/Munich, FGR/9-17 June 1984
Bureau of ASSITEJ Meeting/Paris, France/2-3 February 1985
Executive Committee of ASSITEJ Meeting/Šibenik, Yugoslavia/22-29 June 1985
Bureau of ASSITEJ Meeting/Prague, Czechoslovakia/4-5 October 1985
Bureau & Executive Committee Meetings of ASSITEJ/Helsinki, Finland and Stockholm, Sweden/3-10 May 1986
Executive Committee of ASSITEJ Meeting/Berlin, GDR/6-11 January 1987

ASSITEJ Commission on Themes & Artistic Activities Meeting/Modena, Italy/3-8 November 1987
Executive Committee of ASSITEJ Meeting/Odense, Denmark/15-22 May 1988
Bureau Meeting of ASSITEJ/Moscow, USSR/16-18 November 1988
Executive Committee Meeting of ASSITEJ/Lyon, France/3-6 June 1989
Bureau Meeting of ASSITEJ/Warsaw, Poland/4-10 November 1989
Bureau & Executive Committee Meeting of ASSITEJ/Havana, Cuba/4-11 February 1990
Executive Committee Meeting of ASSITEJ/Budapest, Hungary/23-27 January 1991
Executive Committee Meeting of ASSITEJ/Lyon, France/5-8 December 1991
Executive Committee Meeting of ASSITEJ/Nairobi, Kenya/8-15 November 1992
Executive Committee Meeting of ASSITEJ/Frankfurt, Germany/1-5 December 1993
Executive Committee Meeting of ASSITEJ/Caracas, Venezuela/19-24 September 1994
Executive Committee Meeting of ASSITEJ/Seattle, Washington, USA/7-14 May 1995
Executive Committee Meeting of ASSITEJ/Brisbane, Australia/9-16 June 1996
Executive Committee Meeting of ASSITEJ/Lima, Peru/13-17 August 1997
Executive Committee Meeting of ASSITEJ/Biel, Switzerland/26-31 October 1997
Executive Committee Meeting of ASSITEJ/Haifa, Israel/ 11-15 April 1998
Executive Committee Meeting of ASSITEJ/London, England/27 February-3 March 1999
Executive Committee Meeting of ASSITEJ/Dallas, Texas, USA/11-13 February 2000
Executive Committee Meeting of ASSITEJ/Harare, Zimbabwe/8-11 December 2000
Executive Committee Meeting of ASSITEJ/Tokyo, Japan/19-24 July 2001
Executive Committee Meeting of ASSITEJ/Rio de Janeiro, Brazil/1-7 March 2002
Executive Committee Meeting of ASSITEJ/Zagreb, Croatia/22-27 October 2002
Executive Committee Meeting of ASSITEJ/Aberystwyth, Wales, UK/25-30 March 2003
Executive Committee Meeting of ASSITEJ/Vienna, Austria/23-28 September 2003
Executive Committee Meeting of ASSITEJ/Amman, Jordan/13-17 April 2004
Executive Committee Meeting of ASSITEJ/Cape Town, South Africa/2-8 September 2004
Executive Committee Meeting of ASSITEJ/Adelaide, Australia/7-12 April 2005
Executive Committee Meeting of ASSITEJ/Frankfurt, Germany/2-6 December 2005

APPENDIX E
Volume III
LIST OF MEMBERS OF THE EXECUTIVE COMMITTEE OF ASSITEJ BY TERMS
(1965–2005)

1965–1966 (The Provisional Committee) – 12 Members
Belgium (José Géal), **Canada** (Olivia Hasler), **Czechoslovakia** (Vladimir Adamek), **FGR** (Hanswalter Gossmann), **France** (Rose-Marie Moudoués), **GDR** (Ilse Rodenberg), **Great Britain** (Gerald Tyler), **Italy** (Maria Signorelli), **Netherlands** (Hans Snoek), **Romania** (Margareta Barbutza), **USA** (Sara Spencer), and **USSR** (Konstantin Shakh-Azizov).

1966–1968 (The 1st Election) – 12 Members
Belgium (José Géal), **Canada** (Betty Anderson, Florence James, Joyce Doolittle), **Czechoslovakia** (Vladimir Adamek), **FGR** (Hanswalter Gossmann), **France** (Rose-Marie Moudoués), **GDR** (Ilse Rodenberg), **Great Britain** (Gerald Tyler), **Italy** (Don Rafaello Lavagna), **Netherlands** (Hans Snoek), **Romania** (Margareta Barbutza), **USA** (Nat Eek), and **USSR** (Konstantin (Shakh-Azizov).

1968–1970 – 12 Members
Belgium (José Géal), **Canada** (Joyce Doolittle), **Czechoslovakia** (Vladimir Adamek), **FGR** (Hanswalter Gossmann), **France** (Rose-Marie Moudoués), **GDR** (Ilse Rodenberg), **Great Britain** (Gerald Tyler), **Italy** (Benito Biotto), **Netherlands** (Hans Snoek), **Romania** (Ian Cojar), **USA** (Nat Eek), and **USSR** (Konstantin Shakh-Azizov).

1970–1972 – 12 Members
Belgium (José Géal), **Canada** (Joyce Doolittle), **Czechoslovakia** (Vladimir Adamek), **FGR** (Hanswalter Gossmann), **France** (Rose-Marie Moudoués), **GDR** (Ilse Rodenberg), **Great Britain** (Gerald Tyler), **Italy** (Benito Biotto), **Netherlands** (Hans Snoek), **Romania** (Ian Cojar), **USA** (Nat Eek), and **USSR** (Konstantin Shakh-Azizov).

1972–1975 – 16 Members
Belgium (José Géal), **Bulgaria** (Victor Georgiev), **Canada** (Joyce Doolittle), **Czechoslovakia** (Vladimir Adamek), **FGR** (Hanswalter Gossmann), **France** (Rose-Marie Moudoués), **GDR** (Ilse Rodenberg), **Great Britain** (Gerald Tyler), **Israel** (Orna Porat) **Italy** (Benito Biotto), **Netherlands** (Hans Snoek), **Romania** (Ian Cojar), **Spain** (Maria Sunyer), **USA** (Nat Eek), **USSR** (Konstantin Shakh-Azizov), and **Yugoslavia** (Ljubiša Djokič).

1975–1978 – 11 Members
Bulgaria (Victor Georgiev), **Canada** (Joyce Doolittle), **Czechoslovakia** (Vladimir Adamek), **France** (Rose-Marie Moudoués), **GDR** (Ilse Rodenberg), **Italy** (Benito Biotto, Don Raffaello Lavagna, and Ottorino Negri), **Romania** (Ion Lucian), **Spain** (Maria Sunyer), **USA** (Patricia Snyder), **USSR** (Natalya Sats and Ivan Voronov), and **Yugoslavia** (Zvjezdana Ladika).

1978–1981 – 15 Members
Bulgaria (Victor Georgiev), **Canada** (Joyce Doolittle, resigned in 1978, replaced by Susan Rubes, then Sara Lee Lewis, then Dennis Foon), **Czechoslovakia** (Vladimir Adamek), **FGR** (Kathrin Türks), **France** (Rose-Marie Moudoués), **GDR** (Ilse Rodenberg), **Great Britain**

(John English, replaced by Shaun Hennessey in 1980), **Israel** (Orna Porat), **Italy** (Ottorino Negri), **Romania** (Ion Lucian), **Spain** (Maria Sunyer), **Switzerland** (Elisabeth Cozona), **USA** (Patricia Snyder, replaced by Ann Shaw in 1980), **USSR** (Natalya Sats), and **Yugoslavia** (Zvjezdana Ladika).

[At the 1981 International Congress in Lyon, France, the Statues were amended to raise the total membership of the EC to 17. This now officially allowed the countries of the Secretary General and the Treasurer to be in addition to a 15 Member EC.]

1981-1984 - 17 Members
Australia (Andrew Bleby and Geoffrey Brown); **Bulgaria** (Victor Georgiev); **Canada** (Sara Lee Lewis, Diane Bouchard, and Peter J. Gallagher); **Cuba** (Eddy Socorro): **Czechoslovakia** (Ladislav Knížátko); **France** (Rose-Marie Moudoués); **FGR** (Kathrin Türks and Hildegard Bergfeld); **GDR** (Ilse Rodenberg); **Great Britain** (Shaun Hennessey); **Italy** (Ottorino Negri); **Portugal** (Joao Luiz Brites); **Romania** (Ion Lucian); **Spain** (Maria Sunyer); **Switzerland** (Elisabeth Cozona); **USA** (Ann Shaw); **USSR** (Natalya Sats and Alexei Borodin); and **Yugoslavia** (Zvjezdana Ladika and Bereslav Frkič).

1984-1987 - 17 Members
Australia (Andrew Bleby, Michael FitzGerald as of 1985); **Bulgaria** (Vladimir Georgiev); **Canada** (Peter J. Gallagher resigned in 1987); **Cuba** (Eddy Socorro); **Czechoslovakia** (Ladislav Knížátko and Vladimir Adamek); **FGR** (Hildegard Bergfeld); **Finland** (Nena Stenius); **France** (Rose-Marie Moudoués); **GDR** (Ilse Rodenberg); **Great Britain** (Shaun Hennessey); **Japan** (Kazuto Kurihara); **Portugal** (Joao Brites), **Romania** (Ion Lucian); **Spain** (Maria Navarro); **USA** (Ann Shaw); **USSR** (Natalya Sats); and **Yugoslavia** (Zvjezdana Ladika and Bereslav Frkič).

1987-1990 - 17 Members
Australia (Michael FitzGerald); **Bulgaria** (Zdravko Mitkov); **Cuba** (Eddy Socorro); **Czechoslovakia** (Ladislav Knížátko and Marián Lucky); **FGR** (Hildegard Bergfeld); **Finland** (Nena Stenius); **France** (Rose-Marie Moudoués); **GDR** (Ilse Rodenberg); **Great Britain** (David Johnston and Paul Harman); **Italy** (Franco Passatore); **Poland** (Halina Machulska); **Portugal** (Luiz Pisco); **Spain** (Maria Navarro); **Sweden** (Mårten Harrie); **USA** (Nancy Staub/Harold Oaks after May 1988); **USSR** (Natalya Sats and Alexei Borodin); and **Yugoslavia** (Zvjezdana Ladika).

1990-1993 - 13 Members
Australia (Michael FitzGerald), **Czechoslovakia** (Marián Lucky), **Cuba** (Eddy Socorro), **Denmark**)Michael Ramløse), **France** (Rose-Marie Moudoués), **Germany** (Jürgen Flügge), **Italy** (Franco Passatore), **Japan** (Yohei Hijikata), **Portugal** (Joao Luiz Sousa), **Sweden** (Mårten Harrie), **UK** (Paul Harman); **USA** (Harold Oaks), and **USSR** (Adolf Shapiro).

1993-1996 - 14 Members
Australia (Michael FitzGerald), **Canada** (Marjorie MacLean), **Cuba** (Eddy Socorro), **Denmark**)Michael Ramløse), **France** (Maurice Yendt), **Germany** (Jürgen Flügge),**Italy** (Graziano Melano), **Japan** (Yohei Hijikata), **Korea** (Kim Woo Ok), **Norway** (Helge Andersen), **Russia** (Adolph Shapiro), **Slovakia** (Marián Lucky), **USA** (Harold Oaks), and **Vietnam** (Pham Thi Thanh).

1996-1999 - 13 Members
Australia (Michael FitzGerald), **Austria** (Ullide Plichta), **Canada** (Marjorie MacLean), **France** (Maurice Yendt), **Germany** (Jürgen Flügge), **Japan** (Yoshige Kagawa), **Korea** (Kim Woo Ok),

Norway (Helge Andersen), Peru (Myriam Reategui), Sweden (Judit Benedek), UK (Vicky Ireland), USA (Harold Oaks), and Zimbabwe (Tisa Chifunyise).

1999-2002 - 16 Members

Australia (Lou Westbury), Canada (Rémi Boucher), Croatia (Ivica Šimić), Germany (Wolfgang Schneider), Israel (Hagit Rehavi Nikolayevsky), Japan (Yoshishige Kagawa), Korea (Kim Woo Ok), Netherlands (Kim van der Boon), Norway (Helge Andersen), Poland (Jan Skotnicki), Sweden (Niclas Malmcrona),Switzerland (Peter Rinderknecht), Uganda (Jackson Ndawula), UK (Vicky Ireland), USA (Harold Oaks), and Zimbabwe (Tisa Chifunyise).

2002-2005 - 15 Members

Australia (Tony Mack), Austria (Stephan Rabl), Brazil (Luiza Montiero), Canada (Rémi Boucher), Croatia (Ivica Šimić), Denmark (Klaus Eggert), Germany (Wolfgang Schneider), Israel (Hagit Rehavi-Nikolayevski), Japan (Yuriko Kobayashi), Korea (Kim Woo Ok), Russia (Mikhail Bartenev), Sweden (Niclas Malmcrona), Switzerland (Peter Rinderknecht), UK (Jeremy Turner), Zambia (Cheela Chilala – co-opted).

2005-2008 - 17 Members

Argentina (María Inés Falconi), Australia (Tony Mack), Austria (Stephan Rabl), Croatia (Ivica Šimić), Denmark (Klaus Eggert), Finland (Katariina Metsälampi), Germany (Wolfgang Schneider), Israel (Razi Amitai), Japan (Yuriko Kobayashi), Korea (Young Ai Choi), Rwanda (Hope Azeda), Sweden (Niclas Malmcrona), Switzerland (Peter Rinderknecht),Turkey (Tülin Sağlam), UK (Jeremy Turner), USA (Kim Peter Kovach), Zambia (Cheela Chilala).

2008-2011 - 13 Members

Argentina (Maria Inés Falconi), Australia (Noel Jordan), Austria (Stephan Rabl), Croatia (Ivica Šimić), Denmark (Søren Ovesen), Germany (Wolfgang Schneider), Finland (Katariina Metsälampi), Israel (Razi Amitai), Korea (Young Ai Choi), South Africa (Yvette Hardie), Mexico (Marisa Gimenez Cacho), UK (Paul Harman), USA (Kim Peter Kovac).

[At the Copenhagen/Malmö World Congress in 2011 an Amendment to the Constitution was approved that limited the Membership in the Executive Committee to exactly 15.]

2011-2014 - 15 Members

Argentina (María Inés Falconi), Australia (Noel Jordan), Cameroon (Etoundi Zeyang), Croatia (Ivica Šimić), Germany (Stefan Fischer-Fels), Iceland (Vigdis Jakobsdottir), India (Imran Khan), Japan (Asaya Fujita), Mexico (Marina Gimenez Cacho), Russia (Marina Medkova), Serbia (Diana Krzanic Tepavac), South Africa (Yvette Hardie), UK (Nina Hajjiyanni), and USA (Kim Peter Kovac). Counselor – Austria (Stephan Rabl).

APPENDIX F
Volume III
THE CONSTITUTIONS OF ASSITEJ

The First Constitution (1965)
Approved at the Constitutional Conference in Paris, France on 9 June 1965.

CONSTITUTION OF ASSITEJ

INTERNATIONAL ASSOCIATION OF THEATRE FOR CHILDREN
AND YOUNG PEOPLE

CHAPTER I
CREATION
Since theatrical art is a universal expression of mankind, and possesses the influence and power to link large groups of the world's peoples in the service of peace, and considering the role theatre can play in the education of younger generations an autonomous international organization has been formed which bears the name of the International Association of Theatre for Children and Young People.

ARTICLE I
1. This Association proposes to unite theatres, organizations, and individuals of the world, dedicated to theatre for children and young people.

2. This Association is free from political, religious, or racial commitment of any kind.

3. Official languages in constitutional meetings will be English, French, and Russian. On the occasion of international conferences, the languages of the inviting country will be added.

ARTICLE II – AIMS
This Association is created to facilitate the development of theatre for children and young people, on the highest artistic level. Its aims are:

1. To promote contacts and interchange of experience between all countries, encouraging theatre artists to become mutually acquainted so as to estimate their own work, and in this spirit influence their own public.

2. To promote study tours for individuals and groups, as well as engagements for producing companies traveling abroad.

3. To introduce and support, at its discretion, proposals made to competent national authorities, for the furtherance of its work.

4. To promote the formation, in countries where there is none, of national associations uniting all organizations and persons interesting themselves in theatre for children and young people.

ARTICLE III – MEANS
The means of achieving these aims are:

1. Organizations of international congresses, conferences, festivals, study courses, exhibitions and other activities, and participation in such projects.

2. Assistance in the publication and distribution of books, magazines, legitimate stage plays, musical plays and other literary works dramatic or musical to do with theatre for children and youth.

3. Promotion of theatre for children and young people through the press, films, radio, recording, television, and other means.

4. Encouragement of translation and exchange of plays, texts, or other literature pertaining to theatre for children and young people.

5. Foundation of institutions for research and study purpose—such as libraries, museums, collections of records, etc.—on the subject of theatre for children and young people.

6. Participation in the studies of other international organizations with related interests.

7. Acquisition of the necessary property and equipment.

CHAPTER II
ARTICLE IV – MEMBERS

Members of this Association are National Centers of Theatre for Children and Young People. The following categories of membership for National Centers are acceptable to the International Association:

1. Professional companies of adult actors playing for children and young people.

2. Adult non-professional companies, community theatre companies, college and university theatre companies playing for children and young people.

3. Institutions, organizations or individuals actively engaged in the work of theatre for children and young people.

4. Supporting organizations – institutions, associations, or persons interested in theatre for children and young people.

To qualify for Full Membership in the Association a national Center must have at least one member as defined in Category 1 or 2.

Other National Centers are Corresponding Members.

ARTICLE V – RIGHTS AND OBLIGATION

1. **Full Members** have the right to participate in activities mentioned in Article III, to make proposals in constitutional meetings, to allow their representatives to elect, to be elected, and to vote according to the rules declared in Article IX.

2. **Corresponding Members** have the right to participate in the activities mentioned in Article III, and have a consultative voice in the General Assembly, but have no right to vote.

3. **All Members** have the obligation to work to achieve the aims defined by the Association, to maintain its statutes, to act upon the decisions taken by the Association, and to pay their membership fees.

ARTICLE VI – APPLICATION, RESIGNATION, EXPULSION

1. Written applications for membership shall be addressed to the Secretary General. In the case of a denial by the Executive Committee, the candidate may appeal to the next General Assembly.

2. Any member who wishes to resign should inform the Secretary General in writing for it to take effect from 1st January in the following year.

3. The Executive Committee may decide, by a majority of two-thirds, on the rejection or expulsion of any member whose work conflicts with the fundamental aims of this Association, or who has filed several time in one of the obligations mentioned in Article V.

4. Any rejected or expelled member may appeal to the General Assembly.

CHAPTER III
ARTICLE VII – FINANCE

1. This Association is financed from the subscriptions of members, as well as from bequests, gifts, and subsidies accepted by the General Assembly.

2. The fiscal year of this Association runs from 1st January to 31st December.

3. Membership fees, which are determined by the General Assembly, are due to 1st January of each year, and are payable to the Treasurer.

CHAPTER IV
ARTICLE VIII – STRUCTURE

The governing body of this Association consists of:
  The General Assembly
  The Executive Committee
  The Officers

ARTICLE IX – FUNCTIONS OF THE GENERAL ASSEMBLY
1. The General Assembly consists of delegates of all National Centers.
2. Each national delegation has three (3) votes
   Two (2) votes for its professional companies
   One (1) vote for its non-professional companies
3. Voting by proxy is permitted.
4. The General Assembly shall meet at least once every two years, and will be called at least six months in advance by the Secretary General upon instruction of the Chairman. Normally it will decide the location where the next General Assembly shall meet—but if it should be unable to take a decision on this matter, or if a change of location should prove necessary, this decision may be left to the Executive Committee.
5. An extraordinary meeting of the General Assembly will be called by the Secretary General three (3) months in advance on the request of two-thirds of the members or at the discretion of the officers of the Executive Committee in the case of an emergency.
6. The General Assembly has final control over the Constitution, and decides on any changes or additions necessary. Any member wishing to amend the Constitution must give notice in writing to the Secretary General at least three (3) months before the date of the General Assembly. Any decision taken upon a proposal to amend the Constitution shall require a majority of two-thirds of the members of the Association.
7. The General Assembly establishes the broad outlines of the Association's policy.
8. The General Assembly receives for approval the report of the activities and the financial report which are submitted by the Executive Committee.
9. The Chairman of this Association is by right Chairman of the General Assembly. In the event of his absence, he will be replaced by a Vice-Chairman, or in the absence of all the Vice-Chairmen, by a member of the Executive Committee elected for this purpose by the General Assembly.
10. All decisions unless otherwise stated are taken by simple majority vote. In the case of a tie the Chairman will cast the deciding vote.
11. The General Assembly determines the membership fees and other charges to be levied on the members of the Association.
12. A meeting of the General Assembly can only be held if the delegates of half the National Centers express in writing to the Secretary General their determination to be present and to participate, either in person or by proxy. This decision must be sent to the Secretary General three (3) months in advance of the meeting. The General Assembly can only take decisions if half the members participate.
13. The General Assembly shall elect the Executive Committee and out of their members the Chairman and three Vice-Chairmen. Nominations must be submitted to the Secretary General three (3) months before the date of the meeting of the General Assembly for circulation to the members. It appoints the Secretary General and the Treasurer on the recommendation of the Executive Committee. The officers and members of the Executive Committee shall be chosen to represent all the interests as fairly as possible.
14. The General Assembly shall decide upon the acceptance of, and shall hold, all gifts, bequests, and subsidies made to the Association.
15. The General Assembly shall appoint two professional auditors to the Association.

ARTICLE X – FUNCTIONS OF THE EXECUTIVE COMMITTEE
1. The Executive Committee is composed of a maximum of fifteen members, having the right to vote, including:
   The Chairman and Vice-Chairmen

The Secretary General
The Treasurer, appointed by the General Assembly

2. In the event of the death or resignation of one of its members, the Executive Committee shall authorize the National Center which nominated the member, to appoint a deputy for the remaining period of his office.

3. The Executive Committee has the power to co-opt up to two additional members. It also has the power to co-opt advisors.

4. Any member who cannot attend a meeting of the Executive Committee may appoint a deputy, by giving notice to the Secretary General, in writing.

5. A meeting of the Executive Committee may be called only if at least half of the members express in writing to the Secretary General their determination to be present and participate, either in person or represented by a deputy. The presence of half the members shall constitute a quorum.

6. The Executive Committee will meet at least once a year: the Committee will decide by majority vote if it is necessary to hold additional meetings, and will choose the places and dates of such meetings. The Committee must be called three months in advance. Meetings will be called by the Secretary General at the request of the Chairman.

7. The Executive Committee may decide upon urgent matters by correspondence if it proves impossible to hold a special meeting. In this case the Secretary General, by agreement with the Chairman, shall send to each member of the Executive Committee a questionnaire, to which each member will reply in writing. Decisions will be made by two-thirds majority. The decisions will come before the Executive Committee at their next meeting for ratification. The replies will be placed in the records of the Association where they will be available for examination by members of the General Assembly.

8. Each member of the Executive Committee possesses one vote which he can use in person, or by deputy, or by letter. Voting by proxy is not permitted.

9. The Chairman of this Association is also Chairman of the meetings of the Executive Committee. In the event of his absence, he will be replaced by a Vice-Chairman, or if all Vice-Chairmen are absent, by a Chairman elected for this purpose by the Executive Committee.

10. All decisions are taken by a simple majority vote, except decisions taken by correspondence.

11. The Chairman of the meeting has the right to vote in his own right as a member of the Committee. If a majority decision cannot be established by this means, the Chairman may cast a second vote to decide the issue.

12. The Executive Committee shall deal with the affairs of the Association between meetings of the General Assembly and carry out the decisions taken by the General Assembly. The Executive Committee shall remain in office for the two years or thereabouts and its members shall be eligible for re-election.

13. The Executive Committee will accept or reject new applications for membership made to the Secretary General.

14. The budget is administered by the Executive Committee according to a program established by the General Assembly.

15. The Executive Committee entrusts to the Treasurer the administration of funds, the preparation of the budget, and the accounts. The accounts of the Association must be audited every two years by two professional auditors, appointed by the General Assembly on the recommendation of the Executive Committee.

16. The Executive Committee may take the initiative in matters not anticipated by the General Assembly, providing that these matters are in keeping with the aims and character of this Association, and providing that the Executive Committee takes the first opportunity to report on

these matters to the General Assembly.
ARTICLE XI – THE OFFICERS
The Officers of this Association are elected for two years or thereabouts and as follows:
The Chairman, elected
The Vice-Chairmen, elected
The Secretary General, appointed
The Treasurer, appointed

1. The Officers are charge with carrying out the Association's program and rendering reports to the Executive Committee.

2. In the case of any urgent matters not foreseen by the Executive Committee, the Officers are given power to act at their discretion and will take the first opportunity to report on these matters to the Executive Committee.

CHAPTER V
ARTICLE XII – DURATION

1. This Association is created for an unlimited period.

2. This Association shall cease to function when, for any reason, three-fourths of the members (National Centers) on the basic number of votes shall express in writing to the Secretary General, the desire to dissolve the Association. In this event, the Executive Committee shall be authorized to declare the Association dissolved, and any funds remaining in the Association's treasury shall be given to international organizations pursuing similar aims.

ARTICLE XIII – ADOPTION OF STATUTES
This Constitution shall come into force at the moment of its approval by a Constituent General Assembly of delegations from all interested countries called for this purpose. From that moment the Association may accept as members the national Centers who send their applications to the Secretary General.

The Constitution (1996)
This Constitution of ASSITEJ was revised and approved by the EC and the General Assembly over the years with the latest changes (1996) being approved at the XIIth World Congress in Rostov-on-Don, Russia in 1996.
CONSTITUTION OF ASSITEJ

INTERNATIONAL ASSOCIATION OF THEATRE FOR CHILDREN
AND YOUNG PEOPLE

CHAPTER I
CREATION
Since the theatrical art is a universal expression of mankind and possesses the influence and power to link large groups of the world's peoples in the service of peace, and considering the role theatre can play in the education of younger generations, an autonomous international organization has been formed which bears the name of the International Association of Theatre for Children and Young People.

This Association shall be known by the acronym ASSITEJ (Association International du Théâtre pour l'Enfance et la Jeunesse).

ARTICLE I – Mission

1. This Association proposes to unite theatres, organizations, and individuals of the world dedicated to theatre for children and young people.

2. This Association is free from political, religious, or racial commitment of any kind.

ARTICLE II – Aims
This Association is created to facilitate the development of theatre for children and young people on the highest artistic level. Recognizing that children make up a large part of the world's population and that children are the future of the world, the aims of the Association are:

To work for children's right to artistic experiences especially designed and created for them.

To work for the recognition and acknowledgment of theatre for children and young people.

To work for the improvement of the conditions of theatre for children and young people all. over the world.

To improve the common knowledge of theatre for children and young people worldwide, thus drawing the attention of international and national authorities to the importance of taking children and young people and the work created for them seriously.

To give people working with theatre for children and young people possibilities of getting acquainted with the work of colleagues from other countries and cultures, thus enabling them to enrich theatre for children and young people in their own country.

To help form in all countries, ASSITEJ centers which function in accordance with the mission, constitution and policies of the Association. These national centers shall unite all theatres, organizations and people interested in theatre for children and young people.

ARTICLE III – Means
The means of achieving these aims are:

1. Organization and promotion of national, regional, and international congresses, conferences, festivals, study tours, exhibitions and other activities, and participation in such projects.

2. Promotion of contact and interchange of experience between all countries.

3. Encouragement of translation and exchange of plays, texts, and other literature pertaining to theatre for children and young people.

4. Collection of material and documentation on theatre for children and young people.

5. Promotion of theatre for children and young people through the press, film, radio, television, recording, the internet, and other means.

6. Co-operation with other international organizations with related interests.

7. To introduce and support proposals made by the centers in order to advance the work of theatre for children and young people to appropriate national and international authorities and agencies.

ARTICLE IV – Members
Members of this Association are national centers representative of theatre for children and young people in their own country. No theatre, organization or individual can be refused admittance to any national centre of ASSITEJ on the basis of political conviction, cultural identity, ethnicity, or religion.

The following categories of membership for national centers are acceptable to the International Association:

1. Professional companies of adult actors performing for children and young people or professional theatre artists working in theatre for children and young people. "Professional" is defined as companies or individuals who devote the major portion of their work to theatre for children and young people.

2. Adult non-professional companies, community theatre companies, college and university theatre companies performing for children and young people, as well as college and university programs for the study of theatre for children and young people.

3. Institutions, organizations or individuals actively engaged in the work of theatre for children and young people.

4. Supporting organizations, institutions, associations, or persons interested in theatre for children and young people.

To qualify for full membership in the Association a national centre must have at least three (3) members as defined in category 1 or five (5) members with at least two (2) members as defined in categories 1 and 3 and three (3) members as defined in category 2.

Other Centers with less than two (2) members in category 1 or less than five (5) members, with at least two (2) members in category 1 and three (3) members in category 2 or only members as defined in categories 3 or 4 are corresponding members.

ARTICLE 5 – Rights and Obligations

1. Full Members have the right to make proposals at constitutional meetings, to be elected, to be elected to the Executive Committee, and to vote according to the rules detailed in Article 9.

2. Corresponding Members have the right to make proposals at constitutional meetings and to vote according to the rules detailed in Article 9. Corresponding members do not have the right to be elected to the Executive Committee at constitutional meetings.

3. All Members have the obligation to work to achieve the aims defined by the Association, to maintain its statutes, to act upon the decisions taken by the Association, to pay their membership fees, to keep the Secretary General informed of the activities in their centers, to appoint a correspondent, and to give their National Centre a permanent address, and to communicate to its national members the information sent from the General Secretariat.

4. All national centers must use the acronym "ASSITEJ" as part of the name of the centre.

ARTICLE 6 – Application, Resignation, Suspension, Expulsion

1. Written applications for membership shall be addressed to the Secretary General. In the case of a denial by the Executive Committee, the applicant may appeal to the next General Assembly.

2. Any member centre which wishes to resign from the Association should inform the Secretary General in writing. The resignation will take effect from 1st January in the following year.

3. The Executive Committee may decide, by a majority of two-thirds, on the rejection, suspension or expulsion of any member whose work conflicts with the fundamental aims of this association, or who has failed several times in one of the obligations mentioned in Article 5. Any centre which has been rejected, suspended or expelled loses the right to use the acronym "ASSITEJ".

4. Any rejected, suspended or expelled member may appeal to the General Assembly.

ARTICLE 7 – Finances

1. This Association is financed from the membership fees, as well as subsidies or grants accepted by the Executive Committee.

2. The fiscal period of this Association runs from one General Assembly to the next.

3. Membership fees, which are determined by the General Assembly, are due on 1st January of each year, and must be sent to the Treasurer. Centers more than six months in arrears lose the right to vote in the General Assembly.

ARTICLE 8 – Structure

The governing body of this Association consists of:

1. The General Assembly
2. The Executive Committee
3. The Bureau (consisting of the Officers: President, three Vice-Presidents, Secretary General, and Treasurer).

ARTICLE 9 – Functions of the General Assembly

1. The General Assembly consists of delegations of all National Centers.

2. A delegation from a centre with full membership has three (3) votes. A delegation from a centre with corresponding membership has one (1) vote.

3. Voting by proxy is permitted, and must be given in writing. A national delegation can hold proxy for only one other National Centre.

4. The General Assembly shall meet at least once every third calendar year, and will be called at least six months in advance by the Secretary General upon instruction of the President. Normally, it will decide the location where the next General Assembly shall meet, but if it should be unable to make a decision on this matter, or if a change of location should prove necessary, this decision may be left to the Executive Committee.

5. An extraordinary meeting of the General Assembly will be called by the Secretary General three (3) months in advance on the written and justified request of two-thirds of the members or at the discretion of the Bureau of the Executive Committee in the case of an emergency.

6. The General Assembly has final control over the Constitution, and decides on any changes or additions necessary. Any member wishing to amend the Constitution must give notice in writing to the Secretary General at least three (3) months before the date of the meeting of the General Assembly. Any decision taken upon a proposal to amend the Constitution shall require a two-thirds majority.

7. The General Assembly establishes the broad outlines of the Association's policy.

8. The General Assembly receives for approval the report of the activities and the financial report, which are submitted by the Executive Committee.

9. The President of this Association is by right President of the General Assembly. In the event of his or her absence, he or she will be replaced by a Vice-President, selected by vote of the Executive Committee, or, in the absence of all the Vice-Presidents, by a member of the Executive Committee elected for this purpose by the General Assembly.

10. All decisions, unless otherwise stated, are taken by simple majority vote. In the case of a tie, the President will cast the deciding vote.

11. The General Assembly determines the membership fees and other charges to be levied on the members of the Association.

12. A meeting of the General Assembly can only be held if the delegates of half of the National Centers express in writing to the Secretary General their determination to be present and to participate, either in person or by proxy. This decision must be sent to the Secretary General three (3) months in advance of the meeting. The General Assembly can only make decisions if half the members participate themselves or by proxy.

13. The General Assembly shall elect the Secretary General and the Treasurer in this order: The Secretary General is elected first and presides over the election of the Treasurer, representatives of additional countries to the Executive Committee and of the President. Candidatures for the offices of the Secretary General and Treasurer should be sent in writing to the Secretary General, three (3) months before the date of the General Assembly in order to circulate nominations to the members of ASSITEJ. If no centre has presented candidates for these offices, the Executive Committee at its last meeting before the General Assembly shall recommend a candidate for each of the offices and inform all centers of this recommendation.

14. The General Assembly shall elect the members of the Executive Committee as representatives of their particular countries. A country may have only one representative on the Executive Committee.

Each centre, on its own behalf, should send to the Secretary General, in writing, the name of its candidate three (3) months before the date of the meeting of the General Assembly in order to circulate nominations to the members of ASSITEJ.

15. From amongst the members of the Executive Committee, the General Assembly shall elect the President and Vice-Presidents, who shall be nominated in a meeting of the new Executive Committee. They shall be elected in a personal capacity. The officers and members of the Executive Committee shall be chosen to represent as fairly as possible the interests of the organization and the diversity of all the national centers, taking into account such factors as geography, aesthetics, ethnic origin, gender, and cultural identity.

16. The General Assembly on the recommendation of the Executive Committee can give the titles of President of Honor and Member of Honor for exceptional service given to the Association. The Members of Honor have a consultative voice, but no right to vote, and they cannot represent their country.

17. The General Assembly shall appoint an auditor to the Association on the recommendation of the Executive Committee.

18. The agenda, with its enclosures and candidates for the Secretary General, the Treasurer and the Executive Committee, should be sent from the General Secretariat to all centers no later than two (2) months in advance of the General Assembly.

19. Only the questions, which are set down on the agenda, may be voted upon in the General Assembly.

ARTICLE 10 – Functions of the Executive Committee

1. The Executive Committee is composed of a maximum of seventeen (17) members having the right to vote, including, the President, and three (3) Vice-Presidents, the Secretary General and the Treasurer.

2. In the event of the death or resignation of a member of the Executive Committee, the Executive Committee shall authorize the National Center which nominated the member, to appoint a deputy for the remaining period of the term of office. The exceptions are: in the case of the President, where the replacement shall be from amongst the Vice-Presidents; and in the case of one of the Vice-Presidents, where the Executive Committee is authorized either to leave the office vacant or, if it judges it necessary, to elect a replacement from amongst its own members.

3. The Executive Committee has the power to co-opt persons as members of the Executive Committee. The Executive Committee also has the right to appoint Counselors for the period of its mandate. The Counselors may attend, without voting rights, meetings of the Executive Committee during their time in office.

4. Any member who cannot attend a meeting of the Executive Committee can be replaced only by a permanent deputy nominated by his or her Center for the duration of his or her term of office. The Secretary General must be notified of the deputy's name as soon as possible after the General Assembly.

5. A meeting of the Executive Committee may be held only if at least half of the members express in writing to the Secretary General their determination to be present and participate, either in person or represented by a deputy from their own National Center. The presence of half the members shall constitute a quorum.

6. The Executive Committee will meet at least once each calendar year: the Committee will decide by majority vote if it is necessary to hold additional meetings, and will choose the places and dates of such meetings. The Committee must be notified three months in advance. Meetings will be called by the Secretary General at the request of the President.

7. The Executive Committee may decide upon urgent matters by correspondence if it proves impossible to hold a special meeting. In this case the Secretary General, by agreement with the President, shall send to each member of the Executive Committee a questionnaire, to which each

member will reply in writing. Decisions will be made by a two-thirds majority vote. The decisions will come before the Executive Committee at their next meeting for ratification. The replies will be placed in the records of the Association where they will be available for examination by members of the General Assembly.

8. Each member of the Executive Committee possesses one vote, which he or she may use in person unless delegated to his or her permanent deputy.

9. The President of this Association is also President of the meeting of the Executive Committee. In the event of the President's absence, he or she will be replaced by a Vice-President, selected by vote of the Executive Committee or if all the Vice-Presidents are absent, by a Chairperson elected for this purpose by the Executive Committee.

10. All motions are carried by a simple majority vote, except decisions taken by correspondence or regarding Article 6, item 3.

11. The Chairperson of the meeting has the right to vote as a member of the Committee. If a majority decision cannot be established by this means, the Chairperson may cast a second deciding vote.

12. The Executive Committee will submit a plan of activities to the General Assembly. It manages the affairs of the Association between the meetings of the General Assembly and carries out the decisions of the General Assembly. The Executive Committee will remain in office for the period between one General Assembly and the next, which will be three years or thereabouts, at which time its members shall be eligible for re-election.

13. The Executive Committee will accept or reject new applications for membership made to the Secretary General. A rejection may be appealed by the applicant at the next General Assembly.

14. The budget is administered by the Executive Committee according to a program or a working plan established by the General Assembly.

15. The Executive Committee entrusts to the Treasurer the administration of funds, the preparation of the budget, and the accounts. The accounts of the Association must be audited by the auditor before the presentation in the General Assembly (Article 9, item 17).

16. The Executive Committee may take the initiative in matters not anticipated by the General Assembly, provided that these matters are in keeping with the mission and aims of this Association, and providing that the Executive Committee takes the first opportunity to report on these matters to the General Assembly.

ARTICLE 11 – Functions of the Officers and the Bureau

The Officers of this Association—together forming the Bureau are as follows:
The President
Three (3) Vice-Presidents
The Secretary General
The Treasurer.

1. The Officers are charged with carrying out the Association's program and submitting reports to the Executive Committee.

2. In the case of any urgent matters not foreseen by the Executive Committee, the Bureau is given power to act at its discretion and will take the first opportunity to report on these matters to the Executive Committee.

ARTICLE 12 – Languages

1. Working languages at the General Assembly will be the language of the host country, English, and at least one other language as determined by the Executive Committee according to the needs of the meeting. On the occasion of international events, the working languages will be the language of the host country and English, with the option of one more language according to need.

When the host country is English-speaking, it must provide at least two other languages for the General Assembly. For other international events, at least one other language must be provided if so determined by the Executive Committee according to the needs of the event.

The working language of the Association for written communication will be English.

2. International Events are defined as:
Executive Committee meetings
Seminars and forums as part of an ASSITEJ/Int'l Festival or ASSITEJ/Int'l Projects
Activities which take place officially in the name of ASSITEJ/Int'l apart from the General Assembly

ARTICLE 13 – Duration

1. This Association is created for an unlimited period.

2. This Association shall cease to function when, for any reason, three-fourths of the members (National Centers) on the basis of their number of votes shall express in writing to the Secretary General the desire to dissolve the Association. In this event, the Executive Committee shall be authorized to declare the Association dissolved, and any funds remaining in the Association's treasury shall be given to international organizations pursuing similar aims.

ARTICLE 14 – Adoption of Statutes

This Constitution shall come into force at the moment of its approval by a Constituent General Assembly of delegations from all interested countries called for this purpose. From that moment the Executive Committee may accept as members the National Centers who send their applications to the Secretary General.

The Current Constitution (2005)

The current Constitution of ASSITEJ was revised and approved by the EC at their meeting in Adelaide, Australia in March of 2005. The chief authors of the revisions were Klaus Eggert (Denmark) and Kim Peter Kovac (USA). Others who assisted were Michael Ramløse (Former Secretary General – Denmark) and Niclas Malmcrona (Current Secretary General – Sweden).

It was then presented to the General Assembly at the XVth World Congress in Montreal, Canada in 2005, where it was passed with little further comment.

The changes from the previous amended Constitution are printed in bold type, and this is the Constitution under which ASSITEJ served as of 2005.

CONSTITUTION OF ASSITEJ

INTERNATIONAL ASSOCIATION OF THEATRE FOR CHILDREN AND YOUNG PEOPLE

CHAPTER I
Creation

Since the theatrical art is a universal expression of mankind and possesses the influence and power to link large groups of the world's peoples in the service of peace, and considering the role theatre can play in the education of younger generations, an autonomous international organization has been formed which bears the name of the International Association of Theatre for Children and Young People.

This Association shall be known by the acronym ASSITEJ/Int'l (Association International du Théâtre pour l'Enfance et la Jeunesse). [139]

Article 1– Mission

1. This Association proposes to unite theatres, organizations, and individuals **throughout the world** dedicated to theatre for children and young people.

2. This Association is **dedicated to artistic, humanitarian, and educational efforts and no decision, action or statement of the Association shall be based on nationality, political conviction, cultural identity, ethnicity, or religion.**

Article 2 – Aims

This Association is created to facilitate the development of theatre for children and young people on the highest artistic level. Recognizing that children **and young people**[140] make up a large part of the world's population and that children **and young people** are the future of the world, the aims of the Association are:

To work for **the rights of children and young people** to artistic experiences especially designed and created for them.

To work for the recognition and acknowledgment of theatre for children and young people.

To work for the improvement of the conditions of theatre for children and young people all over the world.

To improve the common knowledge of theatre for children and young people **worldwide**, thus drawing the attention of international and national authorities to the importance of taking children **and young people and the work created for them seriously.**

To give people working with theatre for children and young people possibilities of getting acquainted with the work of colleagues **from** other countries and cultures, thus enabling them to enrich theatre for children and young people in their own country.

To help form **in all countries**, ASSITEJ centers **which function in accordance with the mission, constitution and policies of the Association.** [141] These national centers shall unite all theatres, organizations and people interested in theatre for children and young people.

Article 3 – Means

The means of achieving these aims are:

1. Organization and promotion of national, **regional**,[142] and international congresses, conferences, festivals, study tours, exhibitions and other activities, and participation in such projects.

2. Promotion of contact and interchange of experience between all countries.

3. Encouragement of translation and exchange of plays, texts, **and** other literature pertaining to theatre for children and young people.

4. Collection of material and documentation on theatre for children and young people.

5. Promotion of theatre for children and young people through the press, **film**, radio, television, recording, **the internet**, and other means.

6. Co-operation with other international organizations with related interests.

7. To introduce and support proposals made by the centers **in order to advance the work of theatre for children and young people to appropriate national and international authorities and agencies.**

Article 4 – Members

Members of this Association are national centers representative of theatre for children and young people in their own countries. No theatre, organization or individual can be refused admittance to **any** national centre of ASSITEJ on **the basis of political conviction, cultural identity, ethnicity, or religion.** [143]

The following categories of membership for national centers are acceptable to the International Association:

1. Professional companies of adult actors **performing** for children and young people or professional theatre artists working in theatre for children and young people. **"Professional" is defined as companies or individuals who devote the major portion of their work** to theatre for children and young people.

2. Adult non-professional companies, community theatre companies, college and university

theatre companies **performing** for children and young people, **as well as college and university programs for the study of theatre for children and young people.**

3. Institutions, organizations or individuals actively engaged in the work of theatre for children and young people.

4. Supporting organizations, institutions, associations, or persons interested in theatre for children and young people.

To qualify for full membership in the Association a national centre must have at least 3 members as defined in category 1 or five 5 members with at least 2 members as defined in categories 1 and 3 and 3 members as defined in category 2.

Other Centers with less than 2 members in category 1 or less than 5 members, with at least 2 members in categories 1 and 3 members in category 2 or only members as defined in categories 3 or 4 are corresponding members.

Article 5 – Rights and Obligations

1. Full Members have the right to make proposals at constitutional meetings, to be elected **to the Executive Committee**, and to vote according to the rules **detailed** in Article 9.[144]

2. Corresponding Members have the right to make proposals at constitutional meetings and to vote according to the rules **detailed** in Article 9. Corresponding members do not have the right to be elected **to the Executive Committee** at constitutional meetings.[145]

3. All Members have the obligation to work to achieve the aims defined by the Association, to maintain its statutes, to act upon the decisions taken by the Association, to pay their membership fees, to keep the Secretary General informed of the activities in **their centers**, to appoint a correspondent, and to give their National Centre a permanent address, **and to communicate to its national members the information sent from the General Secretariat.**[146]

4. **All national centers must use the acronym "ASSITEJ" as part of the name of the centre.**[147]

Article 6 – Application, Resignation, Suspension,[148] Expulsion

1. Written applications for membership shall be addressed to the Secretary General. In the case of a denial by the Executive Committee, the **applicant** may appeal to the next General Assembly.

2. Any member **centre which** wishes to resign **from the Association** should inform the Secretary General in writing. The resignation will take effect from 1st January in the following year.

3. The Executive Committee may decide, by a majority of two-thirds, on the rejection, **suspension**[149] or expulsion of any member whose work conflicts with the fundamental aims of this association, or who has failed several times in one of the obligations mentioned in Article 5. **Any centre which has been rejected, suspended or expelled loses the right to use the acronym "ASSITEJ".**[150]

4. Any rejected, **suspended** or expelled member may appeal to the General Assembly.

Article 7 – Finances

1. This Association is financed from the **membership fees**, as well as subsidies **or grants** accepted **by the Executive Committee.**[151]

2. The fiscal **period** of this Association runs from **one General Assembly to the next.**[152]

3. Membership fees, which are determined by the General Assembly, are due on 1st January of each year, and must be sent to the Treasurer. Centers more than six months in arrears lose the right to vote in the General Assembly.

Article 8 – Structure

The governing body of this Association consists of:

1. The General Assembly
2. The Executive Committee

3. **The Bureau** (consisting of the Officers: President, three Vice-Presidents, Secretary General, and Treasurer)[153]

Article 9 – Functions of the General Assembly

1. The General Assembly consists of delegations of all National Centers.

2. A delegation from a centre with full membership has three (3) votes. A delegation from a centre with corresponding membership has 1 vote.

3. Voting by proxy is permitted, and must be given in writing. A national delegation can hold proxy for only one other National Centre.

4. The General Assembly shall meet at least once **every third calendar year**,[154] and will be called at least six months in advance by the Secretary General upon instruction of the President. Normally, it will decide the location where the next General Assembly shall meet, but if it should be unable to **make** a decision on this matter, or if a change of location should prove necessary, this decision may be left to the Executive Committee.

5. An extraordinary meeting of the General Assembly will be called by the Secretary General three (3) months in advance on the written and justified request of two-thirds of the members or at the discretion of the **Bureau**[155] of the Executive Committee in the case of an emergency.

6. The General Assembly has final control over the Constitution, and decides on any changes or additions necessary. Any member wishing to amend the Constitution must give notice in writing to the Secretary General at least three months before the date of the meeting of the General Assembly. Any decision taken upon a proposal to amend the Constitution shall require **a two-thirds majority**.

7. The General Assembly establishes the broad outlines of the Association's policy.

8. The General Assembly receives for approval the report of the activities and the financial report, which are submitted by the Executive Committee.

9. The President of this Association is by right President of the General Assembly. In the event of his **or her** absence, he **or she** will be replaced by a Vice-President, selected by vote of the Executive Committee, or, in the absence of all the Vice-Presidents, by a member of the Executive Committee elected for this purpose by the General Assembly.

10. All decisions, unless otherwise stated, are taken by simple majority vote. In the case of a tie, the President will cast the deciding vote. **If two Centers apply to host the next Congress, the winner shall be the Centre that receives the most votes. If more than two Centers apply for hosting, and neither receives a majority, a second vote shall be taken between the two leading candidates, and the winner shall be the Centre that receives the most votes.**

11. The General Assembly determines the membership fees and other charges to be levied on the members of the Association.

12. A meeting of the General Assembly can only be held if the delegates of half of the National Centers express in writing to the Secretary General their determination to be present and to participate, either in person or by proxy.

This decision must be sent to the Secretary General 3 months in advance of the meeting. The General Assembly can only **make** decisions if half the members participate themselves or by proxy.

13. The General Assembly shall elect the Secretary General and the Treasurer in this order: The Secretary General is elected first and presides over the election of the Treasurer, representatives of additional countries to the Executive Committee and of the President.

Candidatures for the offices of the Secretary General and Treasurer should be **sent in writing to the Secretary General, three months before the date of the General Assembly in order to circulate nominations to the members of ASSITEJ.**[156]

If no centre has presented candidates for these offices, the Executive Committee at its last meeting before the General Assembly shall recommend a candidate for each of the offices and inform all centers of this recommendation.

14. The General Assembly shall elect the members of the Executive Committee as representatives of their particular countries. A country may have only one representative on the Executive Committee.

Each centre, on its own behalf, should send to the Secretary General, **in writing**, the name of its candidate three months before the date of the meeting of the General Assembly in order to circulate nominations to the members of ASSITEJ.[157]

15. From amongst the members of the Executive Committee, the General Assembly shall elect the President and Vice-Presidents, who shall be nominated in a meeting of the new Executive Committee.

They shall be elected in a personal capacity.

The officers and members of the Executive Committee shall be chosen to **represent as fairly as possible the interests of the organization and the diversity of all the national centers, taking into account such factors as geography, aesthetics, ethnic origin, gender, and cultural identity.**

16. The General Assembly on the recommendation of the Executive Committee can give the **titles of President of Honor and Member of Honor for exceptional service** to the Association.

The Members of Honor have a consultative voice, but no right to vote, and they cannot represent their country.

17. **On the recommendation of the Executive Committee, the General Assembly shall appoint a national centre to conduct the audit of the accounts.**

18. **The agenda, with its enclosures and candidates for the Secretary General, the Treasurer and the Executive Committee, should be sent from the General Secretariat to all centers no later than two months in advance of the General Assembly.**

19. Only the questions, which are set down on the agenda, may be voted upon in the General Assembly.

Article 10 – Functions of the Executive Committee

1. The Executive Committee is composed of a maximum of seventeen (17) members having the right to vote, including, the President, and three (3) Vice-Presidents, the Secretary General and the Treasurer.

2. In the **event of the**[158] death or resignation of a member of the Executive Committee, the Executive Committee shall authorize the National Center which nominated the member, to appoint a deputy for the remaining period of **the term of office. The exceptions are: in the**[159] case of the President, where the replacement shall be from amongst the Vice-Presidents; and in the case of **one of** the Vice-Presidents, where the Executive Committee is authorized either to leave the **office** vacant or, if it judges it necessary, to elect a replacement from amongst its own members.

3. The Executive Committee has the power to co-opt **persons as members of** the Executive Committee. **The Executive Committee also has the right to appoint Counselors for the period of its mandate. The Counselors may attend, without voting rights, meetings of the Executive Committee during their time in office.**[160]

4. Any member who cannot attend a meeting of the Executive Committee can be replaced only by a permanent deputy nominated by his or her Center for the duration of his or her term of office. The Secretary General must be notified of the deputy's name as soon as possible after the General Assembly.

5. A meeting of the Executive Committee may be held only if at least half of the members

express in writing to the Secretary General their determination to be present and participate, either in person or represented by a deputy from their own National Center. The presence of half the members shall constitute a quorum.

6. The Executive Committee will meet at least once **each calendar**[161] year; the Committee will decide by majority vote if it is necessary to hold additional meetings, and will choose the places and dates of such meetings. The Committee must be **notified** three months in advance. Meetings will be called by the Secretary General at the request of the President.

7. The Executive Committee may decide upon urgent matters by correspondence if it proves impossible to hold a special meeting. In this case the Secretary General, by agreement with the President, shall send to each member of the Executive Committee a questionnaire, to which each member will reply in writing. Decisions will be made by **a two-thirds majority vote**. The decisions will come before the Executive Committee at their next meeting for ratification. The replies will be placed in the records of the Association where they will be available for examination by members of the General Assembly.

8. Each member of the Executive Committee possesses one vote, which he **or she** may use in person **unless delegated to** his or her permanent deputy.[162]

9. The President of this Association is also President of the meeting of the Executive Committee. In the event of **the President's** absence, he **or she** will be replaced by a Vice-President, selected by vote of the Executive Committee or if all the Vice-Presidents are absent, by a **Chairperson** elected for this purpose by the Executive Committee.

10. All motions are carried by a simple majority vote, except decisions taken by correspondence or regarding Article 6, **item 3.**

11. The **Chairperson** of the meeting has the right to vote as a member of the Committee. If a majority decision cannot be established by this means, the Chairperson may cast a second deciding vote.

12. The Executive Committee will submit a plan of activities to the General Assembly. It manages the affairs of the Association between the meetings of the General Assembly and carries out the decisions of the General Assembly. The Executive Committee will remain in office for the period between one General Assembly and the next, which will be three years or thereabouts, **at which time** its members shall be eligible for re-election.

13. The Executive Committee will accept or reject new applications for membership made to the Secretary General. A rejection may be appealed **by the applicant at**[163] the next General Assembly.

14. The budget is administered by the Executive Committee according to a program **or a working plan** established by the General Assembly.

15. The Executive Committee entrusts to the Treasurer the administration of funds, the preparation of the budget, and the accounts. The accounts of the Association must be audited **by the auditor before the presentation in the General Assembly (Article 9, item 17)**.[164]

16. The Executive Committee may take the initiative in matters not anticipated by the General Assembly, provided that these matters are in keeping with the **mission and aims** of this Association, and provided that the Executive Committee takes the first opportunity to report on these matters to the General Assembly.

Article 11 – *Functions of the Officers and the Bureau*

The Officers of this Association – together forming the Bureau are as follows:
 The President
 Three Vice-Presidents
 The Secretary General
 The Treasurer.

1. The Officers are charged with carrying out the Association's program and **submitting** reports to the Executive Committee.

2. In the case of any urgent matters not foreseen by the Executive Committee, **the Bureau is** given power to act at **its**[165] discretion and will take the first opportunity to report on these matters to the Executive Committee.[166]

Article 12 – Languages

1. Working languages[167] at the General Assembly will be the language of the host country, **English, and** at least one other language as determined by the Executive Committee according to the needs of the meeting. On the occasion of international events, the working languages will be the language of the host country and English, with the option of one more language according to need. **When** the host country is English-speaking, it must provide at least two other languages for the General Assembly. **For other international events**[168]**, at least one other language must be provided if so determined by the Executive Committee according to the needs of the event.**

The working language **of the Association for written communication will be English.**[169]

2. International **Events** are defined as:

Executive Committee meetings

Seminars and forums as part of an **ASSITEJ/Int'l Festival and ASSITEJ/Int'l Projects**[170]

Activities which take place officially in the name of **ASSITEJ/Int'l** apart from the General Assembly

Article 13 – Duration

1. This Association is created for an unlimited period.

2. This Association shall cease to function when, for any reason, three-fourths of the members (National Centers) on the basis of their number of votes shall express in writing to the Secretary General the desire to dissolve the Association. In this event, the Executive Committee shall be authorized to declare the Association dissolved, and any funds remaining in the Association's treasury shall be given to international organizations pursuing similar aims.

Article 14 – Adoption of Statutes

This Constitution **and amendments or changes** shall come into force at the moment of its approval by a Constituent General Assembly of delegations from all interested countries called for this purpose. From that moment **the Executive Committee** may accept as members the National Centers who send their applications to the Secretary General.

Adopted by the Executive Committee at their meeting in Adelaide, Australia, March 2005.

Adopted by the General Assembly at the XVth World Congress in Montreal, Canada, September 2005

Definitions (etc.):

General Assembly (GA): attending delegations from National Centers (Art. 8, 9)

Secretary General (officer): elected directly by the General Assembly (Art. 9, 13)

Treasurer (officer): elected directly by the General Assembly (Art. 9, 13)

Executive Committee (EC): elected directly by the General Assembly, maximum – 17 members (Art. 9,14, 10)

President (officer): elected by GA on the recommendation of EC, among members of EC (Art. 9, 15)

3 Vice-Presidents (officers): elected by GA on the recommendation of EC, among member of EC (Art. 9, 15)

Co-opted (full) member of EC: appointed by EC (Art. 10, 3)
Counselor: appointed by EC (Art. 10, 3)
Deputy (for an EC member): nominated by the EC-members National Center (Art. 10, 4)
President of Honor: appointed by GA on recommendation of EC (Art. 9, 16)
Member of Honor: appointed by GA on recommendation of EC (Art. 9, 16)
Auditor: elected by GA on recommendation of EC (Art. 9, 17)
Bureau: the officers jointly (Art. 8, 11)

The Current Constitution of ASSITEJ (2011)

The Constitution of ASSITEJ (2005) was amended and approved by the General Assembly at the XVIIth World Congress held in Copenhagen, Denmark/Malmö, Sweden on 20-29 May 2011, and is now in force.

Major Constitutional changes were:
a) An international network with members in at least 7 countries can apply to be a full voting Member, and an international network with slightly less (explained in the Constitution) can apply to be a Corresponding Member. They would have the same status as any national center.

b) ANY person, theater, or school can apply to be a Non-voting Member of ASSITEJ.

What was voted down was a proposal that a 'constitutionally independent entity claiming independence' (such as Kosovo or Taiwan) could be a Voting Member.

These were to open up the organization.

The new EC will be reviewing procedures for a) and b) above – certainly any membership application will have to be voted on by the EC.

Other changes include:
1) The term "bureau" and its creation is eliminated.
2) A congress must be held "at least once in every three year period", not "every three years".

CONSTITUTION OF ASSITEJ – (2011)

INTERNATIONAL ASSOCIATION OF THEATRE FOR CHILDREN
AND YOUNG PEOPLE

Preamble
Since the theatrical art is a universal expression of mankind and possesses the influence and power to link large groups of the world's peoples in the service of peace, and considering the role theatre can play in the education of younger generations, an autonomous international organization has been formed which bears the name of the International Association of Theatre for Children and Young People. The Association shall be known by the acronym **ASSITEJ** (L'Association International du Théâtre pour l'Enfance et la Jeunesse).

ASSITEJ recognizes the right of all children and young people to enrichment through the arts and their own cultural traditions, especially theatre culture. Theatre respects its young audiences by presenting their hopes, dreams, and fears; it develops and deepens experience, intelligence, emotion, and imagination; it inspires ethical choices; it increase awareness of social relationships; it encourages self-esteem, tolerance, confidence, and the free expression of opinions. Above all, it helps future generations find their place and voice in society. To this end, **ASSITEJ** endorses Article 31 of the 1989 United Nations Convention of the rights of the Child that affirms the right of children to leisure time and the enjoyment of arts and cultural activities. It shares common values with UNESCO's Cultural Policy, calling for the rights of children and young people to cultural participation and activity. It holds with the belief of the 2005 UNESCO Convention about Cultural Diversity, that children and young people must be allowed a cultural identity and to be visible everywhere in society. **ASSITEJ** is an advocate for the promotion of theatre for young audiences in principle and practice. It calls on all national and international organizations that recognize the potential of children and young people and their capacity to contribute to the development of society to recognize and support this Constitution.

Article 1 – Mission

1.1. ASSITEJ proposes to unite theatres, organizations, and individuals throughout the world dedicated to theatre for children and young people.

1.2. ASSITEJ is dedicated to artistic, cultural, political, and educational efforts and no decision, action, or statement of the Association shall be based on nationality, political conviction, cultural identity, ethnicity, or religion.

1.3. ASSITEJ promotes international exchange of knowledge and practice in theatre in order to increase creative co-operation and to deepen mutual understanding between all persons involved in the performing arts for young audiences.

Article 2 – Aims

Recognizing that children and young people make up a large part of the world's population and that they represent the future, the aims of the Association are:

2.1. To work for the rights of children and young people to artistic experiences especially designed and created for them.

2.2. To work for the recognition and acknowledgment of theatre for children and young people.

2.3. To work for the improvement of the conditions of theatre for children and young people all over the world.

2.4. To improve the common knowledge of theatre for children and young people worldwide, thus drawing the attention of international and national authorities to the importance of taking children and young people and the work created for them seriously.

2.5. To give people working with theatre for children and young people possibilities of getting acquainted with the work of colleagues from other countries and cultures, thus enabling them to enrich theatre for children and young people in their own country.

2.6. To help to form in all countries, ASSITEJ centers and networks which function in accordance with the mission, constitution, and policies of the Association. These centers and networks shall unite all theatres, organizations, and personas interested in theatre for children and young people.

2.7. To help to establish international artistic networks to explore different aspects of artistic work for children and young people, to increase the artistic competence of artists and to benefit them.

Article 3 – Means

The means of achieving these aims are:

3.1. Organization, promotion, and support of national, regional, and international programs, congresses, conferences, festivals, study tours, exhibitions and other activities.

3.2. Promotion and support exchange of experiences between artists from all countries.

3.3. Encouragement of circulation and exchange of plays, texts, and other literature pertaining to theatre for children and young people.

3.4. Collection of material and documentation on theatre for children and young people.

3.5. Promotion of theatre for children and young people through all media.

3.6. Co-operation with other international organizations with related interests.

3.7. Introduction and support of proposals made by centers in order to advance the work of theatre for children and young people to appropriate national and international authorities and agencies.

Article 4 – Members

ASSITEJ is created to facilitate the development of theatre for children and young people at the highest artistic level and no theatre, organization or individual can be refused admittance to membership of ASSITEJ on the basis of age, gender, ethnicity, disability or ability, sexual orientation, cultural identity, national origin, or political or religious conviction.

4.1. Members of the Association are:

1. *National centers* representative of theatre for children and young people in their own countries;

2. *Professional, international networks* of theatres, organizations, and persons who share a common artistic need or interest that serves the growth of theatre for children and young people;

3. *Individual members* (theatre companies, organizations, or persons) dedicated to theatre for children and young people, who are not able to participate in other forms of ASSITEJ membership.

4.2. Categories of Membership:

1. **Full membership**

National centers and networks

2. **Corresponding membership**

Those national centers and networks that are unable to meet the full criteria for membership, but can meet less stringent criteria as defined in Article 4.3.

3. **Non-voting membership**

Individual members (theatre companies, organizations, or persons) dedicated to theatre for children and young people, who are no able to participate in other forms of ASSITEJ membership.

4.3 Definitions of Members:

4.3.1 National Centers

1. **National centers** are networks of theatre companies, organizations, and persons, working in that country in the field of theatre for children and young people.

2. **Categories of membership within national centers are:**

2.1. Professional theatre companies or artists performing for children and young people.

2.2. Non-professional theatre companies or artists performing for children and young people.

2.3. Organizations, institutions, associations, or persons actively engaged in the work of theatre for children and young people.

2.4. Supporting organizations, institutions, associations, or persons interested in theatre for children and young people.

3. **Criteria for full or corresponding membership:**

3.1. To qualify for full membership in the Association, a national center must be a network comprising at least three (3) professional members (2.1), or five (5) members with at least two (2) professional members (2.1) and three (3) non-professional members (2.2).

3.2. To qualify for corresponding membership, a national center must be a network of theatre companies, organizations, and persons which does not achieve the above criteria.

4.3.2 Professional Networks

1. Professional networks are formal, international networks of theatre companies, organizations, and/or persons working in and supporting the field of theatre for children and young people.

2. Professional networks can be formed on the basis of common interests or needs related to the work of theatre for children and young people.

3. Criteria for membership

3. 1. To qualify for **full** membership in the Association, a professional network should be a global network which includes members from at least seven (7) countries from two (2) or more continents.

3. 2. Those professional networks which do not meet the above criteria, but include members from a minimum of five (5) countries, may apply for **corresponding** membership.

4.3.3 Individual Members

1. Individual members are theatre companies, organizations, or persons dedicated to theatre for young audiences, who are not able to participate in other forms of ASSITAJ membership.

2. Individual members are non-voting members.

Article 5 – Rights and Obligations

5.1 Full Members have the right to make proposals at constitutional meetings, to be elected to the Executive Committee, and to vote according to the rules detailed in Article 9.

5.2 Corresponding members have the right to make proposals at constitutional meetings and to vote according to the rules detailed in Article 9. Corresponding members do not have the right to be elected to the Executive Committee.

5.3 Non-voting members have the right to participate in the work of the Association, including giving proposals at constitutional meetings, but do not have the right to vote according to the rules detailed in Article 9. Additionally, non-voting members do not have the right to be elected to the Executive Committee.

5.4 All members, full, corresponding, and non-voting have the following obligations:

- to work to achieve the aims defined by the Association,
- to maintain its statutes,
- to act upon the decisions made by the Association,
- to pay their membership fees,
- to keep the Secretary General informed of their activities on a regular basis,
- to appoint a correspondent,

- to provide a permanent address,
- and to communicate to their members the information sent from the Secretary General's office.

5.5 All full and corresponding members must use the acronym "ASSITEJ" either in the name of the center or network or in the description in the subtitle.

Article 6 – Application, Resignation, Suspension, Expulsion

6.1. Written applications for membership shall be addressed to the Secretary General. These applications will be considered, approved, or denied by the Executive Committee. In the case of a denial by the Executive Committee, the applicant may appeal to the next General Assembly.

6.2. Any member that wishes to resign from the Association should inform the Secretary General in writing. The resignation will take effect from 1st January in the following year.

6.3. The Executive Committee may decide, by a majority of two-thirds, on the rejection, suspension, or expulsion of any member whose work conflicts with the fundamental aims of this Association, or who has failed several times in one of the obligations mentioned in Article 6. 4. Any centre which has been rejected, suspended or expelled loses the right to use the acronym "ASSITEJ".

6.4. Any rejected, suspended or expelled member may appeal to the next General Assembly.

Article 7 – Finances

7.1. This Association is financed from the membership fees, as well as from subsidies or grants accepted by the Executive Committee.

7.2. The fiscal period of this Association runs from one General Assembly to the next.

7.3. Membership fees, which are determined by the General Assembly, are due on 1st January of each year, and must be sent to the Treasurer. Members more than six (6) months in arrears lose the right to vote in the General Assembly.

Article 8 – Structure

The governing body of this Association consists of:
1. The General Assembly
2. The Executive Committee

Article 9 – Functions of the General Assembly

9.1. The General Assembly consists of delegations of all full and corresponding members.

9.2. A delegation from a center or network with full membership has three (3) votes. A delegation from a center or network with corresponding membership has (1) vote.

9.3. Voting by proxy is permitted, and must be given in writing. A center or network wishing to transfer its proxy must do so in writing. A delegation from a national center can hold proxy for only one (1) other national center. A national center with full membership can hold proxy for any full or corresponding member. A national center with corresponding membership can hold proxy only for a national center with corresponding membership. A network with full membership can hold proxy only for another network or full or corresponding membership.

9.4. Non-voting members are invited to participate in the work of the General Assembly. These members are encouraged to find ways to formally associate with others to become part of the voting membership of ASSITEJ/Int'l.

9.5. The Association shall meet in General Assembly at the World Congress at least once in every three (3) calendar years, with the formal announcement of this meeting made at least six months in advance by the Secretary General upon instruction of the President. The General Assembly will decide on the location of the next General Assembly and World Congress, but if it should be unable to make a decision on this matter, or if a change of location should prove necessary, this decision will be left to the Executive Committee.

9.6. The Association may meet between two World Congresses. members may propose an already existing event of international or regional significance for selection as an "ASSITEJ/Int'l Meeting". These events will be selected by the General Assembly at the World Congress.

9.7. A special meeting of the General Assembly may be called by the Secretary General three (3) months in advance on the written and justified request of two-thirds of the members or at the discretion of the Executive Committee in the case of an emergency or extraordinary circumstance.

9.8. The General Assembly has final control over the Constitution, and decides on any changes or amendments. Any member wishing to amend the Constitution must give notice in writing to the Secretary General at least three (3) months before the date of the meeting of the General Assembly. Any decision to amend the Constitution shall require a two-thirds majority.

9.9. The General Assembly establishes the broad outlines of the Association's policy.

9.10. The General Assembly receives for approval the report of the activities and the financial report, which are submitted by the Executive Committee.

9.11. The President of this Association is by right President of the General Assembly. In the event of his or her absence, he or she will be replaced by a Vice-President, selected by vote of the Executive Committee, or, in the absence of all the Vice-Presidents, by a member of the Executive Committee elected for this purpose by the General Assembly.

9.12. All decisions, unless otherwise stated, are taken by simple majority vote. In the case of a tie, the President will cast the deciding vote. If two centers apply to host the next Congress, the host shall be the center that receives the most votes. If more than two centers apply for hosting, and neither receives a majority, a second vote shall be taken between the two leading candidates, and the host shall be the center that receives the most votes.

9.13. The General Assembly determines the membership fees and other charges to be levied on the members of the Association.

9.14. A meeting of the General Assembly can only be held if the delegates of at least 1/3 of the full and corresponding members state in writing to the Secretary General their determination to be present and to participate, either in person or by proxy. This notification of attendance must be sent to the Secretary General three (3) months in advance of the meeting.

9.15. The General Assembly can only make decisions if one-third (1/3) of the members participate in person or by proxy.

Article 9.16 – Elections:

9.16.1. Elections for the Executive Committee of the Association are held at a meeting of the General Assembly at least once in every three (3) calendar years.

9.16.2. General Assembly shall elect the President and the Secretary General from those standing for the Executive Committee, in this order: the President is elected first and presides over the election of the Secretary General and representatives to the Executive Committee. Candidacies for the offices of the President and the Secretary General should be sent in writing to the Secretary General, three (3) months before the date of the General Assembly in order to circulate nominations to the members of ASSITEJ.

If no center or network has presented candidates for these offices, the Executive

Committee at its last meeting before the General Assembly shall recommend a candidate for each of the offices and inform all members of this recommendation.

9.16.3. The General Assembly shall elect the members of the Executive Committee as representatives of centers or networks with full membership. A center or network with full membership may have only one representative on the Executive Committee. Where a center and a network nominate candidates from the same country, the candidate of the national center takes preference and may stand for election. Each full member, on its own behalf should send to the Secretary General, in writing, the name of its candidate three (3) months before the date of the meeting of the General Assembly in order to circulate nominations to the members of ASSITEJ.

9.16.4. From amongst the members of the Executive Committee, the General Assembly shall elect thee Vice-Presidents and Treasurer, who shall be nominated in a meeting of the new Executive Committee. They shall be elected in their personal capacity.

9.16.5. The officers and members of the Executive Committee shall be chosen to represent as fairly as possible the interests of the organization and the diversity of all the centers and networks, taking into account such factors as geography, ethnic origin, gender, aesthetics, and cultural identity. They should also reflect strengths that serve the concerns and priorities of the working plan for the elected term.

9.17. The General Assembly, on the recommendation of the Executive Committee, can give the titles of Honorary President and Honorary Member of Honor for exceptional service to the Association. Both shall have a consultative voice, but no right to vote, and they cannot represent their country.

9.18. On the recommendation of the Executive Committee, the General Assembly shall appoint an accredited financial officer to conduct the audit of the accounts.

9.19. The agenda, with its enclosures, and candidates for the President, the Secretary General, and the Executive Committee, should be sent from the General Secretariat to all centers no later than two (2) months in advance of the General Assembly.

9.20. Only those items which are set down on the agenda may be voted upon in the General Assembly.

Article 10 – Functions of the Executive Committee

10.1. The Executive Committee is composed of a maximum of fifteen (15) members having the right to vote, including, the President, and three (3) Vice-Presidents, the Secretary General, and the Treasurer.

10.2. In the event of the death or resignation of a member of the Executive Committee, the Executive Committee shall authorize the center or network which nominated the member to appoint a deputy for the remaining period of the term of office. The exceptions are: in the case of the President, where the replacement shall be from amongst the Vice-Presidents; and in the case of one of the Vice-Presidents, where the Executive Committee is authorized either to leave the office vacant or, if it judges it necessary, to elect a replacement from amongst its own members. In the case of the death or resignation of the Secretary General, the Executive Committee will appoint a suitable person to the office in an acting capacity, until the next General Assembly.

10.3. The Executive Committee has the right to co-opt persons as members of the Executive Committee. The Executive Committee also has the right to appoint Counselors for the period of its mandate, who may attend, without voting rights, meetings of the Executive Committee during their time in office.

10.4. Any member who cannot attend a meeting of the Executive Committee can be replaced only by a permanent deputy nominated by his or her center for the duration of his or her term of office. The Secretary General must be notified of the deputy's name as soon as possible after the General Assembly.

10.5. A meeting of the Executive Committee may be held only if at least half (1/2) of the members express to the Secretary General their determination to be present and participate, either in person or represented by a deputy. The presence of half (1/2) the members shall constitute a quorum.

10.6. The Executive Committee will meet at least once each calendar year; the Committee will decide by majority vote if it is necessary to hold additional meetings, and will choose the places and dates of such meetings. The Committee must be notified three (3) months in advance. Meetings will be called by the Secretary General at the request of the President.

10.7. The Executive Committee may decide upon urgent matters by correspondence if it proves impossible to hold a special meeting. In this case the Secretary General, by agreement with the President, shall send to each member of the Executive Committee a questionnaire, to which each member will reply in writing. Decisions will be made by a two-thirds majority vote. The decisions will come before the Executive Committee at their next meeting for ratification. The replies will be placed in the records of the Association where they will be available for examination by members of the General Assembly.

10.8. Each member of the Executive Committee possesses one vote, which he or she may use in person, unless delegated to his or her permanent deputy.

10.9. The President of the Association is also Chairperson of the meetings of the Executive Committee. In the event of the President's absence, he or she will be replaced by a Vice-President, selected by vote of the Executive Committee, or if all the Vice-Presidents are absent, by a member elected for this purpose by the Executive Committee to chair the meeting.

10.10. All motions are carried by a simple majority vote, except decisions taken by correspondence or regarding Article 6. 3.

10.11. The Chairperson of the meeting has the right to vote as a member of the Committee. If a majority decision cannot be established by this means, the Chairperson may cast a second, deciding vote.

10.12. The Executive Committee will submit a working plan of activities to the General Assembly. It manages the affairs of the Association between the meetings of the General Assembly and carries out the decisions of the General Assembly. The Executive Committee will remain in office for the period between one General Assembly and the next, which will be three years or thereabouts, at which time its members shall be eligible for re-election.

10.13. The Executive Committee will accept or reject new applications for membership made to the Secretary General. A rejection may be appealed by the applicant at the next General Assembly.

10.14. The budget is administered by the Executive Committee according to a working plan established by the General Assembly.

10.15. The Executive Committee entrusts to the Treasurer the administration of funds, the preparation of the budget, and the accounts. The accounts of the Association must be audited before the presentation to the General Assembly (Article 9.18).

10.16. The Executive Committee may take initiative in matters not anticipated by the General Assembly, provided that these matters are in keeping with the mission and aims of this Association, and provided that the Executive Committee takes the first opportunity to report on these matters to the members.

Article 11 – Functions of the Officers

The Officers of this Association are as follows:

The President
Three Vice-Presidents
The Secretary General
The Treasurer.

11.1. The Officers are charged with specific functions in carrying out the Association's program and submitting reports to the Executive Committee.

11.2. In the case of any urgent matters not foreseen by the Executive Committee, the Officers are given the right to act at their discretion and will take the first opportunity to report on these matters to the Executive Committee.

Article 12 – Languages

12.1. Working languages at the General Assembly will be the language of the host country, English, and at least one other language as determined by the Executive Committee according to the needs of the meeting. On the occasion of international events, the working languages will be the language of the host country and English, with the option of one more language according to need.

When the host country is English-speaking, it must provide at least two other languages for the General Assembly. For other international events, at least one other language must be provided if so determined by the Executive Committee, according to the needs of the event.

12.2. The working language of the Association for written communication will be English.

Article 13 – Duration

13.1. This Association is created for an unlimited period.

13.2. This Association shall cease to function when, for any reason, three-fourths (3/4) of the members, on the basis of their number of votes, shall express in writing to the Secretary General the desire to dissolve the Association. In this event, the Executive Committee shall be authorized to declare the Association dissolved, and any funds remaining in the Association's accounts will be given to international organizations pursuing similar aims.

Article 14 – Constitutional Amendments

All amendments or changes to the Constitution shall come into force at the moment of their approval by a General Assembly.

Adopted by the General Assembly at the XVIIth World Congress in Copenhagen, Denmark/Malmö, Sweden, May 2011.

Definitions, etc.

General Assembly (GA) consists of attending delegations from centers and networks at a World Congress – Art. 8, 9.
President (officer) elected directly by General Assembly – Art. 9.13
Secretary General (officer) elected directly by General Assembly – Art. 9.13
Executive Committee (EC) elected directly by the General Assembly – Art. 9.14 & Art. 10
Treasurer (officer) elected by the GA on the recommendation of EC, among members of EC – Art. 9.15
3 Vice-Presidents (officers) elected by GA on the recommendation of EC, among members of EC – Art. 9.15
Co-opted (full) member of EC, appointed by EC – Art. 10.3
Counselor appointed by EC – Art. 10.3
Deputy (for an EC-member) nominated by the EC-member's Center or Network – Art. 10.4
Honorary President appointed by GA on the recommendation of EC – Art. 9.16

Honorary Member appointed by GA on the recommendation of EC – Art. 9.16
Auditor: An accredited financial officer elected by GA on the recommendation of EC – Art. 9.17 & Art. 10.15
International events are, for example, international festivals, conferences, seminars, workshops, forums, and other activities which take place officially in the name of ASSITEJ, apart from the General Assembly – Art. 12
An ASSITEJ World Congress and Performing Arts Festival is a meeting of the General Assembly taking place at least once every three (3) years, which included both the business of the Association and artistic exchange – Art. 9
An ASSITEJ/Int'l Meeting is an international event where the Executive Committee is present and where all members of ASSITEJ are invited to attend. It is primarily an artistic meeting of the organization and occurs between World Congresses – Art. 9.6

APPENDIX G
Volume III
THE HISTORY OF THE FORMATION & SUSPENSION OF NATIONAL CENTERS (1991–2005)

Because of the current number of National Centers it was no longer pertinent to try to show the yearly changes in the membership of ASSITEJ/Int'l. Accordingly, the active centers are now grouped every few years by continent.

ASSITEJ began with a total of twelve (12) National Centers whose representatives were elected to the Provisional Committee at the Constitutional Conference in Paris, France in June of 1965.

1990

At the Stockholm Congress of ASSITEJ in 1990 there were a total 45 Full National Centers and 5 Corresponding Centers for a total of 50 Centers. They were:

Full Members

AFRICA
Algeria

NORTH AMERICA
Canada
Cuba
Mexico
USA

SOUTH AMERICA
Argentina
Brazil
Ecuador
Paraguay
Peru
Uruguay
Venezuela

MID-EAST
Iran

Iraq
Israel
Turkey

ASIA
Japan
South Korea
Sri Lanka
Taiwan

Vietnam

AUSTRALIA

EUROPE
Austria
Belgium
Bulgaria
Czechoslovakia
Denmark
FGR

Finland
France
GDR
Great Britain
Greece
Hungary
Ireland
Italy
Netherlands
Norway
Poland
Portugal
Romania
Spain
Sweden
Switzerland
USSR
Yugoslavia

CORRESPONDING CENTERS:
India
Kenya
Madagascar
Mongolia
Sri Lanka

1996

As of 1 May 1996, the following countries had national centers for a total of 53 Full National Centers and 2 Corresponding Centers:

Full Members

AFRICA
Kenya
Madagascar
Tanzania
Uganda
Zaïre
Zimbabwe

NORTH AMERICA
Canada
Cuba
Mexico
Nicaragua
USA

SOUTH AMERICAN
Argentina
Brazil
Chile
Peru
Uruguay
Venezuela

ASIA
China
India
Iran
Iraq
Israel
Kyrgyzstan
Korea
Japan
Mongolia
Philippines
Sri Lanka
Thailand
Turkey
Vietnam

AUSTRALASIA
Australia
New Zealand

EUROPE
Austria
Belgium
Bulgaria
Croatia
Cyprus
Czech Republic
Denmark
Estonia
Finland
France
Georgia
Germany
Greece
Hungary
Iceland
Ireland
Italy
Netherlands
Norway

Poland
Portugal
Romania
Russia
Slovakia
Spain
Sweden
Switzerland
Ukraine
United Kingdom

Corresponding Centers
Angola
Singapore

2005
As of 2005, the following 69 countries were listed as Full National Centers and 10 as Corresponding Centers making a total of 79.[171]

Full Members
AFRICA
Benin
Cameroon
Kenya
Mozambique
Namibia
Nigeria
South Africa
Swaziland
Tanzania
Uganda Zambia
Zimbabwe

NORTH AMERICA
Canada
Mexico
USA

SOUTH AMERICA
Argentina
Bolivia

Brazil
Uruguay

MID-EAST
Armenia
Iran
Israel
Jordan
Turkey

ASIA
Bangladesh
China
India
Japan
Korea
Sri Lanka
Vietnam

AUSTRALASIA
Australia
New Zealand

EUROPE
Albania
Austria
Belgium
Croatia
Cyprus
Czech Republic
Denmark
Estonia
Finland
France
Georgia
Germany
Greece
Hungary
Iceland
Ireland
Italy
Latvia
Lichtenstein
Lithuania
Macedonia
Netherlands
Norway
Peru

Philippines
Poland
Romania
Russia
Serbia & Montenegro
Slovakia
Slovenia
Spain
Sweden
Switzerland
United Kingdom
Ukraine
Uzbekistan

Corresponding Members
Angola
Botswana
Madagascar
Malaysia
Mauritius
Nepal
Rwanda
Singapore
Thailand
Tunisia

APPENDIX H
Volume III
THE CURRENT ELECTION PROCESS OF ASSITEJ (2005)
Written by Nat Eek, Michael Ramløse, and Kim Peter Kovac

Over the years, an elaborate election process had emerged and been codified. This lists the process which incorporates all the changes in the Constitution up through 2005. An entire new process was voted in by the General Assembly in 2011.

1. The President appoints a 3-person Committee of Tellers whose responsibility is to count the election ballots, verify the results, and give the results to the Presiding Officer. The General Assembly votes to approve these appointments.

2. In the General Assembly with the Elections on the Agenda the Presiding Officer announces publicly those centers present and which are eligible to vote. This means that each center has had acceptable statutes in conformity with the ASSITEJ Constitution, has a corresponding delegate and address, and has paid its dues. Each center so approved may be present in person, or may give its proxy to another center. However, by the current Constitution no center can have more than one (1) proxy.

3. First, the delegates vote on whether the Secretary General and the Treasurer are to be retained. If not, nominations are accepted from the floor for replacements. In Stockholm in 1990 Rose-Marie Moudoués (France) was defeated as Secretary General and Michael Ramlöse (Denmark) was nominated from the floor and elected.

4. The Presiding Officer reads in English the names of the National Centers, in alphabetical order, who have nominated themselves and who are willing to stand for election. This can be any number. At this same time the Presiding Officer announces any proxies and what Centers hold them. The total number of votes is announced, as well as the majority of votes required for election. In order to be elected a Center must receive at least the majority of the votes which can be cast (51%). Also, according to the current (2005) Constitution there can only be seventeen (17) members on the EC. With the Centers of the Secretary General and the Treasurer automatic members of the EC, the delegates can only vote for a total of fifteen (15) Centers. This means that by *not* voting for all 15 Centers or for a particular Center, a Center may be defeated for election since it will not have a majority vote (51%). Several times there has been a proposal to require all Centers to vote for a total of the current 15, but it has been defeated twice. On the positive side, this voting procedure guarantees that every Center on the EC has a majority vote of confidence.

5. Three (3) identical ballots with the name of each nominated Center on them are distributed to each Center, one for each of their potential three (3) votes (2 professional and 1 amateur), again in alphabetical order.

6. Each center marks the ballots accordingly, and the ballots are deposited in the ballot box, again each center being called to the ballot box for deposit in alphabetical order.

7. The Presiding Officer is given the result by the Tellers, and he/she announces the results of the elections to the General Assembly. Those elected are announced by name starting

with the highest number of votes continuing until a total of fifteen (15) National Centers are reached. The number of votes received by each candidate is always announced. Ties are automatically accepted within the fifteen. If there is a tie at 15, then a run-off election is held between the two. If less than fifteen (15) Centers receive a majority vote, the EC would be comprised of only that number who received a majority vote.

8. A recess is declared; the new EC retires; and in executive session they select a slate of officers by name, not by country: a President and 3 Vice-Presidents from among the fifteen individuals on the EC. They may present more than one name for each office. Returning to the General Assembly in session, the Presiding Officer reads off the names; there can be nominations from the floor for any office as long as the person is on the new EC and has agreed to the nomination; ballots are prepared; and the Centers vote on those names. Each name must receive at least 51% of the total eligible vote. If a name receives less than the majority vote, the EC retires to come up with a new slate; or additional nominations can be made from the floor; or if it is among the Vice-Presidents, they may just have fewer than three.

9. Again, the three (3) tellers count the ballots and give the vote totals to the Presiding Officer for announcement of the election results.

10. Only the EC can co-opt a Center to sit on the EC with or without vote, and it can co-opt no more than two (2) by the Constitution. However, the delegates have made their wishes known to the EC, who usually follow that advice. Recently the EC has also created the office of counselor without vote for a single person whose advice will be sought in their deliberations. Co-opted Centers and Counselors do not have to be appointed. If it so wishes, the EC can do without, or appoint them at a later date as need arises. The EC also has the right to invite any person to attend the EC Meeting, if it so wishes. This has usually been used as a method to introduce leaders from new centers to the ASSITEJ process, or to provide advice from a recognized expert.

11. In 1996 at the Rostov-on-Don World Congress this entire election process was adopted in a series of amendments, and which were written into the Constitution. this process was in force through 2005. In 2011 the entire process was revised to take electronic voting into consideration, which speeded up the process considerably.

THE CURRENT ELECTION PROCESS OF ASSITEJ (2011)
by Nat Eek and Kim Peter Kovac

At the XVIIth World Congress of ASSITEJ, held in Copenhagen, Denmark and Malmö, Sweden from 20–29 May 2011 major changes were voted into the current Constitution. (See this Constitution in Appendix F.) These changes were in two areas: 1) the process of the election, and 2) the need to open up the membership. These election changes were passed unanimously by the General Assembly. Since all Nominations are announced by e-mail, regular mail, and the ASSITEJ Website at least three (3) months in advance, there can no longer be any nominations from the floor.

1. The first major change limited the number to serve on the EC at 15, instead of the previous 17 members.

2. At the General Assembly prior to the election all the candidates for the EC (National Centers who had put themselves in nomination) are introduced, and each gives a short presentation about his/her qualifications.

3. The current President announces the Elections, and then the Secretary General announces the names of those National Centers that are entitled to vote, the proxies as well as the total number of votes to be cast. Each National Center with Full Membership now has three (3) votes, and each Center with Corresponding Membership has one (1) vote. Proxy votes are allowed, but each National Center is allowed to hold only one (1) proxy vote.

4. The Secretary General announces the total number of votes which can be cast, and in turn the majority number of votes required for election (at least 50%).

5. The President is elected first. The current President announces the names in alphabetical order of those members who have put themselves in nomination for the Presidency. Each candidate makes a small presentation of his/her qualifications, and then the National Centers are asked to cast their ballots. At the 2011 Congress an electronic system of voting was used. The Election Commission, previously elected, then certifies the vote. The new President is announced, and the ceremonial gavel is given to the new President by the past President.

6. The Secretary General is elected next. The new President announces in alphabetical order the names of those members who have put their names in nomination for Secretary General. Each candidate makes a personal presentation of his/her qualifications. The President asks for the vote. The Election Commission certifies the vote, and the President announces the name of the new Secretary General, who then assumes his/her place on the podium. At the 2011 Congress there was only one candidate, but who still made a presentation and had to be elected.

7. The President then announces the voting for the remaining 13 members to be elected to the new EC. The Election Commission certifies the vote, and the names of all the centers in nomination are announced along with each of their votes. At the 2011 Congress this was announced by being shown on a large screen fairly rapidly. However, there is still no regulation requiring a Center to vote for all 13 positions, so a "white ballot" vote is still possible. (A white ballot occurs when the voting member turns in a "blank ballot", in the hopes that a candidate will get less than the majority of votes required for election.)

8. The new EC retires and returns with their recommendations for the positions of the 3 Vice-Presidents and the Treasurer, all chosen from the newly elected members of the EC. These names are put to the vote, and the top three become Vice-Presidents in no particular order of seniority, along with the Treasurer. At the 2011 Congress only three (3) candidates for Vice-President were proposed to the General Assembly, and one name for Treasurer.

9. This completes the election process.

APPENDIX I
Volume III
THE ASSITEJ INTERNATIONAL AWARD FOR ARTISTIC EXCELLENCE
[Formerly The Honorary President's Award]
Rules and Regulations (as of 2005)

PART 1: HISTORY AND CRITERIA

History

In 1990 at the Stockholm World Congress, Nat Eek realized that ASSITEJ/Int'l had no official Award to give to its members that honored their artistic excellence in theatre for young audiences. Wishing to honor the memory of his wife Patricia Fulton Eek who died in 1989, and who was a lighting designer and an ardent advocate of theatre for young people as well as ASSITEJ, he established the Honorary Presidents Award of ASSITEJ/Int'l.

It is named and presented on behalf of all the Honorary Presidents of ASSITEJ/Int'l – Gerald Tyler (Great Britain), Konstantin Shakh-Azizov (Russia), Nat Eek (USA), Vladimir Adamek (Czech Republic), Ilse Rodenberg (Germany), Michael FitzGerald (Australia), Harold Oaks (USA), those past and those yet to come.

This ASSITEJ Honorary Presidents Award was established and accepted by the Executive Committee (EC) at the 1993 World Congress in Cuba. Since then it has been given four times – first in 1996 in Rostov-on-Don, Russia; in 1999 in Tromsø, Norway; in 2002 in Seoul, Korea; and most recently in 2005 in Montreal, Canada. [As of this writing the Award was also given at the Australia Congress in 2008, and in the Copenhagen/Malmö Congress in 2011.] At the EC Meeting in Frankfurt, Germany on 5 December 2005, these Rules and Regulations were approved, and the name of the Award was changed to the ASSITEJ/Int'l Award for Artistic Excellence.

Definition and Criteria

The purpose of the Award is to recognize artists in the profession of theatre for children and young people in the national centers, to encourage membership in the international organization among all national centers, and to give those artists some financial assistance in their work. It is not intended to honor those artists well established in their field, many of whom have already been well honored by their associates and their governments. A financial reward can mean much more to a younger or emerging artist.

The Jury is responsible to judge the nominees based on the remarkable and unique nature of the artistic work of the individual or theater company. These qualities must be represented in the past three (3) years of artistic work.

The criteria for the receiving of the Award are:
1. The Award is given every three years in an appropriate ceremony at the current World Congress.
2. The Award is given to one individual creative artist or theater company that has achieved remarkable artistic excellence in theatre for children and young people.
3. Only the creative work of the previous three years by an individual artist or group can be considered for the Award.

4. Once an artist or theater company has received the Award, the national center of the recipient's country may not nominate an artist or theater company from their country again until six years later, or for the second World Congress after receiving the Award.

5. No individual artist or theater company may receive the Award more than once.

The Award

The Award consists of:
1. A check for 5,000 US$.
2. A printed Certificate attesting to the winning of the Award.
3. An engraved goblet along with a bottle of champagne for appropriate celebration.
4. The donor hopes in 2008 to increase the Award to 10,000 US$.

Each of the Nominees for the Award receives a printed Certificate which declares the following:

[Name] was nominated by [country] National Center for ASSITEJ
for the [Year] ASSITEJ/Int'l Award for Artistic Excellence
The Honorary Presidents Award for remarkable achievement in the profession of Theatre for Children and Youth and is due congratulations and high commendation for that nomination.

PART 2: NOMINATION AND SELECTION

Nomination Process

1. At each World Congress, the Secretary General will make available to all national centers the announcement of the award for the next Congress, a list of the history, rules, and regulations, along with a nomination form. All this information will also be available on the ASSITEJ Website.

2. The nomination form includes the following: (see p. 7). All artists or theater companies must be nominated by a national center. Each center is allowed one nomination per award cycle.

3. Samples of the announcement and the nomination form are attached. (See pp. 8–9).

4. All completed nomination forms must be received by the Secretariat by the deadline date indicated on the form.

Jury Selection

1. The President of ASSITEJ/Int'l, with the approval of the EC, selects and appoints the five-member Jury.
2. The Jury meets to review the nominations and to select an Awardee during the EC Meeting prior to the next World Congress.

Jury Deliberation Process

1. Prior to the meeting, all members of the Jury will receive access to the nomination materials.
2. Upon meeting, the Jury first reviews all the nominees to see if there is any conflict of interest between the nominees and their centers, and a member of the Jury. Examples are: a Jury member from the nominating country, or a Jury member from a neighboring country. This is resolved by the Jury

member in conflict excusing him or herself from voting on that nomination. However, they are expected to participate freely in the discussion.
3. The Jury discusses the merits of each nominee based on the submitted materials, and each Juror's personal experience and knowledge of the candidates and their artistic work.
4. The Jury's deliberations must focus on the previous three years of artistic work.
5. The Jury narrows the nominees down to two or three of the most meritorious.
6. The Jury then agrees or votes on the Awardee.
7. Once a decision has been reached, the Jury forwards their decision to the EC and the Secretary General notifies all concerned of the decision.

Notification
1. Once an Awardee has been selected, it is the responsibility of the Chair of the Jury to notify:
   a. The Secretary General
   b. The President
2. It is then the responsibility of the Secretary General to notify:
   a. The donor
   b. The Awardee
   c. All other nominees and their nominating centers

The Donor's Responsibilities
1. To provide the money for the cash Award to be given to the Awardee.
2. To provide the engraved goblet and the bottle of champagne for the Awardee.
3. To provide the appropriate Certificates of Nomination and Awards for all the Nominees.
4. To be present at the Award Ceremony to assist with the presentation of the Award, or to appoint an appropriate person to assist with the presentation.

ASSITEJ/Int'l 's Responsibility to the Donor
1. To send a copy of the award announcement and nomination form to the donor at the time of their issue.
2. To send a copy of the Jury's Selection Report to the donor, to ensure adherence to the criteria of the award and to allow the donor the necessary time to produce the required certificates and awards.
3. To notify the donor of the time and place of the Awards Ceremony, and to request his presence.

Changes to these rules and regulations
   Changes to these rules and regulations can only be made in consultation and through agreement between ASSITEJ/Int'l and the donor.

APPROVED: EC Meeting in Frankfurt, Germany dated 5 December 2005.

   The following people and companies have won the ASSITEJ/INTERNATIONAL AWARD FOR ARTISTIC EXCELLENCE in the past:

   1996 – XIIth ASSITEJ World Congress – Rostov-on-Don, Russia
Mikhail Bartenev, playwright (Russia)
The Barking Gecko Theatre Company (Australia)
Volker Ludwig, director (Germany)
Ray Nusselein, artist (Denmark)

The Award was $250 for each winner, a total of $1,000 US

    1999 – XIIIth ASSITEJ World Congress – Tromsö, Norway
Arena Theatre Company (Australia)
Eva Bergman, director (Sweden) – Honorable Mention
The Award was $2,000 US

    2002 – XIVth ASSITEJ World Congress – Seoul, Korea
Suzanne Osten, director & playwright (Sweden)
The Award was $5,000 US

    2005 – XVth ASSITEJ World Congress – Montreal, Canada
The Zeal Theatre (Australia)
Kim Woo Ok (South Korea)
The Award was $2,500 each winner, a total of $5,000 US

    2008 – XVIth ASSITEJ World Congress – Adelaide, Australia
Teatro Testoni Ragazzi "La Baracca" (Italy)
Lutz Hübner (Germany) – Honorable Mention
The Dance Theatre "Hurjaruuth" (Finland) – Honorable Mention
Theatre Company "Baran" (Iran) – Honorable Mention
The Award was $5,000 US

    2011 – XVIIth ASSITEJ World Congress–Copenhagen, Denmark–Malmö, Sweden
NIE (New International Encounters) Cambridge, Great Britain & Oslo, Norway
Teatret Gruppe 38 (Denmark)
The Award was $2,500 each winner, a total of $5,000 US

APPENDIX J
Volume III
THE 30TH ANNIVERSARY OF ASSITEJ (1965–1995)
(Speeches by Former Secretary General Rose-Marie Moudoués and Former President Dr. Ilse Rodenberg)

The following speeches were delivered at the EC Meeting/One Theatre World Festival in Seattle, Washington, USA/7-14 May 1995 by former Secretary General of ASSITEJ Rose-Marie Moudoués. She gave her speech in French, and the French Center provided this translation. Dr. Ilse Rodenberg gave her speech in English.

'65 – '95 — ASSITEJ IS THIRTY YEARS OLD[172]
by Mme. Rose-Marie Moudoués (France)
Secretary General of ASSITEJ (1965–1990)
Honorary President of ATEJ
Honorary Member of ASSITEJ

If we are to appreciate ASSITEJ's early days and understand how significant its founding was, we should remember that historically speaking, we were living in the so-called "cold-war period", and that politically, the world was split in two.

ASSITEJ was brought into the world by the single-mindedness of a determined group of women and men from the theatre who cherished the humanistic values of their art and shared the vision of a stage of international co-operation regardless of race, politics or religion that would be founded solely on the need to develop or create, if not already in place, high quality performance theatres for children and young people.

But the road from ambition to reality is long.

Founding an international association has never been an easy task. The groundwork was laid during a number of informal meetings organized by Leon Chancerel, a friend of Stanislavsky, and the first to translate the latter's works. At the beginning of the thirties Leon Chancerel had founded the first performing theatre for young audiences in Paris, and in 1957, he created ATEJ – Association du Théâtre pour l'Enfance et la Jeunesse – (which was to become ASSITEJ's Centre in France). A meeting was held in Paris in 1962 attended by participants from three countries (Belgium, England, and France), at which the project to organize a broad international conference was hatched. Having heard that a similar meeting to ours had taken place in Prague in 1960, we were anxious to set up links as soon as possible so that we could work together on a common project. First contacts were made in July 1962 which continued in 1963 in Prague.

The work enabled both parties, East and West, to meet in Paris in September 1963, to look into and discuss draft articles of association. I was called in to draw them up because of my experience in this type of document.

Our strengthened embryonic group moved on to the next phase when we met in London [1964] on the occasion of the International Festival and Commonwealth Conference and opened up to the whole of the international community.

Our informal period was to give way to a formal period because at the close of the London meeting:

- A 12-member preparatory committee had been setup to draw up the articles
- France had invited the countries involved to a constitutional conference to be held in Paris in June 1965

The preparatory committee had just one year to complete its mission: we had to work on a first text drafted in Paris. I provided secretarial services to the preparatory committee to pool observations sent in through the post. We were fortunate to be invited to attend the Venice Biennale which in those days included a young people's Festival, which provided the opportunity to meet at the end of September 1964, to write the final version of the articles of association. This version was revised again before the Paris conference. It should be borne in mind that right from the start, the association tried to combine the administrative tasks with artistic activity: festivals, symposia, round table discussions, etc.

Having got so far in the story, I should mention some fundamental principles that guided the founder's work:

- The association insisted in writing into the foreword of the statutes the beginning of the ITI charter (International Theatre Institute). This action both confirmed its intention to work for peace and understanding between nations and its determination to work within the NGO (Non-Governmental Organization) set up.
- The association had decided that its members should be national centers responsible for bringing together people involved in the various aspects of theatre for young audiences in their countries for the sake of national culture and efficiency. The centers that subscribed to the international articles of the ASSITEJ, turned out to be steadfast partners when it came to organizing exchanges and common activities planned by the association. We drew on the benefit of the experience of the ITI (International Theatre Institute) for these events.
- We had to ensure that our organization had a unique identity to differentiate it from organizations that had long existence: for example, UNIMA (Union Internationale de la Marionnette) for puppets, AITA (Association Internationale du Théâtre Amateur) for amateur theatre with its "theatre in education" section.
- ASSITEJ set itself the aim of enlisting troupes of adult actors who acted for children and young people to the national centre. To cater for the diverse situations in the various countries, ASSITEJ national centre member troupes could either be troupes of professional or amateur actors with the proviso that they were adult actors and not children's troupes.
- The choice of the association's name ASSITEJ (Association Internationale du Théâtres pour l'Enfance et la Jeunesse / International Association of Theatre for Children and Young People), was unambiguous. It was theatre for children and not by children. Contrary to the remark our association's current secretary general [Michael Ramløse] has just made, the acronym ASSITEJ is not an odd name and is no harder to pronounce than other international association acronyms.
- Within the framework of the ITI, whose secretary general had taken part in the final session of the preparatory committee, ASSITEJ was to become part of the NGO scene and establish links with UNESCO.

The upshot was that we had no alternative but to choose at least two official languages to meet the international rules and requirements. English and French were selected, but we had to bear in mind that all the Soviet satellite countries had thriving theatres for children and young people and that at that time Russian was the lingua franca between those countries. ASSITEJ thus selected Russian as its third official language, it being understood that depending on usage, any country hosting as ASSITEJ event would temporarily be able to use its own language officially.

These are the articles that were voted for unanimously by the representatives of 25 countries in Paris at the constituent Conference, presided over by Leon Chancerel, who thus had the immense joy of seeing his dream come true very shortly before his death.

The statutes endorsed on 7 June 1965 form ASSITEJ's Constitutional Articles. The original version was drawn up in French and registered legally in Paris.

The preparatory committee was to make way for a "provisional committee" that was set up just before the first general assembly. The president for this event was Gerald Tyler (Great Britain) with K. Shakh-Azizov (USSR) as his vice-president and I took up the post of secretary general. The office had no treasurer at the time because we had no funds to manage!

The first general assembly took place in Prague in May 1966. In the year following the Paris conference, 17 national centers had been founded, 14 of them were represented at Prague (Belgium, Czechoslovakia, GDR, France, Great Britain, Italy, Netherlands, Norway, Romania, Spain, USSR, USA, West Germany and Yugoslavia), 3 countries presented their apologies (Brazil, Canada, and Israel).

Observers had been sent from 12 countries from Europe, America, Asia and Africa. We were encouraged, hoping that they would soon become members of the association.

With the elections of its first Executive Committee, ASSITEJ brought its emergent and infancy phase to a close. It was [now to] embark on its years of apprenticeship and youth.

I would like to close by emphasizing the drive to explore and innovate artistically, the spirit of friendship, and tolerance that moved these women and men from countries of very distinct political and cultural leanings, who had been united in a new extended humanistic theatrical family by the art of the theatre and the respect for young audiences.
—Rose-Marie Moudoués

THE DREAM OF ASSITEJ[173]
by Dr. Ilse Rodenberg (Germany)
President of ASSITEJ (1978–1987)
Honorary President of ASSITEJ

A copy of the above speech was not available, but the following interview with Dr. Rosenberg in 1994 covers much of the same information. On 22 November 1994 in Berlin Christel Hoffman (formerly GDR) and Jürgen Flügge (formerly FRG) interviewed Dr. Ilse Rodenberg at the age of 88, Past President of ASSITEJ and one of the Founding Members of ASSITEJ/Int'l. The following are excepts from that interview. Edited by Nat Eek.

Interview with Dr. Ilse Rodenberg[174]

Rodenberg: It is still my endeavor to take interest in all fortunes of ASSITEJ. When I think of ASSITEJ today, or its beginning and its development, two things especially come to my mind. First, the ASSITEJ in its beginning had been like a big family. This has got to do with the fact that the number of members had then been much smaller and that times have changed since then – it had been a quite different atmosphere at that time. Nowadays ASSITEJ is a large institution. Then it had been an international family, today it is an international institution. And that, of course , means different kinds of meetings and encounters. Second, today I realize that I feel a huge respect towards ASSITEJ as well as towards ourselves. Because we set an example of community at the peak of the Cold War period. Although all the people were contradictory and all their ideas were inconsistent, we succeeded in building a sense of community which gave everybody the chance to save his or her face without making false promises. In a word, this cooperation was working – you can easily tell this by looking at its beginning and its present situation.

This was only possible because everybody involved in the work of ASSITEJ kept his or her mind on the aim of this organization: to accomplish good and professional theatre for children all over the world – as the statutes of ASSITEJ say. This common matter did permit that people who had an own point of view which they defended with tolerance could compromise without losing their face.

A big contribution to this, of course, our General Secretary Rose-Marie Moudoués, the various presidents from different countries as well as the Executive Committee. Of course, the members of the General Assembly had different opinions and sometimes they pursued a policy—but the leading bodies were always able to achieve the principles of ASSITEJ as they are written in its statutes.

We are no political organization. this organization which assembles various artistic organization in itself, reconciles persons who were humanists. That was the basis on which ASSITEJ could grow in an age which actually had a tendency to breaking-ups.

I remember that the Ministry of Culture of the GDR had the wish to establish such a national organization. The children's theatre makers of course were most enthusiastic about this idea. But we couldn't join the ASSITEJ because of the difficulties the Soviet Union had concerning its own accession to ASSITEJ. the Soviet Union has not been one of the first countries joining! Only after the Soviet Union joined the ASSITEJ the GDR got the green light for its own accession.

In 1964 a preparatory committee for the foundation of a children's and young people's theatre organization was set up. The following countries were included in it: Belgium, Canada, Czechoslovakia, GDR, FRG, Great Britain, France, Italy, Netherlands, Romania, USA, and the USSR.

At the beginning of the 60's [1964] the preparatory committee was set up in London. This happened after a lot of preliminary discussions of various single persons. With this preparatory committee in London the ASSITEJ actually was set up. For this reason a lot of countries were invited, amongst them the FRG and the GDR. I tried to travel to London as representative of the GDR but I couldn't. The reason was not that I couldn't leave the country. The reason lay in a different direction. At this time there existed a so-called "travel office" in West Berlin. this travel office decided to which citizen of the GDR the permission was given to enter a member state of the NATO. When you were planning a journey to London you had to go to this office first, to ask for permission—otherwise you couldn't go there. That was the "travel office." I still keep the passport I received from this office. But I didn't receive permission at this time. As a result of this the Czechs represented the interests of the GDR. Anyway, this was the beginning of the well-functioning cooperation of West and East. When the proposals for an Executive Committee were elaborated, the Czechs of course wanted to propose the GDR, all countries wanted to. But, they didn't really love to propose the GDR—even though not firstly for political reasons; two German states meant two seats in this committee. It were often reasons like these which were an obstacle for such movements. By the way, the representative of the FRG in those days pleaded for the participation of a representative of the GDR. The consequence of this was that the President – at that time it was Mr. Gerald Tyler [UK] who wasn't elected then but who was designated for the presidency after the future constitution of the Executive Committee—made the remark: "When Mrs. Rodenberg isn't able to come to us then we will go to Mrs. Rodenberg."

In 1966 the GDR organized the first big meeting with a lot of international participants. Within framework of this meeting the provisional Executive Committee met as well. The meeting of this committee took place in Berlin. It was a very good meeting. As I remember, about 350 to 400 people from various countries participated. a Lot of representatives from Western states came to a socialistic state for the first time in their life. They weren't disappointed—at least they said so. In my opinion this had one reason: they saw children's theatres which they didn't have in their own countries at that time. Coming from the Soviet Union, a lot of good children's theatres had been founded within many socialistic states. So as well in the GDR and in Berlin, like "Theater der Freundschaft." [See *The History of ASSITEJ, Volume I*, pp. 52-53 re: this EC Meeting.]

At this point, I would just like to say that I—in my position as President—very often used this argument against Western politicians. I asked them: "Why do you leave the children's Theatre to the Eastern states, why don't you establish them in your own countries?" And then they always argued against this view: "You only maintain these children's theatres because you try to disseminate your ideology among the children. "That wasn't true as you can verify by reading the programs, but I answered "What prevents you from building up such theatres in order to spread your ideology among the children?"

This festival in Berlin was a great success for ASSITEJ and of course at that time a great success for the GDR as well. Anyhow, it was the first big conference about children's theatre in Berlin. It was really the first big international meeting, too—although this never has been appreciated properly by ASSITEJ.

In May 1966 the General Assembly was held in Prague, Czechoslovakia. Fourteen national centers of ASSITEJ took part. In fall 1966 the International Bulletin was published. These meetings have always been meetings of theatre people, theatre makers. It was the same with the sittings of the Executive Committee. There have never been any meetings of officials only.

The meetings of the Executive Committee always has been combined with theatre performances, at least from the host country, sometimes from other countries as well. But the country which hosted the Executive Committee always presented a few performances.

Of course, it was an initialization—all big festivals were initializations. That in the beginning the initializing effect was bigger in the Eastern states seems logical to me. That didn't change until the meeting in Munich in 1970, which was really a huge festival.

Of course in the first time ASSITEJ was an European foundation. One main reason was that most theatres were located in Europe. Therefore the European theatres were represented first. But some member countries of ASSITEJ had contacts all over the world, caused by the colonial times. The problems of these countries were then brought into ASSITEJ. In the beginning no one was keen on the integration of these countries. After all it gave no professional children's theatres in these countries there. In addition, no one was interested in imposing the European style of theatre on these countries. So in the beginning it gave only a few singular contacts with representatives of these countries, even fewer with theatre makers. The latter happened only late, when more of these countries became involved in ASSITEJ. But some countries like the USA and later Australia as well were insistent that more relations to so-called Third World countries were established. They even tried to admit these countries as members of ASSITEJ.

At the time when I was President and Vice-President a lot of people from all countries came to see me. I was always eager, nearly fanatically keen to draw their attention to the fact that there existed an organization like ASSITEJ which they should support—no matter whether it already gave professional children's theatres in their country or not. In addition, I very often asked representatives from UNESCO coming to the GDR why their country wasn't a member of ASSITEJ yet. Such countries were courted from all directions. In particular from the Secretary General and the Executive Committee. A member of the Executive Committee, a President or Vice-President with good contacts—personally or via his or her own country—to these countries endeavored to extend and consolidate this contact.

I think no one participating in the large festival as well as in the preparation and implementation of the Executive Committee meeting which took place in the GDR in 1966 could imagine to elect me President. In the first place nobody was eager to have a President from the GDR. I think that's understandable. Secondly, I was bad at English. thirdly, Everybody was eager to become president. Despite all my various positions, as President, Vice President, member of the Executive Committee, I was a canvasser for ASSITEJ all over the world. Wherever I went I tried to enlist support. i always tried to draw all the representatives' attention, especially of those from Western states, to the necessity to setup and to subsidize such theatres like those in the Eastern states. And that had probably got about. At the same time I quit my career as a director general and received my own office for our ASSITEJ. So I wasn't Director General any longer but President of the GDR National Center of ASSITEJ and had my own office with several employees. this position permitted to travel all over the world in order to promote the ASSITEJ. All the others, particularly my colleagues in the Western countries, were so involved in their daily work that they could do this "recruiting work" only on the side. In addition, the existence of children's and youth theatres in the GDR which became well-known because of all the guest appearances and visits, may as well have lead to my being elected President. Nevertheless, my election was quite a surprise for me. The first time it happened in Spain in 1978. Thanks to my own office I could give this task my undivided attention.

Naturally the existence of professional theatres for children in the Eastern states and in the GDR set a good example to the colleagues in other countries to try hard to achieve the same standard—of course, just for the love of it. I too was only interested in one thing: the foundation of good and qualified children's theatre all over the world. For two reasons: on the hand for the artistic reason—after all it was me who had been director general of a children's theatre for years. On the other hand I was convinced that the more money a country spends for children's theatre the less money it will spend for weapons. It was one of my main principles to argue: "Every penny given to children's theatres will not be wasted for all the work was honorary. Nobody was reimbursed his or her travel costs besides the Secretary General, nobody received any wages, everything was done voluntarily. In my opinion that's the reason why ASSITEJ has been enjoying a good reputation until today. The people always have been interested in the subject itself.

With pleasure, I remember President Vladimir Adamek from Czechoslovakia. He was such an intelligent president and a wise adviser having such a good view of the situation. He could turn things in the right direction and make good and creative proposals. I really liked him. We had a good relationship. And never in my life I will forget how he acted when my husband died. When I came to the next meeting of the Executive Committee he just held me in his arms, comforting me, and said quietly: "Ilse, that had to happen some time." That consoled me. He was just a good man. And he was so full of the joys of life, loving wine very much. Certainly some of his ideas arose when he drank his beloved wine in the evening.

Within ASSITEJ it was wonderful that in the beginning the presidency of the Western and Eastern states alternated. That worked even without statutes. So Konstantin Shakh-Azizov from the USSR and Nat Eek from the USA both became President.

In the USA existed a lot of ignorance concerning the division of Germany—not necessarily among the members of ASSITEJ but among those people who invited us. I remember one episode in Albany [New York, USA in 1972 at the World Congress]. On invitation of the University we met with professors and assistant teachers and talked with them. They asked me where I came from. When I answered: "From the German Democratic Republic", they said: "Then you are Russian." Then I answered: "Excuse me, but there are two German states." Nevertheless they replied again: "No, no, when you come from there then you are a Russian." I asked the representative of the FRG for help and together we explained to them that here were two German states and that we both were representatives from those German states. These were events not very important to ASSITEJ but nevertheless they demonstrated how little many people in other countries knew about this divided Germany.

During my Presidency I invested a lot of power and I always exerted all my energies. It was such a great strain because this East-West-structure seemed to be so fragile. And it really was. So I always thought: "It must not happen anything which could separate us." I was always concerned about uniting for the sake of unification, about not permitting any separation. Always immediately after our Executive Committee's meetings in various countries I had the feeling: "Fine, everything went very well, we understand each other, the matter is going on." This feeling I often had after these meetings, after this strain. The most moving feelings I had, of course, were when I was elected President of ASSITEJ. That happened in Madrid. In my opinion, I hadn't done anything extraordinary or special. And I was as well emotionally so moved when I was elected President the second time, again unanimously. I thought: "You must have done your work quite well." And it was a moving moment when I stepped onto the platform and saw all the people sitting in front of me. All the people I had to thank too not as President who helped make ASSITEJ grow, but all the comrades and co-workers who—no matter from which state they came—but who had supported me in my work and made all the things go on well. At that moment I only had one thought, and that it was so sad that my husband didn't live to see that moment.

To this day ASSITEJ is an organization with the same humanistic ideals. Without people with humanistic feelings nothing would have worked during the time of the opening of the Wall. This period of time which came along with the abolition of the German separation held many dangers. If now the Western states try to consider themselves superior to the former socialist states then there would arise again separation and opposition. Well, because that didn't happen up to now within ASSITEJ, it becomes apparent that these humanistic thoughts and work done from the standpoint of humanity have a favorable effect to this day. Of course, the separation was a danger, but the reunification was dangerous too. Internationally, i.e. between the USA and the USSR, and nationally, i.e. between the GDR and the FRG, all is continued what was already successful in the beginning of ASSITEJ: Let the other one be him or herself and co-operate well for the sake of the matter. This is how it worked in the divided Germany and how it works nowadays in the united Germany and on the international level equally.

[In the early days of ASSITEJ] there were fewer people. We talked more about personal things and we became more easy in closer contact than nowadays where about 50 [National Centers] are members of ASSITEJ. We were like a family. We were interested in each other, in everybody's personal matters, and we were much more connected with all the things the others were personally involved in. Of course, the organization has lost some of these characteristics in the course of its institutionalization. Well, it's not that the people don't care for each other anymore but there isn't either enough time or the possibility to continue this intimacy just as it used to be.

Once it gave contacts amongst the socialist states and amongst the Western states, too. I think that's normal, because both had its own matters of concern. And for this you need allies and you look for them within your own level. That didn't interfere with the work. It didn't lead to complications or separations. The co-existence of the socialist states was as complicated or easy as one of the Western states. Because they weren't a unit but every country had its own matter of concern within this composition.

The General Assemblies were very exciting: who will be elected whenever there was more than one candidate for a position. And then, of course, every country tried to get its candidate into the Executive Committee. And then there were always several candidates for the presidency, too. But, because the change between both sides was laid down already some things could be avoided. That only changed when I was elected President three times. I was elected unanimous twice, the third time only with the "normal" majority. At this point one should sing my competitor's praise. It was the American Ann Shaw who was out-numbered. But she did everything possible in order to avoid any discord. For the sake of the organization she accepted me as President and as a human being equally. And we always had a good relationship, although we knew from each other that she had a completely different approach to life.[175]

It wasn't necessary to comment on political matters within ASSITEJ. We only gave our opinion on one topic: the necessity of building up children's theatres all over the world. And in this opinion we were united. Anyhow, it wasn't necessary to comment on anything politically. It was necessary to work politically, as it were. Those states in which we were holding our meetings, had to take care of the support of children's theatre, had to promote such support.

We had our Constitution, and in those Statutes were laid the requirements for the membership of any theatre. What is good and what is poor? We didn't interfere in the domestic affairs of the theatres, but we got to know them on the occasion of our international festivals.

There we talked about our impressions, what we liked and what we disliked. But we as ASSITEJ never had the power to say: "You must not do this or that." We can't dictate to the members what they have to do or not. The statutes helped us avoid quarrels. Although it gave fights during the discussions on the occasion of the festivals. They gave expression to all the different points of view. That's natural—how could it be otherwise? Some members argued very hard and these fights had an ideological basis, too. But when it was over it was okay. The fact that two people meant two opinions meant two opinions was accepted and respected. But, both argued for the sake of good and professional children's theatre.

We noted many countries who pressed ahead in the field of amateur theatre and theatre with children as performers equally. But we always referred them to the Statutes and said that it would be impossible. And there existed an organization for amateurs and we always tried not to intimidate the other organizations. And theatre with children was impossible because we were only competent knowing good professional children's theatre. Of course, that didn't exclude one child acting on stage once. Theatre with children didn't exist as part of ASSITEJ at my time. I wouldn't approve relaxing the Statutes and working with children, but I can't do anything about it if it's done now. But this relaxation I only apply to the professionalism. If you think Africa where no professional Children's theatre exists—you either can exclude a whole continent or accept that there are highly skilled amateur groups with music or dance. You simply have to accept such groups as theatres. That are decisions we had to make within the Executive Committee and which are made today more often.

I cannot give ASSITEJ advice any longer. I only ask ASSITEJ to continue in the same spirit of humanity which has been forming its work not only in the past but nowadays too. That's even more necessary nowadays with all the wars not only being a threat but a reality. The more ASSITEJ looks after its task to convince people and to convince the governments of the necessity of good children's theatre and the necessity to spend money on it – then there will be fewer weapons on earth.

One single piece of advice: Stay as humanistic as always and help the weaker ones. More advice I cannot give nowadays.

APPENDIX K
Volume III
SPEECH BY MICHAEL FITZGERALD
President of ASSITEJ

The following welcoming speech was delivered at the opening of the General Assembly of the XIIth World Congress of ASSITEJ at Rostov-on-Don, Russia on 4 October 1996, and at the time of the retirement of Michael Ramløse as Secretary General.[176]

Colleagues and friends, good afternoon and welcome.

When I was elected President at the Havana Congress [in 1993], I assured you that I would stand accountable for the Executive Committee and its work on your behalf during these last three years. The agenda we are now going to deal with sets out this account, which I trust you will find acceptable.

I do, however, wish to draw your attention to some important features.

The Committee has applied itself most diligently to the tasks in hand as set out in the Working Program, 1993-96 and, indeed, our meetings have been among the most productive I have attended since my involvement in the Executive Committee in 1985. I believe our achievements are considerable and that we have been successful in streamlining the efficiency of the organization, undertaking activities that will advance the world presence and profile of ASSITEJ and providing an impetus and focus for all our future endeavors.

Firstly, we were careful in inviting co-options and counselors to the Committee to allow international voices and perspective to be included. The holding of our meetings in Germany, Venezuela, the United States of America, and Australia further reinforced this. In these ways ASSITEJ was able to see and be seen, hear and be heard in many different parts of the world. This is most important and should continue if we are to be the international association which our name attests to. It is a particular factor for consideration in voting for the new Executive Committee. In this regard, it is pleasing to note that the under-representation of women in the retiring Committee has been redressed in nominations for the next Committee.

In particular our work through the Commissions has given ASSITEJ for the first time a logo, a brochure, and a year book; a sensible and inventive fee structure (though it is interesting to note the extent to which the Committee's intention for those more financially able complementing those less financially able has been realized); sound proposals for amendments to the constitution which, if accepted—and I hope they will be—will allow the diversity of theatre practice across the world and particularly in Africa to be included in the membership; and a strong proposal to change the now called official language of the organization. This is based on a system which takes into account the internationalism of ASSITEJ, principles of cultural equality and language empowerment, and practical considerations. These and other matters are big steps towards making ASSITEJ a contemporary organization of relevance and significance in world affairs.

Above all, the Committee has been at pains to keep you informed at all times and to seek your advice and opinions so that you, the membership, can appropriately guide the organization. This has been done through surveys, questionnaires, particular requests, festival guides and regular bulletins including the excellent *Information* publication, produced by the General Secretariat. However, the responses to these have been less than satisfactory. They have been limited in number (and never even half the membership) and mostly from the same countries. Curiously, request for membership fees have met with a good response—a provocative contradiction to requests in other areas.

And this brings me to three major concerns I wish to share with you. Firstly, this limited response to the Committee's requests for input means in effect that many of you are not contributing. Is this because you don't care or what? It further means that a certain few are guiding the organization. Maybe this is what you want and you are content with it. But it raises in my mind the critical question of communication across the organization and within the centers. Is correspondence actually received and if not, why not, and is there a way of rectifying this? Who receives information and what do they do with it?

Does it sit on one person's desk or is it shared with members? ASSITEJ can only be as strong and effective as a base which gives the "drive from beneath"—and you, the members, are that base. Without your contribution, ASSITEJ is less strong, less effective. It is strongly recommended that the next Executive Committee investigates this whole matter, including the use of modern technology in facilitating the distribution and receipt of information.

This issue has opened up the second matter of attention—the future of ASSITEJ. Indeed, this matter has impinged into many of the Committee's deliberations and, in fact, in Brisbane aroused considerable debate. It provokes such questions as why should ASSITEJ continue to exist? Why should anyone join ASSITEJ? What does membership really offer? What are members expectations? Where should the organization be in the next century? Essential questions which need to be asked and answered if we are to survive and continue. Again, it is recommended that this subject be part of the working program, 1996–1999.

And the final point is the Executive Committee itself. It is clear from an examination of the report of this last triennium, and the working program to come, that being a member of the Executive Committee involves considerable work for all members, not only the officers, in preparation for meetings and in being involved in the many tasks between meetings. This requires considerable time and effort over and above one's occupation. A trip abroad is one thing, to be a working member of a working committee is another. Committee members now should be, indeed must be, prepared to commit voluntary time and energy to represent member interests and to serve the organization. The old Committee acknowledges this through the hard work it has done. To assist its tasks, it has defined job specifications for each of the officers and committee members as guidelines for now and future committees. I trust that nominees for the next Committee present themselves in full understanding of what will be required of them.

It has been my privilege and pleasure to be President for this term. I acknowledge the Australia Council and the Department of Foreign Affairs and Trade which have supported me in this role. I have represented ASSITEJ on various occasions, often more than once, in Canada, Denmark, France, Great Britain, Germany, Italy, Japan, Poland, Russia, Singapore, Thailand, Turkey, Venezuela, and the United States of America where I have been able to publicize and promote the organization and assist its undertakings. I have been particularly attentive to new membership especially in the Asian region where I am confident we shall have an increasing number of centers in the next period of time. I have been well supported by the Executive Committee, including the Counselors, which have worked willingly and well in mutual purpose. I thank them sincerely for their efforts, particularly the Chairs of the Commissions who have undertaken considerable work in producing the positive outcomes as set out in the agenda.

However, neither I nor the Committee could have achieved these results without the extraordinary drive of the Secretary General and his office. And this in turn is the truly remarkable story of a number of exceptional agencies and people. First, the governments of Denmark, Finland, Iceland, Norway, and Sweden were prevailed upon by the ASSITEJ centers in the respective countries to provide the money to support the General Secretariat for 6 years. Generous, exceptional, most special. This is real patronage which is an example to us all and one to be talked about and emulated. I know I have your agreement to write and thank them.

This financial generosity in co-operation with the Danish Teatercentrum enabled the setting up of the first ever full-time professional ASSITEJ secretariat. In Copenhagen, in Denmark, in 1990 where ASSITEJ Danish members made a commitment to ASSITEJ/Int'l and to themselves to take on the Secretariat and see it through. It brought together, some from the beginning, some later on, Teatercentrum staff who formed the wonderful; team of ASSITEJ/Denmark—Peter Manscher, Bjarne Thanning, Ann Berit Sourial, Kate Bryrup, and Else Marie Mandøe, Executive Assistant 'par excellence' to the Committee. Their work, individually and collectively, has driven us forward. On behalf of ASSITEJ/Int'l , I thank the Danish staff one and all for this.

And finally, I must say some words about the splendid work of Michael Ramløse. Michael finishes at this Congress his second term after six years of outstanding service as Secretary General to ASSITEJ. I first knew of him as an accomplished, renowned playwright, composer and musician—and consummate linguist. An original man of theatre, a creative seminal artist. You now know as well as I that he is also that rare breed of person—the creative administrator, the artist as manager. He has brought to his Secretary Generalship the same flair, originality, enthusiasm, and leadership which he has exhibited in his professional life. His organizational abilities are inspirational—and I speak as one old teacher in recognition—and awe—of another. Michael has reformed and revolutionized the practice and process of administration of our organization. ASSITEJ remains eternally in his debt. He has established a modern, efficient base from which ASSITEJ can move forward with confidence and assertion. It has been a rare pleasure for me to have worked with someone so good and he has inspired me to do my best.

And at this juncture, and in keeping with language empowerment I wish to say a few words to Michael in his own language—which in his case is putting the boot on the other foot, so to speak.

(Spoken in Danish) *Michael. Dear friend. Shakespeare wrote "Some are born great, some achieve greatness, and some have greatness thrust upon them." I believe you were born great, ASSITEJ is most fortunate to have your greatness thrust upon it and, because of this, the organization will achieve greatness. Thank you so much.*

(Oh—and I look forward to the scripted, musical version of "The M and M Show", the play of the Fax relationship we have practiced over the last three years. First we wrote it. Now we can act it. It will be a sell-out!)

ASSITEJ Members. I know you join me in thanking Michael for his sterling contribution and wishing him well in his 'after ASSITEJ life' back in the theatre and creative work. I ask you now to stand with me and by our acclimation acknowledge Michael's remarkable work as Secretary General. [Huge standing ovation!]

Thank you. And on this exuberant note I shall now hand [the meeting] over to Michael and ask him to begin the business of this Rostov Assembly!

APPENDIX L
Volume III
"The Tromsø Declaration"

ASSITEJ/INTERNATIONAL
The International Association of Theatre for Children and Young People

The 64 member nations of The International Association of Theatre for Children and Young People: advocate the development of children and young people through the performing arts. The Centers share common values relating to the social, cultural, and physical well-being of children and young people. Therefore, ASSITEJ/Int'l supports the proposal presented by CANADA "The Tromsø Declaration" relating to the human security of children and the protection of their human rights. "The Tromsø Declaration" is against any sort of exploitation, abuse, and violence that can lead to physical, psychological, and social harm that may impair the integral growth of the child. This proposal is declared at the 1999 International Congress of ASSITEJ in Tromsø, Norway, 15 June 1999.

The Tromsø Declaration

Whereas, ASSITEJ/Int'l and its member nations, through their work as children's theatre professionals, formally advocate the protection of the human security for children and young people and the observance of their human rights. ASSITEJ/Int'l and its member nations, in accordance with its constitutional mandate, therefore declare that:

1. The human security of children and young people, throughout the world, should be a priority issue of international concern.
2. That children and young people, throughout the world, must be protected from exploitation in all forms but especially as:
    child soldiers
    child laborers
    victims of war

Therefore, ASSITEJ/Int'l and its member nations support the enhancement of human rights and the security of children and young people through active partnerships with business, government, international organizations, non-governmental organizations, and private persons. The members of ASSITEJ will also actively work towards the implementation of the rights of children and young people in the world through theatre arts.

And that:

To achieve the objectives of "The Tromsø Declaration" ASSITEJ/Int'l members will not participate in or support the exploitation of children and young people as child soldiers or child laborers, and will protect children from becoming or who are victims of war.

"The Tromsø Declaration" is presented to the international assembly of ASSITEJ/Int'l member nations, 15 June 1999 by ASSITEJ/Canada in support of the **"Norway-Canada Partnership for Actions"** ("The Lysøen Declaration") signed in Bergen, Norway on 11 May 1998 advocating human security issues as a priority of international concern.

APPENDIX M
Volume III
A PRESENTATION

The following presentation by Marián Lucky (Czechoslovakia) was made at the Xth Congress in Stockholm, Sweden on 21 May 1990, and was requested to be included in these Appendices.

"To end this up, allow me to describe one experience which proves that theatre can have an immense effect in these days, not only on young audiences, but on the whole society, on civil values of the whole state as well. A year ago I was deeply convinced that theatre cannot make any revolution, it cannot provoke citizens to run into streets and change the social order, or better to say disorder. It is the audience who come to see entertainment and enjoyment in theatres. The actor is a clown, a jester, a comedian and a not very serious person to the former. The actor is here to cheer the viewer up, to fill his thinking with excitement. Such was the way of behavior until November 17, 1989. This is a revolutionary date for my country. After 40 years of totalitarian, directive, and administration centered government it was the youth who revolted against the rule of one party, the rule of the communist regime. After the brutal steps of the police against the peaceful demonstration of youth in Prague, Czechoslovakia, a wave of protests broke out. The first to join the students were theatre people. Theatres went on strike. It was a very extraordinary strike, though. Theatre house and halls changed themselves into life theatre—theatre of life. The citizens used to come to theatres for discussions, for public dialogues. The stories of persecuted people reverberated from the stage. Everybody represented himself. The citizens were coming with resolutions and declarations. Actors, directors, and theatre engineers were organizing meetings and manifestations.

"For example, our Theatre for children and youth in Trnava changed into a centre of citizen's support against the incapable and rude rule of the communist party in the town and its surroundings. Every day, from morning until evening, thousands of people were coming to us, informing us about the situation in factories, schools, and offices. Both children and elders were appearing. Some 10-year-old boys reported to us what were their teachers doing; who were against us; who were with us. For two weeks, every afternoon thousands of citizens gathered in front of the theatre. Our actors led manifestations, explained the people our demands for the government's stepping down and for the abolition of the old regime. Hundreds of times, applauding reverberated in front of the theatre. We visited factories, offices, schools, and we were informing both adults and children about the truth of our protest. The TV, radio, and press blamed us for undercover activities. We had nothing except our voices and our experience in addressing the public. The totalitarian rule liquidated such abilities in its subjects on purpose. For us, this meant profession, thank God. That was the creation of the revolution of children, the revolution of theatre people, the velvet revolution in the whole country. It is not by chance that the revolutionary president, head of state, Mr. Vaclav Havel is a theatre fellow, a dramatist, and a writer. This is the theatre and life experience I will never forget in my life, because I experienced it myself."

APPENDIX N
A Letter Of Concern By Jan Skotnicki[177]

The following undated letter was addressed to Wolfgang Schneider as President of AS-SITEJ. The transcript of it, sent to Niclas Malmcrona, Secretary General, was dated 5 September 2000 with the hand-written reservation "Only for your eyes dear Niclas!" Apparently the Warsaw, Poland EC Meeting never transpired, but Skotnicki's Letter was circulated to the EC, and was much discussed in several of the EC meetings after these dates. Edited for clarity by Nat Eek.

This might be a serious letter. I came back from Dallas [EC Board Meeting in Dallas, Texas, USA on 11-13 February 2000; Skotnicki's letter was written seven months later] with very bad feelings and many doubts, about the sense of what we were and are doing. I was tired of flying, spending not my own money, and most of all I was annoyed, by Harold's [Oaks] simple statement, which was "We have done a good job." I was not feeling like that. After our meeting in Lucerne, I came back with different feelings. I was thinking then, that something useful was being born, that we were beginning a good job. Then after a lot of troubles and difficulties we have managed the money for my trip to Dallas. After nineteen hours of flight around the world I came here to stay three days in an awkward room talking about using internet and the web, which I could have learned drinking a beer with my computer specialist next to the room where I work everyday. But never mind, except for the useful information about the Seoul Congress, and some quite good meals, we were wasting our time, and the money could be spent on much more useful things. You see, I am not a man spoiled by international conferences, state sponsorships, neither in the Communist time nor after that. I was working from 16 years of age, and never took anything for granted. Thus, I like to spend my time intelligently. I was so tired after coming home. I don't want to be one more UNESCO world traveler, roaming from one end of the world to another, drinking soft drinks and flying those awful aeroplanes. I hate airports, (lines and those people happy that they are pretending something). I have seen too much in my life.

Well, because of all that I started thinking, what could be done to make our work really fruitful and worth all this stupid flying. and I will try to make myself clear with all I have managed to make clear to myself.

1. ASSITEJ, in the state it is now, has no authority. That is because people doing children's theatre are always on the margin of real artistic life in our national and international communities. This is due to the state of mind that children's theatre is not considered as a serious theatre art. I will not bother You with all the reasons why we have not managed to create a children's theatre Strehler, Stein, or Bergman, and why shows for children are not being shown in the great theatre festivals, although their theatrical value very often surpasses the so-called "grown up" performances. We have to be conscious of that.

2. This lack of authority is also due to a common ignorance about the character of Theater for the Young People and its fundamental role in the process of elevating (not educating) a young person in the contemporary society. This is due to many historic reasons. The Russians at one period were close to understanding this, but they used their wisdom and big financial possibilities for political aims, trying to create something very artificial and dangerous. Many governments in our time are concerned mostly in creating a society of welfare, but very few are really concerned about the vision of a human being able to face the problems of our complex

world. First of all, they don't consider human imagination as one of the most creative elements in human nature. The world nowadays wants to create a human being starting from its grown-up period. Thus, they don't really understand what it is to start at the very beginning. In this respect maybe the Americans are in some way very close to letting young people pursue their natural imaginations. But as always their system is disorganized and their theatre reduced to clichés formed by their overwhelming show business empire. This all leads us to the need for a deep study of regional cultures and their long traditions.

3. Theatre for Young People is also very often commercialized in many respects in this world. Do you remember our visit to the amusement park in Dallas and all that we saw there. Theatre for Young People is also (and that is our fault—I mean ASSITEJ's fault) trying artificially to stay separate from the major trends of national cultures. When I visited Denmark (which was a very positive experience) I was trying to get some knowledge about theatre in Denmark as a whole. It was very difficult; as if the children's theatre world existed apart from the National Gallery in Copenhagen or the National Theatre there. More than a few years ago we started to understand that culture can be considered as a combination of special independent cultures....as it happens in our field with puppet theatre and "our theatres." This is idiotic because children in the audience are the same.

4. The educational systems in respective countries are naturally different because of different traditions, because of different cultures, but each of these respective systems must stress more or less on developing human imagination, human liberty, or making choices, the human need to teach how to depend on an individual, and how an individual is dependent on the group. This is theatre in the process of education.

5. Last but not least, our anti-democratic tradition, which means ASSITEJ, like many other international organizations was born in the special atmosphere of the world divided after the second world war. The leftist tendencies pursued by the Soviets, French, people's republics in Europe, leftist movements all over the world were petrified by the prospect of the next war. In some way all these international organizations were dominated by:

a) A very dangerous tolerance and liberalism which was naturally very "human", very "anti-totalitarianism," but at the very end neglectful of the most dangerous problems of our times.

b) This created the possibility that our representatives to ASSITEJ were people politically secure. I know it well from my country.

c) As our organization is spreading very quickly, this does not mean that the idea of the world divided among those who have to have right and those who must not have right, is dead. It stays in our mind, and can be traced very often, even if we don't want it to happen.

These are my main doubts. What can we do?

I think that the first thing we have to consider is HOW TO BUILD UP THE AUTHORITY OF ASSITEJ?

We will not succeed doing as we did in Dallas. During that meeting we were not able to publish any statement about our activities; we finally did not meet any important person whom we would be able to influence about the problems of theatre for the Young People. As You have noticed, theatre for young people is considered in Dallas as something not very important, just a pastime. We were very well accepted, we international guests, but it meant really nothing. We came there, we have spent a short period of time, and we went back. We were "social" like we should be in America. We made an impression as very nice people. Is this enough?

First of all, a meeting of the Executive Committee has to deal with one main and very well selected subject. A statement based on this should be made known to those who are really important in this specific respect. Let's say for example "the introduction of theatre into respective educational programs". This should result in a serious statement about the necessity of introducing theatre as a means of education. This also should be sent to respective theatres as a mean of education. This also should be sent to respective international organizations with a survey about the state of this in different countries with a very serious application for action on this subject.

This item should be presented by someone invited by ASSITEJ, someone very important either in scientific or artistic life. This kind of statement should be also published in as many magazines as possible all over the world. It should be also sent to ministries of education and respective organizations like UNESCO for example. The authority of ASSITEJ should be created by the items we deal with, and by the formulating of our statements. These items have to be serious and very valid, based on a solid knowledge of what is going on in the world. Our statements should have such weight that no one could not take them seriously into account. Or we will remain, as we are now, one of those many international organizations which exist just because they exist. Like the "old nice ladies" who were very important because they were important. Nothing more, nothing less. They seemed nice to everybody. This all came to my mind when we were discussing the yearly edition of our bulletin. No one was sure what it serves.

And the magnificent activity of children's theatre all around the world finally is not represented by us in a proper sense. For example, in Dallas we should have been meeting the representatives of the authorities not only in Texas but also in the United States, authorities giving them the report about many magnificent things happening all around the world, trying to persuade them to use their money in a better way than they use it now.

To be frank and short, we have no real idea for what we are pursuing the ASSITEJ existence. We go from one festival to another festival, being nicely hosted with no responsibility at all. We are poor; these few dollars we have can help Galina [Kolosova] to come to Dallas and that is all. We can not even sponsor a performance; we are in great difficulties in editing our bulletin. Harold says there are no means to get more money. If we are poor, let's be wise, wiser, and wiser.

If we are to go to Rio de Janeiro, why are we going there, what purpose? I would be very glad to see Rio de Janeiro beaches and drink a glass in a small cafe. Maybe it is my last chance to visit Brazil, but not with someone else's money with no purpose at all.

Well, I could be writing very long like this. All that I have written is to prepare our eventual meeting in Warsaw. What is the state of our affairs? Halina Machulska has finally gotten some money for the festival. As You know she is also going to organize the interplay meeting just after the festival. Our artistic commission meeting has to be organized during the three days of the Festival. I have made a financial plan and I have left it at the Ministry of Culture, I hope they will add this money to the festival budget. But this is only money. The main problem is the program of the autumn meeting. All that I have written about supports this. You are the boss, and it is up to You to decide what we should be doing here. I would like to know how much of the given time You want to spend discussing ASSITEJ problems, how much time to meet important people in the theatre world, or maybe meet at the Ministry of Culture and Ministry of Education, how many shows are You interested in seeing. I would like to know it as soon as possible because You know there is going to be only two weeks after our summer vacations are over. Poland is like France—those two months—June and July—are lost. Everything has to be arranged before the end of June. Thus we must stay in close contact. In this respect E-mail will be very useful.

As we have stated the meeting is to take place the 14th, 15th, 17th of September (arrival possible on the 13th). I will try to arrange to have the hotel not very far from the centre. Machulska was opposing the idea of taking You to Radziejowice. It seems to her that it will spoil Your visiting of the festival shows. She is right maybe, but we might have very little time for discussion. I want Your opinion about this. Another problem is this—should we discuss general problems during this meeting? I would very much like this, but otherwise we will of course have no time to discuss anything else. If we were to discuss general ASSITEJ problems I should change the program. This would mean I would organize it the way I have been writing about.

Wolfgang, I am staying in Warsaw till the end of June. Then I have to go to France for a couple of days. Then I want to go somewhere to rest, but it will be always possible to come to Warsaw and do the work for the meeting. One thing is necessary if we are to meet, the main schedule has to be finished by mid-June We may have not much time to work afterwards.

You have all my addresses and phone numbers, and my E-mail address to the theatre. You know how to find me. I will do my job here. I have not Yet written Niclas and can not do this before getting some news from You.

I will send this letter by fax and by normal post.

—/s/ Jan Skotnicki

NOTES

1. *The Tale of Haruk* was performed at the XIVth ASSITEJ World Congress in 2002, and was an epoch-making play in the history of Korean children's theater. Since 2002 it has been performed continuously abroad as well as locally, winning awards and acclaims. E-mail to Nat Eek from Kim Woo Ok dtd 2 September 2013.

2. *The World Almanac and Book of Facts 1991*, Pharos Books, A Scripps Howard Company, 200 Park Avenue, New York, NY 10166, USA.

3. Michael FitzGerald, E-mail to Nat Eek dtd 28 April 2013.

4. *The History of ASSITEJ*, Volume II, p. 349. The total was listed as 51, which unfortunately erred by counting the number of Corresponding Centers twice (Ed.).

EC Meeting, January 1991

5. Official Minutes, EC Meeting in Budapest, Hungary on 23-27 January 1991, Secretariat, Copenhagen, Denmark.

6. Michael Ramløse, E-mail to Nat Eek dtd 27 May 2013.

EC Meeting, December 1991

7. Harold R. Oaks, "Notes from the ASSITEJ Executive Committee Meeting", p. 41–43 (*TYA Today, Vol. 7, No. 1*, Spring 1992, 72 pages). Archives, Child Drama Collection, Hayden Library, Arizona State University, Tempe, AZ, USA.

EC Meeting, November 1992

8. Official Minutes, EC Meeting in Nairobi, Kenya on 8-11 November 1992, Secretariat; Handwritten Notes and other documents, November 1992. Harold Oaks Archives, Child Drama Collection, Hayden Library, Arizona State University, Tempe, AZ, USA.

9. James M. Mudavadi, "The Report on the work of ASSITEJ/Kenya Centre, Nairobi, Kenya" dtd 8 November 1992, duplicated, 7 pages.

EC Meeting & World Congress, February 1993

10. Official Minutes, XIth General Assembly of ASSITEJ, 22-27 February 1993, Havana, Cuba. Secretariat.

11. The ASSITEJ/USA *One Theatre World* Program for the 30th Anniversary of ASSITEJ dtd 10 May 1995; Official Minutes, EC Meeting on 21 February 1993 in Havana, Cuba. Secretariat.

12. The Minutes say 104 possible votes, but it doesn't add up. Perhaps the other 2 votes were for Corresponding Centers (1 per Center).

13. Nominations were now sent to the Secretariat on an announced time schedule, and the Award had been increased to 5,000US$. See Appendix I.

14. Official Minutes, EC Meeting in Havana, Cuba on 27-28 February 1993. Secretariat.

EC Meeting, December 1993

15. Official Minutes, EC Meeting in Frankfurt, Germany on 1-5 December 1993. Secretariat.

16. Michael Ramløse, E-mail to Nat Eek dtd 27 May 2013.

EC Meeting, September 1994

17. Official Minutes, EC Meeting in Caracas, Venezuela on 19-24 September 1994. Secretariat; "ASSITEJ Information – 12" dtd October 1994. Secretariat; "Report From the President" ASSITEJ/USA dtd Fall 1994.

EC Meeting, May 1995

18. Official Minutes, EC Meeting in Seattle, WA, USA on 8-12 May 1995, Secretariat; Program of *One Theatre World/30th Anniversary of ASSITEJ*. Archives, Child Drama Collection, Hayden Library, Arizona State University, Tempe, AZ, USA.

EC Meeting, June 1996

19. Official Minutes, EC Meeting in Brisbane, Australia on 9-16 June 1996. Secretariat. Distributed 1 November 1996, only 4 months later.

EC Meeting & World Congress, October 1996

20. Official Minutes, EC Meeting in Rostov-on-Don, Russia on 2 October 1996, Secretariat; Official Minutes of the XIIth ASSITEJ World Congress at Rostov-on-Don, Russia on 4,5, & 7 October 1996. Secretariat; Kim Peter Kovac Archives, Child Drama Collection, Hayden Library, Arizona State University, Tempe, AZ, USA.

21. Harold Oaks, E-mail to Nat Eek dtd 20 April 2011.

22. Official Minutes, New EC Meeting in Rostov-on-Don, Russia on 7 October 1996. Secretariat.

23. According to the Minutes only these five Commissions were identified, and Finance & Statutes were combined. Apparently they did not appoint a Policy Commission at that time.

24. Joyce Doolittle (Canada), critiques excerpted from "RETURN TO RUSSIA", dtd January, 1997, Calgary, Canada. A personal description of performances she saw at the Rostov-on-Don Congress. Kim Peter Kovac Archives, Child Drama Collection, Hayden Library, Arizona State University, Tempe, AZ, USA.

25. Witnessed by Nat Eek.

A Summary of 1991-1996

26. Wikipedia, Internet, USA.

27. Michael Ramløse, E-mail to Nat Eek dtd 7 May 2013, and another dtd 14 May 2013.

28. Michael Ramløse, E-mail to Nat Eek dtd 27 May 2013.

29. "Report on the activities [of ASSITEJ] May 1990-February 1993", The Secretariat.

30. Secretariat's Official Correspondence dtd January 1993 to August 1994. Courtesy of Michael Ramløse. ASSITEJ/International Archives, Dept. Information and Documentation, Children's and Young People's Theatre Center in the Federal Republic of Germany, Frankfurt (Main), Germany.

31. Michael Ramløse, E-mail to Nat Eek dtd 27 May 2013.

The World of 1996-1997

32. The World Almanac and Book of Facts 1997. An Imprint of K-III Reference Corporation, One International Boulevard, Suite 444, Mahwah, New Jersey 07495-0017.

EC Meeting, August 1997

33. Harold Oaks, hand-written notes and papers dtd 13-16 August 1997. Oaks Archives, Child Drama Collection, Hayden Library, Arizona State University, Tempe, AZ, USA.

34. Michael FitzGerald, E-mail to Nat Eek dtd 28 May 2013.

EC Meeting, October 1997

35. Harold Oaks, handwritten notes. Archives, Child Drama Collection, Hayden Library, Arizona State University, Tempe, AZ, USA.

36. Ramløse challenges this statement of Plichta, since during his six years as Secretary General only 2 centers had sent in reports. Also at the Rostov Congress in 1996, the General Assembly had eliminated the annual Report requirement in the Statutes. Michael Ramløse, E-mail to Nat Eek dtd 29 May 2013.

Interim/1997–1998

37. Michael FitzGerald, E-mail to Nat Eek dtd 2 May 2011.
38. Harold Oaks, E-mail to Nat Eek dtd 20 April 2011.
39. FitzGerald, op. cit.
40. Harold Oaks, handwritten notes. Archives, Child Drama Collection, Hayden Library, Arizona State University, Tempe, AZ, USA.
41. Copy of letter from ASSITEJ/Austria dtd 9 February 1998. Harold Oaks Archives, Child Drama Collection, Hayden Library, Arizona State University, Tempe, AZ, USA.
42. Michael FitzGerald , copy of FAX to Christa Horvort dtd 4 December 1997. Oaks Archives, Child Drama Collection, Hayden Library, Arizona State University, Tempe, AZ, USA.
43. Helge Andersen, copy of letter to Michael FitzGerald dtd 27 March 1998. Oaks Archives, Child Drama Collection, Hayden Library, Arizona State University, Tempe, AZ, USA.
44. Harold Oaks, E-mail to Nat Eek dtd 20 April 2011.

EC Meeting, April 1998

45. Official Minutes, EC Meeting at Haifa, Israel in April 1988 dtd 26 June 1998. Secretariat.
46. Ibid.
47. Ibid.
48. Ibid.

EC Meeting, March 1999

49. Agenda mailed to the EC dtd 19 January 1999. Secretariat. Official Minutes, EC Meeting in London, UK dtd 29 March 1999, Secretariat. Oaks Archives, Child Drama Collection, Hayden Library, Arizona State University, Tempe, AZ, USA.

World Congress, June 1999

50. Official Minutes, EC Meeting in Tromsø, Norway on Wednesday, 16 June 1999. Secretariat.
51. "ASSITEJ/USA INTERNATIONAL HOT LINE" dtd July 1999. Oaks Archives, Child Drama Collection, Hayden Library, Arizona State University, Tempe, AZ, USA.

The World of 2000 (The Millennium)

52. *The World Almanac and Book of Facts 2000*, and *2001*, An Imprint of PRIMEDIA Reference Inc. , One International Boulevard, Suite 630; Mahwah, New Jersey 07495–0017; USA.

EC Meeting, February 2000

53. Robyn Flatt Archives, Child Drama Collection, Hayden Library, Arizona State University, Tempe, AZ, USA; Official Minutes, EC Meeting in Dallas, TX, USA on 11-13 February 2000, sent by E-mail to its Members dtd 7 March 2000. Secretariat.

EC Meeting, December 2000

54. Official Minutes, EC Meeting in Harare, Zimbabwe, Africa dtd 8-11 December 2000, 10 pages. Secretariat in Sweden. Archives, Child Drama Collection, Hayden Library, Arizona State University, Tempe, AZ, USA.

EC Meeting, July 2001

55. Official Minutes, EC Meeting, Tokyo, Japan dtd 19-24 July 2001. Secretariat.

Archives, Child Drama Collection, Hayden Library, Arizona State University, Tempe, AZ, USA.

EC Meeting, March 2002

56. Official Minutes, EC Meeting, Rio de Janeiro, Brazil, South America on 1-7 March 2002. Secretariat. Archives, Child Drama Collection, Hayden Library, Arizona State University, Tempe, AZ, USA.

EC Meeting & World Congress, July 2002

57. Official Minutes, XIVth World Congress of ASSITEJ, Seoul, Korea dtd 20-28 2002. Secretariat.; Kim Peter Kovac, "Report on World Congress and Festival in Seoul, Korea, July 2002" to the ASSITEJ/USA Board dtd 4-5 October 2002, Nashville, TN, USA; An informal report on the Congress by President Harold Oaks, undated, 3 pages, Archives, Child Drama Collection, Hayden Library, Arizona State University, Tempe, AZ, USA.

58. Official Minutes, EC Meeting, Seoul, Korea dtd 21 July 2002. Secretariat. Archives, Child Drama Collection, Hayden Library, Arizona State University, Tempe, AZ, USA.

59. Oaks, op. cit.

60. "...my strong memory is that only Cheela and I had 69 votes, that Tülin had 68, and I think Elisabeth 67." Kim Peter Kovac, E-mail to Nat Eek dtd 21 May 2013. [Minutes wrote that all four had 69 votes – Ed.]

61. Oaks, Ibid.

62. Ibid.

63. Kim Peter Kovac (ASSITEJ/USA), "Minutes of the EC Meeting following the election in Seoul", E-mail to Ann Shaw dtd 18 October 2002.

A Summary of 1997–2002

64. Henri Brugat, E-mail to Michael FitzGerald dtd 15 January 1999. Oaks Archives, Child Drama Collection, Hayden Library, Arizona State University, Tempe, AZ, USA.

65. Kim Peter Kovac, E-mail to Nat Eek dtd 16 April 2011.

66. Michael Ramløse, E-mail to Nat Eek dtd 8 June 2013.

67. Ibid.

68. Ibid.

69. Ed.

70. Michael FitzGerald (Australia), Email to Nat Eek dtd 1 August 2002.

71. Michael Ramløse, E-mail to Nat Eek dtd 8 June 2013.

72. Scot Copeland (USA), Email to Ann Shaw and others dtd 12 August 2002.

73. However, Kovac wrote that he asked for Jordan's proxies in the elections of the Congresses in 2005, 2008, and 2011 in order to help maintain cultural and geographic diversity. Kim Peter Kovac, E-mail to Nat Eek dtd 20 May 2013.

74. Kim Peter Kovac, Email to Scot Copeland and others dtd 12 August 2002.

75. Ibid.

EC Meeting, October 2002

76. Official Minutes, EC Meeting, Zagreb, Croatia on 22-27 October 2002. Secretariat Internet.

Interim Fallout/2002

77. E-mail from Kim Peter Kovac to Ann Shaw dtd 9 August 2002 re: the Seoul Congress, 5 pages.

78. Kim Peter Kovac, E-mail to Nat Eek dtd 21 May 2013.

EC Meeting, March 2003
  79. Official Minutes, EC Meeting, Aberystwyth, Wales, UK, on 25-30 March 2003. Secretariat Internet.
EC Meeting, September 2003
  80. Official Minutes, EC Meeting, Vienna, Austria on 23-28 September 2003. Secretariat Internet.
EC Meeting, April 2004
  81. Official Minutes, EC Meeting, Amman, Jordan on 13-17 April 2004. Secretariat Internet.
  82. Kim Peter Kovac, E-mail to Nat Eek dtd 24 July 2013.
  83. The authors and the Sec, Gen. could find no record of, or a report from the proposed WG8—War in Iraq. Malmcrona suggested that any report might have just been oral.
  84. Kim Peter Kovac, E-mail to Nat Eek dtd 21 May 2013.
EC Meeting, September 2004
  85. Official Minutes, EC Meeting, Cape Town, South Africa on 2-8 September 2004. Secretariat Internet.
EC Meeting, March 2005
  86. Official Minutes, EC Meeting, Adelaide, Australia on 6-12 March 2005. Secretariat Internet; Kim Peter Kovac, Report to Board of ASSITEJ/USA dtd 23 March 2005, 5 pages.
  87. Kim Peter Kovac, "Report to the ASSITEJ/USA Board" dtd 23 March 2005.
World Congress, September 2005
  88. *ASSITEJ/International, 15th General Assembly and World Congress, Montreal, Canada, September 20th-30th 2005 (Agenda, enclosures and other material)* Secretariat, ASSITEJ/Int'l, Box 6033, S–121 06 Johanneshov, Sweden; World Congress materials distributed by ASSITEJ/Canada at the Congress; Notes taken by Nat Eek in attendance; edited with additions and corrections by Kim Peter Kovac, President of ASSITEJ/USA, Ann Shaw, and Joyce Doolittle.
  89. Joyce Doolittle (Canada), E-mail to Nat Eek dtd 16 November 2005.
  90. Kim Peter Kovac, E-mail to Nat Eek dtd 29 May 2013.
  91. For the History and the Rules of the Award see Appendix I.
  92. Under the new Amendments to the Constitution, the EC now consisted of 17 Members. However, only 16 were nominated and elected at this 2005 Congress.
  93. The Minutes are obviously in error, since the total comes to 149 instead of 147. However, Schneider's election was decisive.
  94. Joyce Doolittle (Canada), E-mail to Nat Eek dtd 16 November 2005.
  95. Ibid.
  96. Ibid.
  97. Joyce Doolittle (Canada), E-mail to Nat Eek dtd 16 November 2005. Notes and editing by Nat Eek.
EC Meeting, December 2005
  98. Agenda from Niclas Malmcrona, E-mail to Nat Eek dtd 30 May 2013.
A Summary of 2003–2005
  99. Kim Peter Kovach, E-mail to Nat Eek dtd 21 May 2013.
  100. Ibid.
  101. Kim Peter Kovac, "Report to the ASSITEJ/USA Board" dtd 23 March 2005, 5 pages, p. 4.
  102. Kim Peter Kovac, E-mail to Nat Eek dtd 21 May 2013.

The World of 2005
103. *The World Almanac and Book of Facts 2006*, World Almanac Books, A Division of World Almanac Education Group, Inc., A WRC Media Company; 512 Seventh Ave. ; New York, NY 10018, USA.

Appendix A
104. Nat Eek: "In March 1984 I received a letter from Maria Sunyer (Spain – Vice-President) informing me that the EC had recommended that I be given the title Honorary President of ASSITEJ. From that point on I assumed that I had the right to that title. However, the General Assembly at the 1984 Congress in Moscow, USSR apparently never voted upon it, although I have dated my title as of 1984.

"It was still the time of the "cold war" and certainly no American should be given such a prestigious title, especially to have it conferred in public in Moscow, USSR. Apparently Secretary General Moudoués and President Rodenberg never brought it up for a vote at that 1984 Congress. Since I was not able to be there, I assumed it was a "done deal", and was never contradicted.

"However, our Leader, scholar, and researcher Dr. Wolfgang Schneider discovered the error, assembled the current EC, and voted the title to be given to me properly in 2002, informing me accordingly. It was an act of kindness for which I will ever be indebted, and I am no longer a sheep in wolf's clothing, or a bearer of a false honor. Thank you Wolfgang!"

105. "that's the truth, nothing else...." E-mail to Nat Eek from Wolfgang Schneider dtd 2 September 2012.

Appendix B
106. Razi Amitai, E-mail to Nat Eek dtd 5 June 2011.
107. Galina Kolosova, E-mail to Nat Eek dtd 1 November 2012.
108. CIS unites former Soviet Republics of the USSR (Armenia, Moldavia, Turkmenia, Uzbekistan, etc. besides Georgia and 3 Baltic Republics).
109. Judit Benedek, E-mail to Nat Eek dtd 30 October 2012.
110. Dr. Cheela F. K. Chilala, E-mail to Nat Eek dtd 21 August 2011.
111. Klaus Eggert, E-mail to Nat Eek dtd September 2006, and E-mail dtd 25 June 2011.
112. Michael FitzGerald, E-mail to Nat Eek dtd 13 November 2006.
113. Paul Harman, E-mail to Nat Eek dtd 6 November 2008, and E-mail dtd 25 June 2011.
114. Biography of Mårten Harrie submitted to the Secretariat in his nomination for the EC in 1990.
115. Vicky Ireland, E-mail to Nat Eek dtd 12 December 2008, and edited by E-mail dtd 16 May 2013.
116. Fusako Kurahara, E-mail to Nat Eek dtd 23 August 2011, and E-mail dtd 26 August 2011.
117. Kim Woo Ok Biography given by him to Nat Eek at the XVIIth World Congress, May 2011.
118. Yuriko Kobayashi, letter to Nat Eek dtd 20 August 2011.
119. Galina Kolosova Biography, "Who's Who in ASSITEJ", the Czech Bulletin, 1977 (3). Edited by the Theatre Institute, 110 01 Prague 1, Celetná 17, for the Czechoslovak Centre for ASSITEJ, and Galina Kolosova, E-mail to Nat Eek dtd 10 January 2007, and E-mail dtd 5 August 2013.

120. Kim Peter Kovac, E-mail to Nat Eek dtd 24 July 2013.
121. Fusako Kurahara, E-mail to Nat Eek dtd 5 February 2010.
122. Ibid.
123. Tony Mack, E-mail to Nat Eek dtd 30 October 2012.
124. Marjorie E. MacLean, E-mail to Nat Eek dtd 16 November 2008.
125. Niclas Malmcrona, E-mail to Nat Eek dtd 23 September 2011.
126. Katariina Metsälampi, E-mail to Nat Eek dtd 19 September 2011.
127. Hagit Rehavi Nikolayevski, from www. assitej-israel. com.
128. Harold Oaks, E-mail to Nat Eek dtd 10 September 2006.
129. Anne van Otterloo, E-mail to Nat Eek dtd 23 June 2011.
130. Michael Ramløse, E-mail to Nat Eek dtd 8 September 2006, and E-mail dtd 24 June 2011.
131. Dr. Tülin Sağlam, E-mail to Nat Eek dtd July 2011.
132. Galina Kolosova, E-mail to Nat Eek dtd 29 August 2006.
133. Wolfgang Schneider, E-mail to Nat Eek dtd 30 July 2013, one dtd 22 August 2013, and one dtd 29 August 2013. Edited by Nat Eek, Meike Fechner, and Sabine Karmrodt. Dr. Schneider's complete Biography is in the ASSITEJ Archives in Frankfurt, Germany, and the ASSITEJ Archives in the Child Drama Collection, Hayden Library, Arizona State University, Tempe, AZ, USA.
134. Galina Kolosova, E-mail to Nat Eek dtd 18 September 2011.
135. Ivica Šimić, E-mail to Nat Eek dtd 28 August 2011.
136. Jeremy Turner, E-mail to Nat Eek dtd 12 November 2012.
137. Maurice Yendt, E-mail to Nat Eek dtd 7 September 2011. Translated from the French by Eek.
138. Choi Young Ai, E-mail to Nat Eek dtd 9 September 2011.

Appendix F
139. In the original Constitution, the term ASSITEJ was not defined, as the document was in French, and it didn't need to do so.
140. We're now always using "children and young people", not just children.
141. Added clearer statement about following ASSITEJ's rules and procedures.
142. Added the word because we now have many regional conferences and associations.
143. Expanded the definition, changed some terms to more common current usage.
144. Clarification of practice.
145. Ibid.
146. Making sure the national centers communicate with their members.
147. New item – wanting to "brand" the word ASSITEJ
148. Added suspension as an intermediate step.
149. Current practice allows suspensions.
150. Following Article 5, No. 4, protects the name ASSITEJ.
151. Practice is that the Executive Committee can accept funding.
152. Since we do budgets in 3-year cycles, it makes more sense to think in those terms, not a calendar year.
153. The Bureau was never defined in the old Constitution.
154. Clarification of present practice.

155. Consistency.
156. Clarifying nominations in writing.
157. Language to represent the organization's overall mission, also clarifying the co-opting done after Seoul elections.
158. Correcting typo, clearer English.
159. Clarifying terms.
160. Clarifying that there are no limits to numbers of counselors.
161. Clarification of year as calendar year.
162. Adding female or neutral.
163. Term used in Seoul (and perhaps earlier).
164. Clarifying practice.
165. Consistency.
166. The old Item 3 was incorporated in Article 10, item 3.
167. Moved from Article 1.
168. Adding other events.
169. Specifying current practice.
170. New definitions added.

Appendix G

171. *The ASSITEJ Book 2004/2005*, Ed. by Wolfgang Schneider and Tony Mack, Published in Germany, Printed in Croatia, p. 182-197.

Appendix J

172. Harold Oaks, Archives, Child Drama Collection, ASU, Tempe, AZ, USA.
173. ASSITEJ/International Archives, Dept. Information and Documentation, Children's and Young People's Theatre Centre in the Federal Republic of Germany, Frankfort (Main), Germany.
174. Copy of Interview with Dr. Ilse Rodenberg dtd 22 November 1994. Nat Eek Archives, Child Drama Collection, ASU, Tempe, AZ, USA.
175. See *The History of ASSITEJ, Volume II*, pp. 170-174. 1) Rodenberg's Minister of Culture had informed her that she must run for a third term, even though she had initially refused citing health concerns; 2) in a special Soviet meeting during the Congress in Moscow in 1984, the Eastern delegates were told to vote for Rodenberg, or their subsidies would be questioned; 3) Shaw was held incommunicado for several hours the evening before the election where they tried to convince Shaw to withdraw her nomination, which she refused to do; 4) Rodenberg was re-elected to a third term, but not unanimously.

Appendix K

176. Copy of President Michael FitzGerald's Speech on 4 October 1996. Kim Peter Kovac's Archives, Child Drama Collection, Hayden Library, ASU, Tempe, AZ, USA.

Appendix N

177. *The History of ASSITEJ*, Vol. 3, MS Archives of Nat Eek, Child Drama Collection, Hayden Library, Arizona State University, Tempe, AZ, USA

BIBLIOGRAPHY
Volume III

Works Cited
Ann M. Shaw, The Formation of ASSITEJ, ASSITEJ Annual 1996/97, Ed. Wolfgang Schneider, Druckerei Heinrich, Frankfurt am Main.

References
The World Almanac and Book of Facts – *1991*, Pharos Books, A Scripps Howard Company, 200 Park Avenue, New York, NY 10166, USA.
The World Almanac and Book of Facts – *1994*, published by Funk and Wagnalls and distributed by St. Martin's Press.
The World Almanac and Book of Facts – *1997*. An Imprint of K–III Reference Corporation, One International Boulevard, Suite 444, Mahwah, New Jersey 07495–0017.
The World Almanac and Book of Facts – *2000*, and *2001*, An Imprint of PRIMEDIA Reference Inc. One International Boulevard, Suite 630; Mahwah, New Jersey 07495–0017; USA.
The World Almanac and Book of Facts – *2003*, World Almanac Books, A Division of World Almanac Education Group, Inc., A WRC Media Company; 512 Seventh Ave. ; New York, NY 10018, USA.
The World Almanac and Book of Facts – *2006*, World Almanac Books, A Division of World Almanac Education Group, Inc., A WRC Media Company; 512 Seventh Ave. ; New York, NY 10018, USA.
The History of ASSITEJ, Volume I
The History of ASSITEJ, Volume II.
Wikipedia, Internet, USA.

Archives
ASSITEJ/International Archives, Dept. Information and Documentation, Children's and Young People's Theatre Centre in the Federal Republic of Germany, Frankfurt (Main), Germany.
Doolittle, Joyce, and Eek, Nat, Minutes and Notes taken (1975). Special Collections. Dept. of Archives and Manuscripts. University Libraries. Arizona State University, Tempe, AZ, USA.
Mudavadi, James M., "The Report on the work of ASSITEJ Kenya Centre, Nairobi, Kenya" dtd 8 November 1992. Duplicated, 7 pages, ASU.
Oaks, Harold, "Excerpted Notes from the ASSITEJ Executive Committee Meeting", Reported by Harold R. Oaks, p. 41–43 (*TYA Today*, Vol. 7, No. 1, Spring 1992, 72 pages). Archives, Child Drama Collection, Hayden Library, Arizona State University, Tempe, AZ, USA.
_____. Minutes of the EC Meeting in Nairobi, Kenya on 8-11 November 1992, Secretariat; and Handwritten Notes and other documents, November 1992. Harold Oaks Archives, Child Drama Collection, Hayden Library, Arizona State University, Tempe, AZ, USA.
Shaw, Ann, Report 1984. Special Collections. Dept. of Archives and Manuscripts. University Libraries. Arizona State University, Tempe, AZ, USA.

Documents (in chronological order)
(**1991**) Official Minutes of the EC Meeting in Budapest, Hungary on 23-27 January 1991, printed and distributed by the Secretariat in Copenhagen, Denmark.
(**1992**) Official Minutes, EC Meeting in Nairobi, Kenya on 8-11 November 1992, Secretariat.
(**1993**) Official Minutes of the 11th General Assembly of ASSITEJ, 22-27 February 1993, Havana, Cuba. The Secretariat, Copenhagen, Denmark.

Official Minutes of the EC Meeting in Havana, Cuba dtd 27-28 February 1993. The Secretariat.
Official Minutes of the EC Meeting in Frankfurt, Germany dtd 1-5 December 1993. The Secretariat.
"Report on the activities [of ASSITEJ] May 1990-February 1993", The Secretariat.
(**1994**) "ASSITEJ Information – 12" dtd October 1994. The Secretariat
"Report From the President" ASSITEJ/USA dtd Fall 1994
Official Minutes of the EC Meeting in Caracas, Venezuela dtd Fall 1994 and distributed by the Secretariat.
"Report on the activities [of ASSITEJ] May 1990 – February 1993", The Secretariat.
(**1995**) ASSITEJ/USA *One Theatre World* program for the 30th Anniversary of ASSITEJ dtd 10 May 1995.
Official Minutes of the EC Meeting in Seattle, WA, USA on 8-12 May 1995. The Secretariat.
(**1996**) Official Minutes of the EC Meeting in Brisbane, Australia dtd 9-16 June 1996. The Secretariat.
Official Minutes of the EC Meeting in Rostov-on-Don, Russia on 2 October 1996 and the Rostov Congress, 4,5, & 7 October 1996.
Kim Peter Kovac Archives, Child drama Collection, Hayden Library Arizona State University, Tempe, AZ, USA.
Official Minutes, New EC Meeting in Rostov-on-Don, Russia on 7 October 1996. Secretariat
(**1997**) "RETURN TO RUSSIA", by Joyce Doolittle (Canada) dtd January, 1997, Calgary, Canada.
Harold Oaks, handwritten notes. Archives, Child Drama Collection, Hayden Library, Arizona State University, Tempe, AZ, USA.
Michael FitzGerald, copy of FAX to Christa Horvort dtd 4 December 1997. Oaks Archives, Child Drama Collection, Hayden Library, Arizona State University, Tempe, AZ, USA.
(**1998**) Copy of letter from ASSITEJ/Austria dtd 9 February 1998. Harold Oaks Archives, Child Drama Collection, Hayden Library, Arizona State University, Tempe, AZ, USA.
Helge Andersen, copy of of letter to Michael FitzGerald dtd 27 March 1998. Oaks Archives, Child Drama Collection, Hayden Library, Arizona State University, Tempe, AZ, USA.
Official Minutes of the EC Meeting in April 1988 in Haifa, Israel dtd 26 June 1998. Secretariat.
(**1999**) Official Agenda mailed to the EC by the Secretariat dtd 19 January 1999, and the Official Minutes of the Meeting dtd 29 March 1999.
Official Minutes, EC Meeting in Tromsø, Norway on Wednesday, 16 June 1999. Secretariat.
"ASSITEJ/USA INTERNATIONAL HOTLINE" dtd July 1999. Oaks Archives, Child Drama Collection, Hayden Library, Arizona State University, Tempe, AZ, USA.
(**2000**) Official Minutes of the EC Meeting in Dallas, TX, USA on 11-13 February 2000. Robyn Flatt Archives, Child Drama Collection, Hayden Library, Arizona State University, Tempe, AZ, USA.
Official EC Minutes (Secretariat in Sweden), 10 pages, of the Meeting in Harare, Zimbabwe, Africa on 8-11 December 2000.
(**2001**) Official Minutes of the EC Meeting in Tokyo, Japan on 19-24 July 2001.
(**2002**) Official Minutes of the EC Meeting in Rio de Janeiro, Brazil on 1-7 March 2002.
Official Minutes of the XIVth World Congress of ASSITEJ, Seoul, Korea dtd 20-28 July 2002 Secretariat dtd 20-28 July 2002.
The "Report on World Congress and Festival in Seoul, Korea, July 2002" to the ASSITEJ/USA Board by Kim Peter Kovac dtd 4-5 October 2002, Nashville, TN, USA.
An informal report on the Congress by President Harold Oaks, undated, 3 pages.
"Minutes of the EC Meeting following the election in Seoul" letter of Kim Peter Kovach.
Minutes of the EC Meeting, Zagreb, Croatia, 22-27 October 2002. Secretariat Internet.

(**2003**) Official Minutes of the EC Meeting, Aberystwyth, Wales, UK, 25-30 March 2003. Secretariat Internet.
Official Minutes of the EC Meeting, Vienna, Austria, 23-28 March 2003. Secretariat Internet.
(**2004**) Official Minutes, EC Meeting, Amman, Jordan on 13-17 April 2004. Secretariat Internet.
Minutes of the EC Meeting, Cape Town, South Africa, 2-8 September 2004. Secretariat Internet.
(**2005**) Official Minutes of the EC Meeting, Adelaide, Australia, 6-12 March 2005. Secretariat Internet.
Report to Board of ASSITEJ/USA by Kim Peter Kovac dtd 23 March 2005.
ASSITEJ/International, 15th General Assembly and World Congress, Montreal, Canada, September 20th–30th 2005 (Agenda, enclosures and other material) published by the Secretariat, ASSITEJ/International, Box 6033, S–121 06 Johanneshov, Sweden.
World Congress materials distributed by ASSITEJ/Canada at the Congress.
Notes taken by Nat Eek at the 15th General Assembly and World Congress, Montreal, Canada, September 20th–30th 2005; edited with additions and corrections by Kim Peter Kovac, President of ASSITEJ/USA, Ann Shaw, and Joyce Doolittle. Special Collections. Dept. of Archives and Manuscripts. University Libraries. Arizona State University, Tempe, AZ, USA.

Journals
The ASSITEJ Book 2004/2005, Ed. by Wolfgang Schneider and Tony Mack, Published in Germany, Printed in Croatia, p. 182–197.

Newsletters (in chronological order)
"ASSITEJ/USA INTERNATIONAL HOT LINE" dtd July 1999.

Correspondence (in chronological order)
(**1990**) Biography of Mårten Harrie, Secretariat.
(**1993–1994**) Official Correspondence dtd January 1993 to August 1994 of the Danish Secretariat.
(**1997**) Hand-written notes and papers of Harold Oaks dtd 13-16 August 1997.
Copy of FAX to Christa Horvort from Michael FitzGerald dtd 4 December 1997.
(**1998**) Copy of letter from ASSITEJ/Austria dtd 9 February 1998.
Copy of letter from Helge Andersen to Michael FitzGerald dtd 27 March 1998.
(**2011**) Kim Woo Ok Biography, given to Nat Eek at theXVIIth World Congress in Copenhagen/ Malmö.
Letter from Yuriko Kobayashi to Nat Eek dtd 20 August 2011.

Speeches
Ilse Rodenberg, The Dream of ASSITEJ
Michael FitzGerald, President of ASSITEJ, welcoming speech to the General Assembly at Rostov-on-Don, Russia, on 4 October 1996.
Rose-Marie Moudoués, '65–'95 – ASSITEJ Is Thirty Years Old

E-mail
Amitai, Razi, 5 June 2011, E-mail to Nat Eek.
Benedek, Judit, 30 October 2012, E-mail to Nat Eek.
Brugat, Henri, 15 January 1999, E-mail to Michael FitzGerald.

Chilala, Cheela F. K., 21 August 2011, E-mail to Nat Eek.
_____. 5 August 2013, E-mail to Nat Eek.
Choi Young Ai, 9 September 2011, E-mail to Nat Eek.
Copland, Scot, 12 August 2002, E-mail to Ann Shaw and others.
Doolittle, Joyce, 16 November 2005, E-mail to Nat Eek.
Eek, Nat, 16 November 2005, E-mail to Joyce Doolittle
Eggert, Klaus, September 2006, E-mail to Nat Eek.
_____. 25 June 2011, E-mail to Nat Eek.
FitzGerald, Michael, 1 August 2002, E-mail to Nat Eek.
_____. 13 November 2006, E-mail to Nat Eek
_____. 2 May 2011, E-mail to Nat Eek.
_____. 28 April 2013, E-mail to Nat Eek.
_____. 28 May 2013, E-mail to Nat Eek.
Harman, Paul, 6 November 2008, E-mail to Nat Eek.
_____. 25, June 2011, E-mail to Nat Eek.
Ireland, Vicky, 12 December 2008, E-mail to Nat Eek.
_____. 16 November 2013, E-mail to Nat Eek.
Kim Woo Ok, 2 September 2013, E-mail to Nat Eek.
Kobayashi, Yuriko, 20 August 2011, E-mail to Nat Eek.
Kolosova, Galina, 29 August 2006, E-mail to Nat Eek.
_____. 10 January 2007, E-mail to Nat Eek.
_____. 18 September 2011, E-mail to Nat Eek.
_____. 1 November 2012, E-mail to Nat Eek.
_____. 5 August 2013, E-mail to Nat Eek.
Kovac, Kim Peter, 9 August 2002, E-mail to Ann Shaw.
_____. 12 August 2002, E-mail to Scot Copeland.
_____. 18 October 2002, E-mail to Ann Shaw.
_____. 16 April 2011, E-mail to Nat Eek.
_____. 20 May 2013, E-mail to Nat Eek.
_____. 21 May 2013, E-mail to Nat Eek.
_____. 24 May 2013, E-mail to Nat Eek.
_____. 29 May 2013, E-mail to Nat Eek.
_____. 24 July 2013, E-mail to Nat Eek
Kurahara, Fusako, 5 February 2010, E-mail to Nat Eek.
_____. 23 August 2011, E-mail to Nat Eek
_____. 26 August 2011, E-mail to Nat Eek
_____. 4 September 2013, E-mail to Nat Eek
Mack, Tony, 30 October 2012, E-mail to Nat Eek.
MacLean, Marjorie E., 16 November 2008, E-mail to Nat Eek.
Malmcrona, Niclas, 23 September 2011, E-mail to Nat Eek.
_____. 30 May 2013, E-mail to Nat Eek.
Metsälampi, Katariina, 19 September 2011, E-mail to Nat Eek.
Nikolayevski, Hagit Rehavi, www.assitej-israel.com
Oaks, Harold, 10 September 2006, E-mail to Nat Eek
_____. 20 April 2011, E-mail to Nat Eek.
van Otterloo, Anne, 23 June 2011, E-mail to Nat Eek.
Ramløse, Michael, 8 September 2006, E-mail to Nat Eek.
_____. 24 June 2011, E-mail to Nat Eek.

_____. 7 May 2013, E-mail to Nat Eek.
_____. 14 May 2013, E-mail to Nat Eek
_____. 14 June 2011, E-mail to Nat Eek.
_____. 24 June 2011, E-mail to Nat Eek.
_____. 27 May 2013, E-mail to Nat Eek.
_____. 29 May 2013, E-mail to Nat Eek.
_____. 8 June 2013, E-mail to Nat Eek.
Sağlam, Tülin, July 2011, E-mail to Nat Eek.
Schneider, Wolfgang, 30 July 2013, E-mail to Nat Eek.
_____. 22 August 2013, E-mail to Nat Eek.
_____. 29 August 2013, E-mail to nat Eek.
_____. 2 September 2013, E-mail to Nat Eek
Shaw, Ann, 13 August 2002, E-mail to Scot Copland.
_____. 18 October 2002,
Šimić, Ivica, 28 August 2011, E-mail to Nat Eek.
Turner, Jeremy, 12 November 2012, E-mail to Nat Eek.
Yendt, Maurice, 7 September 2011, E-mail to Nat Eek.

Conversations/Interviews
Rodenberg, Dr. Ilse, interview dtd 22 November 1994. Nat Eek Archives, Child Drama Collection, ASU Tempe, AZ, USA.
Shaw, Ann, personal narrative, August 2005.
_____. Conversation with Nat Eek, 10 August 2006 in Santa Fe, NM, USA.

Resource Accreditations
ASSITEJ/Int'l Website
ASSITEJ/International Archives, Dept. Information and Documentation, Children's and Young People's Theatre Centre in the Federal Republic of Germany, Frankfort (Main), Germany.
Archives, Child Drama Collection, Hayden Library, Arizona State University, Tempe, AZ, USA.